Murnaghan

BIRTH OF THE SYMBOL

BIRTH OF THE SYMBOL

ANCIENT READERS AT THE LIMITS OF THEIR TEXTS

Peter T. Struck

PRINCETON UNIVERSITY PRESS

PRINCETON AND OXFORD

COPYRIGHT © 2004 BY PRINCETON UNIVERSITY PRESS
PUBLISHED BY PRINCETON UNIVERSITY PRESS, 41 WILLIAM STREET,
PRINCETON, NEW JERSEY 08540
IN THE UNITED KINGDOM: PRINCETON UNIVERSITY PRESS, 3 MARKET PLACE,
WOODSTOCK, OXFORDSHIRE OX20 1SY
ALL RIGHTS RESERVED

LIBRARY OF CONGRESS CATALOGING-IN-PUBLICATION DATA

STRUCK, PETER, 1965–
BIRTH OF THE SYMBOL : ANCIENT READERS AT THE LIMITS OF THEIR TEXTS /
PETER STRUCK.
P. CM.
BASED ON AUTHOR'S THESIS (DOCTORAL)—UNIVERSITY OF CHICAGO.
INCLUDES BIBLIOGRAPHICAL REFERENCES (P.) AND INDEX.
ISBN 0-691-11697-0 (ALK. PAPER)
1. CLASSICAL POETRY—HISTORY AND CRITICISM. 2. SYMBOLISM IN
LITERATURE. 3. BOOKS AND READING—GREECE. 4. BOOKS AND READING—
ROME. 5. RHETORIC, ANCIENT. 6. ALLEGORY. I. TITLE.
PA3021.S76 2004

881′.010915—DC21 2003048609

BRITISH LIBRARY CATALOGING-IN-PUBLICATION DATA IS AVAILABLE

THIS BOOK HAS BEEN COMPOSED IN SABON

PRINTED ON ACID-FREE PAPER. ∞

WWW.PUPRESS.PRINCETON.EDU

PRINTED IN THE UNITED STATES OF AMERICA

1 3 5 7 9 10 8 6 4 2

For Natalie and Adam

Γελοῖα μὲν οἶμαι φανεῖσθαι, ὦ Ἑρμόγενες, γράμμασι
καὶ συλλαβαῖς τὰ πράγματα μεμιμημένα
κατάδηλα γιγνόμενα· ὅμως δὲ ἀνάγκη.

I suppose it will appear laughable, Hermogenes,
that things are made manifest by imitation in
letters and syllables. Nevertheless, it must be so.
—Plato *Cratylus* 425d

CONTENTS

ACKNOWLEDGMENTS

THIS BOOK began as a dissertation at the University of Chicago. I have been generously supported for research and travel by the University of Chicago, the Whiting Foundation, Ohio State University, the University of Missouri at Kansas City, the University of Pennsylvania, the American Council of Learned Societies, and the National Humanities Center, where I was Robert F. and Margaret S. Goheen Fellow (2002–3). For their generous guidance and inspiration I would like to thank Christopher Faraone, W. Ralph Johnson, Sarah Iles Johnston, Elizabeth Asmis, Françoise Meltzer, Walter Burkert, Anthony C. Yu, Ineke Sluiter, W. Robert Connor, Mark Usher, and Natalie Dohrmann. I have also learned a great deal from brief conversations with Stephen Gersh, Glenn Most, and Dirk Obbink, whose critical reactions to various sections of this work have spurred me to reconsiderations on several levels. T. J. Wellman and Kevin Tracy provided invaluable help in preparation of the manuscript. But thanks are due especially to Michael Murrin, *magister doctissimus*, whose influence will be apparent to all who have been lucky enough to have worked with him.

BIRTH OF THE SYMBOL

INTRODUCTION

THE GENEALOGY OF THE SYMBOLIC

THIS STUDY EXAMINES the ancient history of an idea, or perhaps it is better called a hope or desire. What do we expect from poetry? Is it an entertaining diversion? An edifying tale? A craft whose masters delight and move us with their elegance and fine workmanship? Yes, perhaps. But a few bold souls, ancient as well as modern, have it in mind that poetry will do something more for us. They suspect that the poets' stories might say more than they appear to say, and that their language might be more than just words. Though these readers are likely to concede that the poets work with the mundane stuff of everyday speech, they still hear in their words the faint but distinct promise of some truer resonance, of a subtle and profound knowledge that arrives in a concealed form and is waiting for a skilled reader to liberate it from its code. Some go further and take poetry as a vehicle into a region where more sober minds fear to tread, where the limitations and encumbrances of our regular lives do not exist, and where we might meet, finally face to face, the deathless gods themselves. This realm is familiar to most of us, as a superstition or a moment of insight. It lies just beyond the always receding horizon that circumscribes our day-to-day existence. Though some say it is only a phantom, others are equally sure that it exists and are drawn away by its Siren song toward what they have learned from tantalizing daily experience to be always just out of reach. With a certain regularity, ancient readers find passage to this realm by the same means. They are transported by what they understand to be the inspired poets' most profound and most deeply resonant poetic creations, which they mark with the same Greek term, σύμβολα, or "symbols."

The symbol has a familiar enough standing in contemporary thinking on literature. In most standard reference works, a symbol is a deeply resonant literary image thought to have some special linkage with its meaning: the word "organic" frequently appears in its various definitions. We owe to the Romantics the symbol's modern apotheosis into the role of master literary device. As I will discuss in my concluding chapter, the modern symbol is connected with its ancient legacy, but only through a circuitous and difficult route. This study attempts to retrace the oldest segments of this path. In order to do so, we will pass through an overgrown tangle of debates and discussions, problems and possibilities, cosmologies, theologies, and metaphysical schemes that have long since lost their relevance—and yet whose concerns, motivations, and agendas endure, even to this day, in and through the category of symbolic language. With this in mind, I consider what I present here to be a genealogy, of sorts, of classical notions of the symbol, insofar as they are relevant to its history in literary commentary.

A historian focusing on the large body of texts and scholarship that in recent tradition constitutes the field of classical literary criticism will be tempted to conclude that the symbol is a foundling in the history of criticism, as though it arrived a fully formed orphan on the doorstep of the modern age in the late 1700s. As opposed to metaphor (Greek μεταφορά) which critics of many later periods reconstruct as a regnant trope with explicit attention to Aristotle's *Poetics*, the literary "symbol" has a more obscure classical history. It almost never appears in the texts of the ancient authors that are typically collected in anthologies of classical literary criticism, such as Aristotle, Demetrius, Horace, Quintilian, or Dionysius of Halicarnassus. Indeed, the concerns that are generally seen to be embedded in the modern symbol—to produce a form of representation that has an intimate, ontological connection with its referent and is no mere mechanical replication of the world, that is transformative and opens up a realm beyond rational experience, that exists simultaneously as a concrete thing and as an abstract and perhaps transcendent truth, and that conveys a unique density of meaning—are all quite alien to the concerns of these ancient readers. As has often been recognized within the scholarship that treats these figures, the work of Aristotle is their most prominent touchstone, and it is from rhetoric that they derive their literary-critical categories. They generate an approach to poetry and a method for studying it by adapting conceptual tools first developed for the study of the public delivery of persuasive prose: schemes of tropes, levels of style, figures of speech and thought, criteria of genre, methods of moving the emotions of an audience. This approach leads these critics to generate a particular kind of criticism. Ever mindful of the audience and of the poet's role in communicating a message to his listeners, they tend to value clarity above all as the chief virtue of poetic language. They investigate which tropes are useful and which to avoid, which levels of diction are appropriate to the various types of subject matter, or how to produce a particular effect in an audience, whether fear or pity, delight or awe. The greatest poets, in this reckoning, are those able to achieve these ends most effectively and clearly. They aim at an understanding of poetry in the abstract and in general, considered as a *techne* with its own specifications and characteristics. They proceed mainly by analysis—by identifying, classifying, and investigating the various species of the poetic genus. The rhetorical approach tends toward a criticism that focuses on composition, that is, on producing a "how-to" manual for would-be poets. For the most part these critics see the great poet, something like the great orator, as a master craftsman who produces a finely wrought piece of work with skill and elegance. For these purposes, neither Aristotle nor ancient rhetoricians had much interest in "symbols." The notion is almost entirely absent from the conceptual apparatus they use to analyze texts.

But in trying to understand the literary history of the symbol we find more fruitful ground when we turn to a second body of ancient texts and a second corpus of scholarship. These ancient texts, produced by literary commentators commonly known to modern scholars as the allegorists,[1] display a nearly continuous and lively interest in literary σύμβολα. For reasons that bear some reconsideration, these readers have generally not been included in contemporary studies under the heading of ancient literary criticism. In marked contrast to critics in the Aristotelian tradition, these readers see their task to be primarily interpretive, not analytical.[2] While allegorists emerge from different traditions, and with many differences in the details of their methods, we can make a few general characterizations of ancient allegorical reading.[3] Allegori-

[1] The term allegory has the benefit of an etymological link to an ancient Greek term, ἀλληγορία, which played a part in the tradition, though not the starring role. We will see that the term αἴνιγμα and its cognates are most consistently used by our critics; σύμβολον is the second most common term, followed by the two terms by which the tradition is most often referenced by contemporary scholars, ἀλληγορία and ὑπόνοια. "Allegory" has the disadvantage of invoking a genre of writing, not developed until the early medieval period, in which a writer personifies abstract ideas and encodes a formulaic, one-to-one correspondence between each character and some concept, abstract principle, or element of the physical world. This kind of allegory has only a little to do with the ancient tradition, as will become clearer in the early chapters of this work. While some ancient writers, notably Ovid and Vergil, surely incorporated the insights of allegorical readers in their poems, ancient allegorism is a phenomenon of reading, not writing. See below, chap. 1. Even as late as Eustathius, an ἀλληγορητής is an interpreter of allegories, not a writer of them.

[2] By "analytical" I mean a mode of criticism that is primarily dedicated to locating and mastering various classifications and characteristics of poetry, considered as a *techne* with unique rules and specifications. By "interpretive" I mean a mode of criticism that sees the text primarily as a repository of hidden wisdom and envisions its task as the extraction of these meanings. There is an analogue here, which will come into play in my concluding chapter, to the relationship between modern formalist criticisms and those approaches based on hermeneutics.

[3] Of course this sketch is no more exhaustive than the sketch of rhetorical criticism given above. It rather presents rules of thumb that apply in the production of allegorical commentaries. It will also be noted with some frequency below that many allegorical critics show an equal facility with the tools and approaches of rhetorical criticism—which

cal readers may or may not display interest in generating classificatory schemes for tropes or levels of style, or in any formalist questions at all. Allegorical critics sometimes show an interest in locating and analyzing the mechanics of the poetic craft, considered as a *techne* of composition; sometimes they do not. Nor are they wedded to the idea of poetry as governed by the needs of the poet to communicate to an audience. More consistently in the allegorical commentaries, one sees a view of the individual poet (or some *ur*-mythmaker) in isolation, as a figure with some special insight into the underlying structures that govern the world, the hidden way of things. Allegorists are more likely to approach the poetic text not as a finished example of a craft but as a sui generis artifact. Where rhetorical critics see a polished handiwork, allegorical commentators tend to see a deep well of wisdom, which everywhere nearly vibrates with arcane observations on the structure of the world and the place of humans and gods within it. Allegorists see great poetic language as deeply figurative, with the potential always, even in the most mundane details, to be freighted with hidden messages. They spend the bulk of their critical energy, not on isolating the features of ποιητική in the abstract, but on particular scenes, within the (usually hexametric) lines of the great poets, which they see as murky and allusive puzzles, more precisely enigmas [αἰνίγματα] or symbols [σύμβολα], that carry some hidden message. Precisely reversing the scale of poetic virtues put forward by critics in the Aristotelian line, the allegorists claim that *un*clear language, whose message is by definition obscured, is the chief marker of great poetry.

Whereas the rhetorical approach shares tools and assumptions in common with oratory, we will see that the allegorical approach shares conceptual tools with other well-attested fields of interpretive inquiry in the ancient world, including divination, magic, religious rite, and certain traditions of esoteric philosophy. As their associations with these other fields suggest, allegorists, uniquely among classical readers, see in poetry the promise of conveying complete and fundamental truth. One conclusion to which this study points is that allegorism reveals the literary-critical impact of one of the best-attested popular views of the poets, that the poet is a kind of prophet. (This stance toward literature may sound vaguely familiar to post-Romantic critics. Indeed, I suspect

is to say that the rules of thumb here are not to be taken as excluding other approaches. The critic who produces an allegorical commentary is not barred from other forms of commentary as well, even when those other forms of commentary grow out of a quite different set of opening premises. One often sees rather sober textual criticism alongside exuberant interpretive leaps. The author of the *Life of Homer*, for example, shows a strong interest in formalist questions in one part of his text, but this interest is attributable to a Peripatetic influence and not to an allegorical one (see chap. 4).

that it is not too strong to say that the Romantics reinvented it for the modern period.)[4] Among the ancients it is the distinct domain of readers with allegorical affiliations. Pure Aristotelians do not, in general, have such heady visions of poetry, nor do they expect to find in it such grand truths. Where Aristotle and his followers see a master craftsman, the allegorists tend to see a master riddler and a savant who can lead the skilled reader to the most profound knowledge the world has to offer. This contrast will be worked through in chapter 1.

Among the allegorists we encounter names that are perhaps not as familiar as Aristotle or Horace, in texts and translations that are not as widely available.[5] Among these are, in the classical period, the Derveni commentator and fragments from Metrodorus of Lampsacus and Theagenes of Rhegium; in the Hellenistic period, Chrysippus and Crates of Mallos; in the early Roman, Cornutus, Pseudo-Plutarch, and Heraclitus the Allegorist; in the late Roman, Porphyry, Sallustius, and Proclus. The category of the symbol, I will argue, is one of the allegorists' most distinctive conceptual tools, albeit one that does not arrive on the scene until the Hellenistic period. As we will see in chapter 2, the classical "symbol" is quite a different notion from the later allegorical one. A conclusion reached by Walter Müri in his philological study of σύμβολον some seventy years ago still holds: in the classical period, the word "symbol" is used almost exclusively to mean the token that authenticates a contract. But as we will see in chapter 2, a few unique contexts—in the mysteries, Pythagorean philosophy, and divination—facilitate its move from the marker of social agreements to a pivotal category in the literary imagination of the postclassical ancient world. It is securely attested as a critical term for reading literature in the third century B.C.E., when the Stoic Chrysippus uses it as a term of art of his allegoresis, but we have hints that the notion was in place as early as

[4] In sharp contrast to the Romantics, the ancients did not generally distinguish between the "symbolic" and the "allegorical" mode. As contemporary critics, especially Paul DeMan, have pointed out, the Romantics define their "symbol" in opposition to medieval and Renaissance notions of literary allegory, which struck them as mechanistic. The Romantic reinstatement of the symbol to primary position brings back a classical notion of allegorism in response to a neoclassical criticism that took its cues from the Aristotelians.

[5] The work of Robert Lamberton, from his Yale dissertation forward, has been most influential in changing this situation. See Robert Drummond Lamberton, *Homer the Theologian: The Iliad and the Odyssey as Read by the Neoplatonists of Late Antiquity*, 2 vols. (diss., Yale Univerity, 1979); Porphyry, *On the Cave of the Nymphs*, trans. and intro. Lamberton (Barrytown, N.Y.: Station Hill Press, 1983); Lamberton, *Homer the Theologian: Neoplatonist Allegorical Readings and the Growth of the Epic Tradition* (Berkeley: University of California Press, 1986); Lamberton, and John J. Keaney, eds., *Homer's Ancient Readers: The Hermeneutics of Greek Epic's Earliest Exegetes* (Princeton: Princeton University Press, 1992); [Plutarch], *Essay on the Life and Poetry of Homer*, ed. and trans. John J. Keaney and Robert Lamberton (Atlanta: Scholars Press, 1996).

the second half of the fourth century. It shortly takes its place among the organizing concepts of allegorical commentary and is boosted into preeminence by the Neoplatonists.

While many of the allegorists perhaps remain obscure, a rather large and growing body of scholarly work has been uncovering them. A half-century ago, Jean Pépin and Félix Buffière pioneered the contemporary study of these figures and presented general narratives of these traditions of reading.[6] Both scholars made myth a central category of their investigations and situated their works within the expansive studies of myth being done at that time by philosophers, psychologists, anthropologists, and historians of religion. Pépin's work is especially pronounced in this regard. His masterful introductory section situates ancient allegory within a wide survey of the modern study of myth, from Schelling through Freud and Jung. In more recent years, a series of scholars has been investigating the allegorists from many different approaches. Among the most fruitful works for literary study are those of Michael Murrin, James Coulter, Anne D. R. Sheppard, Robert Lamberton, Jon Whitman, Glenn Most, David Dawson, and James I. Porter.[7] The influence of these scholars' work on my own will be apparent throughout, in particular Lamberton's *Homer the Theologian* and Coulter's "Mimesis: Eicon and Symbol," a section in *The Literary Microcosm*.[8] Were it not for these two prior studies, the present one would probably not have been undertaken.

For several reasons, some worthy and some worth reconsideration, it is perhaps still the exception rather than the rule to find this scholarship, or the presence of allegorism more generally, reflected in the broader scholarship on ancient literary criticism. The allegorists are completely absent, for example, from most of the (now outdated) anthologies of ancient literary criticism, such as D. A. Russell and M.

[6] Félix Buffière, *Les mythes d'Homère et la pensée grecque* (Paris: Belles Lettres, 1956); Jean Pépin, *Mythe et allégorie* (Paris: Éditions Montaigne, 1958).

[7] Michael Murrin, *The Veil of Allegory* (Chicago: University of Chicago Press, 1969) and *The Allegorical Epic* (Chicago: University of Chicago Press, 1980); James A. Coulter, *The Literary Microcosm* (Leiden: E. J. Brill, 1976); Anne D. R. Sheppard, *Studies on the 5th and 6th Essays of Proclus' Commentary on the Republic*, Hypomnemata, vol. 61 (Göttingen: Vandenhoeck and Ruprecht, 1980); Robert Lamberton, *Homer the Theologian: Neoplatonist Allegorical Reading and the Growth of the Epic Tradition* (Berkeley: University of California Press, 1986); Jon Whitman, *Allegory: The Dynamics of an Ancient and Medieval Technique* (Cambridge: Harvard University Press, 1987); Glenn W. Most, "Cornutus and Stoic Allegoresis," *ANRW* 2.36.3 (1989): 2014–65; David Dawson, *Allegorical Readers and Cultural Revision in Ancient Alexandria* (Berkeley: University of California Press, 1992); James I. Porter, "Hermeneutic Lines and Circles: Aristarchus and Crates on the Exegesis of Homer," in *Homer's Ancient Readers*, ed. Robert Lamberton and John J. Keaney (Princeton: Princeton University Press, 1992).

[8] Coulter, 32–72.

Winterbottom's *Ancient Literary Criticism: The Principal Texts in New Translations* (New York: Oxford University Press, 1972), J.W.H. Atkins's *Literary Criticism in Antiquity* (1934; reprint, Gloucester, Mass.: Peter Smith, 1961), and J. D. Denniston's *Greek Literary Criticism* (New York: E. P. Dutton, 1924). The perhaps standard contemporary work, *Classical Criticism*, (volume 1 of *The Cambridge History of Literary Criticism*) was edited by one of the great scholars of the rhetorical tradition, George Kennedy; it gives the allegorical tradition ten pages in a late chapter and treats it as though it were an aberration of late antiquity. Kennedy himself treats the early tradition, from the Presocratics to the classical period, again in only a few pages, without mentioning that the early material has a continuous legacy throughout the remainder of antiquity, and he invites the reader to skip the chapter and move on to the mainstream tradition.[9]

These works and the field of study of ancient literary criticism in general tend to begin from the premise that the parameters of literary criticism as an ancient discipline are defined by Aristotle's *Poetics*. The allegorists' interpretive exuberances, of course, fall outside of literary criticism as Aristotle defined it, so one is more likely to see allegorism classified as speculative philosophy, naive science, or theology. The work of Buffière and especially Pépin, which identified myth—the coin of the realm in the study of religion in the 1950s—as the proper context for understanding allegoresis continues to have a strong influence on the field. The allegorists' interest in poetry is often characterized as only incidental to their philosophical and religious interests or agendas. In the strongest formulations of this view, the allegorists are seen as only "using" poetry to pursue their agendas in these other fields, not as interested in literature for its own sake.[10] But this is, of course, a complicated claim. I will turn to it in a moment.

Such views on allegorism run somewhat counter to what one finds in the current scholarship on allegorism itself. While I am not aware of an

[9] "Readers whose interests in criticism are not theoretical may, however, prefer to skip to chapter 3" (78). The allegorists are seen to be doing theoretical criticism, where the rhetorical critics, apparently, operate on the theoryless plane of common sense.

[10] This view is pervasive. See, for example, George Kennedy, *Cambridge History of Literary Criticism,* vol. 1, *Classical Criticism* (New York: Cambridge University Press, 1989), 86, where allegory is cast as a "tool" of philosophical and religious rhetoric; D. A. Russell, *Criticism in Antiquity* (Berkeley: University of California Press, 1981), 42, where the Stoic allegorists are said to "use" poetry as a propaedeutic for philosophy, and 95, where allegory is said to "have to do more with the history of religion and ethics than with that of literary criticism"; G.M.A. Grube, *The Greek and Roman Critics* (Cambridge: Hackett, 1968), 55–56, where the allegorists are said to "use" the poets as authorities "for their own ideas"; and finally, Michael Burney Trapp, "Allegory," in the *Oxford Classical Dictionary*, 3d ed. (New York: Oxford University Press, 1996).

explicit reappraisal of the question of whether it is appropriate to consider allegorism within more general studies of "literary criticism," a quite positive "yes" seems to animate some of the recent scholarship, where literary issues are often close to the surface. One thinks especially of Coulter's and Lamberton's pathbreaking work in this vein.[11] An article on the best-known early allegorist appeared in *TAPA* in 1986 under a title that also reflects this view: "The Derveni Commentator as Literary Critic."[12] A change can also be observed in the evolving views of perhaps the single most important recent scholar of ancient literary criticism, D. A. Russell. His article on "Literary Criticism in Antiquity," in the second edition (1970) of the *Oxford Classical Dictionary*, stated quite broadly that "Most ancient criticism is a byproduct of rhetoric," and goes on to call Aristotle "the fountain-head of most later criticism." He nowhere mentions allegorism. But in the third edition of the *OCD* (1996), while he maintains the fundamental importance of rhetorical criticism, he also includes several references to allegorical strategies of reading and drops the characterization of ancient criticism as a "byproduct" of rhetoric. Andrew Ford's recent *Origins of Criticism*, which appeared as this manuscript was in the final stages of preparation, gives thorough consideration to allegorism as one of the roots of classical aesthetics.[13] I follow these cues, and place the allegorists within a rather broad context of ancient literary criticism.

Of course, the positions we take on these issues depend entirely on what we mean by literary criticism. I will here work from the premise that ancient literary criticism comprises the whole collection of ancient theories, practices, and techniques of reading literary texts. Whether the readers I examine have other, secondary (or even primary) motivations is for me less important than the role they play in generating influential and normative rules for reading literature. I have taken this approach not only because it is impossible to understand the development of the literary symbol without it but also on account of the (well-known) difficulty in sorting out more exclusive rules from the ancient categories. It is hard to find a self-conscious genre of "literary criticism" in antiquity. The ancient terminology provides little help. The idea of a literary κριτικός was mainly an Alexandrian one, designating a scholar who makes judgments about who should be included in a canon and who should

[11] See, e.g., Coulter, 5–31. Lamberton seriously entertains such a view of Porphyry (120) but expresses mixed views about Proclus in this regard (179, 185).

[12] Madeleine Henry, "The Derveni Commentator as Literary Critic," *TAPA* 116 (1986): 149–64.

[13] Andrew Ford, *Origins of Criticism: Literary Culture and Poetic Theory in Classical Greece* (Princeton: Princeton University Press, 2002), 67–89.

not.[14] If we made our category stick to this native criterion, not many ancient readers would be included. For example, while Quintilian would surely count as a κριτικός, many other rhetorical critics would not; neither would Aristotle himself, for that matter, since he inaugurates his "poetics" by uncovering the mechanisms by which the poetic craft functions, not by making canonical judgments. It is even more difficult to find an ancient analogue for our notion of the "literary." Rather, one finds ποίησις. But once again this category confounds our consideration of several rhetorical critics who are primarily interested in prose speeches rather than poetic texts. It will similarly disqualify the allegorists, who regularly use their interpretive tools on esoteric philosophers (writing in prose more often than in hexameters) and cultic practices, as well as on Homer.

But even according to a broader notion of literary criticism, can any of the allegorists legitimately be counted as "literary critics"? We ought first to consider the important allegorical tracts produced by figures who have no clear nonliterary interests and no identifiable philosophical axes to grind. The author of the *Life of Homer* and Heraclitus the Allegorist are rather single-minded in their devotion to Homer and attempt a full account, by their own ingenuous measures, of his greatness. They might then be called "literary critics" before they are called anything else. But often, to be sure, one would be hard-pressed to label a given allegorical reader a literary critic in any exclusive sense. It would be absurd to insist that the Derveni commentator, for example, a temple priest likely from the late fifth century B.C.E., should be considered (or considered himself) *more* a "literary critic" than a mystic figure, a mediator of the divine, with special insight into the world through a close affiliation with a certain Orphic poem. (Ten centuries later, remarkably enough, the same description would aptly fit a Neoplatonist like Proclus, perhaps the most important figure within the tradition of the ancient symbol, whose work will occupy us in chapter 7.) For entirely different reasons, Stoics like Chrysippus or Cornutus make odd fits under the heading "literary critic." If a discrete label for these figures is required, one feels no need to call Chrysippus anything other than what he is usually called, a philosopher, while Cornutus might best be described as a cultural anthropologist.[15] Like other allegorical readers, they see the poetic text as one among several significant sources of in-

[14] For usage of the term, see Gregory Nagy, "Early Greek Views of Poets and Poetry," in *The Cambridge History of Literary Criticism*, ed. George A. Kennedy vol. 1, *Classical Criticism* (Cambridge: Cambridge University Press, 1989), 1, 68.

[15] See A. A. Long, "Stoic Readings of Homer," in *Homer's Ancient Readers*, ed. Robert Lamberton and John J. Keaney (Princeton: Princeton University Press, 1992), 55; cf. Most (1989), 2026.

sight into philosophical and theological questions. In the case of the Stoics, Glenn Most (in his criticism of Steinmetz) has taken the allegorists' application of their methods to nonliterary materials as well as literary as sufficient evidence that they are not interested in "*Dichtung als Dichtung*."[16] However, we may then feel some need for an explanation of the overwhelming preference for literary evidence in the allegorical sources. Typically, for every interpretation of a cultic practice one finds a dozen readings of the poets. Even Cornutus, who picks up more nontextual evidence than the other allegorists, draws most of his information from the poets, and his explicit statements of theory focus on poetic issues. This tendency is pervasive. Whatever a particular allegorist is after (and there is no universal answer), he tends to see poetry as the most potent source of it.[17] We have to conclude that allegorical readers see something of distinctive value in poetry.[18]

A judgment that decides allegorical readers are not literary critics on the grounds that they turn their tools on sources beyond poetic texts is further complicated by the general lack of critical purity in antiquity. After all, an extended line of such reasoning could just as easily prevent us from considering readers like Dionysius of Halicarnassus or Quintilian, for example, as ancient literary critics—for these writers' primary interest is unequivocally rhetoric and *not* poetry. (An analogous argument would rule Freud out of the history of twentieth-century criticism.)[19] We are of course right to allow that Quintilian deserves a cen-

[16] Most (1989), 2023–26.

[17] This view needs to be modified somewhat for the post-Plotinian Neoplatonists, whose texts of choice are usually the prose works of Plato. Two mitigating factors should be considered. First, as in Cornutus's case, the most detailed statements of theory appear under the consideration of poetic texts (in Proclus's study of Homer in the *Commentary on the Republic*). Second, this is not much different from the sorts of variations one sees within rhetorical literary criticism, where some critics focus nearly exclusively on the poets (Demetrius) and others are much more weighted toward prose speeches (Dionysius of Halicarnassus).

[18] If one is looking for an equivalent of Aristotle in the extant allegorical tradition, that is, someone who self-consciously codifies a definition of poetry that excludes all other forms of discourse, one has to wait until the fifth century C.E., when Proclus produces, in the *Commentary on the Republic*, the most thoroughly articulated of the extant allegorical theories of poetry. See chap. 7.

[19] One would, of course, be reluctant to call Freud a "literary critic," but even more reluctant to leave him out of a general consideration of twentieth-century literary criticism. Rather than saying that Freud was not interested in literature for its own sake, it seems more satisfying to say that he introduced a new vision of what literature is: he presented it as a near epiphenomenon of the mechanisms of repression and displacement. This view is, of course, persuasive to some later readers (whether explicitly Freudian or not), and they begin to see literature as an opening into the otherwise hidden components of the mind's interior life. Further, Freud helps us to better understand developments in the history of literature itself—since critical approaches have their effects on writers as well as readers. Our understanding of Joyce's *Ulysses*, for example, would suffer greatly

tral position in histories of criticism, even though he produces literary commentary nearly always within the context of rhetorical investigation. This has to do with our understanding that many in the ancient world thought rhetoric and poetry share a great deal. In a rather similar way, I am claiming, the allegorists begin from the premise that poetic questions are deeply intertwined with philosophical and theological ones, and that to neglect the latter is to neglect what is distinctive and unique, indeed definitional, about great poetry. There is, after all, nothing to prevent a reader from a view that poetry *as poetry* is a font of philosophical and theological insight. In a well-known passage, the early Stoic philosopher Cleanthes says something close to this:

> Poetic and musical models are better than philosophical language and—while the language of philosophy is on the one hand sufficiently able to express things human and divine, it is on the other hand inarticulate and unable to express a language befitting the divine magnificence—the meters, the melodies, the rhythms as much as possible approach the truth of the contemplation of divine things.[20]

> ὅς φησιν ἀμείνονά τε εἶναι τὰ ποιητικὰ καὶ μουσικὰ παραδείγματα καί, τοῦ λόγου τοῦ τῆς φιλοσοφίας ἱκανῶς μὲν ἐξαγγέλλειν δυναμένου τὰ θεῖα καὶ ἀνθρώπινα, μὴ ἔχοντος δὲ ψελλοῦ τῶν θείων μεγεθῶν λέξεις οἰκείας, τὰ μέτρα καὶ τὰ μέλη καὶ τοὺς ῥυθμοὺς ὡς μάλιστα προσικνεῖσθαι πρὸς τὴν ἀλήθειαν τῆς τῶν θείων θεωρίας. (Cleanthes, SVF 1.486)[21]

Cleanthes asserts that poetic language carries a special aptitude for handling stories about the divine. One can point to a certain dignity that poetry's musicality will accord the gods, but Cleanthes goes slightly further than that; he suggests that poetry's unique characteristics have epistemological implications as well. They have a bearing on how close human language is able to get to "the truth" of the divine. We will find this view to be a working assumption in several of the allegorical tracts under investigation here. In fact, though the allegorical tracts differ in

without Freud. Similarly, ancient allegorical criticism had an impact on writers. Michael Murrin has shown that Vergil self-consciously fashioned his Juno in book 1 of the *Aeneid* under the influence of traditional allegorical readings of Hera. See Murrin, *Allegorical Epic*, chap. 1; cf. Joseph Farrell, *Vergil's Georgics and the Traditions of Ancient Epic* (New York: Oxford University Press, 1991), 257–58 and Robin Schlunk, *The Homeric Scholia and the Aeneid* (Ann Arbor: University of Michigan Press, 1974), 107–15.

[20] Unless otherwise indicated, all translation are my own.

[21] While there is likely a problem with this text, the main point is not in doubt. Arnim follows Kemke (*Philodemi De Musica Librorum* ed. Johannes Kemke, [Leipzig: Teubner, 1884], 97 [col. 28, line 9]) and reads ψειλοῦ, which faces morphological difficulties, where I have ψελλοῦ. Kemke represents a lacuna directly above the form. While not fully satisfying, ψελλοῦ is at least attested.

important ways, they are united in the idea that poetry has as its defining characteristic an ability to convey grand truths that more discursive forms of language are incapable of capturing. Such a vision of poetry is vigorously disputed by some ancient thinkers, Plato not the least. It is out of step with Aristotle's approach. To some modern philologists, it may seem overly Romantic. For contemporary literary critics, reattuned to this view by the Romantics and steeled against it by critiques from deconstruction, it may seem at the same time overzealous and oddly familiar. However it strikes us, this approach to poetry is common and unmistakable among ancient readers; it is among the most consistently attested premises of the allegorical stream of ancient reading.

Finally, on this point, it is probably still sometimes the case that the question of whether the allegorists count as sufficiently literary in their approach is confounded with a quite different one: whether a given allegorical reading seems acceptable or plausible. If it is not, this line of thinking goes, then the reader reveals him- or herself to be not interested in literature for its own sake. Of course, if one's ultimate goal is to generate a proper reading of a particular literary text, one will disregard certain interpretations and mark down others as tendentious or not useful. But if, on the other hand, one is a historian reconstructing ancient approaches to reading, it is counterproductive to invoke some general notion of plausibility of interpretation (or our own sense of justice to a text) as a criterion for judging whether a particular ancient reader is sufficiently interested in literature. The critical commentary of any generation of readers more often than not seems outlandish to the succeeding one.

In the end, such classifications, like generic boundaries, run to the limits of their usefulness if they prevent us from seeing the cross-fertilization of ideas and intellectual practices from one field to the next. A quick look at one particular ancient reader of poetry will show the difficulty of developing exclusive categories for classifying ancient commentators. An A-scholion on *Iliad* 1.197 discusses the moment where the goddess Athena graphically intervenes in the action and restrains Achilles by his hair:

> "By the yellow hair she grabbed the son of Peleus": [Homer] says that she grabbed "the son of Peleus by the hair," not "the hair of the son of Peleus." Some ignorant scribes write "She grabbed the hair of the son of Peleus." Through this he allegorizes the heat and passion of the hero. For people suffering from jaundice are like this.

"ξανθῆς δὲ κόμης ἕλε Πηλείωνα" ὅτι οὕτως λέγει, τὸν Πηλείωνα τῆς κόμης εἶλεν, οὐχὶ τοῦ Πηλείωνος τὴν κόμην. ἀγνοήσαντες δέ τινες γράφουσι "ξανθῆς δὲ κόμης ἕλε Πηλείωνος". διὰ τούτου δὲ αἰνίττεται τὸ θερμὸν καὶ ὀργίλον τοῦ ἥρωος· οἱ γὰρ ξανθόχολοι τοιοῦτοι.[22]

Here the critic disagrees with those who suggest a variant textual reading (the genitive of the Greek word meaning "Peleus's son" for the accusative) and at the same time offers an allegorical reading of Achilles' yellow hair. To say that the first observation is literary criticism but the second is not strikes me as somewhat forced. This scholion is not atypical of the mixed approaches one finds in allegorical texts.

What then is to be gained from the debate over whether to classify allegorical commentary as literary as well as (not to the exclusion of) religious and philosophical? First and most relevant for the immediate purposes of this study, as I have already mentioned, the ancient history of the literary symbol is nearly invisible unless we reconsider the issue. Without reckoning the ancient developments of allegory within the context of literary criticism more generally, it becomes impossible to discern the history that runs from ancient to modern symbol theories. Though I will do little more than suggest the connections in the concluding chapter, it will be clear throughout that what are usually thought of as strictly modern concerns—ontological linkage between signs and their referents, the notion that language is autonomous and creates a world rather than passively labeling it, and the view of the poet as a solitary genius attuned to the hidden truths of the cosmic order—all these positions have their roots in ancient thought and can be tracked through the study of the symbol. Second, the general definition of allegory that I have been suggesting, that allegorical readers are those that view the poet as primarily a font of subtle insight into the basic workings of the world, is visible only when set in the context of the ancient schools of literary criticism. This characteristic of allegorism is hardly noticeable when, for example, we view it solely within the traditions of physical and theological speculation that emerge with the philosophers. In these other contexts allegorical reading will not be much more than science manqué. It is often that, but it is always also more than that. As a corollary to this position, and as I hope is made clear in chapter 1, an investigation of the allegorists in literary-critical contexts gives us a place outside the more familiar Aristotelian currents, from which we are able to see aspects of Aristotelian criticism that are otherwise difficult to spot. In particular I will be suggesting that Aristotle's notions of poetic language, which value clarity above all, are actually part of a decidedly anti-allegorical project that sits at the head of rhetorical criticism.

The view of allegorical reading that emerges in a literary context is more satisfying, in my opinion, than one that is often found in standard

[22] *Scholia Graeca in Homeri Iliadem*, ed. Erbse (Berlin: De Gruyter, 1969), 1.64.

reference sources, though not as often in the scholarship on allegorism. One regularly reads that there are two forms of ancient allegorism, "defensive" and "positive," both of which are motivated exclusively by extratextual concerns. Michael Burney Trapp's article on Greek allegory in the third edition of the *OCD* presents this widely held view concisely: "Throughout the early period it is hard to be sure what the balance was between 'defensive' allegoresis (rescuing the poets and their myths from charges of intellectual naïveté and impiety) and 'positive' allegoresis (claiming the poets' authority for the interpreter's own doctrines)." While one can surely observe examples of defensiveness and forced reading in various allegorical commentaries, the defensive/positive split as an organizing principle has no ancient attestation and is beset with difficulties.

First, "defensive" motivations on the part of the reader and "positive" imposition of the reader's own ideas are of course not mutually exclusive, and the conceptual boundary between them is in practice very difficult to arbitrate. To situate defensiveness properly, one must resort to some notion of the general state of mind of the interpreter: was he engaged in a polemic with some critic of Homer or not? While the polemical dimension is sometimes plain—for example, in certain interpretations of the tryst of Ares and Aphrodite, a scene which we know to have been offensive to some famous ancient readers—many allegorical readings (in my estimation, most of them) have no clearly identifiable defensive origin. And even in cases where defensiveness is present, more often than not this observation hardly scratches the surface of explaining what the reader is up to. What does it add to our understanding of allegorical reading, for example, if we could determine which of the following standard treatments had a polemical origin: the production of Achilles' shield as a statement on the creation of human society,[23] Apollo's arrows as the sun's rays carrying plague,[24] the cave of the nymphs as a microcosm of the material world,[25] or the adventures of Odysseus as a human being's journey through life to acquire wisdom and self-control?[26]

The emphasis on defensiveness also relies on a standard and probably erroneous history of allegorism, according to which it arose in direct response to philosophers like Xenophanes who first launched attacks on Homer. But as Jonathan Tate pointed out some time ago, the works of

[23] Heraclitus the Allegorist *Homeric Allegories* 43–51, drawing from Crates of Mallos.

[24] Pseudo-Plutarch *Life of Homer* 202; Heraclitus *Homeric Allegories* 8; Cornutus *Compendium* 32.

[25] This is the subject of perhaps the most famous example of ancient allegorical reading, Porphyry's essay on *Cave of the Nymphs*.

[26] Heraclitus the Allegorist *Homeric Allegories* 70.

other figures, like Pherecydes of Syros, make such a narrative dubious and suggest that allegorical reading predates the philosophers' attacks.[27] Robert Lamberton also doubts that allegorism rose in response to philosophical detractors.[28] Moreover, and more importantly, defensive reading is not exclusive to allegory. One can defend Homer with all manner and means of critical tools, but it would not be useful to situate a binary of "defensive" versus some other category at the head of each critical approach whose tools are used to answer Homer's detractors. A figure like Aristarchus, for example, commonly "defends" Homer, if you like, but to create a large category of defensive readings might lead us to overstress his extratextual motivations and underappreciate the richness and importance of his methods. The sources attest to works titled *Homeric Problems* that likewise seek to exonerate Homer. Aristotle and Porphyry both wrote such books. Porphyry, who leaves us with our chief extant example, thought text-critical and Peripatetic methods and *not* allegorism to be his most useful tools in producing this work, though he was thoroughly familiar with all of these methods. Since nearly every kind of critical approach can be used to exonerate Homer from his detractors, and many approaches have been so used, in order to justify maintaining defensive allegorism as a primary organizing category, one should address the question of whether allegorism was used defensively to a greater degree than other ancient approaches. This has not been satisfactorily established.

On the other side of the binary, "positive" allegoresis, the problems are more severe. It is, after all, rather blunt to claim that *all* allegorical reading that is not defensive is an imposition of a reader's own views onto a text. This characterization of allegory is very old indeed. Cicero first put it in the mouth of the allegorists' detractors in his dialogue *On the Nature of the Gods* (1.41). As that work makes clear, it is useful polemic, but it is not much more than a caricature. We might compare, for example, one famous allegorist's reductive treatment of the stylistic interests of critics in the Aristotelian fashion: Lamberton has already pointed out that the great Neoplatonic commentator Proclus accuses them of missing the real point of writers like Homer and Plato and

[27] J. Tate, "On the Beginnings of Allegory," *Classical Review* 41 (1927): 214–15. Tate concludes that allegory was "originally positive, not negative," and that the primary motivation of early philosophical allegory was an attempt to appropriate and rewrite traditional mythic authority on the nature of things for a newly emerging philosophical discourse. "Thus allegory was originally positive, not negative, in its aim." See also, Tate, "On the History of Allegorism," *Classical Quarterly* 28 (1934): 105–7; and Tate, "Plato and Allegorical Interpretation," *Classical Quarterly* 23 (1929): 142.

[28] Lamberton, 15, n. 40.

dismisses their "quibbling about style," which he is happy to leave to others [τὴν περὶ τὴν λέξιν πολυπραγμοσύνην ἄλλοις ἀφέντες].[29] The classification of "positive" allegory glosses over the rather obvious point that a critic who is charged with reading something into a poem sees the text differently than the one who levels the charge. We can be sure that *no* reader (ancient or modern) understands himself or herself as foisting ideas onto a text that do not belong there. The one who proposes a reading, I think we are safe to assume, thinks the text will bear it. More interesting questions present themselves at this point: What is different about these readers' vying notions of the text? What can we learn from them? What effect do these visions have on the history of reading? The answers to these questions are consistently more complex and interesting than we have yet appreciated.

In any case, a binary mapping of allegorism as motivated *either* by an attempt to save a poet from critics *or* by an attempt to enlist his authority for the allegorist's own dogma claims that only extratextual motivations produce this rather large genre of ancient commentary and leaves out even the possibility that allegorists read poetry allegorically for no more complicated motivation than that they thought they were following the dictates of poetry itself.[30] Rather than focusing on a particular reader's motivations, or exposing hermeneutical mischief, it is in my view more satisfactory to define allegorism by what all its practitioners have in common and what is observable in their commentaries and theoretical statements—whether they are defending Homer, twisting his words, or just reading him the way they thought he ought to be read. Whatever their differences, those who read allegorically share an approach that sees the defining characteristics of a poetic text as its surplus of meaning, its tendency to transmit these extra messages in a specifically enigmatic and symbolic fashion, and its need for a skilled reader who is attentive to poetry's allusiveness and density of meaning.

By situating the allegorists and their symbols in a broader context of ancient approaches to literature, we see that they help us to modify not only our understanding of literary theory in the classical period but our overall view of the history of literary criticism.[31] These observations will

[29] *In remp.* 1.164.8; cited by Lamberton, 178.

[30] A. A. Long has shown such a view to be operative in the writings of the Stoics of the formative period, though he argues that on this basis we should not call their reading "allegory" (Long, "Stoic Readings of Homer"). In my view, such a corrective can be applied to many readers commonly cited within the allegorical tradition, which suggests that our definition of allegory needs to be revised.

[31] The work of Jon Whitman has been especially important in this regard. See, most recently, Jon Whitman, ed., *Interpretation and Allegory: Antiquity to the Modern Period* (Leiden: E. J. Brill, 2000). Especially worth noting in this volume are Whitman's introduc-

occupy us briefly in the concluding chapter. General histories tend to treat the classical period as consisting of a few precursors—Plato, Aristotle, Longinus—to the great epochs and movements of literary criticism: the Renaissance, neoclassicism, Romanticism, and the modern period. This view leads to several problems: (1) The classical period can too easily be reduced to an Aristotelian monolith, with a few Platonic objections; (2) ancient criticism appears to be only marginally troubled by the question of mimesis, or the adequacy of language to capture certain fundamental truths about the world; (3) we have a distorted view of which "Plato" the Renaissance rediscovered; and (4) the Romantics are seen as rejecting "classical" principles with their embrace of the "symbol," when it is probably closer to the truth to say that they are displacing one classical model with another, equally well-attested one (while introducing a myriad of refinements and innovations, to be sure). In all the observations that follow I hope to show that literary symbols have existed since ancient times, in forms that are sometimes strange, and with powers that are sometimes exotic, but nearly always displaying recognizable features and making claims that cast an instructive light on the problems and possibilities, verities and illusions, that animate even contemporary visions of the power of poetry. The case study presented here, of an ongoing debate in ancient criticism over theories of representation and the power of poets and their texts, will I hope suggest how much more is waiting to be done. While distant and sometimes arcane, the habits of reading developed here left an enduring legacy to later periods, and even to our own.

Finally, this study will implicitly question a view expressed among some scholars that allegorism is rare in the extant evidence, outside the main currents of ancient reading, and generally concentrated in the later periods. For reasons that are not at all clear to me, for example, Tate, who did the most important work on the allegorists early in the last century, assures us that allegory was "never, be it noted, popular among the Greeks."[32] However, if one is counting simple numbers of surviving texts, it is hard to say that allegorism is at all rare. At least half a dozen major allegorical tracts survive from the ancient period, roughly equivalent to the number of major tracts that survive from the rhetorical traditions of reading, and allegorical commentary is as well represented in the scholia as other kinds. Among ancient philosophers, opinion is decidedly split, with Aristotle and Plato clear opponents of allegoresis, but

tion and Robert Lamberton's masterful "Language, Text, and Truth in Ancient Polytheist Exegesis," 73–88.

[32] Jonathan Tate, "Allegory, Greek," in *The Oxford Classical Dictionary*, 2d ed. (Oxford, 1970), 46.

with ardent support coming from the Stoics and their followers, whose work we will explore in chapters 3 and 4, and the Neoplatonists, to whom we will turn in chapters 6 and 7. Considering time distribution, a large group of allegorical works survives from the early and late Roman periods — but this is not much different from the distribution of tracts of rhetorical criticism. (One wonders what our notions of classical criticism would be had Aristotle's *Poetics* perished!) Furthermore, with the discovery of the Derveni Papyrus some decades ago, alongside the fragments of other famous allegorists from the classical period, we have indication enough that allegoresis forms a more or less continuous strand of literary thinking through the classical, Hellenistic, and early- and late-Roman periods. For these reasons it is difficult to accept that this method of reading was "never very popular," that it was exotic or clearly outside of the mainstream, or that it was concentrated in late periods of literary thought.

It may be useful at this point to offer three final caveats. First, though I will from time to time emphasize certain inherent tensions between allegorical premises and the premises of rhetorical reading, we will see repeatedly that *most* literary commentators who suggest allegorical readings demonstrate an interest in and facility with a range of approaches to criticism: rhetorical, philological, and text-critical as well as allegorical. Some scholars take a critic's interest in textual or other forms of criticism as evidence that he could not have been interested in allegorical reading, or vice versa. For me, on the other hand, the opposition between allegorical and rhetorical readers is a heuristic one and not by any means a hard and fast division in the ancient sources. Prominent allegorists — including Metrodorus of Lampsacus, the Derveni commentator, Chrysippus, Pseudo-Plutarch, Cornutus, and Porphyry — show varying degrees of facility with several different ways of reading, not excluding rhetorical criticism. I would not want my approach, of highlighting through contrast, to reinforce the mistaken notion that we will find allegoresis in a remote archipelago, tucked away from the Aristotelian mainland.

Second, in looking more closely at allegoresis, I do not at all propose that one reading is just as good as the next, that any text will bear any interpretation, and that we ought to abstain from comparative critical judgment. In fact, I claim just the opposite. Comparative critical judgment is absolutely necessary for highlighting the insights and blindnesses of the multitude of possible approaches to the task of reading. Bringing allegorism into conversations with other modes of literary criticism, in my view, only heightens and reawakens our sensitivity to such questions. For example, our reexamination of the ancient allegorists and the question of whether they recreate texts in their own image, might also sharpen our scrutiny of all who take on the heavy burden of giving exhaustive readings of texts as dense and distant as those of the ancient epic poets. For example, we might also wonder whether the recent generations of Homeric critics were exerting themselves too much when they tried to make Homer out to be a master reader of the "human condition." Did such a notion—decked out as it is in universalist urges accreted from modernism, Romanticism, the Enlightenment, humanism, and ironically enough, from Stoicism—occur to Homer? It is highly dubious. Are these critics wrong to find it in Homer's works? Maybe, but maybe not. Furthermore, any reading or any misreading may have something instructive to tell us about the preconceptions and expectations of the critics who forward it, the community in which they read, and the legacies of their views to later periods of literary and literary-critical history.

Third, I do not propose to lay bare some essential referent that lies behind the term "symbol," in its Greek or English (or Latin, German, French, or Italian) variants. Any such claim would be tenuous indeed. Rather, the literary term is a critical tool, constructed by theorists of literature, in order to meet the needs of the work that they do. It does not label some stable, abstract mode of looking at the world that exists in nature and is waiting for us to discover it, like an element in some mythical periodic table of literary criticism. But it seems clear to me at this point that the term itself, which is perhaps to say the concept itself, considered as a particular unit of the historically linked Greek, Latin, Romance, and Germanic languages, has a history. The concept has been constructed and reconstructed over centuries, across cultures, and always for particular purposes, but never ex nihilo. This study attempts to locate and trace the earliest constructions and reconstructions in that history. Closer inspection of the various traditions of symbolic reading will reveal a series of complicated and rich debates, varied lines of thinking, and several precursors to crucial later developments in the history of the interpretive urge in literary criticism.

Michel Foucault writes in his essay "Nietzsche, Genealogy, History" that "Genealogy is grey, meticulous, and patiently documentary. It operates on a field of tangled and confused parchments, on documents that have been scratched over and recopied many times." While I hope that I have been meticulous and patient, I would alert the reader that the other portions of Foucault's characterization may apply to some of the following pages as well. The debates covered here take us into territories that are sometimes unfamiliar. Though these contestations focus on concerns and questions from a remote past, argued for their own idiosyncratic purposes, they nevertheless have more than antiquarian interest. They have something to say for the visions that inform contemporary thinking about literature. Mindful of Cicero's charge, however, I have tried as much as possible to remain faithful to the thoughts and arguments of the ancient critics themselves and to refrain from reading into their debates current issues that may have only tangential bearing on the ancient ones. A faithfulness to particularity is crucial lest we reduce the past to the role of precursor for some as yet unimagined future. This approach has necessitated a good bit of context building and a reliance on the work of many other scholars. But in my estimation, there is something more to be gained from a look at the large assemblage of evidence from many fields. I will have undoubtedly made mistakes, but with luck they have not effaced the main points: the interpretive urge in literary criticism has deep classical roots and the *telos* of this view points toward the divine. What we will find here are only the early stages of an enduring hope that lingers in many ages: the hope that we might find in poetry some palpable trace, at last, of the transcendent.

1

SYMBOLS AND RIDDLES: ALLEGORICAL READING AND THE BOUNDARIES OF THE TEXT

Textual Difficulties

IN BOOK 5 of the *Iliad*, Homer relates a scene that drew the interest of ancient commentators.[1] Homer has Diomedes stab the goddess Aphrodite on the battlefield, an incident troublesome enough in itself. But when Aphrodite retreats, Dione consoles her by telling an even stranger tale (*Il.* 5.381–90). She reminds the goddess that she is not alone in her sufferings at the hands of mortals. Once, the giants Ephialtes and Otos overpowered Ares, chained him up, and locked him in a bronze cauldron for three months. Ares could have died [καί νύ κεν ἔνθ' ἀπόλοιτο Ἄρης], Dione says, had Hermes not caught wind of the situation and sprung him loose. A D-scholion on this section of Homer's text attributes the following opinion to Aristarchus (c. 215–c. 143 B.C.E.), the head of the Alexandrian library and one who can lay claim to being the principal textual critic of the ancient world:

> Aristarchus thought that readers ought to take things told by the poet as more like legends, according to poetic license, and not bother themselves about what is outside the things told by the poet.

> Ἀρίσταρχος ἀξιοῖ τὰ φραζόμενα ὑπὸ τοῦ ποιητοῦ μυθικώτερον ἐκδέχεσθαι, κατὰ τὴν ποιητικὴν ἐξουσίαν, μηδὲν ἔξω τῶν φραζομένων ὑπὸ τοῦ ποιητοῦ περιεργαζομένους. (D-scholion, *Il.* 5.385)

When critics run into something troubling or out of the ordinary in the narrative, Aristarchus counsels that they ought not to expend a great deal of energy generating imaginative explanations for it. We should keep in mind that the poets are wont to flights of fancy, which they

[1] See Félix Buffière, *Les mythes d'Homère et la pensée grecque* (Paris, 1956), 299–301. The story sticks in the imagination of the poets as well as the critics. See Horace, *Odes* 1.6.16; Vergil, *Aeneid* 11.276.

include for their entertainment value.[2] The critic who spends time trying to interpret the oddity runs the risk of reading into the poem what properly belongs on the outside [ἔξω]. This same concern about reading something into the text animates the most famous of Aristarchan principles. We ought to read "Homer from Homer" [Ὅμηρος ἐξ Ὁμήρου] and rely on parallels within the Homeric corpus, rather than any outside criteria, to guide our reading. For Aristarchus here, and for a long tradition of readers in antiquity, strange or fantastic happenings in Homer's narrative invite the closure of interpretive activity.[3]

Porphyry (233–c. 305 C.E.), a Neoplatonist educated at Athens and Rome four and a half centuries later, takes precisely the opposite stance toward another passage that traditionally provoked commentators' interest, the cave of the nymphs episode in *Odyssey* 13.96–112. In this scene, Homer tells matter-of-factly of a sacred grotto where nymphs weave purple cloth on stone looms, where bees use stone bowls and jars to store their honey, and where there are two gates, one for mortals and one for immortals. As in the account of the binding of Ares, Homer's narrative marches on without elaboration or even a hint that he has said anything out of the ordinary. In the opening sentence of *On the Cave of the Nymphs*, Porphyry asks "What on earth does the cave in Ithaca mean for Homer . . . ?" [Ὅτι ποτὲ Ὁμήρῳ αἰνίττεται τὸ ἐν Ἰθάκῃ ἄντρον . . . ;]. And he introduces his commentary proper this way: "Given that the description is full of such obscurities, it is not, in fact, a random fiction created for our amusement" [τοιούτων ἀσαφειῶν πλήρους ὄντος τοῦ διηγήματος πλάσμα μὲν ὡς ἔτυχεν εἰς ψυχαγωγίαν πεποιημένον μὴ εἶναι] (Antr. 4).

In sharp and, I will argue, self-conscious contrast to Aristarchus, Porphyry takes a strange description in Homer's poem as a place to initiate critical activity. For Porphyry here and, as we will see, for a long tradition of reading different from the one to which Aristarchus belongs, the critic should pay attention precisely to those places in the poem that are

[2] One can see this famous position also in Eratosthenes. After Strabo summarizes Eratosthenes' maxim that poetry aims at entertainment only [ψυχαγωγίας μόνον] not instruction, [διδασκαλίας οὔ] he gives a colorful characterization of Eratosthenes' view: "poetry is a fable-blathering old hag, who has been permitted to make up whatever appears to it to be suitable for entertainment" [τὴν ποιητικὴν γραώδη μυθολογίαν, ᾗ δέδοται πλάττειν, φῄς, ὃ ἂν αὐτῇ φαίνηται ψυχαγωγίας οἰκεῖον] (Strabo 1.2.3).

[3] James I. Porter remarks rightly that this passage "has no sense at all unless it is directed against allegorizing interpretations of the passage." "Hermeneutic Lines and Circles: Aristarchus and Crates on the Exegesis of Homer," in Robert Lamberton and John J. Keaney, eds., *Homer's Ancient Readers* (Princeton: Princeton University Press, 1992), 70. See Eustathius (ad loc., cited in Porter): "It *is* an allegory, even if Aristarchus thought it inappropriate to waste time on any of the mythical elements in the poetry by interpreting them allegorically, beyond what the poet has said."

unclear or obscure and that appear to run counter to our common sense. The strange elements in Homer's narrative are proof not that he was indulging in a flight of fancy but that he wished to convey some hidden significance. Therefore, these passages will repay the efforts of a diligent and careful interpreter.

Porphyry's treatise is perhaps the most impressive example of allegorical reading in the ancient period. In trying to convince his fellow readers that there is more to Homer's cave than meets the eye, Porphyry uses the distinctive conceptual tools of allegoresis. He begins his commentary with the tradition's most durable notion, that of the "riddle" or "enigma": Homer's cave is "riddling" [αἰνίττεται] some hidden meaning that we readers are justified in trying to decode. This term is central for nearly every major allegorical commentator from the classical period down through late antiquity. More important for our narrower purposes, Porphyry repeatedly calls the cave in Ithaca a "symbol" [σύμβολον]. The term and its variants appear emphatically, twenty-seven times, in his short treatise—more than once a Teubner page. Along with the better-known ἀλληγορία [other-speaking] and ὑπόνοια [under-meaning], σύμβολον and αἴνιγμα and their cognates form the central concepts of ancient allegorical reading.

We begin by trying to illuminate through contrast, placing allegorical strategies of reading in conversation with literary ideas found in the traditions that flow from Aristotle, which is for the most part understood as the mainstream of ancient literary criticism.[4] While the purpose of the contrast is to highlight the allegorists and thus to gain an understanding of the poetics in which the ancient literary symbol is born, we will find that we also gain a few clarifications of what Aristotle was up to in developing his approach to reading poetry. Others have given the general outline of Aristarchus's inheritance from Aristotle;[5] I will focus on only one aspect of it: the view that clarity is the governing virtue of poetic language.

It surely stands to reason that a critic who approaches poetry through the lens of oratory, where persuasion in the open light of the agora is paramount, should hold clarity of diction in high esteem.[6] However, it is less often remarked that as Aristotle argues for an elevated sort of clarity as the truly excellent poetic mode (λέξεως δὲ ἀρετὴ σαφῆ καὶ μὴ

[4] See introduction.

[5] See Porter, 74–80; cf. M. Van Der Valk, *Researches on the Text and Scholia of the Iliad*, pt. 2 (Leiden: E. J. Brill, 1964), 84–85; and Roos Meijering, *Literary and Rhetorical Theories in the Greek Scholia* (Groningen, 1987).

[6] On the prominence of clarity in Aristotle's discussion of style, see Stephen Halliwell, *Aristotle's Poetics* (Chapel Hill: University of North Carolina Press, 1986), appendix 4, "Aristotle on Language (*lexis*)," 344–49.

ταπεινὴν εἶναι [*Poet.* 1458a18]—on which more below), he is arguing *against* something else at the same time. The extant evidence for "poetics" before Aristotle attests beyond doubt to the rather widespread currency of an opinion in stark contrast to his. Diverse witnesses point to a commonsense view in the archaic and classical periods, well before the time Aristotle is writing, that great poetry is by definition unclear, or more precisely, that it is made up of αἰνίγματα, riddles hinting at some hidden truth.[7] Such a predisposition, which sees poetry as enigmatic and defines the reader chiefly as a decipherer, is part and parcel of allegorical reading, not only in this early period but throughout its whole history. As we will see in the next chapter, some time in the second half of the fourth century B.C.E., the notion of the symbol steps in as a synonym for enigma and begins to take its place within the vocabulary of ancient allegorism—a position that grows and expands until it reaches exalted status among the later Neoplatonists such as Porphyry. A solid understanding of the classical notion of the "enigmatic" is therefore necessary for understanding its later trajectories into the "symbolic."

With these considerations in mind, when Aristotle defines a sort of elevated clarity as the mark of greatness in poetic language and, as we will see, simultaneously redefines the αἴνιγμα, the centerpiece of allegorical poetics, as a *flaw* of style, we are right to take notice. In fact, he places the enigma on a par with a barbarism, a use of Greek that is so nonstandard as to be no longer recognizable. It degenerates into babble. Where others see murky riddles hinting at profound truths Aristotle sees murky nonsense. The skillful poet will avoid such constructions, and, one can infer, the sensible critic will pass over them without much comment. Aristotle's new scale of poetic value knocks the legs out from under an allegorical approach to reading. By redefining the main focus of the allegorists' energies as a flaw of style, he suggests at a stroke that many of his predecessors in the field of poetic commentary have been wasting their time. Reconstructing the background of this development enlightens not only our understanding of Aristotle but also our understanding of the poetics of the enigma, from which allegorism proceeds. Each provides a context against which new aspects of the other's significance emerges.

[7] For general treatments of allegory in this period, see James Tate, "On the History of Allegorism," *Classical Quarterly* 28 (1934): 105–14; Jean Pépin, *Mythe et allégorie*, 2d ed. (Paris: Études Augustiniennes, 1976), 95–105; N. J. Richardson, "Homeric Professors in the Ages of the Sophists," *Proceedings of the Cambridge Philological Society* 201 (1975): 65–81; Robert Lamberton, *Homer the Theologian* (Berkeley: University of California Press, 1986), 10–44; and Andrew Ford, "Performing Interpretation: Early Allegorical Exegesis of Homer," in Margaret Beissinger, et al., eds., *Epic Traditions in the Contemporary World* (Berkeley: University of California Press, 1999), 33–53.

Pre-Aristotelian Literary Commentary

The evidence for literary commentary before Aristotle is fragmentary, and one has a difficult time making sweeping statements about it. I will here be following a view that N. J. Richardson developed in looking at the Sophists and that Andrew Ford's recent work has confirmed: though many early commentators on Homer practiced textual and other forms of criticism, allegorical approaches are a central piece of the early picture.[8] I will here make a brief review of the allegorical evidence in this period, beginning with three of the most substantial fragments from early readers and giving particular attention to the poetics generated by the assumption that great poetry is by definition obscure and enigmatic. Next, we will give consideration to the Derveni Papyrus, a fifth-century interpretation of an Orphic poem recovered from a papyrus that dates to the fourth century.[9] André Laks and Glenn Most have pointed out the stunning importance of this text for our understanding of early allegory.[10] I will attempt to work out a literary-critical context for the Derveni Papyrus, supplementing the work that has already been done to develop its philosophical and religious contexts.[11] While nearly all of our other evidence for poetic commentary in the period before Aristotle comes from second- and third-hand references to shadowy figures, and in texts removed from the period by many centuries, the Derveni text is of a different order of magnitude: over twenty columns of it survive, and its authenticity is beyond doubt. I will then reread certain characterizations of poetry and poetics from the classical sources in light of the information gained from the Derveni text in order to see how the poetics of the enigma, which informs the Derveni author's text, might have been received and viewed in the broader classical world. Plato's corpus in particular offers us slightly more information here than is commonly appreciated.

[8] Richardson, 1975. See esp. Richardson's summary statements, 77, 79, 81. Andrew Ford, *Origins of Criticism* (Princeton: Princeton University Press, 2002), 67–89.

[9] I follow Burkert in this dating; see below. The papyrus has still not been published in its entirety.

[10] André Laks and Glenn Most, eds., *Studies on the Derveni Papyrus* (New York: Oxford University Press, 1997), 4: "The Derveni Papyrus permitted scholars to glimpse for the first time directly and concretely a literary genre to which access had previously only been indirect and abstract." Laks and Most would prefer to contextualize this text as primarily "religious and initiatory." I am trying to show here that this text also contributes significantly to our understanding of the ancient tools of "literary criticism."

[11] For a previous attempt, on which the following relies, see Madeleine Henry, "The Derveni Commentator as Literary Critic," *TAPA* 116 (1986): 149–64. Her individual insights are invaluable, though the larger emphasis on a "practical" criticism is less satisfying.

Fragments

A few fragments remain of allegorical readings from pre-Aristotelian literary commentators, including Pherecydes of Syros, Metrodorus of Lampsacus, Theagenes of Rhegium, Anaxagoras,[12] and Stesimbrotus of Thasos.[13] We will look here at the first three authors. In *Against Celsus* 6.42, Origen testifies to an allegorical reading by Pherecydes, a figure from the first half of the sixth century B.C.E.[14] The text at hand discusses the threats that Zeus makes near the end of *Iliad* 1 and at the beginning of *Iliad* 15.

> Celsus, interpreting the verses of Homer, says: "The words of Zeus to Hera are the words of god to matter, and the words of god to matter indicate in an enigmatic way that god grasped hold of matter, which right from the beginning was in a confused state, and bound it by certain proportions and ordered it; and that the *daimones* that were present in it, as many as were evil doers, he tossed them out and punished them by a journey to this world." And he says, "Pherecydes understood these verses of Homer in this way and said that beneath this region, Earth, there is the region Tartarus, and the Harpies, the daughters of Boreas, and Thyella guard it, whither Zeus thrusts down any of the gods, whenever one of them is rebellious."

> καὶ διηγούμενός γε τὰ Ὁμηρικὰ ἔπη φησὶ λόγους εἶναι τοῦ θεοῦ πρὸς τὴν ὕλην τοὺς λόγους τοῦ Διὸς πρὸς τὴν Ἥραν, τοὺς δὲ πρὸς τὴν ὕλην λόγους αἰνίττεσθαι, ὡς ἄρα ἐξ ἀρχῆς αὐτὴν πλημμελῶς ἔχουσαν διαλαβὼν ἀναλογίαις τισὶ συνέδησε καὶ ἐκόσμησεν ὁ θεός, καὶ ὅτι τοὺς περὶ αὐτὴν δαίμονας, ὅσοι ὑβρισταί, τούτους ἀπορριπτεῖ κολάζων αὐτοὺς τῆι δεῦρο ὁδῶι. ταῦτα δὲ τὰ Ὁμήρου ἔπη οὕτω νοηθέντα τὸν Φερεκύδην φησὶν εἰρηκέναι τό "κείνης δὲ τῆς μοίρας ἔνερθέν ἐστιν ἡ ταρταρίη μοῖρα· φυλάσσουσι δ' αὐτὴν θυγατέρες Βορέου Ἅρπυιαί τε καὶ Θύελλα· ἔνθα Ζεὺς ἐκβάλλει θεῶν ὅταν τις ἐξυβρίσηι." (D-K 7 B5)

Pherecydes (fl. c. 544 B.C.E.), about whom we now have valuable information, thanks to the work of Hermann Sadun Schibli, remains a difficult figure to discern.[15] He is our first extant writer of Greek prose, and his interests tend to confound the categories of "mythic" and "philo-

[12] See Pépin, *Mythe et allégorie*, 99. Diog. Laert. 2.11 is the most important text. For a dissenting view on whether this counts as allegory, see Ruth Scodel, "Tantalus and Anaxagoras," *Harvard Studies in Classical Philology* 88 (1984): 13–24.

[13] Xenophon, *Symposium* 3.5–6. See Richardson's discussion of this evidence, and Stesimbrotus, in particular 71–73.

[14] Tate was the first to point this out. J. Tate, "The Beginnings of Greek Allegory," *Classical Review* 41 (1927): 214–15. Schibli is overly cautious about calling Pherecydes' reading an allegory; see Hermann Sadun Schibli, *Pherekydes of Syros* (New York: Oxford University Press, 1990), 99–100, incl. n. 54.

[15] Schibli, 1990.

sophical." He seems to be writing at a time when the two were not stabilized as separate categories of inquiry. Origen's thirdhand citation of him, if genuine, is our earliest known instance of allegorical reading. Diels and Kranz consider the citation authentic; if so, the claim that Homer uses language "enigmatically" may come directly from Pherecydes, although it is impossible to establish this based on the fragmentary evidence. Was Pherecydes involved in a polemic, as Celsus surely was, and was he trying to exonerate Homer from detractors? Did he have some already conceived philosophy that dictated his reading of Homer, or did he generate his views on the cosmos from his reading of Homer? Did he think that Homer made an early adumbration, through myth, of a scientific observation that he (Pherecydes) knew to be true through his research? We have no information on these questions. What we can say, without speculation, is that Pherecydes had an interest in Homer's poem as a source of wisdom about the fundamental structure of the cosmos.

In his *Homeric Questions* Porphyry preserves a discussion on the theomachy at the beginning of *Iliad* 20. We hear that certain myths concerning the gods are unseemly, and that some people answer the charge by claiming that myths are to be understood allegorically. He then cites Theagenes' (fl. 525 B.C.E.) view that the scenes in which Homer has gods battle one another carry hidden messages about struggles between great elemental forces:

> The story concerning the gods is held universally to be infelicitous and inappropriate. For it tells myths about the gods that are not fitting. In the face of this charge, some resolve it from the standpoint of language, by considering everything to have been spoken as an allegory concerning the nature of the elements, for example, in the case of the oppositions of the gods. For indeed, they say that the dry battles the wet, the hot the cold, and the light the heavy. Furthermore, water extinguishes fire, but fire dries out water. Likewise also in the case of all the elements, from which the universe is joined, opposition arises and destruction is admitted once in a while, but all things endure eternally. The story sets forth battles by naming fire "Apollo," "Helios," and "Hephaistos," water "Poseidon" and "Scamander," the moon "Artemis," the air "Hera," and the rest. The case is similar when the story attributes the names of the gods also to dispositions: Athena to sensibleness, Ares to senselessness, Aphrodite to passion, Hermes to reason, and they assign them to these. Such is the method of explanation from language, then, which is very ancient, even coming from Theagenes of Rhegium, who first wrote about Homer.

> τοῦ ἀσυμφόρου μὲν ὁ περὶ θεῶν ἔχεται καθόλου λόγος, ὁμοίως δὲ καὶ τοῦ ἀπρεποῦς· οὐ γὰρ πρέποντας τοὺς ὑπὲρ τῶν θεῶν μύθους φησίν. πρὸς δὲ τὴν τοιαύτην κατηγορίαν οἱ μὲν ἀπὸ τῆς λέξεως ἐπιλύουσιν, ἀλληγορίαι πάντα

εἰρῆσθαι νομίζοντες ὑπὲρ τῆς τῶν στοιχείων φύσεως, οἷον <ἐν> ἐναντιώσεσι τῶν θεῶν. καὶ γάρ φασι τὸ ξηρὸν τῶι ὑγρῶι καὶ τὸ θερμὸν τῶι ψυχρῶι μάχεσθαι καὶ τὸ κοῦφον τῶι βαρεῖ. ἔτι δὲ τὸ μὲν ὕδωρ σβεστικὸν εἶναι τοῦ πυρός, τὸ δὲ πῦρ ξηραντικὸν τοῦ ὕδατος. ὁμοίως δὲ καὶ πᾶσι τοῖς στοιχείοις, ἐξ ὧν τὸ πᾶν συνέστηκεν, ὑπάρχειν ἐναντίωσιν, καὶ κατὰ μέρος μὲν ἐπιδέχεσθαι φθορὰν ἅπαξ, τὰ πάντα δὲ μένειν αἰωνίως. μάχας δὲ διατίθεσθαι αὐτόν, διονομάζοντα τὸ μὲν πῦρ Ἀπόλλωνα καὶ Ἥλιον καὶ Ἥφαιστον, τὸ δὲ ὕδωρ Ποσειδῶνα καὶ Σκάμανδρον, τὴν δ' αὖ σελήνην Ἄρτεμιν, τὸν ἀέρα δὲ Ἥραν καὶ τὰ λοιπά. ὁμοίως ἔσθ' ὅτε καὶ ταῖς διαθέσεσιν ὀνόματα θεῶν τιθέναι, τῆι μὲν φρονήσει τὴν Ἀθηνᾶν, τῆι δ' ἀφροσύνηι τὸν Ἄρεα, τῆι δ' ἐπιθυμίαι τὴν Ἀφροδίτην, τῶι λόγωι δὲ τὸν Ἑρμῆν, καὶ προσοικειοῦσι τούτοις· οὗτος μὲν οὖν <ὁ> τρόπος ἀπολογίας ἀρχαῖος ὢν πάνυ καὶ ἀπὸ Θεαγένους τοῦ Ῥηγίνου, ὃς πρῶτος ἔγραψε περὶ Ὁμήρου, τοιοῦτός ἐστιν ἀπὸ τῆς λέξεως. (D-K 8 A2)

Alongside this text, we also consider a fragment of Metrodorus (sixth to fifth century B.C.E.) that survives in Philodemus's work:

> Agamemnon is aether, Achilles is the sun, Helen is the earth and Paris the air, Hector is the moon, and the others are named analogically to these. But among the gods, Demeter is the liver, Dionysius is the spleen, and Apollo the bile.
>
> τὸν Ἀγαμέμνονα μὲν αἰθέρα εἶναι, τὸν Ἀχιλλέα δ' ἥλιον, τὴν Ἑλένην δὲ γῆν καὶ τὸν Ἀλέξανδρον ἀέρα, τὸν Ἕκτορα δὲ σελήνην καὶ τοὺς ἄλλους ἀναλόγως ὠνομάσθαι τούτοις. τῶν δὲ θεῶν τὴν Δήμητρα μὲν ἧπαρ, τὸν Διόνυσον δὲ σπλῆνα, τὸν Ἀπόλλω δὲ χολήν. (D-K 61 A4)

These citations reveal an assumption that Homer's text has hidden layers of meaning that are unclear and obscure. His odd stories should provoke readers to look deeper into his tales. Further, his hidden meanings unfold systematically, revealing patterns and consistencies from one to the next. The bare outline preserved of Metrodorus's reading is especially enticing. He proposes an interlacing of the human and divine realms, equating mortals with cosmic realities and immortals with parts of the human body.[16] Richardson is surely right to connect this aspect of the text with Anaxagorean tendencies to link microcosm and macrocosm thinking. He and several scholars before him have even made slightly less satisfying attempts to correlate these positions to tenets of Anaxagorean physics, though in an admittedly conjectural fashion.[17]

[16] On the basis of this shard of evidence, which does not claim to be anything other than a reductive summary, some scholars conclude that Metrodorus was "extreme" in his allegorical orientation. In my view the paucity of sources does not provide us with an adequate basis for making such a judgment.

[17] Richardson, 69, with citations.

The fragment of Theagenes suggests, though not conclusively, that he was engaged in a polemic, and that certain allegorists were defending Homer from his critics. Porphyry, who preserves the citation some seven centuries after the fact, refers to a debate, lively in his own time, in which Theagenes' methods are used. The Metrodorus text does not reference such polemics.

Aside from these few observable points, a great and provocative silence surrounds these bits of text. Of immediate interest, did Pherecydes, Theagenes, and Metrodorus organize their poetics around the notion of the "enigma"? The texts are simply too mediated and fragmentary to draw either positive or negative conclusions. But surely the kind of reading these texts exhibit will, by the late fifth century B.C.E., be governed by the αἴνιγμα. A host of other questions are unresolved. Did these readers suggest that Homer intentionally included these meanings in his tale? Did they suggest some other source behind the oblique messages, such as that the meanings preexisted Homer's particular rendition and resided in the mythic tales that Homer retells, that they resided in the very nature of things, or that they came from some other source? Did Pherecydes, Theagenes, and Metrodorus have preconceived theories of physics into which they fitted Homer's text? Or did they build their notions of the cosmos, humans, and gods from their readings of Homer? Even in the case of Metrodorus we cannot be sure. What was their view of Homer as a poet? Was he inspired by the gods? Or was he merely a gifted observer of the world who subtly built his observations into his work? As we will see in later chapters, their better-documented successors offer us variously nuanced answers to these questions. Because the record is so fragmentary, we simply do not have direct evidence of how these early allegorists viewed these issues.

Derveni Papyrus

One extant allegorical text offers evidence on an entirely different scale. In 1962 a papyrus, preserved by carbonization, was found at Derveni in the funeral pyre of a tomb that must date to before 300 B.C.E.[18] The script has been assigned to the period from 340–320 B.C.E.,[19] and the

[18] Those interested in the Derveni Papyrus have been greatly aided by the publication of the first book dedicated to the still unpublished text. This collection of articles, an extensive bibliography, seven introductory columns edited by K. Tsantsanoglou, and a full translation are the first resource for anyone interested in the papyrus. See André Laks and Glenn W. Most, eds., *Studies on the Derveni Papyrus* (New York: Oxford University Press, 1997). Maria Serena Funghi's article, "The Derveni Papyrus" (25–37), provides a lucid introduction to the papyrus and the scholarship on it to date.

[19] See Funghi, 25–26.

ideas expressed by the writer were current in the era before 400 B.C.E.[20] Any firm conclusions about the details of the Derveni Papyrus must await the long-delayed publication of a critical edition of the text, but a few preliminary statements can be made. The text is a running allegorical commentary on an Orphic cosmogonical poem. Burkert's suggestion that Stesimbrotus is the author behind it is tantalizing.[21] The first seven columns published by Tsantsanoglou, supplemented by the provisional reconstruction of the remainder of the text as it appeared in the *ZPE* (47 [1982], appendix) indicate that the interpretation of αἰνίγματα is the commentator's central concern.[22] The term and its cognates appear—as noun, verb, adjective, and adverb—three times in column VII,[23] and once each in columns IX, XIII, and XVII—all in about two hundred lines of text, many of them fragmentary. Lines 5–6 from column XIII lay out the text's program most generally: "Since he [the poet] riddles concerning his subject matter throughout all his poem, it is necessary to discuss it word by word" [ὅτι μὲν πᾶ[σ]αν τὴν πόησιν περὶ τῶν πραγμάτων αἰνίζεται[24] κ[α]θ' ἔπος ἕκαστον ἀνάγκη λέγειν].[25] Rusten has pointed out that these lines are marked off by *paragraphoi*, which in this papyrus generally indicate the direct quotation of a lemma, though in his view this text does not appear to be such a quotation.[26] Dirk Obbink repeats Burkert's suggestion that in this instance the mark may only indicate a strong grammatical pause, but this would be a departure from what Obbink describes as the scribe's "relatively consistent" use

[20] I agree with Burkert on this dating, see Walter Burkert, "La genèse des choses et des mots," *Les Études Philosophiques* (Oct.–Dec. 1970): 443.

[21] Walter Burkert, "Der Autor von Derveni: Stesimbrotos Περὶ τελετῶν?" *Zeitschrift für Papyrologie und Epigraphik* 62 (1986): 1–5; see also Charles Kahn, "Was Euthyphro the Author of the Derveni Papyrus?" in Laks and Most, 55–63. For a review of the bibliographies around these questions, see Maria Serena Funghi, "The Derveni Papyrus," in Laks and Mosts, 36.

[22] For a survey of the technical terminology in the commentary, see A. Lamedica, "La terminologia critico-litteraria dal Papiro di Derveni ai Corpora scoliografici," in *Lessici Tecnici Greci e Latini*, Atti del 1° Seminario di Studi, "Accademia Peloritana dei Pericolanti," *Cl. Lett. Filos.* 66 (1990), supp. 1: 83–91.

[23] In column numeration, I am following the translation in Laks and Most, which will (gods willing) be the definitive one. The *ZPE* text followed a different numeration; M. L. West made still another. For columns I–VIII, I am working from text produced by Tsantsanoglou in the Laks and Most volume and for subsequent columns, from the provisional *ZPE* text.

[24] I follow Jeffrey S. Rusten in reading αἰνίζεται as a variant of αἰνίττεται. See his "Interim Notes on the Papyrus from Derveni," in *Harvard Studies in Classical Philology*, vol. 89 (Cambridge: Harvard University Press, 1985), 121–40. See, e.g., θοάζω for θοάσσω at Soph. *OT* 2. Laks and Most's translation also reflects such a reading.

[25] Translations my own, though I have consulted the work of Laks and Most, and, in this passage, Rusten, 133. The papyrus has πόησις for ποίησις throughout.

[26] Rusten, 133–34.

of the *paragraphos* to mark quotations.[27] It also leaves unexplained the unanswered μέν, which Rusten noted. If the sentence is in fact a quotation, it would presumably be a well-known saying, a kind of principle or maxim. This would set it on a par with, and in an inverse relation to, the Aristarchan maxim, "Homer from Homer," and would speak for a rather broad and firmly established context of allegorical reading in the commentator's time. (We will see corroborating evidence of such a context in the classical period in a moment.) In any case, the lines reveal a stance toward the poem that is wholly different from the one that motivates the Aristotelian or Aristarchan opinions with which we began. Rather than expecting clarity from a poet and being suspicious of obscurity, this commentator expects the poet to be unclear—systematically. Further, these obscurities are not at all flaws of style to be noted and passed over; they are, on the contrary, the necessary [ἀνάγκη] focus of the diligent reader's attention. This suggests a wholly different view of the poet from Aristotle's master craftsman.

Lines 3–8 of column VII give us more detail:

> And it is not possible to articulate the solution of the words, even though they are spoken. The poem is [oracular?] and riddling for humans. Orpheus did not mean to say in it riddles that are contestable, but rather great things in riddles. Indeed, he speaks like an oracle from the first all the way to the last word.

> [κ]αὶ εἰπεῖν οὐχ οἷόν τ[ε τὴν τῶν ὀ]νομάτων
> [λύ]σιν[28] καίτ[οι] ῥηθέντα. ἔστι δὲ [μαντικὴ ἡ][29] πόησις
> [κ]αὶ ἀνθρώ[ποις] αἰνι[γμ]ατώδης. [ὁ δ]ὲ ['Ορφεὺ]ς αὐτ[ῆι]
> [ἐ]ρίστ' αἰν[ίγμα]τα οὐκ ἤθελε λέγειν, [ἐν αἰν]ίγμασ[ι]ν δὲ
> [μεγ]άλα. ἱερ[ολογ]εῖται[30] μὲν οὖν καὶ ἀ[πὸ το]ῦ πρώτου
> [ἀεὶ] μέχρι οὗ [τελε]υταίου ῥήματος.

This column contains difficulties. It has been suggested that the pieces on either side of the seam running from the suggested kappa of the initial καί to the suggested τελε of τελευταίου simply do not belong together.[31] Regardless of this concern, the fragments of which this column

[27] Obbink, "Cosmology as Initiation vs. the Critique of the Orphic Mysteries," in Laks and Most, 44–45.

[28] Following Tsantsanoglou rather than Laks and Most (see Laks and Most, 12).

[29] In the Laks and Most volume, Tsantsanoglou has ἔστι δὲ ξ[ένη τις ἡ] πόησις. See below for discussion.

[30] We lack early enough attestation of ἱερολογέω to be confident of its precise meaning here; however, a notion of oracular speech is surely plausible. Laks and Most opt for "uttering a holy discourse."

[31] I thank Albert Henrichs for sharing his views with me on this issue. In discussion, he has pointed out difficulties with the syntax, which Burkert also acknowledges. The

has been assembled show at least two, and more likely three, secure attestations of αἴνιγμα terms. This confirms the centrality of the enigma in this author's poetics. But the column might also go further. If we rely on the reconstruction in the Laks and Most volume, the Derveni author claims that the riddles of the poet transmit "great things." They are not side interests but truths of large proportions. Also, and perhaps more interesting, the Derveni author appears to associate the poetic riddle with oracular speech. A statement in column V prepares us for such a view. The author claims to be a divinatory priest who acts as intermediary between the suppliant and the gods. He says the divine words are hard for the laypeople to understand and therefore require his interpretive insight. (Even so, he bemoans, the suppliants don't always follow his advice.) As Henry has pointed out, the papyrus shows the commentator turning his interpretive tools on poetic texts, dreams, and oracles, without any self-conscious difficulty, suggesting a parallelism between these objects of his attention.[32] We will see below, in chapter 5, a rather broad classical context attesting to a certain parallelism between allegorical and divinatory hermeneutics, but one parallel witness is helpful here. In the *Timaeus*, Plato states that the priests at divinatory shrines serve as interpreters of the frenzied utterances of oracles, which, interestingly, Plato characterizes as enigmas (τῆς δι' αἰνιγμῶν[33] οὗτοι φήμης καὶ φαντάσεως ὑποκριταί [*Tim.* 72b]). So our commentator, in his professional life, was very much engaged in the reading of enigmatic speech (presumably hexameters), which he was able to decode with his interpretive skills. We are very close here to an allegorical stance toward the literary text. With such considerations in mind, then, the ἱερ[ολογ]εῖται of column VII, an unusual term otherwise unattested in the classical period, likely indicates an association with prophetic speech.[34] I have suggested a change in the lacuna of line 4, where I have μαντικὴ ἤ, from Tsantsanoglou's ξένη τις ἤ. Tsantsanoglou places the xi outside the brackets, though he calls it "admittedly quite uncertain."[35] He adduces a parallel to Aristotle's comments on "riddles" in the *Poetics* (1458a) but does not take into account that Aristotle, as I will detail below, values αἴνιγμα as well as τὸ ξενικόν in a negative way, as flaws of style. This could not be farther from the Derveni commentator's position.

ῥηθέντα appears in the accusative though it seems to depend grammatically on the genitive plural τῶν ὀνομάτων, and the sense of middle ἱερ[ολογ]εῖται is difficult to discern.

[32] See Henry, 152.

[33] Plato uses a rare masculine form; see discussion in chap. 5.

[34] *LSJ* finds two meanings for it in later Greek, one of which is "prophesy."

[35] K. Tsantsanoglou, "The First Columns of the Derveni Papyrus," in Laks and Most, 121.

And while τὸ ξενικόν appears in proximity to αἴνιγμα in Aristotle, it actually marks a different flaw of style, the overuse of foreign words (as opposed to overuse of metaphor). As we will see in chapter 5, an association between divinatory and allegorical interpretation is attested in a variety of sources. On this basis, I have here suggested μαντικὴ ἤ, which is at least plausible and does fit the gap in the papyrus.[36]

Before considering the Derveni commentator's individual interpretations of the Orpheus poem, we should remark two further features of his text. First, he shows an interest in the cryptic philosophies of Heraclitus (column IV):[37]

> Heraclitus disguises common meanings and clothes them in strange ones; he speaks like a mythmaker in this line: "The sun by nature is the width of a man's foot, not overstepping its boundaries; for if it in some way goes out of its own widths, the Erinyes will search him out, the assistants of justice."
>
> Ἡράκλ[ε]ιτος με[τασκευάζων] τὰ κοινὰ
> κατ[αστέλ]λει[38] τὰ ἴδ[ι]α· ὅσπερ ἰκελ[οῖ μυθο]λόγωι λέγων [ὧδε]·[39]
> "ἥλι[ος ἑωυ]τοῦ κατὰ φύσιν ἀνθρω[πηίου] εὖρος ποδός [ἐστι]
> τοὺ[ς οὔρου]ς οὐχ ὑπερβάλλων· εἰ γά[ρ τι εὔ]ρους ἑ[ωυτοῦ]
> [ἐ]κ[βήσετα]ι, Ἐρινύε[ς] νιν ἐξευρήσου[σι, Δίκης ἐπίκουροι."

According to this passage, the philosopher Heraclitus speaks like a mythmaker. Not only does he refer to traditional mythological characters but he also tends to hide his meanings and speak in an oblique fashion. This characteristic is precisely that claimed for the Orpheus poem that is the commentator's main focus. The comparison with Heraclitus sets up a kind of equivalence between the texts. The esoteric philosopher and the poet-savant (as well as the oracle) produce texts that might equally be the subjects of allegorical inquiry. The crucial

[36] I recently asked Martin West, in correspondence (March 2001), whether such a reading is possible. He replied that in a letter to Tsantsanoglou in June 1984 he had already suggested MANTIKH, and after checking the papyrus, Tsantsanoglou replied that it fit the lacuna perfectly.

[37] On this text, see most recently, David Sider, "Heraclitus in the Derveni Papyrus," in Laks and Most, 129–48.

[38] Following A. V. Lebedev's reconstruction for the lacuna in line 6 ("Heraclitus in Derveni," *ZPE* 79 [1989]: 39).

[39] Sider suggests an even more provocative ending for this line: ὅσπερ ἴκελ[α ἱερο]λόγωι λέγων [ἔφη]. Should this be accurate, it would provide an even stronger tie between this writer, allegory in general, and prophetic discourse (Sider, 129). Sider also adduces (albeit late) texts that fold together ἱερολόγος with allegory. See Sider, 135, n. 17. Until there is more consensus on this term and also on the integrity of column VII, the matter remains somewhat difficult to judge.

similarity is that they contain hidden messages that the skilled interpreter can decode.[40] Again, as I see it, this multiple application of the approach does not on its own remove this kind of reading from "literary criticism" any more than the flexibility of rhetorical approaches (which are employed with equal ease on rhetorical speeches in prose histories and on poetic texts) compromises their "literariness."

In addition to divination and esoteric philosophy, the Derveni commentator shows a strong interest in a third allied field, which he also submits to his tools of analysis: cultic practice. The commentary gives several indications of a ritualized *Sitz-im-leben*. The text itself may have played some role in the funeral rites for the corpse with which it was buried. We have already mentioned column V, where the commentator discusses oracle reading at his shrine. In column XI he interprets a section of text dealing with an oracle proclaimed from a temple's *adyton*. Laks and Most characterize the papyrus as a whole as being "in the service of a project which was religious, and more particularly initiatory in character,"[41] a view that Dirk Obbink has presented at some length.[42] It is not at all surprising, then, that in column VI the Derveni commentator generates an interpretation of a particular ritual element: the fact that sacrificial knobby cakes are innumerable accords with the notion that souls are also innumerable. In column XX, the author expresses strong opinions on ritual performance. He sets up a contrast between the truly pious, who have a full (allegorical) understanding of texts/rituals and suppliants who perform the rites thoughtlessly. This contrast is one we will meet again in later Stoic and Neoplatonic material, where allegorical understanding is contrasted with mere performance.[43] We see here in a nascent form a long and enduring bias that uses allegorism to situate true piety in text and its interpretation rather than in ritual praxis. (The Pauline texts form another late analog here.) We will see various other kinds of overlapping between poetic myth, cult practice, and esoteric philosophy, and the interpretive possibilities that they all yield. Among allegorical commentators, all three cultural forms regularly come under the same general interpretive approach.

As with Porphyry, the Derveni commentator's enigma marks a kind of sense-shifting. In column X, the commentator devotes ten lines to teasing out the meaning of the form πανομφεύουσαν, an epithet that appears in the Orphic poem he is reading. Since the meaning of this

[40] Sider comments as follows: "Heraclitus—and this would be one of the Commentator's more perceptive observations—writes (prose) just like Orpheus's enigmatic sacred discourse" (Sider, 135).

[41] Laks and Most, 4.

[42] Obbink, 39–54.

[43] See chaps. 3 and 4.

term is difficult, the commentator follows a string of synonyms until a more serviceable sense is arrived at. He claims that τὸ λέγειν (to say) is the same as τὸ φωνεῖν (to speak), and the idea of teaching, τὸ διδάσκειν, is contained in the idea of τὸ λέγειν; therefore, πανομφεύουσαν (which literally means something like "all-proclaiming") is equivalent to πάντα διδάσκειν (to teach everything). This technique of reading appears exotic, but it actually has several contemporary *comparanda.* At *Cratylus* 398b–c, Plato attests that such a method was current enough in his day for Socrates to adopt it playfully. Socrates addresses the question of what Hesiod means by the "golden" race, and by the claim that the golden race became the spirits, or *daimones* (*WD* 122ff.). He says that when Hesiod called this race "golden" he meant that they were good; and those who are good are wise; and those who are wise are knowing [δαήμονες]. And so when Hesiod says that the golden race became the race of *daimones* he actually means that they were knowing. The Hippocratic treatise *On Regimen* puts the same technique to use. The author strings together a series of paired terms, declaring each of them in turn to be "the same" (*On Reg.* 1.4). Rusten also cites Thucydides 2.43.4, where happiness is freedom, freedom is bravery, and so to be happy, one ought to be brave.

Later in the commentary, in column XIII, we are offered a reading of the term αἰδοῖον, which appears in the poem. He begins by setting out a line from the poem:

> *he swallowed down the reverend one* [αἰδοῖον], *who was the first to leap forth into the aether.*

> Since he [the poet] riddles concerning his subject matter throughout all his poem, it is necessary to discuss it word by word. Since he saw that men consider birth to be dependent upon the genitals [αἰδοῖα], he used this word [i.e., αἰδοῖον]—it does not happen without the genitals—and likened the sun to "the reverend one" [αἰδοῖον]. For without the sun, it is not possible for such things that exist. . . .

> *αἰδοῖον κα[τ]έπινεν, ὃς αἰθέρα ἔχθορε πρῶτος.*
> ὅτι μὲν πᾶ[σ]αν τὴν πόησιν περὶ τῶν πραγμάτων
> αἰνίζεται κ[α]θ' ἔπος ἕκαστον ἀνάγκη λέγειν.
> ἐν τοῖς α[ἰδοίο]ις ὁρῶν τὴν γένεσιν τοὺς ἀνθρώπου[ς]
> νομίζο[ντας εἶ]ναι τούτωι ἐχρήσατο, ἄνευ δὲ τῶν
> αἰδοίων [οὐ γίν]εσθαι, αἰδοίωι εἰκάσας τὸν ἥλιο[ν]·
> ἄνε[υ γὰρ τοῦ ἡλίου] τὰ ὄντα τοιαῦτα οὐχ οἷόν τε. . . .

West and Rusten have both concluded that the Orphic poem that the Derveni commentator is interpreting must have used αἰδοῖον as an adjective in the sense of "reverend," modifying Protogonos, whom Zeus swallows, according to the Orphic legends.[44] But this reader finds further layers of meaning operative in the poet's word choice.[45] He suggests that the epithet "reverend" was chosen precisely because it has another common use as a noun, where it means "genitals."[46] The commentator then claims that this epithet, with its generative undersense, further points to the sun, since no generation of any kind is possible without the sun. The commentator assumes that the poet knew this fact and made use of it to convey a hidden meaning: Zeus swallowing the reverend one (Protogonos) is an enigma for him subsuming generative power as embodied in the sun/penis. Claude Calame has situated this rearranging of Hesiodic elements in a "typically Orphic vein of polemic against traditional theology."[47] In the commentator's theology, actions that Hesiod divides among major deities—the swallowing (Kronos swallows the stone) and castration (Ouranos castrated by Kronos)—are now centered on Zeus.

I think we can safely conjecture that Aristarchus would judge this type of reading to be ἔξω τῶν φραζομένων ὑπὸ τοῦ ποιητοῦ. The Derveni commentator, of course, would not share this view. More likely he believed that when, for example, the poet inserted the word πανομφεύουσαν into his poem, he at the same time brought in φωνεῖν, λέγειν, and διδάσκειν. Similarly, along with αἰδοῖον, "reverend," comes αἰδοῖον, "penis," and also the notion of generation in general, and finally other particular manifestations of the generative property, like the sun. We enrich our sense of the premises of such interpretive approaches if we take a broader look, such as Walter Burkert has done, at the philosophical underpinnings of the author's understandings of the cosmos and language. Burkert makes a compelling reading of the metaphysics behind the commentator's linguistic views and suggests that we see here a cosmogony (specifically, an Anaxagorean cosmogony) as onomatogony.[48] We have Nous operating as a grand, overarching principle that puts things in motion (P. Derv. XVI, cf. Anaxagoras D-K 59 B 13) and an early stage, where air and aether prevail, followed by a later stage in which motion separates all things. The separation, however, is

[44] M. L. West, *The Orphic Poems* (New York: Oxford University Press, 1983), 85; Rusten, 125. Burkert has suggested a connection with the Kumarbi story and is followed by Kirk, Raven, and Schofield. See Rusten, 125, n. 9, for references.

[45] On this section of text, see Claude Calame, "Sexuality and Initiatory Transition," in Laks and Most, 66–70.

[46] It usually appears in the plural in this sense, but the singular is used as well (Herodotus 2.30).

[47] Calame, 68.

[48] Burkert 1970, 450. Funghi also gives a perceptive reading of Burkert's article, in Laks and Most, 33. See also M. L. West, "Hocus-Pocus in East and West," in Laks and Most, 88.

not total: each thing has a share of every other thing in it (implied in P. Derv. XIX, cf. B 11). According to this metaphysical scheme, we identify things, and therefore assign names to them, not as wholly discrete entities, but rather on the basis of the predominating element in them (P. Derv. XIX, cf. B 12).

Such a metaphysics has profound implications for language, and sets up the preconditions for an expansive approach to literary interpretation. Crucially, the world is thought to have an underlying unity: the principle of all things in all things, plus the overarching interventions of the agitating Nous. In the face of such a universalist metaphysics, names take on a more provisional character, as designators of an underlying reality that is more synthetic and permeable than our words would have us believe. Sense shifting is here premised on connections through an underlying substance, and, to extend Burkert's observation, onomatology becomes intricately implicated in ontology. The study of words and their true referents always provokes a reconsideration of the true nature of things. On this view, the categories of language for the Derveni commentator hardly appear to be labels of simple, discrete entities in the world—a view that Aristotle champions. They are rather designations of a reality that has less stable boundaries. A word set inside a poem will itself pull at the other words that surround it; our attempt to cut apart these aspects of reality by making different words for them may or may not be completely successful. At several key points in the history of allegorical reading, we will see a similar cluster of ideas emerge. Some form of universalist ontology forms the basis for interpretive leaps from a surface sense to a hidden sense. The movement from one sense to the next is anchored through an assertion of ontological linkage. Such a universalist ontology is evidenced in three major schools of thought that are the most important engines of allegorical reading: the Anaxagoreans (P. Derv., Metrodorus), the Stoics (see chap. 3), and the Neoplatonists (see chap. 7). Such a metaphysics is also perhaps the most important presupposition standing behind the development of the notion of the poetic "enigma," which will, within a century of the Derveni commentator, lend itself to the creation of the "symbol."

Several of the Derveni commentator's interpretations demonstrate the importance of a universalist ontology in his methods. Zeus is the name for the air (for they both dominate all things), and Moira is his wisdom.[49]

[49] The Derveni commentator shares the interpretation of Zeus as air, though not the reasoning for it, with another Anaxagoras-influenced commentator, Diogenes of Apollonia: Διογένης ἐπαινεῖ τὸν Ὅμηρον ὡς οὐ μυθικῶς ἀλλ' ἀληθῶς ὑπὲρ τοῦ θείου διειλεγμένον. τὸν ἀέρα γὰρ αὐτὸν Δία νομίζειν φησίν, ἐπειδὴ πᾶν εἰδέναι τὸν Δία λέγει (D-K 64 A 8). Diogenes commends the view that Homer discoursed on the divine not in a mythic way but in a true one. For he claims that Homer considered the air to be Zeus, since he says that Zeus knows all.

These always existed, we are told, but they received their names when they emerged and separated themselves from the whole (columns XVII, XVIII). In column XXI we hear that when all things that exist now were mixed together, the name Aphrodite was applied to the whole. "Persuasion" was the name applied when they yielded to one another, and "Harmony" when they each were fitted together. These names emerge as part of the cosmogonic picture and will reemerge in different aspects of the universe as they evidence mixture, yielding, and harmony. These readings give us a conceptual meta-level above the specific reading of αἰδοῖον that we saw above: the generative principle, once invoked by αἰδοῖον, manifests itself in penis and sun. Column XXII adds a further consideration to these processes and tells us that the human invention of language produces a multiplicity of names for larger single entities. All names reflect the nature and limitations of humans, we are told. Since humans are corrupted by their own passions and ignorance and look at things according to their own idiosyncrasies, we get a multiplicity of names for a single reality: Ge, Meter, Rhea, and Hera are actually all designations of the earth. She was called Ge (Earth) by convention; Meter (Mother) because all things are born from her; Gaia (from Ge) because of a shift in dialect; Demeter from Ge + Meter with a corruption of the initial sound; Deio because she was cut [ἐδηιώθη] during sexual intercourse. The commentator then cites a line from the Orphic *Hymns*, "Demeter Rhea Ge Meter Hestia Deio," whose asyndeton suggests a vivid equivalence between these names. Each of these examples shows the Derveni commentator inhabiting a notion of the world whose basic premises confound human vocabularies, whose connections and unities escape normal language. Furthermore, the poet/savant is aware of this and conveys his knowledge of hidden connections in a code, which lies waiting for the perceptive interpreter to restore and reassemble.

In the Derveni text the most important notion that embraces this type of shape shifting is the αἴνιγμα. The repeated appearance of enigma terms in the Derveni commentary adds precious information to our fragmentary and mediated evidence of pre-Aristotelian approaches to reading literature. In this text the notion is the most prominent marker of an overall stance toward the poetic text as a repository of great (and even sacred) hidden truths, which are conveyed in riddles through the whole poem, in a manner that resembles the semantically dense language of oracular speech, esoteric philosophy, and cultic practice, and so requires an expansive interpretation to unpack the significance of each word. This constitutes a wholly different notion of what one does when one reads poetry than the one we know from Aristotle. For the Derveni commentator—and a whole line of allegorical readers after him—the poem is a riddle to be solved. For Aristotle, it is the masterwork of a craftsman to be appreciated. Of course the chance survival of a single papyrus does not allow us to conclude anything about how broadly its approach was used. To get a sense of this, we now turn to a wider range of evidence. Against the background picture that this next step will fill in for us, the Derveni text emerges as an invaluable close-up look at a single practitioner of a general approach to the poets that was not at all isolated to him.

Poetics of the Enigma

The Derveni text indicates that the enigma was surely a part of the conceptual apparatus of early allegorical reading. While our commentator likely has idiosyncratic views on some matters, especially on particular interpretations, it is unlikely that he invented the poetics of the riddle. He references it often, and in contexts that assume his audience will recognize what he means. Furthermore, as we will now see, when we consider the Derveni commentator within the larger corpus of classical authors, we find that several witnesses attest to poetic "enigmas" that, when read with attention to the term's connection with allegorism, further illuminate the wider currency of the approach at roughly the time the commentator is writing. The Derveni text does not prove that all early "enigmas" are connected with allegorical reading. However, we will see suggestive echoes of this in the broader testimony below. (This is a point to which we will return in chapter 5.) The absence of the term from the extant fragments of allegorical reading, all of them tiny and consisting of second- or third-hand materials, tells us very little. These scraps of evidence are simply too few and too mediated. As we will see here and in the rest of this study, the most common and enduring conceptual category within allegorical reading is not ἀλληγορία,[50] which Plutarch says is a neologism in his time (*De aud. po.* 19e–f), nor is it ὑπόνοια, which appears in a prominent location in Plato but is not very prominent in the allegorical texts themselves. Rather, αἴνιγμα terms are the real conceptual engines of allegorism.[51] They form the terrain onto which the symbol will enter as a synonym some time in the second half of the fourth century B.C.E., as we will see in chapter 2.

Aristophanes' mocking at the beginning of *Peace* (line 38 and following) is a good place to begin looking at the broader classical references

[50] One notable exception here is Heraclitus the Allegorist, whose commentary on Homer is clearly anchored by the notion of ἀλληγορία, though the other standard features of the vocabulary of allegorism appear there also.

[51] For references and discussion, good places to start are Buffière, 45–65, and Sheppard, 145.

to a poetics of the enigma. Here two servants wonder what deep meanings the whiz kids of their day will find in the disgusting dung beetle to which they are forced to attend.

SECOND SERVANT: What an indecent, stinking, gluttonous beast! I don't know what angry god let this monster loose upon us, but of a certainty it was neither Aphrodite nor the Graces.

FIRST SERVANT: Who was it then?

SECOND SERVANT: No doubt Zeus, the God of the Thundercrap.

FIRST SERVANT: But perhaps now some spectator, some beardless youth, who thinks himself a sage, will say, What is this? What does the beetle mean? And then an Ionian, sitting next to him, will add, I think he refers this enigmatically to Cleon,[52] who so shamelessly feeds on filth all by himself.

SECOND SERVANT: But now I'm going indoors to fetch the beetle a drink.[53]

ΟΙΚΈΤΗΣ Β:
μιαρὸν τὸ χρῆμα καὶ κάκοσμον καὶ βορόν·
χὤτου ποτ' ἐστὶ δαιμόνων ἡ προσβολὴ
οὐκ οἶδ'. 'Αφροδίτης μὲν γὰρ οὔ μοι φαίνεται,
οὐ μὴν Χαρίτων γε.

ΟΙΚΈΤΗΣ Α:
τοῦ γάρ ἐστ';

ΟΙΚΈΤΗΣ Β:
οὐκ ἔσθ' ὅπως
τοῦτ' ἔστι τὸ τέρας οὐ Διὸς καταιβάτου.

ΟΙΚΈΤΗΣ Α:
οὐκοῦν ἂν ἤδη τῶν θεατῶν τις λέγοι
νεανίας δοκησίσοφος, "τὸ δὲ πρᾶγμα τί;
ὁ κάνθαρος δὲ πρὸς τί;" κᾆτ' αὐτῷ γ' ἀνὴρ
'Ιωνικός τίς φησι παρακαθήμενος·
"δοκέω μέν, ἐς Κλέωνα τοῦτ' αἰνίσσεται,
ὡς κεῖνος ἀναιδέως τὴν σπατίλην ἐσθίει."

ΟΙΚΈΤΗΣ Β:
ἀλλ' εἰσιὼν τῷ κανθάρῳ δώσω πιεῖν.

This text, together with the Derveni Papyrus, makes a rather powerful witness. Derveni unmistakably shows enigma poetics to be part of the technical language of the professional allegorical interpreter. The Aristophanes text attests, equally unmistakably, that the methods of such

[52] A comparison with the syntax of *Birds* 970 suggests this rendering; see below, chap. 5.

[53] Modified from Eugene O'Neill's translation of Aristophanes, *Peace*, in *The Complete Greek Dramas* (New York: Random House, 1938), 2: 672.

professionals were familiar enough to an Athenian audience to get a laugh in the popular medium of comedy. So when Aristophanes mocks professional interpreters, he is doing it in their own terms. They must have been a recognizable "type" in Athens by the time he was writing. It is surely significant that the beardless youth has fallen under the spell of an Ionian. Ralph Rosen has pointed to a connection with the animal fable [αἶνος].[54] It could also of course be a general reference to the influx of philosophers from this region during the fifth century, who would be parodied for their general tendency to find deep meanings in things.[55] However, in light of the Derveni Papyrus, it seems more likely that Aristophanes was spoofing the followers of one particular famous Ionian immigrant of the fifth century, Anaxagoras. Anaxagoras spent time in Athens (c. 480–c. 450) and we know his followers to have been famous for their allegoresis.[56] Perhaps the "beardless youth, who thinks himself a sage," was someone like Metrodorus, whose interpretations we saw above, though his dates may be off. One candidate is Diogenes of Apollonia, who was part of Anaxagoras's circle, took an allegorical approach to Homer, and had already been a target of Aristophanes' satire in the *Clouds*.[57]

We find further witnesses to the poetics of the enigma in the Socratic dialogues.[58] Plato gives markers that his contemporaries are engaged in allegorical reading. The point is highlighted when set against the near absence, in his engagement with poetic texts, of the criteria and critical concerns that we recognize from Aristotle's work. Socrates' dismissive treatment of such Aristotelian issues in the poetry of Simonides in the *Protagoras* is telling:

> There are many things in the various expressions of the poem that demonstrate how finely it is composed—for it is very elegant and carefully wrought—but it would take too long to go through all this.

[54] Ralph Rosen, "The Ionian at Aristophanes *Peace* 46," *Greek, Roman and Byzantine Studies* 25.4 (1984): 389–96. Rosen explores the connection between αἶνος and αἰνίττομαι through the links of epinician praise poetry and the Ionian *iambos*. His work prompts a second look at an overlap between the traditions of Aesopean fable, epinician poetry, and allegorism, as attested by the etymological link. In chap. 5 I will attempt such an exploration, extending Gregory Nagy's observations on an "ideology of exclusiveness" (Nagy, *Best of the Achaeans* [Baltimore: Johns Hopkins University Press, 1979], 239–40).

[55] On this line of scholarship, see Rosen, 389–90.

[56] D-K 61 A 1.

[57] Specifically, his view that thinking operates by *aêr*. See *Clouds* 223–34, and note ad loc. by Jeffrey Henderson in his translation of the play (Newburyport, Mass.: Focus, 1993).

[58] On this topic, the work of J. Tate remains helpful ("Plato and Allegorical Interpretation," *Classical Quarterly* 23 [1929]: 142–56; continued in *CQ* 24 [1930]: 1–10).

πολλὰ μὲν γὰρ ἔστι καὶ περὶ ἑκάστου τῶν ἐν τῷ ᾄσματι εἰρημένων ἀποδεῖξαι ὡς εὖ πεποίηται—πάνυ γὰρ χαριέντως καὶ μεμελημένως ἔχει—ἀλλὰ μακρὸν ἂν εἴη αὐτὸ οὕτω διελθεῖν. (*Prot.* 344a–b)

Whatever irony could be present is mitigated by the fact that Plato, indeed, shows very little interest in such questions, either in the *Protagoras* or anywhere else. He is much less concerned with genre, techniques of producing plots, stylistic questions, etcetera, than he is with the epistemological status of the poets' claims. Plato is working within the paradigm that primarily sees poets as producers of insights into the nature of the divine, the structure of the cosmos, and the place of humans within it. This aspect of Plato's work sometimes strikes us as priggish and beside the point of literary analysis as Aristotle defines it. It is often and rightly placed in the context of the debate between poetry and philosophy, especially to illuminate the early emergence of philosophy as an authoritative discourse. Plato's difficulties with the poets tell us a little about the poets themselves but much more about how poets were commonly viewed during his time, and about the kinds of questions that would animate the "Homeric professors" of the day. Plato's criticisms are, in fact, indicative of just the kinds of concerns one would have if one were generating a critique of the poetics of the enigma. Here the poet as font of knowledge is the dominant model, and Plato's lavish critiques of this view show him rather deeply engaged, on the negative side, in a literary debate whose terms and premises are distinctly allegorical.

Allegorical reading is not foreign to Socrates and his interlocutors. In an often-cited passage from *Republic* 2, Socrates is willing to concede that allegorical meanings exist. He is excising from the guardians' curriculum a list of jarring poetic scenes: various bindings, rapes, and battles that happen among the gods. Traditional allegorical readings of such scenes survive, but Plato bars these sections of the text "whether they are written with hidden meanings or without them" [οὔτ' ἐν ὑπονοίαις πεποιημένας οὔτε ἄνευ ὑπονοιῶν], "for a young man [νέος] is unable to judge [κρίνειν] what is a hidden sense and what is not" (378d). With no apparent irony, Socrates allows that such hidden meanings might lurk in poetry, and perhaps even believes that the poets themselves produced these undersenses. (The designing hand of the poet seems to be at work in the passive participle πεποιημένας.) Xenophon attributes a similarly ambivalent stance to Socrates: Socrates does not question that "ὑπόνοιαι" exist (*Symp.* 3.5–6); indeed, he holds that there is no more foolish class of men [ἠλιθιώτερον ἔθνος] than rhapsodes, since they are ignorant of undermeanings, and pokes fun at Niceratus for paying great sums to Stesimbrotus and others to learn them.

The poses Socrates assumes in these texts attest more to the attitudes of his audience than to his own beliefs, but his audience's attitudes are precisely what helps us to determine the more general picture.

Plato's most concentrated treatment of poetry appears in the short dialogue, *Ion*. It is rarely remarked that the view of the poet that Plato assumes to be common, and on which he heaps ridicule, is one particularly characteristic of allegorical readers. Ion is locked into the view of Homer the savant:

> I consider myself to speak best among men about Homer, since neither Metrodorus of Lampsacus nor Stesimbrotus of Thasos nor Glaukon nor anyone else of those who ever lived were able to articulate so many and such fine meanings concerning Homer as I.
>
> οἶμαι κάλλιστα ἀνθρώπων λέγειν περὶ Ὁμήρου, ὡς οὔτε Μητρόδωρος ὁ Λαμψακηνὸς οὔτε Στησίμβροτος ὁ Θάσιος οὔτε Γλαύκων οὔτε ἄλλος οὐδεὶς τῶν πώποτε γενομένων ἔσχεν εἰπεῖν οὕτω πολλὰς καὶ καλὰς διανοίας περὶ Ὁμήρου ὅσας ἐγώ. (530c–d)

If he had used ὑπονοίας instead of διανοίας, it would have made the point more precisely, but the correlatives οὕτω πολλὰς . . . ὅσας, considered in the whole context of the dialogue, are very suggestive. Ion and his peers measure their skill as commentators by the sheer amount of material they are able to extract from Homer's text. Such a scale of values is worth remarking. It attests to a view that poetry's unique characteristic is a density of meaning, which nurtures a view of the task of the professional reader as primarily an interpretive one. Ion also includes himself in the ranks of readers whom we know from other sources to be famous for their allegorical approach, adding further evidence that the vision of poetry at which Plato pokes fun here is an allegorical one. Also, Ion's claims that Homer knows everything (and that he himself does, too, by transference), will find many echoes in later allegorical readers. Homer the polymath is a recurrent figure in the later material.[59] If during Plato's time the Homeric professors were famous for textual criticism, or grammatical commentary, or the articulation of formalist criteria, we would have expected to see these methods, rather than allegoresis, caricatured in the dialogue in which Plato gives the most specific attention to poetry.

In the *Cratylus*, a dialogue in which Plato toys with etymological allegory, he gives us our first attestation of a few standard readings in the repertoire of allegorical critics. He tells us of the equation of Hera with the air (404c)[60] and later in the dialogue refers to Homer's readers

[59] See discussion of this in chap. 4.

[60] On the equation of Hera and the air, see esp. Michael Murrin, *The Allegorical Epic* (Chicago: University of Chicago Press, 1980), 3–25.

as a class "most of whom" say that Homer made out Athena to be the mind and intellect:

> Indeed, even the ancients seem to think about Athena just as those who are currently skilled concerning Homer do. For the majority of these in interpreting the poet say that he has made out Athena to be mind and thought.
>
> ἐοίκασι δὴ καὶ οἱ παλαιοὶ τὴν Ἀθηνᾶν νομίζειν ὥσπερ οἱ νῦν περὶ Ὅμηρον δεινοί. καὶ γάρ τούτων οἱ πολλοὶ ἐξηγούμενοι τὸν ποιητήν φασι τὴν Ἀθηνᾶν αὐτὸν νοῦν τε καὶ διάνοιαν πεποιηκέναι. (407a–b)

Plato here tells us that Homeric commentators *generally* made judgments such as those we know to be part of the allegorical tradition. Also, the tradition was developed and diffused enough for Plato to remark on one of its standard views. Though the Greek is somewhat ambiguous, one reading of it tells that these critics thought that Homer (αὐτός) has made Athena out to be the mind.[61] This echoes the sentiment hinted at in *Republic* 2.378d and provides us with secondhand evidence that the allegorical critics of Plato's time generally thought Homer himself intended his undermeanings.

In the *Theaetetus*, which questions what knowledge really is, allegoresis pops up several times, reiterating the close tie between poets and epistemological questions in Plato's time. If we assume also that Plato is mimicking the techniques of argumentation of his opponents in order to show their flaws (something he is prone to do), the dialogue also suggests a tie between allegoresis and Ionian philosophy, particularly that of Heraclitus. This carries forward an association we saw exhibited also in the Derveni Papyrus. Socrates and his interlocutors draw their proof texts just as easily from Homer as they do from earlier philosophers, and nearly every time Homer's name comes up in the dialogue, it is in the context of allegorical reading. In favor of the doctrine that all things are constantly in flux, Socrates cites Protagoras, Heraclitus, and Empedocles, but also the "chief poets in the two kinds of poetry, Epicharmus, in comedy, and Homer in tragedy" (*Theaet.* 152e; cf. 160d, 179e). The Homer text he has in mind is *Iliad* 14.201: "Oceanus the origin of the gods, and Tethys their mother." Socrates claims that Homer *really* means "that all things are born from flow and motion." A little later in the dialogue, Socrates reads one of Homer's infamous scenes allegorically. Zeus boasts that all the gods together could not pull him off his lofty post if they tried to drag him by a golden chain, but that he would win the tug of war and dangle them and the earth with them from the peak of Olympus. Socrates interprets the "golden chain" as the "sun" and says

[61] Cf. a nearly identical grammatical construction, using αὐτός, in Diogenes of Apollonia (D-K 64 A 8).

that Homer here makes clear that "as long as the heavens and the sun are in motion all things, both human and divine, exist and are preserved, but if it should stop, as if bound fast, everything would be destroyed and would, as the saying is, be upside down" [ἕως μὲν ἂν ἡ περιφορὰ ᾖ κινουμένη καὶ ὁ ἥλιος, πάντα ἔστι καὶ σῴζεται τὰ ἐν θεοῖς τε καὶ ἀνθρώποις, εἰ δὲ σταίη τοῦτο ὥσπερ δεθέν, πάντα χρήματ' ἂν διαφθαρείη καὶ γένοιτ' ἂν τὸ λεγόμενον ἄνω κάτω πάντα.] (*Theaet.* 153d). And at 180c, we hear a very general characterization of the nature of poetry, as seen from within the allegorical tradition. In returning to the question of whether the whole world is constantly in flux, as the Heracliteans say in maddeningly unclear terms, Socrates states the following:

> Now, is the issue at all different which we have received on the one hand from the ancients, who concealed their meaning from the multitude by their poetry, and said that Oceanus and Tethys, which are things that flow, are the origin of everything else and that nothing is at rest, and on the other hand from the moderns, who since they are wiser declare their meaning openly in order that even shoemakers may learn it by attending lectures and may stop foolishly thinking that some things are at rest and other things are in motion, and after they have learned that everything is in motion, hold their teachers in esteem?
>
> τὸ δὲ δὴ πρόβλημα ἄλλο τι παρειλήφαμεν παρὰ μὲν τῶν ἀρχαίων μετὰ ποιήσεως ἐπικρυπτομένων τοὺς πολλούς, ὡς ἡ γένεσις τῶν ἄλλων πάντων Ὠκεανός τε καὶ Τηθὺς ῥεύματα <ὄντα> τυγχάνει καὶ οὐδὲν ἕστηκε, παρὰ δὲ τῶν ὑστέρων ἅτε σοφωτέρων ἀναφανδὸν ἀποδεικνυμένων, ἵνα καὶ οἱ σκυτοτόμοι αὐτῶν τὴν σοφίαν μάθωσιν ἀκούσαντες καὶ παύσωνται ἠλιθίως οἰόμενοι τὰ μὲν ἑστάναι, τὰ δὲ κινεῖσθαι τῶν ὄντων, μαθόντες δὲ ὅτι πάντα κινεῖται τιμῶσιν αὐτούς; (*Theaet.* 180c–d)

The irony is rich, but the poses Socrates strikes here and elsewhere in the *Theaetetus* are not at all far from the positions we see in the Derveni text, and not out of step with the other information Plato gives us when he adopts the manner of an expert in myth and poetry. We find a similar stance taken by the Egyptian priest in the *Timaeus* as he reads the myth of Phaethon. When the story says that Phaethon drives his father's chariot awry, it really means that the sun periodically swerves too close to the earth and consumes it by fire: "This is told in the form of a myth, but the truth of it lies in a shifting of the bodies that travel around the earth throughout the heavens and after great stretches of time there arises a destruction of those on earth by a great fire" [τοῦτο μύθου μὲν σχῆμα ἔχον λέγεται, τὸ δὲ ἀληθές ἐστι τῶν περὶ γῆν κατ' οὐρανὸν ἰόντων παράλλαξις καὶ διὰ μακρῶν χρόνων γιγνομένη τῶν ἐπὶ γῆς πυρὶ πολλῷ φθορά.] (*Tim.* 22c–d).

Often in the Platonic corpus, we find this kind of reading marked with cognates of αἴνιγμα, which situates the idea that poetry is a source of hidden knowledge within the poetics of the enigma. In the *Theaetetus* Plato has Socrates draw a connection between the heart and wax. He explores the theory that the soul receives impressions and is literally molded by them. In this context he makes a reference to Homer's language for heart [κέαρ (contracted form = κῆρ)] and points out the similarity with the word for wax [κηρός].

> When the wax in the soul of someone is deep and abundant and smooth and moderately tempered, data that come through the perceptions are imprinted upon this, the "heart" of the soul—as Homer calls it, enigmatically indicating its similarity to "wax"—then . . . the imprints . . . are longlasting. . . .
>
> ὅταν μὲν ὁ κηρός του ἐν τῇ ψυχῇ βαθύς τε καὶ πολὺς καὶ λεῖος καὶ μετρίως ὠργασμένος ᾖ, τὰ ἰόντα διὰ τῶν αἰσθήσεων, ἐνσημαινόμενα εἰς τοῦτο τὸ τῆς ψυχῆς "κέαρ," ὅ ἔφη Ὅμηρος αἰνιττόμενος τὴν τοῦ κηροῦ ὁμοιότητα τότε . . . τὰ σημεῖα . . . πολυχρόνια γίγνεται. . . . (*Theaet.* 194c)

We find similar enigmas attested in the probably spurious *Second Alcibiades*. This author portrays Socrates reading the Homeric *Margites* in much the same way the Socrates of the *Theaetetus* reads Homer. The poetic passage under scrutiny runs as follows: "Many crafts he knew, but he knew them all poorly" [πολλ' ἠπίστατο ἔργα, κακῶς δ'ἠπίστατο πάντα] (Theaet. 147b). The poet, Socrates tells us, has enigmatically given an adverb form that hints at an intended noun form and an infinitive form that hints at a finite form. He interprets it this way:

> For you don't think, I suppose, that Homer, the most divine and wisest poet does not know that it is impossible to know "poorly" . . . but he speaks enigmatically, I think, bringing in the "poorly" to stand for "evil," and "knew" for "to know." So if we put it together, letting the meter go, indeed, but grasping his meaning, we get this: "Many crafts he knew, but it was evil for him to know them all."
>
> οὐ γὰρ δήπου Ὅμηρόν γε τὸν θειότατόν τε καὶ σοφώτατον ποιητὴν ἀγνοεῖν δοκεῖς ὡς οὐχ οἷόν τε ἦν ἐπίστασθαι κακῶς . . . ἀλλ' αἰνίττεται οἶμαι παράγων τὸ κακῶς μὲν ἀντὶ τοῦ κακοῦ, τὸ δὲ ἠπίστατο ἀντὶ τοῦ ἐπίστασθαι· γίγνεται οὖν συντεθὲν ἔξω μὲν τοῦ μέτρου, ἔστι δ' ὅ γε βούλεται, ὡς πολλὰ μὲν ἠπίστατο ἔργα, κακὸν δ' ἦν ἐπίστασθαι αὐτῷ πάντα ταῦτα. (*Alc.* 2, 147c–d)

The shape shifting here takes place not just within schemes of synonyms but across parts of speech. It is difficult to say whether this attests to a particular kind of reading or an ironic *reductio* of a general kind of reading. Even more significant, the *Second Alcibiades* author prefaces this interpretation with a rather sweeping statement of the poetics of the enigma. Socrates here characterizes poetry in general to be the production of riddles.

> Well, this man [the poet of the Margites] is speaking enigmatically, my good fellow, he and nearly all the other poets too. For the whole poetic art is by nature riddling and it is not for just any man to understand it.
>
> ἀλλ' αἰνίττεται, ὦ βέλτιστε, καὶ οὗτος καὶ ἄλλοι δὲ ποιηταὶ σχεδόν τι πάντες. ἔστιν τε γὰρ φύσει ποιητικὴ ἡ σύμπασα αἰνιγματώδης καὶ οὐ τοῦ προστυχόντος ἀνδρὸς γνωρίσαι. (*Alc. 2* 147b)

This is a remarkably broad characterization. Knowing what we do about the role of αἰνίττεται in allegorical reading, it is difficult to imagine such a statement being made absent a rather general currency of such an approach. It is difficult to date this text with certainty, but we find a confirmation of the view in the *Republic*. In that dialogue, Plato gives a mock grandeur to the ideas of the poet Simonides, which turn out to lead to absurdities when read literally. "As it turns out, Simonides was speaking enigmatically, in a poetic manner, about what the just is" [ᾐνίξατο ἄρα, ἦν δ' ἐγώ, ὡς ἔοικεν, ὁ Σιμωνίδης ποιητικῶς τὸ δίκαιον ὃ εἴη] (*Rep*. 332b–c). This text indicates that during Plato's time speaking enigmatically is very closely linked with speaking poetically. Given the word order, the verb and the adverb have an almost appositional character in the sentence.

At several additional places in the corpus, Plato uses the notion of "speaking in enigmas" as a trope of subtle mockery in addressing the ideas (or in his view, dogmas) of others. In these cases, Plato tests a chestnut of wisdom passed down from an ancient authority, a poet or philosopher, runs into aporia, then claims (with tongue firmly in cheek) that the saying must have been an "enigma" for something else, since the ideas turn out to be so far-fetched that the putatively wise speaker simply cannot have meant what he said. These texts set Plato's tone quite close to the Aristophanes reference with which we began. In the *Republic* passage dealing with Simonides that we just examined, Simonides had suggested that the just is "to render to each his due." With typical irony starting to rise, Socrates says that it is not easy to disbelieve this poet, who is a wise and divine man [σοφὸς καὶ θεῖος ἀνήρ], but there are problems in his definition. What if a person does technically owe something to someone but returning it will cause that person harm—that can't be just, can it? No, answers the interlocutor. So, it must be that the poet was speaking in enigmas, as it turns out [ᾐνίξατο ἄρα] (*Rep*. 332b). As is characteristic, Plato uses the ἄρα with subtle but cutting ironic effect—a grace note of mock surprise at an actually well-foreseen conclusion. According to Socrates, the poet enigmatically tells us that actually justice is rendering to each what befits him [τὸ προσῆκον]. The name that he gave to this "thing which is befitting" was the "thing which is due" [τοῦτο δὲ ὠνόμασεν ὀφειλόμενον]. Here αἰνίττομαι marks a shift in sense, where one word evokes another in an oblique fashion. The Derveni text uses the term in precisely this way.

Consistent with this treatment of Simonides, Plato elsewhere mocks supposedly wise authorities by invoking the notion of the enigmatic. At *Charmides* 162a–b, for example, Socrates tests the idea that "temperance" [σωφροσύνη] is "attending to one's own business" [τὸ τὰ αὑτοῦ πράττειν], a definition that has come from some "wise man" (who turns out to be Critias). This definition, Socrates begins, seems to be an enigma. Would we call it intemperance, for example, every time people did something for someone else? Of course not, comes the reply. The person who offered the definition, says Socrates ironically, couldn't have been so foolish [εὐήθης] and idiotic [ἠλίθιος] as to mean it literally. So it seems he was speaking enigmatically, as it turns out [ἠινίττετο ἄρα, ὡς ἔοικεν]. The ἄρα here does the same subtle work of mockery that it did in the *Republic* passage. Socrates concludes: "Then it is certain, in my opinion, that he propounded it as a riddle, in view of the difficulty of understanding what on earth 'attending to one's own business' is" [παντὸς τοίνυν μᾶλλον, ὡς ἐμοὶ δοκεῖ, αἴνιγμα αὐτὸ προύβαλεν, ὡς ὂν χαλεπὸν τὸ τὰ αὑτοῦ πράττειν γνῶναι ὅτι ποτε ἔστιν]. The ὅτι ποτε extends the ironic distance between the supposedly wise enigmatic man and the actual producer of foolery.

Such mockery is also present at *Lysis* 214b–d. Socrates here interprets a maxim, "Like is attracted to like," culled from Homer (*Od.* 17.218) and unnamed other "eminently wise men" [σοφώτατοι] who discuss the natural world and the universe [περὶ φύσεώς τε καὶ τοῦ ὅλου]. The maxim is questionable, Socrates suggests, since those who harm people are repellent to everyone, including people of their own ilk. In fact, it is only people who bring some benefit that are able to attract others. Therefore these eminently wise poets and philosophers must have been speaking enigmatically [τοίνυν αἰνίττονται]; and when they said that like is attracted to like, they really meant that the good alone belongs to the good alone, and that the bad is a friend to no one. In the *Theaetetus* (152a–e), Protagoras's maxim that "man is the measure of all things" is treated identically. First Socrates states "It is likely that a wise man does not prattle foolishly" [εἰκὸς μέντοι σοφὸν ἄνδρα μὴ ληρεῖν]; next he demolishes the position, then he concludes that this "all-wise" man must have "spoken enigmatically" here, since no one could actually mean to say something so foolish. Socrates goes further and suggests a purposeful esotericism: Protagoras must have produced the maxim as an enigma for the common people but told the real truth to his own inner circle in secret [ἆρ' οὖν πρὸς Χαρίτων πάσσοφός τις ἦν ὁ Πρωταγόρας, καὶ τοῦτο ἡμῖν μὲν ᾐνίξατο τῷ πολλῷ συρφετῷ, τοῖς δὲ μαθηταῖς ἐν ἀπορρήτῳ τὴν ἀλήθειαν ἔλεγεν;]. Socrates positions enigmatic language as a method of shielding true insights from the mob (presumably, the mob is unable to deal properly with such powerful wisdom). This aspect of the caricature accords with what we can see in the record of allegorical readers. The esoteric character of philosophical insight will be confirmed regularly in the poetics of the enigma. The enigma (as well as the symbol, we will see) is a language that hides as much as it reveals and produces always two groups, the enlightened and the unenlightened.

In all four of these cases—Simonides in the *Republic*, the wise man in *Charmides*, the sages (including Homer) who know the secrets of the universe in the *Lysis*, and Protagoras in the *Theaetetus*—we have the same basic elements.[62] Socrates examines a nugget of wisdom, finds it faulty, ironically claims that we need to read it as an enigma in order to understand its real message, and then puts forward an interpretation of the saying. In all cases his irony undercuts the authority of the speakers of these maxims as well as the interpreters who look to such figures for hidden wisdom. He casts both sorts as pettifoggers.[63] This attests to Plato's view that such interpretation is the last refuge of the fool but also, once again, to a developed, mature tradition of such a practice among his contemporaries. Plato could not have constructed such a subtly cutting rhetorical position without it, nor would he have returned to this particular form of teasing with such regularity. Again, mockery attests to a common cultural type.

In Plato's corpus most of those who speak in αἰνίγματα are poets, but like the Derveni commentator, he also testifies to the use of the poetics of the enigma to interpret other cultural phenomena. The *Theaetetus*'s treatment of Protagoras and the *Lysis* passage show that certain esoteric philosophers, who discuss great matters obliquely, might be thought to speak in enigmas. Interestingly, like the Derveni commentator, Plato says that ritual actions can also be decoded as enigmas. In the *Phaedo* he claims to find a hidden meaning in the mysteries:

> It is likely that those who established the mysteries were not some trifling men, but in reality they long ago expressed enigmatically that whoever arrives in Hades uninitiated and unsanctified will lie in the mire, but he who arrives there purified and initiated will live with the gods.
>
> καὶ κινδυνεύουσι καὶ οἱ τὰς τελετὰς ἡμῖν οὗτοι καταστήσαντες οὐ φαῦλοί τινες εἶναι, ἀλλὰ τῷ ὄντι πάλαι αἰνίττεσθαι ὅτι ὃς ἂν ἀμύητος καὶ ἀτέλεστος

[62] We could also add *Apology* 27a–d, where Socrates follows the same strategy with his accusers.

[63] Cf. *Theaetetus* 180a, where the Heracliteans are said to use "little enigmatic phrases" to avoid rigorous argument.

εἰς Ἅιδου ἀφίκηται ἐν βορβόρῳ κείσεται, ὁ δὲ κεκαθαρμένος τε καὶ τετελεσμένος ἐκεῖσε ἀφικόμενος μετὰ θεῶν οἰκήσει. (69c)

Added to the Derveni commentator's testimony, this evidence from Aristophanes, Xenophon, Plato, and the *Second Alcibiades* shows a rather developed tradition of reading "enigmas," centered on ancient and authoritative poetic texts but also applicable to ritual and certain kinds of philosophy.

As we will see in more detail in subsequent chapters, for literary critics with allegorical affiliations, the logic of the enigma takes central position. The enigma, and later the symbol and its cognates, live in ongoing tension with central notions of Aristotelian criticism: that the best poetry makes use of clear language, subsumable under a scheme of tropes, to produce an effect on an audience, by a straightforward mimesis of the world. Perhaps this explains the radically different evaluation of the notion of enigmatic language by rhetorical critics. Nearly all of them, beginning with Aristotle (as we will see in a moment), define an αἴνιγμα as a *flaw* of style, one that a skilled poet avoids since it produces unclarity. As we will see in chapter 5, with its attendant senses of riddle, omen, and oracle, the αἴνιγμα marks out an obliqueness of signification, situated outside the concerns of the τέχναι of language and plot and the dictates of genre and character. It hints at hidden connections within reality itself and lays out a particular program of action for the reader of poetry: to decode. As with the sayings of the Sphinx or the Pythia, the point is to solve the riddle. We also find the suggestion that the poets' hidden meanings are underwritten by an underlying entelechy, rather than the logic of mere mimesis or resemblance of the sort that governs the surface meanings of the poem. For the allegorists, the study of diction or plot types or character (such as the Aristotelian critics emphasize) may be important but usually as a preliminary step[64] to what they see as the central task of the reader of poetry: rooting out the deep meanings that are understood to be lurking underneath the mimetic surface of the poem.[65]

[64] Porphyry, *Quaestionum Homericarum*, ed. A. R. Sodano, 1.22–28. The simple arrangement of the books in Pseudo-Plutarch's *Life of Homer*, with lexical issues coming first, followed by allegorical ones, exemplifies the attitude. Cf. Philo *De conf. ling.* 143, cited in J. I. Porter, "Philo's Confusion of Tongues," *Quaderni Urbinati di Cultura Classica* 24 (1986): 55–74.

[65] These observations fit in generally with a picture of early poetics developed by Detienne in his *Homère, Hésiode et Pythagore: Poésie et philosophie dans le pythagorisme ancien* (Bruxelles-Berchem: Latomus, 1962), and also in his *Les maîtres de vérité*. Using the categories that Detienne has uncovered to classify my own conclusions, the allegorical approach to poetry is a stealthy survival of an archaic view of the poet as a "master of truth" who—along with the diviner and the king—is thought to have access to an ex-

Pre-Aristotelians on Language

This reconstruction of the poetics of the enigma can be fruitfully supplemented by a brief look at a few of the more prominent pre-Aristotelian theories of language. Even this cursory examination will show that Aristotle's notion of clear language, sensible as it seems, was actually a radical departure from the intellectual currents of the day. It stands out in stark relief against the extant evidence for the linguistic theories that preceded him. At the same time, it will show that the problematics of the αἴνιγμα, which simply assumes a fraught and nearly always contestable relation between word and world, was actually more in step with the linguistic theories of the time. Given the fragmentary state of the record, none of the theories we will here examine can be considered "representative" in any meaningful sense. Rather, they are pieces of information that give us some sense of what others were saying about language at the time Aristotle wrote. They do, however, attest that before Aristotle the connection between language and the world was often laden with epistemological and ontological consequences. This vision of language further enriches our understanding of an approach to poetry that sees the reader's job as primarily interpretive and focused on digging "underneath" words to their unapparent referents.

Heraclitus: The Word as Riddle

Heraclitus (fl. 500 B.C.E.) understood all the realities of the world to be in a state of continuous flux. Even seemingly solid things, like a bronze sword handle, for example, wear away over time. Plato testifies to the linguistic problems that lurk beneath Heraclitus's ontological theory. Under Heraclitus's scheme, Plato says, the moment we try to pin something down under a name, it flows out from under us and becomes something else (*Crat.* 439b–e). If we cannot step into the same river twice, which Heraclitus was the first to tell us, how will we be able to give any of the world's mercurial realities a name? The fragments that remain of Heraclitus's work show us a philosopher with a keen interest in the linguistic oddities that arise from this ontological situation. He was fond of pointing out places where our language and the world don't quite fit. For example, when we try to discuss something like god,

traordinary range of knowledge through a kind of panoptic sight. The speech of these figures is of a different order from that of other humans: it is efficacious and revelatory. Allegoresis is charged and vivified by such a view of the poet. Though it is not endorsed by most later allegorists, it is clearly present in the Derveni Papyrus and likely provided the ground from which sprang a habit of interpretation that developed a life all its own.

Heraclitus suggests that we speak this way: "God is day night, winter summer, war peace, satiety hunger" [ὁ θεὸς ἡμέρη εὐφρόνη, χειμὼν θέρος, πόλεμος εἰρήνη, κόρος λιμός] (D-K 22 B67).[66] His pairs of opposites constitute less a "naming" than a commentary on naming and its limitations. When it comes to the divine, our language is simply not up to the task. In Heraclitus's thinking, these difficulties present themselves not only with abstract realities, like the divine, but also with mundane objects in the world. In another famous example, he points out that the word for bow [βιός], an instrument of death, has the same letters as the word for life [βίος] (D–K 22 B48). Here Heraclitus suggests that language is a misleading veil and cannot fix its referent in any sure way.

Perhaps more significant, Heraclitus elsewhere says that though humans have heard the divine λόγος, an expansive "language" that underlies and constitutes the world as it really is, they do not understand it (D-K 22 B1). It seems we have to resort to paradoxical riddles to make our language approximate the way things are. Heraclitus expressed all these linguistic concerns most pointedly in his notoriously enigmatic style. His formulations, like "day night," are difficult not just to modern translators; the ancients remarked on it too—and when they did, interestingly enough, at least one of them resorted to language that had long been in use by the allegorists. Timon of Phlius, a third-century B.C.E. satirist, dubbed Heraclitus the "riddler" [αἰνικτής] (Diogenes Laertius 9.6). Through his style Heraclitus reveals a view that language does not do precisely what it sets out to do. Language is an opaque surface whose relationship to the way things really are falls under a heavy burden of suspicion.

Gorgias: The Word as Magic Spell

Though we don't know the full extent to which the Sophists were dedicated students of the philosophy of language, the provocative view of Gorgias of Leontini (c. 485–c. 380 B.C.E.) survives. If we are to judge from the effort Plato devotes to refuting him in the *Gorgias*, he was prominent among these arguers for hire. In the *Encomium of Helen* (D-K 82 B11), he calls language "a great master, who with the tiniest and least visible body achieves the most divine works" [λόγος δυνάστης μέγας ἐστίν, ὅς σμικροτάτωι σώματι καὶ ἀφανεστάτωι θειότατα ἔργα ἀποτελεῖ] (*Hel.* 8). Language is a drug that can drive the humors and end either illness or life. It has the power to "drug" [φαρμακεύω] (*Hel.* 14)

[66] Texts of the Presocratics from H. Diels and W. Kranz, *Fragmente der Vorsokratiker*, 6th ed. (Berlin: Weidmann, 1951).

and "bewitch" [μετέστησεν γοητείαι] (*Hel.* 10).[67] Gorgias here compares the power of language—which was quite evident to the Sophists, who made their living by it—with the irresistible powers of medicaments and spells. He has in mind a quite physical process. Charles P. Segal put it this way: "It is . . . apparent that Gorgias regarded his rhetoric as having more than a superficial effect on the ear, as actually reaching and 'impressing' the psyche of the hearer. All persuasion is thus action upon and manipulation of the psyche of the audience; and the *dynamis* of the *logos* (*Hel.* 14) acts like a real drug in affecting the state of the psyche."[68]

Even more explicitly than Heraclitus, Gorgias indicates his suspicions of the fraught relation between language and world. He tells us, pointedly: "That by which we impart information [μηνύομεν] is language [λόγος], but language is not the things that are or that exist; we do not then impart to others the things that exist, but only language, which is other than the things that exist" (D-K 82 B3 84).[69] This could be a simple assertion, similar to ones that Plato makes, that a representation is not and cannot be the thing itself. But, given the larger context of Gorgias's thought, he is probably remarking on the freedom of language from the world. Segal and Rosenmeyer agree on this point: Gorgias has discovered an "autonomy of speech," where "speech is not a reflection of things, not a mere tool or slave of description, but . . . it is its own master."[70]

Plato: The Word as Drug, Screen, or Tool

In Plato's corpus, we need to take account of several positions. First, despite his thorough critique of Gorgianic views in the *Gorgias*, Plato still thinks language has the power to act as a *pharmakon*.[71] If poetic language was a drug for Gorgias, Plato wants to ensure that it is a prescription drug, carefully regulated and controlled by the state. Like a *pharmakon* (which can be understood as a magic spell as well as a drug),[72] the word enters the body and has the power to produce delu-

[67] This theory recapitulates the view of Gorgias's teacher, the philosopher Empedocles.

[68] Charles P. Segal, "Gorgias and the Psychology of the Logos," *Harvard Studies in Classical Philology* 66 (1962): 105.

[69] Cited in Segal, 109.

[70] Rosenmeyer, "Gorgias, Aeschylus, and *Apate*," *AJP* 76 (1955): 231–32; cited in Segal, 110.

[71] Elizabeth Asmis, "Plato on Poetic Creativity," in R. Kraut, ed., *Cambridge Companion to Plato* (New York: Cambridge University Press, 1992), 348.

[72] See C. Pharr, "The Interdiction of Magic in Roman Law," *TAPA* 63 (1932): 272–74; Fritz Graf, "An Oracle against Pestilence from Western Anatolia," *ZPE* 92 (1992): 276–77. See also A.L.T. Bergren, "Helen's 'Good Drug' (Odyssey 4.305)," in S. Kresic, ed.,

sions by shaping a weak soul.[73] According to Plato, language can introduce phantom realities that distort the truth and lead us away from it. We can see this concern at work in Plato's notorious banishment of the poets in book 10 of the *Republic*. He tells us, over and over again, that the poets make *eidôla* [εἴδωλα], a term that marks the conjuration of spirits, ghosts, and phantoms.[74] Plato's theory grows out of an anxiety provoked by an appreciation of the power of language to invoke a world—an appreciation not far removed from the idea of language as a magic spell. The *eidôlon* theory warns us against the poets' power to delude us through representations, to show us beguiling semblances of things that do not really exist. In this sense the poet is something like a conjurer, with the power to call up phantoms. Such a view casts suspicion on the whole process of linguistic mimesis, in literary and other contexts. In additon to his admonitions about the poets, Plato extends his caveats on language to other unscrupulous wordsmiths, like the Sophists. In several dialogues Plato treats language as a filter, sometimes distorting, that stands *between* us and the phenomenal world.[75] Since we make use of this filter, we run the risk of distorting the world of appearances, and so bringing ourselves even further away from the true realities that underlie the phenomena.[76] This distrust culminates in a call for us to move beyond the screen of words and to apprehend things in themselves.[77]

In the *Cratylus*, named for one of Heraclitus's students, Plato includes a third vision of language, which is of specific importance for Aristotle and so requires a more extended consideration.[78] In the dialogue, he explores, though does not in the end accept, the theory of a natural connection between word and thing. He proceeds, for the most part, by testing the theory of whether the sound of a word might somehow match the idea it conveys—for example, whether the sound of the aspirated rho in the word for "to flow" [ῥεῖν] might convey a sense of

---

Contemporary Literary Hermeneutics and the Interpretation of Classical Texts (Ottawa, 1981), 201–14.

[73] Asmis, 341–48.

[74] *Rep.* 10 598b, 599a, 599d, 600e, 601b, 605c.

[75] The general attitude is apparent in the *Protagoras*, *Cratylus*, and *Phaedrus*.

[76] *Crat.* 438e, 439b.

[77] *Crat.* 439a–b; this stance is also apparent in the terms with which Socrates disparages rhetoric in the *Phaedrus* (234e–235a, 261e–262c, 273d–e). He suspects the rhetorician is focusing only on words and not on the things themselves.

[78] The bibliography on the *Cratylus* is, of course, vast. For an introduction to it, see Allan Silverman, "Plato's *Cratylus*: The Nature of Naming and the Naming of Nature," *Oxford Studies in Ancient Philosophy* 10 (1992): 25–71. My indebtedness to Norman Kretzmann's still classic article, "Plato on the Correctness of Names" (*American Philosophical Quarterly* 8 [April 1971]: 126–38), will be apparent.

movement, since our tongue is agitated when we pronounce it (426d). While the abundance of counterexamples leaves Plato doubtful that certain sounds are naturally linked with certain meanings, he is skeptical too of pure conventionalism. First of all, a person cannot arbitrarily assign to a thing any name he or she pleases. But further, the naming of things is not merely a matter of a group of speakers collectively deciding on one name rather than another (437d, 438c). This would be to engage in the kind of majoritarian reasoning that the Sophists liked to use to further their own ends, and against which Plato is consistently pitched. Socrates will not give up the idea that words must answer not to the community but to reality,[79] that the particular words on which a community agrees make a difference. In fact, in the dialogue, the giving of names remains a rare skill, one reserved for the rarest of the artisans (389a).

It remains difficult to make a final statement of precisely what middle ground there might be between the two pitfalls. But to get a sense of what is at stake here, we need to look at a third of Plato's linguistic theories: the word as tool [ὄργανον]. In the *Cratylus* Socrates considers a range of tools, including the shuttle, which separates, and the awl, which pierces. The word also is a tool.

> SOCRATES: Now do you suppose that we say this also concerning a name. By using the name as a tool, what do we do when we name?
> HERMOGENES: I cannot say.
> SOCRATES: Don't we teach each other something, and separate things according to how they are?
> HERMOGENES: We surely do.
> SOCRATES: Then a name is a sort of teaching tool and one that separates existence, as the shuttle does for the web.
>
> ΣΩ.
> Ἔχεις δὴ καὶ περὶ ὀνόματος οὕτως εἰπεῖν; ὀργάνῳ ὄντι τῷ ὀνόματι ὀνομάζοντες τί ποιοῦμεν;
> ΕΡΜ.
> Οὐκ ἔχω λέγειν.
> ΣΩ.
> Ἆρ' οὐ διδάσκομέν τι ἀλλήλους καὶ τὰ πράγματα διακρίνομεν ᾗ ἔχει;
> ΕΡΜ.
> Πάνυ γε.
> ΣΩ.
> Ὄνομα ἄρα διδασκαλικόν τί ἐστιν ὄργανον καὶ διακριτικὸν τῆς οὐσίας ὥσπερ κερκὶς ὑφάσματος. (*Crat.* 388b–c)

[79] On this point, see Roy Harris and Talbot J. Taylor, *Landmarks in Linguistic Thought: The Western Tradition from Socrates to Saussure* (New York: Routledge, 1989), 18–19.

In keeping with his predecessors, Plato sees the problem of language as implicated in ontological questions. He proposes that a word (or a noun, the Greek is ambiguous) is an instrument that works on Being [ἡ οὐσία] just as a shuttle does its work on a web. This all takes place through the give and take of dialectical conversation. Note that this instrumental function is true not only for language as a whole or for long conversations meant to reach a greater understanding of things but for each unit of language, each individual word. We will return to this point later. Plato tells us that the material of which the word is made, that is, syllables and letters, is analogous to the material of which a craftsman makes a tool. It may vary from tool to tool, but as long as the function is embodied properly, the tool will remain useful:

> Must not the lawgiver [the one who invents language] also know how to embody in sounds and syllables that name which is fitted by nature to each object? Must he not make and assign all names looking to the ideal name, if he is to be an authoritative giver of names? And if each lawgiver does not embody it in the same syllables, the ideal name should not be forgotten on that account; for not every blacksmith embodies the form in the same iron, though they make the same instrument for the same purpose. But so long as they reproduce the same ideal, though in different iron, still the instrument is as it should be, whether someone should make it here or among those who speak other languages, is it not?
>
> Ἆρ' οὖν, ὦ βέλτιστε, καὶ τὸ ἑκάστῳ φύσει πεφυκὸς ὄνομα τὸν νομοθέτην ἐκεῖνον εἰς τοὺς φθόγγους καὶ τὰς συλλαβὰς δεῖ ἐπίστασθαι τιθέναι, καὶ βλέποντα πρὸς αὐτὸ ἐκεῖνο ὃ ἔστιν ὄνομα, πάντα τὰ ὀνόματα ποιεῖν τε καὶ τίθεσθαι, εἰ μέλλει κύριος εἶναι ὀνομάτων θέτης; εἰ δὲ μὴ εἰς τὰς αὐτὰς συλλαβὰς ἕκαστος ὁ νομοθέτης τίθησιν, οὐδὲν δεῖ τοῦτο ἀ<μφι>γνοεῖν· οὐδὲ γὰρ εἰς τὸν αὐτὸν σίδηρον ἅπας χαλκεὺς τίθησιν, τοῦ αὐτοῦ ἕνεκα ποιῶν τὸ αὐτὸ ὄργανον· ἀλλ' ὅμως, ἕως ἂν τὴν αὐτὴν ἰδέαν ἀποδιδῷ, ἐάντε ἐν ἄλλῳ σιδήρῳ, ὅμως ὀρθῶς ἔχει τὸ ὄργανον, ἐάντε ἐνθάδε ἐάντε ἐν βαρβάροις τις ποιῇ. ἦ γάρ; (*Crat.* 389d–390a)

The notion of the "ideal name" does not figure prominently in the rest of the dialogue, but here it is clear: Plato is suggesting some translinguistic entity, independent of the particular combination of sounds one uses to make a word, that the makers of different languages embody into their respective tongues.[80] In this passage the idea of a natural fit between language and the world is tied to proper expression of this

[80] On this, see Kretzmann, 130: "The fact that the correct Greek name for horse does not sound or look the same as the correct French name for horse shows simply that different linguistic authorities are operative in, or constitutive of, different languages. Both those names—*hippos* and *cheval*—are correct in the sense that just such a name, regardless of its appearance, ought to be in use."

translinguistic entity. This is a naturalism of a different order than the idea of a word's sounds somehow mimicking its meaning. The measure of the correctness of a name, then, will be whether the lawgiver has made a tool that "fits" the ideal name, regardless of whether he does it in one group of letters and syllables or another:

> On this basis, then, you will judge the lawgiver, whether he be here or among those who speak other languages, so long as he gives to each thing the fitting form of the name, in whatever syllables, to be no worse lawgiver, whether here or anywhere else.
>
> Οὐκοῦν οὕτως ἀξιώσεις καὶ τὸν νομοθέτην τόν τε ἐνθάδε καὶ τὸν ἐν τοῖς βαρβάροις, ἕως ἂν τὸ τοῦ ὀνόματος εἶδος ἀποδιδῷ τὸ προσῆκον ἑκάστῳ ἐν ὁποιαισοῦν συλλαβαῖς, οὐδὲν χείρω νομοθέτην εἶναι τὸν ἐνθάδε ἢ τὸν ὁπουοῦν ἄλλοθι; (390a)

The best judge of any tool, Plato says, is the user. The sailor should guide the work of the shipbuilder; the weaver should guide the carpenter who makes the shuttle. In the case of names, Plato asserts, the primary user is the dialectician. The role of the dialectician, as Plato articulates in several places, is that of dividing things at the appropriate points.[81] He makes the clearest statement of this view in the *Phaedrus*. There he describes the dialectician in language very similar to that which he used to describe the namegiver. He says that the good dialectician is able to draw things together into one form [εἰς μίαν ἰδέαν] and cut things apart [διατέμνειν] where the natural seams are, in accordance with how the Forms themselves are situated [κατ' εἴδη] (*Phaedr*. 265d–e; cf. *Crat*. 388b).[82] Plato warns that a person who does not understand the world well is like a bad butcher, he does not cut along the joints [κατ' ἄρθρα]. Socrates provides us with an example to illustrate his point. He looks at the divine form of "madness" [μανία] as a single thing, within which are four subgroups: "prophetic," governed by Apollo; "ritualistic," by Dionysus; "poetic," by the Muses; and "erotic," by Aphrodite and Eros (265b). If the one who proposes these subgroups is to be counted as a "good butcher," he must carve reality at the right spots. We arrive at a question like this: Does the word μανία, understood as a unit of the Greek language, match up with a Form that truly exists? Further, do the words μαντική, τελεστική, ποιητική, and ἐρωτική correspond to an actual fourfold division with this form? If so, then the words will match the ideal names, and in that sense be correct, regardless of which particular sounds the word maker uses. But if not, the dialectician will enter into his craft with faulty tools.

[81] See *Phaedrus* 265e, 266b; *Statesman* 262b, 287c; *Sophist* 253d–e.

[82] On the elisions between the worlds of the Forms and of language, see Lamberton, *Homer the Theologian*, 165, and his citation of J. E. Raven.

Here Plato raises the concern that our words *systematically* run the risk of separating reality at the wrong spots.[83] Words might presume a taxonomy that does not match the real one and thereby create a reality that does not exist.[84] By such bad butchering, the Sophists, poets, and others are able to shape-shift and beguile their audiences with phantoms. If our words fail to separate at the right places, Plato suggests, we are like a person who builds a house on a shaky foundation.[85] This, it seems clear, is the kind of concern Plato has in mind when he insists that our words be made to answer not to the consensual agreement of a group of speakers but to things themselves. In sharp contrast with the "autonomy" theory of Gorgias and with the conventionalist theories of language against which Plato is arguing in the *Cratylus*, Plato makes the word answer to reality, not just to language itself, and certainly not just to the whims of the many.

The *Phaedrus* passage helps explain another curious aspect of the *Cratylus*. Plato insists that truth [ἀλήθεια] is at stake, not just in the larger constructions of language (like sentences that make statements, for example), but in the individual word. He leaves uncontroverted in the dialogue the claim that truth, if it is to exist at all, must begin at the level of the individual word (385c; cf. 430d). Though various forms of naturalism are refuted in the dialogue, this claim is not. Aristotle's view is that a single word cannot be either true or false. Unless we propose a predicate, and claim that "madness," for example, *is* something or other, we have not said anything whose truth can be evaluated. But in Plato's view, as exhibited in the *Phaedrus* and the *Cratylus*, individual names are true or false, depending on whether their contours and the seams between them match the contours and seams of reality. It is a question of an isomorphism between the taxonomy of language and the taxonomy of reality.[86] Since the word is a tool to divide reality, it is itself implicated in the process of cutting reality at the joints. It has a taxonomic role to play, and in this sense each individual word makes a

[83] Plato considers this most explicitly at *Crat.* 436b–d, but the concern is clear in the discussion of the ideal name also.

[84] Plato articulates such a concern in the more general setting of the *Protagoras* (349a–b) also. At issue is the proper definition of virtue. Recapping an earlier discussion, Socrates asks whether wisdom, temperance, courage, justice, and holiness are five terms that stand for separate realities or are really divisions of a single one, virtue. Similar concerns haunt the *Philebus* from beginning to end.

[85] *Crat.* 436b–d. Plato believes that, to assign names properly, one must know the world well: "It is clear that the one who first gave names, gave to things the sort of names which he considered those things to be. . . . Then, if he considered incorrectly, and gave such names as he considered, what do you suppose will happen to us who follow him? What else but that we will be deceived?"

[86] See also Kretzmann for this view.

claim about reality.[87] We might just note that this issue is quite independent of the question of comprehensibility. We can say the word μανία all we want, and we can be understood by another speaker who knows our language, and may be under the same delusions we are, but unless the word and the meaning we both accept match up with some independently existing reality, we are simply saying words: we are just communicating the same phantom back and forth. One can hear echoes, but now tinged with anxiety, of Gorgias's understanding of language as "its own master," which has no connection to things as they are.

In general, we are safe to say that among these three major thinkers language is a cause for suspicion and concern. Before Aristotle, the question of whether language is an adequate reflection of things as they really exist was an open and much debated one. Though they approach it in different ways, Heraclitus, Gorgias, and Plato place this issue at the center of their linguistic theories. Of course, legions of other people simply used language and got along well enough in the world not to be bothered with any paralyzing doubts over whether their words were an adequate match for things. But those who made it their business to propose theories about such matters often considered the assigning of words to be a tricky business.

Aristotle on Language and Poetry

Aristotle: The Word as Label

In book 4 of the *Metaphysics*, where Aristotle begins his investigation proper, he tells us that Cratylus became so crippled by the observation that our language may not correspond to the world that, at the end of his life, he no longer spoke but only moved his finger (1010a10–15).[88] And before his words dried up, Cratylus criticized his teacher Heraclitus for being naive. Not only is it impossible to step into the same river twice, but it cannot even be done once. In his survey of his predecessors in book 1 of the *Metaphysics*, one can sense Aristotle's impatience with the state of philosophy as it was handed down to him. The problems

[87] On this aspect of Plato's *Cratylus*, see Giovanni Manetti, *Theories of the Sign in Classical Antiquity* (Bloomington: Indiana University Press, 1993), 61–63, and citations.

[88] "Furthermore, observing that all this nature is in motion, and that no true statement can be made of what changes, they thought it impossible to make a true statement about that which changes in every way and entirely" [ἔτι δὲ πᾶσαν ὁρῶντες ταύτην κινουμένην τὴν φύσιν, κατὰ δὲ τοῦ μεταβάλλοντος οὐθὲν ἀληθευόμενον, περί γε τὸ πάντῃ πάντως μεταβάλλον οὐκ ἐνδέχεσθαι ἀληθεύειν] (*Metaphysics* 1010a7–9). That Cratylus could not easily move on from the problem of language is also clear in Plato. In the *Cratylus*, he tells Socrates and Hermogenes that the subject of language is "one of the most important" (427e).

that had transfixed the thought of his elder colleagues needed to be left behind so that one might get on with the things that it is possible for philosophy to do. Such a sentiment is certainly also true within his thinking on language: Aristotle will remove the burden of suspicion that the Presocratics, the Sophists, and to some extent Plato had placed on it.

Aristotle tells us in the *De interpretatione* that the word is a "token" not of a thing in the world but of a πάθημα (a mental impression produced passively by observation of the world) of the soul, which results from the world pressing itself on us, and that written words are signs of words spoken:

> Spoken words, then, are tokens of affections of the soul, and written words are tokens of spoken ones. And just as written letters are not the same for all humans, neither are spoken words. But the mental affections themselves, of which these words are primarily signs, are the same for everyone, as are also the objects of which those affections are likenesses. These things have been discussed, however, in my writings on the soul—for it is a different matter from the current one.
>
> Ἔστι μὲν οὖν τὰ ἐν τῇ φωνῇ τῶν ἐν τῇ ψυχῇ παθημάτων σύμβολα, καὶ τὰ γραφόμενα τῶν ἐν τῇ φωνῇ. καὶ ὥσπερ οὐδὲ γράμματα πᾶσι τὰ αὐτά, οὐδὲ φωναὶ αἱ αὐταί· ὧν μέντοι ταῦτα σημεῖα πρώτων, ταὐτὰ πᾶσι παθήματα τῆς ψυχῆς, καὶ ὧν ταῦτα ὁμοιώματα πράγματα ἤδη ταὐτά. περὶ μὲν οὖν τούτων εἴρηται ἐν τοῖς περὶ ψυχῆς,—ἄλλης γὰρ πραγματείας· (*De int.* 16a3–9)

This is an extraordinarily rich passage. Aristotle assures us that the things of the world [πράγματα] as opposed to the names we give them are all the same for all people. Furthermore, and pivotal for his theory, these things impress themselves identically on all people and produce in them the same παθήματα—this must be the case regardless of a person's innate powers of observation, his personal experiences, or his language group. Deborah K. W. Modrak's recent book-length treatment of this passage outdoes any earlier consideration of it. She has conclusively shown that Aristotle's linguistic position here is not a tangent or a sidelight in his thought but is deeply implicated in key positions of his psychology, epistemology, and ontology.[89] Briefly, Aristotle's views on language, specifically his relative lack of suspicion of it, are part and parcel of a theory that sees basic concept acquisition to be a rather unproblematic affair.[90] Language is relatively unproblematic for Aristotle because the bearer of the name (the thing "out there") is more or less

[89] Deborah K. W. Modrak, *Aristotle's Theory of Language and Meaning* (New York: Cambridge University Press, 2001).

[90] The key text here is *Posterior Analytics* 2.19. This text has been much debated, but Modrak's view that it refers to basic concept acquisition is entirely persuasive (see Modrak, 95–116).

straightforward in its autonomy and the simple concept of it is available to the normal powers of observation of normal people. Nature no longer systematically hides herself; not every perception falls under intense suspicion; and the discrete elements of existence, the joints between things, are on the whole perceptible to all observers.[91] This could not be farther from the premises of Aristotle's predecessors. Such an ontology and epistemology allow Aristotle to claim that the word is a relatively trustworthy name—what I have called a label. I will add a few observations that are relevant to our present purposes.

In the *De interpretatione* text, Aristotle uses the term σύμβολον, which I have translated as "token." I will justify this translation in the next chapter, which is devoted to understanding "symbol" in the classical period.[92] As we will see there, his particular use of the term in this context could not differ more from later allegorical uses of it. The final sentence of the text, which refers the reader to Aristotle's thoughts on the soul, is also worthy of note. Which issue exactly it is that Aristotle refers to his psychology is not entirely clear, but I agree with Modrak that the reference most likely signals an expansion on the notion of παθήματα: what they are, how they are aquired, and how they function in the soul.[93] In the *De anima* (one of the possible texts he has in mind) he addresses the issue of how individual things make their marks on us (book 3.3–7).[94] Each discrete essence presents itself to the lower, passive part of our minds. Essences are realized in sensible particulars and are impossible to cognize without them. This is a natural process of the human mind and takes place without the application of judgment, which would implicate it in the question of truth and falsity.[95]

Aristotle's terminology emphasizes this passivity. The term πάθημα is already formed from the verb which means to "suffer" or "undergo" something, and this particular noun form, with the -μα suffix, indicates

[91] See also Modrak, 263. For the standard reference to the issue of nature hiding herself, see Heraclitus frag. 208, and discussion, in G. S. Kirk, J. E. Raven, and M. Schofield, eds., *The Presocratic Philosophers: A Critical History with a Selection of Texts* (Cambridge: Cambridge University Press, 1983).

[92] Briefly, this is a unique appearance of the term in a linguistic context in the classical period. Aristotle draws here from the well-established classical sense of the term as a receipt or token of a contract of some kind, where two parties make an agreement and mark it with a token called a "symbol." This fits with Aristotle's insistence on the consensual nature of language. The term will take on a quite different sense, literary and linguistic, for the later allegorists.

[93] Modrak, 221.

[94] For a recent treatment of this text, with citations to the ongoing discussion, see C.W.A. Whitaker, *Aristotle's* De interpretatione (New York: Oxford University Press, 1996), 13–17.

[95] See Modrak's reading of *Posterior Analytics* 2.19, 95–101.

an internal accusative, a result or effect of an action. The existing things of the world, then, take the active role in this process. They do the work of generating our conceptual and linguistic definitions and taxonomies, not words. We may be mistaken in a particular judgment, when, say, we see something far off and think that it is a man when it is not (*De anima* 430b30–32). But Aristotle, in sharp contrast to his predecessors, does not see this problem as generalizable to the formation of the intellectual or linguistic categories by which we divide the world. Such a misrecognition is a mistake of the active faculty of judgment, which decides that an object "is" or "is not" something, and not the passive one, which receives and passes on the taxonomy of the discrete existents that make up the world. This latter faculty, he says explicitly, is never mistaken (430b29–30; cf. 428b12–13). In this way, then, Aristotle arrives at a linguistic theory which very much accords with his urge to move forward, away from the problems that had transfixed earlier thinkers. The grave concern—evident in Heraclitus and Plato and evidently exploited by Gorgias—of systematic delusion in our conception of the joints between things is put to rest. When we are guaranteed a set of essences that is reasonably stable (in contrast to Heraclitus) and more or less obvious (in contrast to Plato), our assignment of words to them becomes a rather perfunctory affair.

We can see two important implications from this basic position, set forth at the very beginning of the *De interpretatione*. If for Plato truth is at stake down to the individual word, Aristotle sees the notion of truth [ἀλήθεια] as only relevant to words in combination. Using a single word is not, he says, overturning Plato, an act of combination or division:

> Nouns and verbs themselves are like a thought without combination or division, for example, "man" or "white," whenever nothing is added. For neither is it true nor false in any way.
>
> τὰ μὲν οὖν ὀνόματα αὐτὰ καὶ τὰ ῥήματα ἔοικε τῷ ἄνευ συνθέσεως καὶ διαιρέσεως νοήματι, οἷον τὸ ἄνθρωπος ἢ λευκόν, ὅταν μὴ προστεθῇ τι· οὔτε γὰρ ψεῦδος οὔτε ἀληθές πω. (16a13–16; cf. *De anima* 430a26–430b5)

Truth or falsity only enters the picture when we add something to a word—for example, "is" or "is not" to a noun. Since it is only a label, Aristotle's word does not in itself make any claim about the world; it does no cutting. Second, and in keeping with the first point, Aristotle explicitly does away with the notion that language is a tool: "All language is significant—not as a tool, but as has been said, by convention" [ἔστι δὲ λόγος ἅπας μὲν σημαντικός, οὐχ ὡς ὄργανον δέ, ἀλλ' ὥσπερ εἴρηται κατὰ συνθήκην·] (*De int.* 16b33–17a1). This opposition of conventionalism to instrumentalism makes little sense unless it is a reference to the *Cratylus*. (A later commentator, Boethius, drawing on Alexander of Aphrodisias, expressly links this passage to the *Cratylus*, as does Proclus in his commentary on the *Cratylus*; Modrak does as well.)[96] With this opposition, Aristotle attempts to relieve the stress that Plato had placed on the assigning of individual names by calling them the very instruments by which we make our understanding of the world. If language makes no taxonomic claims, and we no longer need to concern ourselves with the question of isomorphism between our linguistic mapping of the world and the world itself, it makes no sense to say that a word is a "tool" for doing anything. The creation of language is instead a rather straightforward process in which a group of language users agrees on this or that combination of sounds to label a given reality, which demands no higher cognitive power, and certainly no dialectical genius, to be observed.

In short, Aristotle makes the world much more cooperative with our attempts to name it than it was for the pre-Aristotelians. In Aristotle's thinking, the interesting problems begin to arise only when we string words together and predicate claims about the separate essences that (according to him) we all know to be out there in the world. Aristotle promotes a certain trust in the words we use, and in the collective group of language creators that agreed on them, often appealing to τὸ κύριον (ordinary usage) to advance his arguments. This approach allows him to get on with the task of analyzing the various essences that present themselves to us.[97]

Aristotle and the Poetics of Clarity

Hand in hand with this new theory of language Aristotle is able to develop an approach to poetry different from those that precede him. When language (poetic or otherwise) is not primarily a veil overlying a hidden reality, it follows that the critic's role as interpreter—in the sense of one who digs out hidden significances—is considerably diminished. The question of what the poet *means* by his or her words starts to look increasingly like the question of what any speaker means. Decoding poetic language is not an occasion for diving into the mystified soup of an always receding reality; it is rather an exercise in understanding how language produces effects on audiences. For this task the professional speakers, the rhetoricians (e.g., Isocrates), were already developing a

[96] Boethius, *Commentarii in librum Aristotelis* ΠΕΡΙ ΕΡΜΗΝΕΙΑΣ, ed. Karl Meiser, 2d ed. Pars Posterior (Leipzig: Teubner, 1880), 92.25–94.21; Proclus, *In Platonis Cratylum Commentaria* (Leipzig: Teubner, 1908), 15.27–18.5; 25.17–28.22. Modrak, 52, n. 1.

[97] For a recent discussion of Aristotle's use of the notion of κύριον, see Jacques Derrida, "White Mythology: Metaphor in the Text of Philosophy," in *Margins of Philosophy*, trans. Alan Bass (Chicago: University of Chicago Press, 1982), 207–71.

stock of useful tools. Gorgias, with his theory of language as magic spell, tried to give the orator the power traditionally attributed to poetic speech by mimicking a portentous and obscure style.[98] Aristotle implicitly suggests that the poet should strive to be more like the public orator.[99] In oratory the primary virtues are clarity and precision, and one does not usually expect a public speech to reveal arcane philosophical truths. Aristotle introduces new concerns to poetics and initiates an approach that centers not on the interpretation of obscure messages but on the analysis of a poem's constituent parts. This sets him on a collision course with the poetics of the enigma.

In a move whose significance has hardly been given its due, Aristotle actually defines metaphor, his new central category of poetic language, over and against αἴνιγμα, which we know from the Derveni text to be already fully implicated in allegorical reading and from supporting testimonia to be a generally known term of art. In the section of the *Poetics* that deals with style or diction [λέξις], Aristotle tells us that the best poetic language is no longer the riddling, enigmatic type. He takes a page from his treatise on rhetoric and makes clarity the central value for poetic style as well, although with the proviso that the style is not base.

> Excellence in style is to be clear and not lowly. The style that comes from common words is certainly clearest, but it is lowly. The poetry of Cleophon is an example and that of Sthenelus. The style which uses strange words is majestic because it utterly changes the commonplace. By a "strange" word I mean an obsolete or foreign word or a metaphor or vowel lengthening and everything contrary to proper usage. But if someone composes entirely these sorts of things, it will be either an enigma or babble. If composed from metaphors, an enigma, if from obsolete or foreign words, babble.
>
> λέξεως δὲ ἀρετὴ σαφῆ καὶ μὴ ταπεινὴν εἶναι. σαφεστάτη μὲν οὖν ἐστιν ἡ ἐκ τῶν κυρίων ὀνομάτων, ἀλλὰ ταπεινή· παράδειγμα δὲ ἡ Κλεοφῶντος ποίησις καὶ ἡ Σθενέλου. σεμνὴ δὲ καὶ ἐξαλλάττουσα τὸ ἰδιωτικὸν ἡ τοῖς ξενικοῖς κεχρημένη· ξενικὸν δὲ λέγω γλῶτταν καὶ μεταφορὰν καὶ ἐπέκτασιν καὶ πᾶν τὸ παρὰ τὸ κύριον. ἀλλ' ἄν τις ἅπαντα τοιαῦτα ποιήσῃ, ἢ αἴνιγμα ἔσται ἢ

[98] See Aristotle's remark in the *Rhetoric*: "And as the poets, although their utterances were devoid of sense, appeared to have gained their reputation through their style, it was a poetical style [of oratory] that came into being first, as that of Gorgias." (trans. based on that of John Henry Freese in the Loeb ed.) [ἐπεὶ δ' οἱ ποιηταί, λέγοντες εὐήθη, διὰ τὴν λέξιν ἐδόκουν πορίσασθαι τὴν δόξαν, διὰ τοῦτο ποιητικὴ πρώτη ἐγένετο λέξις, οἷον ἡ Γοργίου] (*Rhet.* 1404a24–26). For the contrast between Gorgias and Aristotle, see Jacqueline de Romilly, *Magic and Rhetoric in Ancient Greece* (Cambridge: Harvard University Press, 1975), 69–88.

[99] The thoroughgoing nature of Aristotle's use of rhetoric in his *Poetics* is well known. For a relatively recent treatment of the topic, see John T. Kirby, "Aristotle's *Poetics*: The Rhetorical Principle," *Arethusa* 24 (1991): 197–217.

βαρβαρισμός· ἂν μὲν οὖν ἐκ μεταφορῶν, αἴνιγμα, ἐὰν δὲ ἐκ γλωττῶν, βαρβαρισμός. (1458a18–26)

This unassuming section of text marks a pivotal moment in the history of classical literary criticism. It allows us to locate precisely within the term αἴνιγμα what was surely a central feature of Aristotle's reaction against earlier approaches to reading the poets. In a move that sides with Aristophanes and Plato and against allegorical commentators, Aristotle characterizes the enigma as a *flaw* of the poetic craft, counterbalanced by the opposite flaw of perfectly ordinary speech. As is typical of his method, Aristotle invents a mean, and in the process labels a group of his predecessors as extremists. Furthermore, Aristotle classifies the whole notion of the enigma, which for allegorical readers placed rather large issues of epistemology and ontology in the balance, under the heading of style, or the packaging in which an idea is wrapped. This classification of the issue removes at a stroke the dynamics and problematics on which the poetics of the enigma depends. Once reduced to a question of style, the enigma can no longer serve as a provocation to peek under the veil of language at the underlying structures of being. Rather, it can only count as an obfuscation, a barrier between the audience and the poet's point. This is a frontal assault on the allegorical conception of great poetry. It reclassifies allegory's term for the highest form of poetic language into a portentous defect.[100] It is also in keeping with a certain desacralizing interest in Aristotle's *Poetics*.[101]

Aristotle sets up the metaphor [μεταφορά], placed at the center of his poetics, to supplant the notion of enigma. His valorization of it, after all, comes at the enigma's expense. The *Rhetoric* makes this point just as bluntly as the *Poetics* does. He simply defines metaphor as an enigma that lacks the defect of obfuscation: "For metaphors indicate enigmatically, such that it is clear that the sense has been transferred well" [μεταφοραὶ γὰρ αἰνίττονται, ὥστε δῆλον ὅτι εὖ μετενήνεκται] (1405b4–5).[102] In the context of this duel between anchoring concepts, we should

[100] We have already mentioned, and will see in more detail in chap. 5, that the enigma has a usage, well attested by the fifth century, as a term in the practice of divination. Aristotle's distaste for using omen language to describe what the poet does can also be seen at *Poetics* 1453b9, where he says that one ought to produce pity and fear and not something portentous [τερατῶδες].

[101] See J. F. García, "Ritual Speech in Early Greek Song," in *Epea and Grammata: Oral and Written Communication in Ancient Greece* (Leiden: E. J. Brill, 2002), 35–41. See also M. Massenzio, "La Poesia come Fine: La desacralizzazione della tragedia: Considerazioni sulla 'Poetica' di Aristotel," *Religione e Civiltà* 1 (1972): 285–318.

[102] We should note that in both the *Poetics* and the *Rhetoric*, Aristotle draws from the tradition of enigma as an intellectual challenge (the Sphinx is the most famous exemplar) and illustrates his remarks both times with the same riddle: "I saw a man weld bronze

also note that the notion of metaphor is likely to have come from the rhetorical tradition; it is already in evidence in Isocrates (9.9). So when Aristotle situates metaphor at the center of his poetics, he is simultaneously engaging in a polemic against contemporary allegoresis; this gives him the fulcrum to shift the field away from the question of interpretation—*what* the poem means—and toward analysis—*how* the poem produces meaning. While nearly all of the later allegorical readers retain in their allegoresis the archaic and early classical view of the centrality of the enigma, nearly all rhetorical critics that follow Aristotle repeat his late classical understanding of enigma as an obscurantist flaw, setting it in a disreputable position in the general scheme of tropes. Good poets avoid it, since it tends to produce an unclear style.[103]

Also in contrast to his allegorical predecessors, Aristotle makes his governing notion definable. His elegant treatment of the transfer theory, and the subgroups he proposes, stands even today as a workable definition of the transfer of sense from a surface meaning to a tropological one (*Poetics* 1457b; cf. *Rhetoric* 1405a–1407a). This kind of specificity of definition is something allegorical critics rarely (if ever) do. Aristotle's treatment suggests that the density of meaning to be found in poetic texts actually is capable of being theorized and subsumed under articulable principles of language, while the allegorical resistance to making such definitions attests to the opposite view. This new, rhetorically minded attempt to systematize shifts in meaning, making them tamer and easier to reckon, is meant to supplant a larger notion of poetry such as we see operative in the Derveni text. This ascendancy of a rationalized view of poetic language is meant, quite literally, to demystify it. (We shall soon—in chapters 2 and 5—see the longstanding connections between traditional allegorical conceptions of poetry and traditional notions of mystery language.) These different visions of what counts as

upon a man with fire." (For further discussion, see chap. 5.) But his referencing of this narrower enigma context is not an impediment to considering a simultaneous and more significant reference to the poetics of the enigma. The secure attestation of poetic enigmas before Aristotle puts it beyond doubt that, however he chooses to illustrate the concept, both he and his audience would have been used to thinking of αἰνίγματα in poetic contexts as the putatively profound nuggets of wisdom that poets express indirectly. In addition, Aristotle has good reasons to sell the poetic enigma short, and by treating the poet's enigmatic constructions as mere brainteasers, he characterizes them as intellectual mind games rather than profound insights.

[103] Quintilian (8.52) will repeat exactly this formulation, specifically in terms of allegory: an allegory that goes too far is an *ainigma*. Demetrius, a critic who follows in a generally Aristotelian tradition, also repeats Aristotle's warning (*On Style* 102). We will return to this point in chap. 4.

poetic underpin profound differences in the questions readers see fit to ask a given poetic text.

One can detect Aristotle's de-emphasis of allegorically oriented questions in other aspects of the *Poetics* also. Aristotle explicitly declares a separation between poetic issues and philosophical ones. Looking for philosophical truths in poetry entails a genre transgression. "Homer and Empedocles have nothing in common except their meter, on account of which it is right to call the one a poet, but the other is an investigator of the physical world rather than a poet" [οὐδὲν δὲ κοινόν ἐστιν Ὁμήρῳ καὶ Ἐμπεδοκλεῖ πλὴν τὸ μέτρον, διὸ τὸν μὲν ποιητὴν δίκαιον καλεῖν, τὸν δὲ φυσιολόγον μᾶλλον ἢ ποιητήν (*Poetics* 1447b17–20). Demarcating a clear genre distinction between Empedocles and Homer has the side effect of undercutting the consistent allegorical inclination to find specifically philosophical kinds of knowledge inside poetic texts, and to read all the ancient wise men (whether poets or philosophers) starting from the same basic assumptions. If esoteric philosophy (the sort which Empedocles produced) really does have *nothing* [οὐδέν] in common with Homer's epic poetry beyond the dactyl, then it makes little sense to use the same interpretive tools on both forms of writing. Aristotle is clearing the ground for his own approach to poetry. In this vein, his treatment of the notion of διάνοια is also suggestive. As we saw above, the *Ion* portrays the extraction of copious διάνοιαι from Homer's work as the entire sum of activity of the Homeric expert. We also saw that that text associated this approach with allegoresis. It is therefore significant that, while Aristotle makes διάνοια one of his six basic elements of poetry, he defines it much more narrowly, spends hardly more than a few sentences on the topic, and even refers questions concerning it entirely to his treatise on rhetoric (*Poetics* 1456a35). In short, he makes Ion's self-proclaimed area of expertise a provocatively bland activity, and not an especially "poetic" one at that. Aristotle is far more interested in the analysis of plot structure and the creation of strong characters.

Aristotle does not mention allegorical commentators directly, but we would be wrong to take this silence as evidence that his arguments did not engage them. Aristotle is equally silent, for example, on Plato's positions on poetry, but they can hardly be ignored in coming to grips with what is new in the *Poetics*. His focus on clarity is in my view as strikingly novel as his ideas on *mimesis* or *katharsis* and serves as another of the foundational building blocks of his decisive contribution to poetics. Plato was unable to change the terms of inquiry in this matter: he quarreled with enigma poetics but on its own terms. Aristotle shifts the ground of the issue and, after having destabilized the old concerns, creates new ones. While the allegorists considered the great poet to be a master riddler, Aristotle supplants this view with a new one: the poet as master craftsman, who produces a finely wrought piece of art marked by clarity and elegance. Aristarchus, to whom we will return in closing, draws a corollary from this position and declares that a great poem will *by definition* convey its meanings in a clear manner. This stance toward the text will foster the opinion that knotty passages will not repay interpretive efforts to extract meaning from them. Difficulties in sense are the mark of an unskilled poet, a textual corruption, or a flight of fancy meant to delight us but not to carry some deeper message. Such a position is logical enough after Aristotle classifies the entire discussion concerning whether a poet speaks enigmatically or clearly as a question of style, not "meaning." A poet departs from common usage to create a lofty air in the poem, not to evoke some meaning more profound than plain language can convey. Early on and consistently, the more sophisticated allegorists embraced the view (implicit in Heraclitus) that obscurity in language is a necessary mode for capturing profundities of meaning that evade common speech. Aristotle and most of his heirs have little patience for this attitude.

Of the many important consequences of Aristotle's new language theory, we should note finally the role it plays in reformulating the notion of poetic mimesis. In Plato's thinking, we need constantly to be on guard lest the poetic *mimêma* turn into an *eidôlon*, that is, lest the poet's words produce a phantom image that leads us away from the truth. Aristotle's scheme alleviates this concern significantly. As he understands it, words do *not* always threaten to slip away from the world as it really is. While madmen face such problems, the rest of us simply do not. This reformulated vision of language allows for fictive products that do not pose severe epistemological threats. We do not have to be on constant guard against misleading phantoms—just as we can no longer expect to find mysterious spirits leading us to the revealed truth. In Aristotle's reckoning, language is firmly enough bound to reality that we need not get overly concerned with the license that the poets sometimes take with it. If we follow Aristotle's wake into the rhetorical tradition, mimesis ceases completely to be a problem of linguistic representation. It becomes, at least by the time of Demetrius (third century B.C.E.?), the name for a rhetorical training exercise—what Cicero and Quintilian will call *imitatio*—the mimicking of earlier literary and oratorical models. Aristotle, not least because of his theory of language, seems to have successfully drained the term *mimêsis* of all the epistemological anxiety it aroused in Plato.

Aristarchus and the Poetics of Clarity

The basic differences between the poetics of the enigma, such as animates the commentary of the Derveni text, and the poetics of clarity, such as Aristotle develops, help to clarify the different approaches to textual difficulties that were evidenced at the beginning of this chapter. Aristotle's central value of clarity is part of Aristarchus's inheritance. Both start from the premise that a poem provides its own internal modes of explication, it makes itself clear and needs no recourse to extrapoetic knowledge about the order of things to convey its messages. The *Poetics* makes clarity a goal that a poet should strive for, as we saw, in part as a polemic against allegorical reading. Similarly, Aristarchus's approach, which looks within poetic texts for their own solutions, takes a position in decided opposition to allegorical readings. The merits of Aristarchus's approach have been well appreciated for the last two centuries, and there is little need to rehearse them here. He is held up, and rightly so, as the great ancient precursor to modern philological methods of textual scrutiny.[104] But it is also perhaps worth reckoning with the interpretive issues such criticism raises, even as it eschews them. In the D-scholion with which I began, Aristarchus attempts to clarify one of the thorniest of ἄτοπα facing the Homeric critic. Aristarchus warns us not to bother about [περιεργάζομαι] the binding [δέω] of a god in the episode where Ephialtes and Otos overpower Ares, chain him up, and lock him in a bronze cauldron for three months. We can compare Aristarchus's treatment of the offending verb δέω in another instance where it appears, during the tryst of Ares and Aphrodite, in *Odyssey* 8. In this scene, also notorious among Homer's commentators, Hephaestus catches his wife, Aphrodite, sleeping with Ares and binds them up in strong bonds. The other gods gather round to laugh at them. Poseidon does not think this a bit funny and bids Hephaestus to set Ares free. Hephaestus answers that if he did, he would have to "bind" [δέοιμι] Poseidon as a surety, and that he could not do.

> How could I bind you, in front of the deathless gods,
> If Ares should go away and slip his debt and his bond?
>
> πῶς ἂν ἐγώ σε δέοιμι μετ' ἀθανάτοισι θεοῖσιν,
> εἴ κεν Ἄρης οἴχοιτο χρέος καὶ δεσμὸν ἀλύξας;
>
> (8.352–53).

According to the scholia at *Odyssey* 8.352, Aristarchus glossed the line. "Aristarchus writes, 'How could I *censure* you'" [ὁ δὲ Ἀρίσταρχος, πῶς

[104] For the modern *locus classicus* of this view, see Rudolph Pfieffer, *History of Classical Scholarship* (New York: Oxford University Press, 1968–1976), 1: 210–33.

ἂν εὐθύνοιμι, γράφει]. The proposed metaphorical meaning of censure rules out the notion that a god might even bring up in anger the possibility of actually binding another god. Aristarchus suggests that either Hephaestus or Homer was speaking in a trope. So, in both the D-scholion on the *Iliad* and the gloss on the *Odyssey*, Aristarchus has the same general notion in mind: to prevent the reader from thinking that immortals and giants actually go around binding one another in Homer's text. In the case of Otos and Ephialtes binding Ares, Aristarchus offers no gloss but falls back on the poetic-license argument. Both these readings reflect the Aristotelian inheritance of clarity as the guiding virtue of great poetry; the commentators believe that the poet is saying what he means—and while he may be speaking in a trope, he is not offering subtle invitations to uncover some supposedly hidden message about the order of things. But when Aristarchus admonishes us to understand binding scenes as flights of fancy that do not teach us about the nature of the gods and men, or to consider them as tropes for a binding pledge, he also risks misreading. We have some reason to believe that in this particular case the poetics of clarity gives an incomplete understanding of the poem. Based on the now recognized ritual practices by which mortals in late Bronze-Age Greece (and later) did bind their gods, as Christopher Faraone has shown, far from being flights of fancy, it is probable that Homer's tales of binding reflect the practice common in the ancient Mediterranean world of ritually binding and burying effigies of hostile divinities.[105] In the Greek world, specifically in Boeotia, Ares was a prime target of such treatment, and this may be reflected in *Iliad* 5. He is also one of the binding targets in *Odyssey* 8. As we will see, the allegorists show themselves to be especially acute at appreciating such congruences between literary representations and religious cult. Cornutus in particular makes such observations regularly and with results that are not easily dismissed as being simply forced reading.[106] Aristarchus's method is perhaps too hasty in rejecting such reading as being "outside" the text.

From this survey of the poetics of clarity, I draw the following general conclusions. First, for critics working in an Aristotelian mode, poets do their work through the transparent medium of language. Their art does not raise grand ontological questions. It is a matter of rather simple *mimesis*, accurate or inaccurate, and in the best examples always clear. One can assume that a poet skilled in his craft will make his meaning

[105] Christopher A. Faraone, "Binding and Burying an Effigy of Evil," in *Talismans and Trojan Horses: Guardian Statues in Ancient Greek Myth and Ritual* (New York: Oxford University Press, 1992), 74–86.

[106] See, for example, Cornutus's reading of the castration of Ouranos as reflecting a priestly castration practice (Corn. *Compendium* 6; see chap. 4 below).

plain, whether through words used in their common meanings or through a tropological language that answers to certain identifiable rules. We should not read with the expectation of semantic trouble that is insoluble by recourse to the knowledge of the internal τέχνη of poetry—no knowledge of the underlying secrets of the world is called upon. Finally, the poet creates as the fully sovereign, independent master. He has full control over what comes into his poem. He chooses precise words that point without undue complication to things in the world, which he assembles into a sound plot that moves the emotions of the audience with skill and elegance.

Porphyry and the Poetics of the Riddle

While Aristotle's approach was convincing to many of the critics who followed him, it was not adopted by everyone. A number of ancient readers share more in common with the general approach, though not necessarily the specific techniques, of the Derveni commentator. Porphyry, a third-century C.E. Neoplatonist, is one of the ancient critics who adopts the approach that a poem might be a repository of enigmatic wisdom. When Odysseus lands at the cave of the nymphs in Ithaca, Homer devotes eleven lines to describing it in detail. After mentioning the cave's stone bowls and jars that bees use to store honey, stone looms where nymphs weave purple cloth, and two gates, one for mortals and one for immortals, Homer continues with his story, as though what he had just described were a perfectly normal setting. In a telling contrast, Aristotle briefly discusses the same scene, but his curiosity is peaked because it seems absurd to him that Odysseus would not have woken up when the ship ran aground and the Phaeacians carried him ashore (1460b). Porphyry, on the other hand, seems to feel that the curious elements within the cave are in need of explanation. As was noted earlier, he opens *On the Cave of the Nymphs* with a question using the verbal form of αἴνιγμα: "What on earth does Homer riddle by the cave?" [Ὅτι ποτὲ Ὁμήρῳ αἰνίττεται τὸ ἐν Ἰθάκῃ ἄντρον].[107] One is forced, Porphyry tells us, to trouble oneself with [πολυπραγμονεῖν ἀναγκάζοντα] a number of bothersome questions (*Antr.* 3). For example: "What is a gate of men and one of gods?" [τίς μὲν ἀνθρώπων πύλη, τίς δὲ θεῶν]; "What is the use of the kraters and amphoras?" [τίς δὲ καὶ ἡ

[107] Text from Porphyry, *The Cave of the Nymphs in the Odyssey*, ed. L. G. Westerink (Seminar Classics 609), Arethusa Monograph: 1 (Buffalo: Department of Classics, State University of New York, 1969), 2–34. For an English translation and lucid introduction, see Porphyry, *On the Cave of the Nymphs*, trans. and with introduction by Robert Lamberton (Barrytown, N.Y.: Station Hill Press, 1983) on which my translations have drawn.

τῶν κρατήρων καὶ ἀμφιφορέων παράληψις]; and "Who could remain credulous when told that the goddesses go around weaving sea-purple cloaks on stone looms in a murky cave. . . ?" [τίς γὰρ ἂν πιστεύσαι θεὰς ἁλιπόρφυρα ἱμάτια ὑφαίνειν <ἐν> σκοτεινῷ ἄντρῳ ἐπὶ λιθίνων ἱστῶν]. Porphyry's πολυπραγμονέω, in this context, carries a connotation—"bother about," "be an inquisitive busybody," or "meddle with"—nearly identical to the verb that Aristarchus uses to warn us away from "bothering about" [περιεργάζομαι] concerns "outside" the poem.[108] Given Porphyry's familiarity with Aristarchus's work, we are likely reading a kind of answer to Aristarchus. He says he is forced [ἀναγκάζοντα] to ask these questions, and the answers are not to be found in the ποιητικὴ τέχνη alone. As we know from his *Homeric Questions*, Porphyry considers analysis by the tools of textual criticism to be one possible solution for a troublesome spot in the text. In his textual commentaries on Homer, Porphyry explicitly reserves the possibility of finding a solution by allegory, indicating that while he sees a difference between the two methods of reading, he has no problem applying both to any given text.[109] Elsewhere he tells us that the first method is a kind of warm-up or preliminary exercise for the real contest, which seems to be a reference to the kind of interpretation he ventures into with the commentary on the cave of the nymphs.[110]

In his commentary, Porphyry exhibits one of the most durable characteristics of allegorical reading. In order to find out what the cave means *in* Homer's text, Porphyry feels it necessary to explore what real caves out in the world are. Such investigations are part and parcel of the view that sees questions of literary interpretation as inextricably bound up with ontological ones. The literary portrayal of the cave provokes a consideration of "caveness." Such a stance leads allegorical commentators to analyses, sometimes lengthy, of various features of the cosmos in an effort to elucidate what hints about these subjects Homer may have revealed to his careful readers. Porphyry surveys the opinions on caves that are attested not only elsewhere in the Homeric corpus but also in the Presocratics, Plato, and the Persians, and adds his own scientific assessment of what caves are and what they do in the world—this latter view is of course steeped in Neoplatonic common sense. He nowhere

[108] The nuance of the two words is slightly different, as befits their respective uses: Porphyry's πολυπραγμονέω suggests troubling oneself, while Aristarchus's περιεργάζομαι suggests wasting effort. But both these verbs have a strong connotation of being a "busybody," of overdoing something and intruding effort where it does not belong.

[109] Porphyry *Quaestionum Homericarum ad Iliadem pertinentium reliquiae* (Shrader, ed.), commentary on *Iliad* bk. 19, line 221; and esp. bk. 20, line 67.

[110] Porphyry *Quaestionum Homericarum*, book 1, ed. A. R. Sodano (Naples: Giannini, 1970), 1.22–28.

suggests that Homer had in mind a particular traditional belief when he constructed the cave. His position is closer to the following: caves themselves have characteristics; these can be researched by examining and evaluating the available opinions on caves from all sources; Homer, possessing an acute understanding of the world, knew about caves and constructed the cave in his poem in accordance with particular aspects of caves as they exist in the world. In other words, the referent of the word ἄντρον is something Porphyry sees as an entirely open topic, worthy of consideration for a reader of Homer who wants to appreciate everything the poem has to offer. The significance of the word is not clear and plain, nor is it reducible to a trope. Porphyry never calls the cave a metaphor—though he has no general aversion to the term. Indeed, his *Homeric Questions*, where his textual criticism and his Aristotelian approach are put to use, contains discussion of dozens of μεταφοραί (23.3, 24.5, 46.6, 52.19, etc. [Sodano, ed.]). The multiplicity of meanings in the cave and its accoutrements seems to defy tidy classification. The cave in Homer, Porphyry suggests in the end, is a crystallization of the material cosmos, the world subject to generation and decay. Each of the elements inside of it adds to this meaning, highlighting particular parts of the world that comes into being and passes away.

One detail of his reading will perhaps give a sense of the whole. Porphyry spends several pages teasing out what Homer might have meant by the honey that the bees store in stone jars (*Antr.* 15). He begins by wondering why Homer told us that the amphoras are filled not with water but with honey. This is strange. The myth tellers [οἱ θεολόγοι] use honey to symbolize many things, he says, since honey has many uses. It has both cathartic and preservative functions. It heals wounds and keeps things from rotting. In the Lion mysteries (the fourth and last stage of the Mithras cult), initiates are cleansed with honey (water would not work, because it is inimical to fire). The Mithraists cleanse the tongue by means of honey and offer honey to Mithras in his role as "preserver of fruit." Furthermore, Porphyry continues, the preservative effect is why some equate honey with ambrosia, Homer's "tawny nectar." But Porphyry is not sure that they should be considered identical and says we can only resolve this question by looking at more texts. According to the Orphics, Zeus used honey to make Kronos drunk so he could bind him, weakening him as Kronos weakened Ouranos by castrating him (Orph. frag. 154). Plato also tells of a similar effect of honey on the mythical figure of Poros, "since wine did not yet exist" (*Symp.* 203b). Orpheus is hinting that divine beings are ensnared by pleasure and pulled down into the world of coming-to-be and passing away. This is why Kronos castrates Ouranos just as he is settling down on the earth to make love to it. Earthy actions will dissolve divine powers. Honey is an earthy pleasure. For the ancients (as Porphyry calls Homer and his contemporaries), the pleasure of honey had the same meaning as sexual pleasure (and is therefore, by implication, not to be equated with ambrosia). To sum up, Porphyry says, the honey in Homer's poem has these properties: it indicates purification, prevention of decay, and the pleasure of descent into the material delights. It is therefore appropriate to the water nymphs, whom Porphyry says live in the cave and preside over the process of bringing souls down into bodies, and to human souls who are caught in the material world that is subject to generation and decay. The honey is further appropriate because the ancients commonly referred to souls as bees. Porphyry cites Sophocles (frag. 795, Nauck): "The swarm of the dead buzzes and rises up." In this long reading, Porphyry nowhere suggests some simple anachronistic prescience on Homer's part. Rather, he sees his job as a critic to be the discovery of what Homer could have meant by introducing honey at this point in his text. In order to do so, the critic must understand everything he can about actual honey, with the goal of seeing what possible resonances it had for Homer. This occasions a long search in a whole array of cultural material, ancient and contemporary, mythic and cultic, Greek and non-Greek. This is not to claim that we ought to endorse the answers Porphyry reaches by his method, only that his method is not *simply* a foisting of his own views onto the text.

From the standpoint of his theoretical position toward the text, most telling for us is Porphyry's treatment of the issue of a poetic fabrication. Porphyry is not uninterested in whether there was a real cave in the harbor of Phorcys or whether this is Homer's flight of fancy. He takes up the question by way of introduction to his interpretation. But he soon leaves it. After examining briefly the evidence for and against such a cave, Porphyry tells us:

> Whether Homer described it as it actually is or embellished it, nonetheless the problems remain. An investigator will still hunt for the intention, either of those who set up the real shrine or for the poet who made it up. Neither would the ancients have established a shrine without mystical symbols, nor would Homer have described them randomly.
>
> εἴτε δ' οὕτως ἔχον ἀφηγήσατο εἴτε καὶ αὐτός τινα προσέθηκεν, οὐδὲν ἧττον μένει τὰ ζητήματα τὴν βούλησιν ἢ τῶν καθιδρυσαμένων ἢ τοῦ προσθέντος ποιητοῦ ἀνιχνεύοντι, ὡς ἂν μήτε τῶν παλαιῶν ἄνευ συμβόλων μυστικῶν τὰ ἱερὰ καθιδρυσαμένων μήτε Ὁμήρου ὡς ἔτυχε τὰ περὶ τούτων ἀφηγουμένου. (*Antr.* 4)

The judgment that a representation is a poetic flight of fancy, then, will not be the end point of the reader's work but the starting point. Aristarchus warns against searching for meanings in such places in a poem, for we risk pulling to the inside of a poem what should be left on the outside. Porphyry and the other allegorical critics share precisely the opposite belief. What appear as poetic flights of fancy are exactly where we should look for the poet's most profound messages.

Does a Work of Literature Need Interpretation?

The kind of criticism in which Porphyry engages in *On the Cave of the Nymphs* has traditionally been considered to be at odds with what he does in the *Homeric Questions*, which more nearly resembles the close textual scrutiny that Aristarchus practices. In fact, one often sees the claim that a critic's interest in allegorism is a defining affiliation and that such an interest would have excluded him from practicing close textual criticism or other forms of commentary.[111] Indeed, this study's placement of rhetorical criticism and allegoresis in an "on the one hand"/"on the other hand" binary may have reinforced this view. But the binary is intended as a heuristic device—in order to highlight a strong demarcation between the two approaches over the issue of clarity in poetic language—and not as a claim that one and the same critic cannot employ both. Surely Porphyry did not consider these methods to be incompatible; he is a critic whose approach to reading poetry took hybrid forms. We will see many other readers, especially in chapter 4, who cannot be exclusively classified as "allegorists." From the beginning we know that many allegorical readers had strong interests in other approaches to reading. Metrodorus of Lampsacus, Chrysippus, Crates of Mallos, Cornutus, Pseudo-Plutarch, Heraclitus the allegorist, and Proclus all exhibit a plurality of approaches—philological, allegorical, Aristotelian—in their commentaries. This is certainly also the case with Porphyry. As we will see, many of these allegorists are indeed interested in close textual scrutiny, but this is usually not the end point of their work. From there they go on to what I have claimed is the distinctive feature of allegorical criticism: the belief that the text's relationship to the world is never reducible to a straightforward representation; that the reality it points to in the world will itself have signifying power and bring along with it, to the inside of the poem, a whole host of attendant significations. The urge to go on with interpretation, when a reader is perched at the limits of the text, emerges from a belief that the poem signifies in a way that is more akin to the language of oracles, esoteric philosophy, and secret rites than to the language of the public orator. The "enigma" and, as we will see in the rest of this work, the symbol too, mark an understanding of how poetry works that draws more from Delphi than from the agora, and a vision of the role of the reader as

[111] See, for example, the remarks regarding Stesimbrotus in Pfeiffer, 35–36, and Jacoby *FGH* 2 D, 349.15ff. For a convincing rebuttal, see Richardson, 67–68.

active interpreter (who now feels forced to tease out meanings understood to be hidden). But the most skilled of these readers will follow this urge entirely in tandem with an attempt at mastering the *techne* of poetic language.

It is perhaps, then, not so surprising that the same critic who produces the best surviving allegorical exegesis from antiquity also preserves what has been understood to be the motto of the critics who practice the textual methods of Aristarchus.[112] Aristarchus's principle that we should interpret "Homer from Homer" survives from a citation in Porphyry's *Homeric Questions*, and may even have been coined by Porphyry himself.[113] There is little doubt that both in the *Homeric Questions* and in *The Cave of the Nymphs*, Porphyry believed that he was being faithful to what Homer said, that he was reading Homer from Homer. Porphyry closes his essay on the cave of the nymphs with a denial that he is doing the kind of thing that Aristarchus would deplore: "This sort of exegesis should not be considered forced or the product of a credulousness or exuberance to find things," he tells us [οὐ δεῖ δὲ τὰς τοιαύτας ἐξηγήσεις βεβιασμένας ἡγεῖσθαι καὶ εὑρεσιλογούντων πιθανότητας] (*Antr.* 36). Aristarchus would clearly think that Porphyry, by going deeply into the question of what caves themselves might mean, was reading into Homer what was not there. Would Porphyry agree? I think the answer is clearly no. So Aristarchus's opinion as we have it in the D-scholion, that we should not bother ourselves with what is outside the text, as well as Cicero's judgment (*De nat.* 1.41; see introduction) that the allegorists read into a poem what is not there, beg the question, as the allegorists see it. The questions we should be asking, if we are to achieve a better understanding of ancient techniques of symbol reading, are these: What counts as being the inside and the outside of a text? Are these two regions stable, and may lexical rules decide the boundary between them? Or does a signification through language always carry the possibility of meaning more than what the rules of language say it means? Or, to simplify matters slightly, Is a "cave" ever just a cave?

[112] George A. Kennedy, "Alexandrian Philology," in Kennedy, ed., *The Cambridge History of Literary Criticism*, vol. 1, *Classical Criticism* (New York: Cambridge University Press, 1986), 208.

[113] Pfeiffer suggests that Porphyry may have coined this phrase drawing inspiration from Aristarchus's work (226). Porter disagrees (73). The spirit of the idea is traceable to Aristotle, as Porter has shown. For a completely different proposal, see the note by Guy Lee, "An Aristarchan Maxim?" *Proceedings of the Cambridge Philological Society* 201 (1975): 63–64. Lee suggests, on the basis of a similar phrase regarding Agathon, that the famous Aristarchan maxim is actually an invention of the Sophists.

2

BEGINNINGS TO 300 B.C.E.: MEANING FROM THE VOID OF CHANCE AND THE SILENCE OF THE SECRET

WHEN PORPHYRY refers (repeatedly) to Homer's cave of the nymphs as a σύμβολον of certain hidden meanings, he is using the term in a sense that appears only in the postclassical period in ancient Greece. The early Greek term meant something quite different—so different, in fact, that we will be forced to wonder just how it developed a literary sense at all. These earliest manifestations of the Greek symbol provide insights into the trajectories the notion later follows. Of course, they do not and cannot be asked to provide some authentic glimpse of the "true" or "real" symbol, as if core identity somehow lay at an originary moment of intellectual coinage. (The dynamics of the early symbol itself confound simple originalist theories of meaning, as we will see shortly.) Nor does this history determine or exhaust the possibilities for the symbol's future, but these early manifestations set out certain parameters and pairs of oppositions that, our evidence suggests, endure in the term's later history as stubborn and durable armatures around which later literary theorists construct and reconstruct a conceptual category for understanding literature.

I will examine the early history in two parts. First I will make a general survey of occurrences of the term in the surviving Greek literature up through the fourth century B.C.E., then discuss three specialized senses that are most relevant to its later literary development: in divination, the mysteries, and Pythagorean philosophy. The survey has aimed to be as nearly comprehensive as possible. Walter Müri produced the definitive philological study of the Greek term, from earliest appearances down through the fourth century C.E. The work presented here is generally consistent with his broader findings but concentrates on the symbol as an object of hermeneutic activity and expands on the possible avenues of generation for the literary symbol. In this sense, it is an extension of the work that Coulter has done.[1]

[1] James A. Coulter, *The Literary Microcosm* (Leiden: E. J. Brill, 1976), 60–68.

The Symbol as Authenticating Device

In its earliest instances, the Greek word σύμβολον does not have anything like the literary sense that it has for Porphyry, nor does it have the breadth of its current English equivalent. Up to about 300 B.C.E., except in a few specialized contexts, a symbol has nothing to do with figurative or suggestive language. Formed off the verb συμβάλλειν (put together), a symbol is one half of an object—usually a piece of cloth, wood, or pottery—that is deliberately split in two and then allocated to the parties to an agreement. It is reassembled at a later time to verify the deal. As Müri has shown, on philological grounds it is more likely that the neuter noun form σύμβολον grew out of the connotation of agreement contained in the verb, rather than from the notion that the symbol itself was "put together" with something else.[2] Müri adduces parallel formations from other -βάλλειν verbs and shows that first-declension forms in -βολη typically mark the abstract nominalization of the verbal idea, while the masculine omicron forms in -βολος typically act as *nomen agentis* and the neuter omicron forms in -βολον as *nomen rei qua agitur*. The symbol begins life as a concrete thing by which the action contained in the verb is performed. The sense of συμβάλλειν, then, which most plausibly stands behind the early symbol is "to agree." We will shortly see the significance of this in the emphasis on social agreement in the early evidence; a symbol in this period (with rare and significant exceptions) indicates what it indicates *by agreement*, or as we might put it in linguistic terms, by convention.[3]

In a survey of the surviving literature down through the fourth century B.C.E., the very general sense of a "tally" that fits with another tally to form a whole appears in the works of comic poets, tragedians, and philosophers.[4] This sense lies behind Plato's famous comment on the

[2] Walter Müri, "Symbolon," in *Griechische Studien* (Basel: Friedrich Reinhardt, 1976), 13–14.

[3] Müri sees three main uses for "symbol" in antiquity: as hospitality token (and uses traceable to that one); as a marker of legal rights granted a foreigner; and as a sign. Müri's first two categories are in keeping with the current findings. His third category strikes me as almost entirely divisible into the first two. It consists of uses of the term that are influenced by the meaning of hospitality token—whose sense Müri himself says is "nearly always beside it" (20, cf. 18)—or that are connected with divination, the Pythagorean texts, and the mysteries. It seems to me a better arrangement of the evidence to split the notion of symbol as sign (= σημεῖον) into the respective categories out of which the more general uses must have grown—be they the authenticating device of the hospitality token or the interpretable enigma of divine speech—as I will do here.

[4] Hermippus frag. 14; Empedocles frag. 63 (from Aristotle *On the Generation of Animals* 722b11); Plato *Symposium* 191d; Sophocles *Philoctetes* 403; Aristotle *Eudemian Ethics* 1239b30; Aristotle *Politics* 1294a35; Eubulus frag. 70; also Aristotle *On Genera-*

nature of lovers in the *Symposium*. Aristophanes sums up his theory that romantic love derives from an early stage in the development of the human species, when all humans were four-legged, four-armed, two-faced creatures, whom Zeus, out of a fit of jealousy, weakened by splitting in two:

> Then each of us is a symbol of a human, since we have been cleaved just like flatfish, two generated from one. So each person forever searches for the symbol of himself.
>
> ἕκαστος οὖν ἡμῶν ἐστιν ἀνθρώπου σύμβολον, ἅτε τετμημένος ὥσπερ αἱ ψῆτται, ἐξ ἑνὸς δύο· ζητεῖ δὴ ἀεί τὸ αὑτοῦ ἕκαστος σύμβολον. (*Symp*. 191d)

This theory, striking in its imagery and wholly idiosyncratic to this dialogue, points out several characteristics of the symbol considered as a token, half of a larger whole. It is, first of all, characterized by lack: a symbol has something missing, and this incompleteness begs to be resolved. The symbol rings with both lack and potential wholeness, something incomplete and something always potentially complete. The symbol is also implicated, as Plato's particular example highlights, in an economy of desire. The symbol itself, precisely in its being a symbol, generates a passion, an inquiry, an investigation, and an examination, or, to employ a term that embraces both lack and desire, the symbol operates according to want.

Most often in the surviving literature, symbols are two halves of a single object and serve as authenticating tokens for the two parties to an agreement. Most important among these uses, to which many others can be traced, is the symbol as a hospitality token and proof of one's status as a guest-friend.[5] A symbol can also be a receipt in a business transaction.[6] This use is widespread enough to generate two adjectives, εὐξύμβολος and δυσξύμβολος, which mark people who are either easy to deal with or difficult to deal with.[7] Commonly among orators and

---

tion and Corruption 331a24–332b29 and Aristotle *Meteorology* 360a, where vapor (moist and cold) and smoke (hot and dry) are called symbols or "complementary factors," which combine in pairs to form air (moist and hot).

[5] *Hymn to Hermes* 527; Archippus frag. 8; Euripides *Medea* 613; Demosthenes *Letter 2* 24.6. See Müri, 2–9, for several other attestations, including later texts and the epigraphical material.

[6] Herodotus *Hist.* 6.86a.5–b.1; Lysias *On the Property of Aristophanes* 25–26 (this passage indicates both a business and a diplomatic usage for the term; see below); Hermippus frag. 61; Plato *Republic* 371b; Aristotle *Politics* 1275a10 and 1280a37.

[7] For δυσξύμβολος, see: Plato *Republic* 486b7; Plato *Letter 13* 362d9; Xenophon *Memorabilia* 2.6.3. For εὐξύμβολος, see Aeschylus *Suppliants* 701; Xenophon *Memorabilia* 2.6.5; and probably Antiphon frag. 74, though the lack of context leaves doubts. One can also note the use of the term at Aeschylus *Libation Bearers* 170 where it marks not easy

historians, the symbol marks a political treaty[8] or a diplomatic credential.[9] In the corpus attributed to Theognis, the term also marks general compacts or agreements, in this case between rogues.[10] These usages in the realms of diplomacy and personal relationships are very closely connected through the diplomatic institution of proxeny, whereby wealthy guest-friends evolved somewhat seamlessly into ambassadors. The symbol is put to use as a proof of something. It authenticates. Various social, commercial, and political spheres put to use the economy of want that it sets in motion. It is a means to secure the benefits of contracts, and it presupposes a set of conventions that make a society work. In this sense, the symbol materializes in a most concrete way social agreement and social commitment, in commercial, political, and personal spheres.

Another significant cluster of uses remains to be considered. The symbol becomes a token that allows entry[11] or the password or watchword of a soldier,[12] which like two halves of a broken token are repeated back

---

business dealings but something easy to understand—an early hint at a sense seen more clearly in Demosthenes. See below, pp. 84–88.

[8] Andocides *Against Alcibiades* 4.18; Antiphon *On the Murder of Herodes* 5.78; Demosthenes *On Halonnesus* 9, 12, and 13; Demosthenes *On the Liberty of the Rhodians* 4; Demosthenes *Against Meidias* 173; Aristotle *Politics* 1280a39; Aristotle *Constitution of the Athenians* 59.6.

[9] Xenophon *Cyropaedia* 6.1.46 and Lysias *On the Property of Aristophanes* 25. An inscription on the Acropolis, which was removed and now resides at Oxford, confirms this sense. See E. L. Hicks, *Greek Historical Inscriptions* (Oxford: Clarendon Press, 1901), 111.19.

[10] Theognis *Elegy* 1150.

[11] Aristophanes *Birds* 1214 (a token that is stamped for admission to Cloudcuckooland); Aristophanes *Plutus* 278 (a ticket that Charon gives a person after death); Theophrastus *Characters* 6.4 (a receipt for the admission fee to a public spectacle). The archaeological record confirms the existence of such identity tokens. See J. H. Kroll and F. W. Mitchel, "Clay Tokens Stamped with the Names of Athenian Military Commanders," *Hesperia* 49 (1980): 86–96. Kroll and Mitchel publish thirty-two small terracotta tokens, excavated mostly from the Athenian agora. They date from the fourth century B.C.E. The tokens carry the name and title of a military officer and probably functioned as the officer's credentials.

[12] Euripides *Orestes* 1130; Euripides *Rhesus* 573; and two uses of the term in Aeschylus's *Agamemnon* require some comment. The signal fire that announces Agamemnon's return from Troy is twice called a "σύμβολον," once in the play's opening passage and once as Clytemnestra announces Agamemnon's imminent return. Translators have handled these sections differently, often relying on the English equivalent and rendering the fire as a "symbol" or a "sign" that the great warrior is coming home. This treatment seems reasonable enough at first glance, but in the second reference Clytemnestra's use of the term locates a rather more precise meaning for it:

> I announce to you such a proof and σύμβολον,
> with my lord having sent it along out of Troy to me.

and forth. Euripides also knows as a symbol any object that marks one's true identity—particularly the secret objects that indicate the true lineages of foundlings.[13] These senses show the term as somewhat broader, but still not overly broad. One could find an equivalent English idiom in the notion of the "calling card." These texts also highlight the nature of the symbol as a secret, an important development to which we will return below. For now, borrowing a phrase that Gregory Nagy has used in another context, we might call this secrecy an "ideology of exclusiveness," an idea that we will see is formative in the poetics of both the symbol and the enigma. Both passwords and Euripides' tokens mark identity in a way that is not open to all. Their purpose is to reveal (to the few) and at the same time to conceal (from the many). Branching off from this use of identity marker we see a few others. Several writers call the token that dicasts use to vote in Athenian court a symbol.[14] In Plato's letters, it is also a distinctive word or heading by which a correspondence is proved genuine.[15] Aristotle and Isocrates also use the term symbol in the sense of a generic proof of something.[16]

We have so far accounted for all but a few of the surviving attestations of the term symbol from the classical period. On the surface, this background seems to be a congenial enough one for the development of a literary idea where one word or idea might provoke another and set a reader off on a trail of literary figuration. But on second look it becomes clearer that the move from the context we have seen so far to the literary symbol would actually have been rather a leap. We must, of

---

> τέκμαρ τοιοῦτο σύμβολόν τέ σοι λέγω
> ἀνδρὸς παραγγείλαντος ἐκ Τροίας ἐμοί. (315–16)

The verb παραγγέλλω is often used in conjunction with a military watchword that is passed along from one soldier to the next. This is a well-attested use of the term σύμβολον. Given the military context and the manner by which the fire is "passed" from post to post along the Aegean coastline, this is surely the sense of σύμβολον in this instance, which may then be translated: "I announce to you such a proof and watchword, / with my lord having sent it along out of Troy to me." Such also must be the sense of the "symbol" in line 8, which comes, after all, from the mouth of a watchman:

> As it is, I keep a lookout for the watchword of the torch light
> a gleam of fire bearing from Troy a rumor
> and the report of capture.

[13] Euripides *Ion* 1386; Euripides *Electra* 577; Euripides *Helen* 291.

[14] Aristophanes *Ecclesiazusae* 297; Aristotle *Constitution of the Athenians* 65.2, 68.2, and 69.2; Demosthenes *On the Crown* 210 (contra the translation in the Loeb volume). Some such legal use seems also to lie behind two puzzling appearances of the term in fragments of Aristophanes (frags. 44, 278).

[15] Plato *Letters* 13.363b and 13.360a.

[16] Isocrates *Panegyricus* 49; Aristotle *Eudemian Ethics* 1237b25; cf. Euripides *Rhesus* 220.

course, work hard to bracket the current English term symbol and allow ourselves only to think with the senses revealed in the cases we have seen so far: receipt, passport, credential, watchword, identity token. Imagining the emergence of a literary term against this background becomes problematic for two reasons. The key function of all of these classical symbols is authentication, and this sense is quite out of place in a literary context. Second, the classical symbol operates by means of consensus. The token is a simple vessel, meaning nothing in itself, which takes on a meaning only insofar as it marks an agreement between two parties, and this meaning is entirely arbitrary. This sets it quite a distance from the idea of hinting, allusive literary language, where a prior agreement is never presupposed. Literary symbols, as we will see, tend to be understood as working (very much like the enigma as we saw it in the previous chapter) by means of hidden connections in nature that exist regardless of whether a group of language users agree on them or not.

Slightly more interesting, in the late classical period, two passages from Aristotle's *Rhetoric* discuss many methods for removing suspicion available to orators in the law courts; one of them is the use of symbols [τὸ σύμβολα λέγειν] (1416b1). He illustrates this (not at all clearly) with an example from Sophocles' *Teucer*, where individual facts are adduced toward a proof. Later in the same treatise Aristotle mentions that orators describe an emotion by introducing its "accompanying features" [ἑπόμενα] (1417a37). These are gestures—such as assuming a grim look, shaking the fist, or covering the face with the hands—that are well known to be characteristics of oneself or one's opponent. Such details produce a persuasive argument, because, being known, they become "symbols" of what is unknown.[17] In these texts the symbol expands its power to authenticate into the law courts, but once again, its meaning remains rather narrow—circumscribed within the conceptual terrain of authentication and proof.

In Aristotle's corpus an even more provocative usage appears as well. As we have already seen, the symbol assumes a prominent place in Aristotle's theory of language, as expressed in the *On Interpretation* (16a4, 16a28, 24b2) and later in both the *Sophistical Refutations* (165a8) and the *On Sense and the Sensible* (437a15), which suggests that the usage

[17] Aristotle's earlier use of the term as meaning reciprocal arguments and his theory of "complementary factors" in *On Generation and Corruption* 331a24–332b29 and *Meteorology* 360a suggest a sense here of a redeemable chit, something to be "cashed in" for something else. Compare two notices, one in an Aesop fable (*Fabulae Aphthonii rhetoris* 24.8) and one in the Hippocratic corpus (*Letters* 16.48), that demonstrate a possible use of the term in medical terminology, as a symptom or as an indication of a medically significant corruption of a plant. However, it is difficult to decide how to value this evidence, since establishing sure dates for these texts is next to impossible.

was not casual. Aristotle tells us in these works that words are symbols of affections in the soul. At the outset of *On Interpretation* he states the theory clearly, in a passage that we examined briefly in the previous chapter:

> Spoken words, then, are symbols of affections of the soul; and written words are symbols of spoken ones. And just as written letters are not the same for all humans, neither are spoken words. But the mental affections themselves, of which these words are primarily signs, are the same for everyone, as are also the objects of which those affections are likenesses.
>
> Ἔστι μὲν οὖν τὰ ἐν τῇ φωνῇ τῶν ἐν τῇ ψυχῇ παθημάτων σύμβολα, καὶ τὰ γραφόμενα τῶν ἐν τῇ φωνῇ. καὶ ὥσπερ οὐδὲ γράμματα πᾶσι τὰ αὐτά, οὐδὲ φωναὶ αἱ αὐταί· ὧν μέντοι ταῦτα σημεῖα πρώτων, ταὐτὰ πᾶσι παθήματα τῆς ψυχῆς, καὶ ὧν ταῦτα ὁμοιώματα πράγματα ἤδη ταὐτά. (16a3–8)

This appears to be a major shift from previous uses of the term. The specificity of its earlier meanings seems at first glance to have disappeared in favor of a general notion of signification, which is emphasized even further by Aristotle's placing the term σημεῖον in apposition to it. Σημεῖον, or "sign," had a history that was not so narrow as the symbol. From early on, it is a general word for anything that stands for something else.[18] It had not occurred to Aristotle's predecessors to introduce the term symbol into discussions of linguistic issues. Such a resistance is explained by our survey of the generally narrow early senses of the term. In almost all cases, as we have seen, the term was as specialized as the English terms "receipt," "treaty," "passport," or "proof." Given this narrow past, why does Aristotle see fit to insert it into this context? He leaves no doubt on this question a few sentences later, when he begins his section on nouns by telling us that a noun is "significant by convention" [ὄνομα μὲν οὖν ἐστὶ φωνὴ σημαντικὴ κατὰ συνθήκην] (16a19), has no reference to time, and has no part that means something on its own. As is typical of his style, he then goes on to explain each part of his definitional statement and soon arrives at κατὰ συνθήκην: "A noun is significant 'by convention,' since no noun is by nature significant, but only when it has become a symbol" [τὸ δὲ κατὰ συνθήκην, ὅτι φύσει τῶν ὀνομάτων οὐδέν ἐστιν, ἀλλ' ὅταν γένηται σύμβολον] (16a26–28). Unless we read the term symbol with attention to its earlier uses, we might miss the true import of this definition of κατὰ συνθήκην. In fact, "symbol" here *cannot* mean, generally, anything that stands for something else. If it did, the opposition between natural meaning and the symbol would make no sense. The key here is Aristotle's distinction between nature and convention. Aristotle clearly as-

[18] LSJ, s.v. II.

sumes that symbols belong *as a matter of definition* to the sphere of convention and social agreement. Since Aristotle's sentence specifically denies the possibility of symbols that have meaning by nature [φύσει], he does not have a broad sense of the term in mind. The final temporal clause here, ὅταν γένηται σύμβολον, securely defines his notion of meaning by conventional agreement among a society of speakers [κατὰ συνθήκην]. Aristotle must have a sense of symbol in mind that is in keeping with the term's earlier uses as a marker of social agreement. He has purposefully imported a term from an uncommon context into his argument in order to highlight what is distinctive about his theory of language: his insistence on its pure conventionality. (As we have seen, this position was troublesome to his predecessor Plato.) Such an introduction of a term in a slightly uncommon context is typical of Aristotle when he wants to emphasize an innovation or clarification that his philosophy brings to an old problem.[19] As is also typical of him, he introduces the term first without explanation, then defines it more precisely in the sentences that follow. The "symbol"—marker of agreements between people in business, politics, and social situations—nicely articulates pure conventionality. It is one of many of the symbol's ironies that it enters its long history in describing linguistic relations as the crux of a polemic for pure conventionalism. The Stoics and later the Neoplatonists, as we will see, make out the symbol to be precisely the opposite: the governor of pure naturalism, specifically as opposed to the conventional agreement of any particular group of speakers.

Demosthenes' Testimony

Near the end of the period under consideration, we have a single use of the term that stands out in contrast to the dozens of attestations we have polled so far. Demosthenes (384–322 B.C.E.) regularly uses "symbol," to mean a political treaty and on single occasions a hospitality token and a voting chit in the courts. However, at one point in the *Against Aristocrates*, while engaged in interpreting a section of a traditional Athenian statute, he employs the term symbol in a context we have not yet seen. In the speech, Demosthenes has the full text read publicly and then proceeds to interpret it at length, phrase by phrase and word by word. During this interpretation, he says:

> "If any man die a violent death," says the legislator. First, by adding the "violent," he has made a symbol by which we understand that he means, "if a man die wrongfully."

[19] See, for example, Aristotle's treatments of the terms μῦθος and ἦθος in *Poetics* 1449b.

"ἐάν τις βιαίῳ θανάτῳ ἀποθάνῃ," φησίν. πρῶτον μὲν δὴ τοῦτο προσγράψας τὸ "βιαίως," σύμβολον πεποίηκεν ᾧ γιγνώσκομεν ὅτι, ἂν ἀδίκως, λέγει. (*Against Aristocrates* 83)]

We note here the absence of both the idea of social convention, which distinguishes this text from Aristotle's, and of the notion of authentication. Demothenes uses the term to mark a figural shift of sense from one word to another, not on the basis of an agreement, but on the basis that the surface sense of violence simply has to do with the notion of injustice. The fact that his audience will be inclined to agree that this is a fair association of ideas is entirely irrelevant to the question of *how* the one idea invokes the other. (We could all agree that the sun is related to daytime, but that does not make social consensus the basis of the link between the two.) Demosthenes is not here making the point (as Aristotle clearly was) that the relation between the signifying thing and what it signifies is simply a matter of convention (which would have meant that the signifier meant nothing in itself and could just as easily have been linked to some other meaning entirely). Instead he is making an interpretive move, teasing out an association from a surface meaning to a hidden undermeaning based on an understanding of the way things are. This is the first text to attest this precise sense of the symbol. It is worth some extended consideration.

Demosthenes wrote the speech for a client who wished to prove that a decree of the Senate proposed by Aristocrates was not in keeping with some of the most cherished legal norms in Athens, particularly the laws of the Areopagus concerning homicide. Aristocrates proposed a protection for a certain mercenary (who had powerful friends in Athens) in terms that were very broad. Anyone accused of killing him would be immediately liable to seizure, and those who seized him were able to do with the accused as they wished. To prove that the decree circumvented the normal procedures for prosecuting homicides, which were enshrined in the laws of the Areopagus, Demosthenes' strategy is to elaborate the precision and care with which the Areopagus laws deal with these grave crimes. They lay out many protections for the accused, including provisions for judicial inquiry before punishment (25), directives that punishment is to be meted out only by lawful institutions and not by individuals (32), limits on where seizures can lawfully take place (32), and a range of gradations in treatment to take into account motivation, from provisions for involuntary manslaughter (47), to accidental death in athletic contests (54), to killing out of rage at catching an adulterer *in flagrante* (55), to killing in self-defense against illegal assault (60). These careful limits placed on the power to punish a homicide make clear that a few acts of killing, in extenuating circumstances, are justified, and the decree of Aristocrates deals cavalierly with these important issues. It sets the mercenary it protects outside the normal legal channels. The decree would deal summarily, and without proper room for defense, with anyone even accused of killing him, notwithstanding actual guilt or innocence nor extenuating circumstances. Should he himself set at someone with lethal force, he would be shielded from a lethal counter-attack, however justified. It would even bar his execution should he one day become an enemy of the city of Athens (17).

The reading that Demosthenes proposes under the heading of the symbol, the notion of injustice as the true meaning of the text's reference to violence, is in keeping with his larger project in this speech of making the Areopagus laws take on their most tailored appearance. The full passage from the statute states that: "If someone dies a violent death, on this account it is permitted for his kinsmen to take hostages, until either the hostages submit to trial for murder, or surrender the killers. Up to three hostages are permitted, but no more" (82). In this particular part of the law, in contrast to the earlier parts he has gone over, no explicit mention is made of whether the killing at issue is justified or not. An adversary of Demosthenes' speech could say that the Areopagus law here makes no mention of justifiable homicide and states that any violent death (including those that take place in the course of self-defense, accidental fatalities in sporting events, etcetera) falls in for the same treatment. This observation could be part of a counterargument that the Areopagus laws were actually not so narrowly tailored and that the decree is therefore not such a departure from them as the prosecution claims. To head off this line of counterattack, Demosthenes' speech finds a "symbol" with a defensible figurative sense.

Given that the context at hand is a law court speech, in which Demosthenes' purpose is to persuade a broad cross-section of the Athenian population, it is highly unlikely that he was minting some new sense for the symbol.[20] Absent much more extensive discussion and explanation, a public speech is not the place to introduce new technical terms, for the dangers of misunderstanding are at a premium. In order for his use of the term in this context not to have jarred his audience, they must have already known the symbol as figurative language. Where did this sense come from? Other, intervening contexts for understanding the term must have been operative.

Based on what we have already seen, one suggestive parallel already calls out. Demosthenes' use of the symbol is difficult to distinguish from earlier uses of the term αἴνιγμα, which we saw in the previous chapter to be central to the vocabulary of allegorical commentary. In just about

[20] I thank the anonymous reviewers of the manuscript for this observation.

every period for which evidence survives, and well before Demosthenes is writing, we have testimony in the allegorical commentators that certain words in a poem by Homer or Orpheus or Hesiod do not have only surface meanings but are actually αἰνίγματα, enigmas, or that they αἰνίττονται some other meaning. Socrates' ironic treatment of allegorical techniques in the *Republic*, which we examined earlier, is useful to reiterate here:

> It seems, then, that Simonides was speaking enigmatically, after the manner of the poets, when he said what "the just" is. For it seems that he meant that "the just" is to render to each what is fitting, but he named this "the due."
>
> Ἠινίξατο ἄρα, ἦν δ' ἐγώ, ὡς ἔοικεν, ὁ Σιμωνίδης ποιητικῶς τὸ δίκαιον ὃ εἴη. διενοεῖτο μὲν γάρ, ὡς φαίνεται, ὅτι τοῦτ' εἴη δίκαιον, τὸ προσῆκον ἑκάστῳ ἀποδιδόναι, τοῦτο δὲ ὠνόμασεν ὀφειλόμενον. (*Rep.* 1.332b–c)

When Demosthenes substitutes dying "wrongfully" for dying a "violent" death on the grounds that the latter is a "symbol" for the former, he precisely parallels the notion of figurative linguistic substitution that Plato and others attributed to enigma. The evidence shows beyond doubt that these two terms are synonyms within a hundred years of Demosthenes' time. Perhaps they were for him as well.

As we discovered in the previous chapter, such interpretations of αἰνίγματα are the common coin of allegorical reading in the classical period. (In chapter 5 we will make the further finding that, while other important clusters of enigma ideas exist, allegorical contexts dominate its usage in the classical period.) We also saw that by means of the vocabulary of the enigma, which the Derveni text shows to be a term of art in allegorism, Plato regularly references (for his own ironic purposes) an allegorical approach to reading. We ought not to overlook that Demosthenes is here reading roughly the same kind of text that we saw to be the typical subject of allegorical reading in the previous chapter, ancient and hoary wisdom put down by original wise men. None of this would make Demosthenes an allegorist any more than the *Republic* passage above makes Plato one; there is, of course, a great distance between allegorical readers of Homer on the one hand and Plato and Demosthenes on the other. But this distance itself is suggestive. If interpretive moves such as we know to have been made by allegorists can be invoked in philosophical as well as legal contexts, in order to round out or punctuate arguments quite isolated from the concerns of literary allegoresis, this would suggest that Athenian audiences were well familiar with them. Given the lack of parallel citations in the rest of Demosthenes' speeches, the link with allegorism in his case can only remain a suggestion, but given the lack of apposite contexts for making sense of Demosthenes' use of the term "symbol," we have no better explanation. Allegorical commentators beginning within a century of Demosthenes' time use the terms σύμβολον and αἴνιγμα interchangeably, without meaningful distinction between the two.

Whatever else it tells us, the *Against Aristocrates* securely attests that the symbol has a sense of figurative language at least back to 352 B.C.E. As we have observed, a token that authenticates is, after all, a far cry from a figurative linguistic sign that carries some hidden message, in which a prior agreement or a convention is not presupposed. A few specialized senses of σύμβολον, to which we will turn next, bridge the gap between these two. First, divination provides us with an interpretable symbol. Here, as we will see, an aspect of the verbal idea συμβάλλειν that is entirely different from "to agree" brings a different kind of noun into being. The symbol Euripides knows as a secret marker of identity has already pointed the way to the second and third specialized senses. In both the mysteries and esoteric philosophy, symbols are passwords of authentication that just happen to be enigmatic, interpretable speech. But before we turn to these other streams of the symbolic, we should take a step back and consider the ground we have covered so far.

Nature, Convention, and Symbolic Meaning

With the exception of Demosthenes' testimony, the symbol as we have seen it is instituted to mark a contractual agreement between parties who have settled on particular terms. The parties in the agreement create a language by fabricating a token whose signifying power lies along its seam. The symbol becomes significant at a beginning moment when two parties make a purposeful rupture in an otherwise seamless whole. The two halves of the symbol acquire significance because a prior moment of wholeness was fragmented by those who needed a signifier. This history cuts two ways. The classical symbol has two referents. First, it does its main job of indication by means of matching, in a very concrete way, its other half. At its first level, the symbol's power as a signifier could not be more straightforward. The parties who come to agreement construct this level of signification with the express purpose of doing away with ambiguity and doubt. The seam between two pieces of broken terra cotta is functionally impossible to duplicate. Who is the beneficiary of this contract? The one that holds the symbol. Among the hordes of piratical raiders that might drop an anchor in my port, who are my family's friends? Those that hold the proper tokens. In this sense the symbol indicates its referent in a wholly unambiguous and, one might say, "natural" way. The symbol's power is built into its physical characteristics. No mistake or miscommunication is possible.

On the other hand, symbols, when reassembled into a proper, completed whole have a second-order referent that is more abstract and difficult. Despite the best efforts of the parties involved to use a language that is free from ambiguity and doubt, nevertheless doubt inevitably threatens to creep in. The symbol is asked to indicate something as ephemeral and difficult as agreement between two human beings in a particular social, political, or business matter. What precisely *did* we agree to? How strong *is* the bond of guest-friendship, or the political imperative of allowing diplomats unharassed passage? The possessor of the symbol must always await the full understanding as well as the good faith of the other party to the agreement. Furthermore, how does one know that the unambiguous signifier, the authorizing "symbol," did not somewhere fall into the wrong hands? Away from the context of its inception, when the parties break open a signifier, the symbol's power to signify is free-floating, and remains completely independent of the integrity of the one who holds it now, in the present. The very naturalism of the symbol makes it vulnerable to the thief. With these things in mind, then, the symbol partakes of *both* nature and convention, and it partakes of these at one and the same time. The semantic stability that those who create the language hope to secure is contingent: it relies on a whole host of normative arrangements negotiated in particular social situations with the aim, but never the guarantee, of doing away with malfeasance, double-dealing, and doubt. But social contingency introduces itself into the well-ordered world of the natural signifier. The natural sign does not solve the problem of semantic instability, it only staves it off until a later moment when the symbol is reassembled and the original contract, one hopes, will be fulfilled.

The two positions, purely natural signification and purely conventional signification, anchor what appear in most theories of language (ancient as well as modern) to be opposite ends of a spectrum. The bipolar question of *whether* language is natural *or* conventional has interested thinkers at least as far back as Plato. The ancient history of the symbol demonstrates the difficulty of maintaining such an opposition in any meaningful way. It reveals that when we say "natural" and "conventional" we may not quite mean what we think we mean. Naturalism in such dichotomies regularly stands for some sort of semantic stability, on the basis that signifiers have meanings built right into them. Conventionalism, on the other hand, usually suggests some contingency, whether it be social or historical or cultural. Behind the conventional also lurks an element of semantic imposition, as if things mean nothing in themselves until some outside observers assign a value to them. This imposition of value, which can always be questioned or renegotiated, raises the specter of instability. The pair naturalism vs. conventionalism, therefore, shows a certain congruence to another pair: reading a meaning that is "just there" and reading a meaning "into" a text. It is perhaps not curious, then, that the notion of the "symbol," as a governing concept for ancient allegorical readers, is deeply implicated in precisely this debate. This topic awaits a fuller consideration, to be taken up after more historical study. For the time being, we can point out that the symbol, which is born from a desire to do away with ambiguity, suggestiveness, and figuration, becomes perhaps the central repository of just such qualities in the postclassical period. Furthermore, the traditional alignments of semantic security with naturalism and ambiguity and doubt with conventionalism are utterly compromised in the symbol's history—throughout the whole of the symbol's history. As we have seen already, the symbol in the classical period is at once the paragon of conventionality (as Aristotle's *On Interpretation* makes clear) and the guarantor of semantic stability (as is reiterated through countless examples of the symbol as an authentication). Conversely, during the later periods, as we will see, the symbol marks natural semantic linkages specifically as opposed to conventional agreement and at the same time carries a consistent inscrutability and ambiguity, and an inexhaustible suggestiveness. In practice then, in the symbol's history, naturalism tends to produce ambiguity and convention semantic stability.

The Symbol as Interpretable Riddle I: Divine Message

In addition to the uses we examined above, the symbol has a marked classical specialization in divination. In fact, in the very early periods this is among the most prominent uses of the term. This divinatory context is crucial for understanding the prominent role that interpretation plays in the later history of the symbolic. Unlike the symbols we have seen so far, the symbol as omen carries no hint of authentication or convention, and it regularly provokes vigorous interpretations. How then did the divinatory sense develop? Here we need to return to the verb. Συμβάλλειν also carries with it a notion of a meeting, as in bumping into someone or something. An array of coincidences had prophetic meaning from the archaic period forward. The neuter noun σύμβολον will appear in this context interchangeably with a masculine form σύμβολος. The ancients themselves were not consistent in distinguishing between the two.[21] Müri demonstrates that the masculine here indicates

[21] See the scholion on Pindar's *Olympian Ode* 12.7, cited below.

"that which one meets," on the basis of parallel formations from other -βάλλειν verbs.[22] He suggests, surely rightly, that the more specific masculine noun (which only appears in the early materials) gets fused with the more broadly used neuter term. In addition, he adduces the tendency to give neuter forms preference in the vocabulary of divine signs.[23]

Before the fifth century, Aeschylus, the author of the *Hymn to Hermes*, Pindar, and Archilochus all speak of the symbol in a divinatory context. In the *Prometheus Bound*, Prometheus produces a long list of the arts that he taught humans, including an array of divinatory techniques. These include the reading of ominous sounds, bird flights, entrails, and something he calls ἐνόδιοι σύμβολοι, "symbols of the road" (487). The sense of this compressed phrase is difficult to determine, but Aeschylus's *Suppliants* (502) fixes it. The symbol there is a chance meeting (though in this case it has no apparent divinatory value): Pelasgus orders that the stranger (Danaus) be taken directly to the altar and that they not stop to talk to "whomever they might meet" [καὶ ξυμβολοῦσιν οὐ πολυστομεῖν χρεών]. The beginning of the *Hymn to Hermes* tells of the god's birth and how he sprang forth from the womb intent on stealing the cattle of Apollo. As he stepped over the threshold, a tortoise fell into his path [ἀντεβόλησεν] right at the courtyard gate. He exclaims upon the abrupt [ἤδη] meeting with the tortoise: "A chance meeting very auspicious for me! I will not slight it" [σύμβολον ἤδη μοι μέγ' ὀνήσιμον, οὐκ ὀνοτάζω] (30). He then consecrates the meeting by constructing the lyre. Xenophon (c. 430–c. 352) confirms the sense of symbol as ominous chance meeting. He produces a list of ways in which the diviner is able to predict the future, including by birds, chance utterances, συμβόλοις, and sacrifices (*Mem.* 1.1.3). The "symbol" is glossed in the following sentence as τοὺς ἀπαντῶντας, leaving no doubt that these divine signs are coincidental meetings with people. A nearly identical list recurs at Xenophon *Apology* 13.5. Aristophanes (b. 460–450, d. c. 386) at *Birds* 721, likely references this sense as well when he lists divination by a chance utterance [φήμη], a sneeze, a ξύμβολον, the cry of beast or human [φωνή], a servant, and an ass.[24] Divination by servant probably had to do with the first servant one saw upon waking up, and meeting an ass in the road could have ominous significance (like a black cat).

Two texts, from Aeschylus and Pindar, deserve more extended attention. The symbol appears in the context of an omen at *Agamemnon* 144. The chorus recounts Agamemnon's fateful sacrifice of Iphigenaia.

[22] Müri, 13–14.

[23] Müri, 25.

[24] A similar list appears at *Apology of Socrates* 13.3.

According to Aeschylus, at Aulis Artemis is angered at the particular means by which Zeus sends a sign to the Greeks: Zeus has eagles maul a pregnant hare, which is supposed to indicate that Agamemnon and Menelaus will conquer Troy. In a section that leads Page to remark "text and interpretation extremely doubtful," the chorus recounts the tale. According to Page, the introductory phrase explains Artemis's anger, which was highlighted in the previous antistrophe.

> The beautiful one [Artemis] being, as she is, so well-disposed
> to the cubs of fierce lions,
> and delighted with the sucklings of all the beasts
> that lurk in the lonely places,
> begs Zeus to fulfill the ξύμβολα of these,
> portents that on the one hand bode well, on the other ill.
>
> τόσον περ εὔφρων ἁ καλά
> δρόσοις ἀέπτοις μαλερῶν λεόντων
> πάντων τ' ἀγρονόμων φιλομάστοις
> θηρῶν ὀβρικάλοισι τερπνά,
> τούτων αἰτεῖ ξύμβολα κρᾶναι,
> δεξιὰ μὲν κατάμομφα δὲ φάσματα· (140–45)[25]

Here the symbol refers to the appearances of the birds. There is no problem with the αἰτεῖ ξύμβολα κρᾶναι. According to Page's interpretation, a lower god appeals to Zeus (unexpressed), who has sent the omen in the first place, to fulfill it. The genitive τούτων, however, gives some pause and seems to twist the sentence slightly. Its antecedent must be the young beasts of which Artemis is so fond, or perhaps the whole set of omens more generally. The ξύμβολα of these things, then, seem to be the events themselves that the omens portend. But the final piece of the sentence places φάσματα in apposition with ξύμβολα, clearly meaning the birds' appearances as portents. These two senses are somewhat difficult to reconcile if we maintain that a symbol must be signifier and never signified. However, perhaps, as we saw above in the wider uses of the term, the symbol here brings two things to the table, both of which are required to complete or fulfill a meaning. On this reading, Aeschylus's symbols in this divinatory context are both the divine omen and the actual events they portend. If this section of text is not corrupt (though it may well be), we can conjecture that these two elements fit together, like the two halves of a broken whole.

Finally, for divinatory symbols, we turn to Pindar (518?–c. 438). In

[25] Text OCT, interpretation to follow draws on Page's notes, Aeschylus, *Agamemnon*, ed. Denys Page and J. D. Denniston (Oxford: Clarendon, 1957).

Olympian Ode 12, Pindar celebrates the victory of Ergoteles of Himera in the long race at Olympia in 472 B.C.E. He opens with an invocation to Tyche, goddess of fortune or chance, and a meditation on the role of chance in all great endeavors. He continues:

> Never yet has anyone who walks upon earth
> found a reliable symbol from god concerning a future matter.
> Intimations of the future are blind.
> Many things fall counter to the mark, sometimes
> contrary to delight, but other people, having met with distressing
> surges, change in a moment a deep goodness for pain.

> σύμβολον δ' οὔ πώ τις ἐπιχθονίων
> πιστὸν ἀμφὶ πράξιος ἐσσομένας εὗρεν θεόθεν·
> τῶν δὲ μελλόντων τετύφλωνται φραδαί.
> πολλὰ δ' ἀνθρώποις παρὰ γνώμαν ἔπεσεν,
> ἔμπαλιν μὲν τέρψιος, οἱ δ' ἀνιαραῖς
> ἀντικύρσαντες ζάλαις ἐσλὸν βαθὺ πήματος ἐν μικρῷ πεδάμειψαν χρόνῳ.
> (7–12)

Here the symbol as omen appears in a context saturated by the language of chance. One may in a moment exchange pleasure for pain, and chance seems to overwhelm our possibility of knowing the future by any secure sign. Pindar here deepens his play between the realms of knowledge and signification, intention and chance, by inserting just the type of omen that tries to make meaning from coincidence, from chance happenings.

Pindar's play between chance and meaningfulness—together with the consistent testimony of Aeschylus, Aristophanes, and Xenophon—confirm the philological observation that σύμβολον indicates a specific form of divine sign: it is whom or what one meets. Such a reading conforms with a scholion on this passage (to which we will turn at the chapter's close). In this use the term points up nicely the suddenness and unexpectedness of any appearance of a divine sign. One later observer confirms these earlier testimonia. Pseudo-Plutarch's *Life of Homer* comments on the passage in *Odyssey* 20 where Odysseus asks Zeus for a word of omen to come out of a nearby house. Zeus obliges him by having a domestic servant utter a general curse against the suitors, which Odysseus overhears. Here, a set of words overheard by chance are imbued with prophetic power for the one who overhears them. The gods who guide the process of divination appear to have steered the suppliant into the right place at the right time, and thereby undergird the surplus meaning that the words have for the one who overhears them. The *Life* author calls this a "symbol." Chance becomes meaningful to a select audience who is "in the know"—the overheard words are "just words" to all but Odysseus. The sense of the symbol as a divine omen reappears in the work of many other figures after the classical period, including Philo,[26] the historian Appian (95–165 C.E.),[27] the second-century novelist Achilles Tatius,[28] Galen (130–200 C.E.),[29] Aelian,[30] Origen,[31] Porphyry,[32] Eusebius,[33] Proclus,[34] and Eustathius,[35] as well as in a scholion on Aristophanes,[36] and in the Suda.[37]

The Semantics of Coincidence

At this point, we might return to our broader speculations on the "symbol"—now considered as a divine sign as well as an authentication of contractual social relations. The possible meaningfulness of coincidences and chance meetings is familiar to all who have felt a chill at crossing paths with a black cat or at seeing a person who has just a moment before been spoken or thought of. But the semantics of coincidence warrant further investigation. The very notion of a meaningful coincidence contains from the beginning a contradiction. It requires both chance and intention. Two things that happen at once become

[26] *De providentia* frag. 2.24 (an oracle [χρησμός] is said to be made up of riddles [αἱ αἰνιγματώδεις φάσεις] that work through symbols).

[27] *Roman History, Iberica* 26 (102) (birds are symbols of Scipio's impending victory); *Syriaca* 56 (286) (Alexander stumbles over a stone being used as an anchor; some say it is a symbol of decay, others of safety).

[28] *Leucippe and Clitophon* 3 6.2 (characters ask a god inside his temple for a symbol).

[29] *In Hippocratis de victu acutorum commentaria* 4 (Kuehn, ed.), 15: 442.1 (list of the different types of μάντεις includes entrail readers, bird readers, and those who predict the future from symbols).

[30] *On the Nature of Animals* 1.48 (mantic symbols [μαντικὰ σύμβολα] are mentioned in a discussion of the raven as a bird attendant upon Apollo).

[31] *Contra Celsum* (Barret, ed.) 4: 88.14 (Origen cites Celsus as describing birds and other mantic animals that foretell the future through symbols).

[32] *Quaestionum Homericarum ad Iliadem pertinentium reliquiae*, scholia on *Iliad* 24.221 "μάντεις" (the diviners foretell the future from meaningful portents, birds, certain symbols [ἔκ τινων συμβόλων], and accidents).

[33] *Demonstratio evangelica* 5, prooem 19.8 (the different kinds of divination use birds, symbols, sacrifices, and coincidences).

[34] *In remp.* (Kroll, ed.) 2: 186.23 (some gain divine knowledge through symbols, dreams, or other signs).

[35] *Commentarii ad Homeri Iliadem* (Van der Valk, ed.) 3. 69.4; 4. 909.13 (where symbols appear in the context of birds).

[36] *Glossae in Plutum* (Tzetzes) on *Plutus* 63 (where a symbol is the mantic bird of a god).

[37] "Ὄρνις," omicron entry 615 (a bird as a mantic symbol); "σύμβολον," sigma entry 1376 (a bird, sign, or oracle).

such a coincidence only when two criteria are met: logic must dictate the event as purely accidental, but the simultaneity must nevertheless tempt one to assume some more remote, mysterious connection between them. Pure chance does not make for a portent; rather, chance must be combined with an uncanny sense of meaningfulness that underwrites the happening. Once again, the symbol sends us in two opposite directions at the same time, directions that can be mapped fruitfully onto the earlier dichotomies we uncovered. First, the symbol as omen mirrors the secure and palpable linkage operative in a symbol as a contract marker. A broken piece of terra-cotta has a physical link with its other half. Similarly, an omen has a secure link with the future events it foretells since its meaningfulness is underwritten by the gods themselves. When Zeus thunders destiny, the future follows without exception or contingency.

On the other hand, the omen's status as an accident points to a contingency that runs parallel to a contingency we saw in the symbol's nondivinatory uses. A divine omen appears to be just put into one's path. Similarly, that two pieces of terra-cotta happen to be a pair means nothing in itself, of course: the potsherds threaten to revert from language into happenstance without careful social constructions and reconstructions of the agreement. From a perspective that is tone-deaf to the divine, the coincidental event is a sudden intervention that we just happen to run across. It is an event that takes place in our own world, whose capacity to carry significance and whose status as an omen grows entirely from its origin with the gods, which is by definition hidden from us. A bird might be just a bird, and a chance meeting becomes a coincidence with meaning only when a god's hand is behind it. In fact, a simple coincidence might be said to be the sine qua non of meaninglessness. The ancient habit of seeing just these crystallizations of randomness as the ultrasignificant language of the divine dramatically points to a certain willful resistance to nonsense, an assertion of sense where none is by any logical definition possible. In the case of both omen and contract marker, significance is pulled from the void of happenstance by looking to an intentionality, social in the one case and divine in the other. These intentional moments are by definition unavailable for direct consultation: the one is past, the other supermundane.

If we map both of these situations onto our earlier, partially articulated pair, naturalness versus conventionality, we see something rather strange. The symbol considered in itself, as either a contractual marker or a divine sign, indicates its referent by its very nature. However, the grounds of possibility for a symbol lie in a set of normative relationships between humans themselves or between humans and gods. In the case of the contract marker, natural signification requires and is predicated on consensual agreement of the parties. In the case of the divine sign, the natural divine sign is lost on those who have not learned the gods' conventional ways of speaking. But the conventional aspect of these symbols is equally dependent on the natural. It is only because the potsherds have the physical property of forming a unique and verifiable seam that they are able to encode social relations within a language. Without such a means of surety, no one in their right mind would redeem the entitlement that the token demands, and the language it speaks would fall apart; all bets would be off, so to speak. And without the first premise, that the gods themselves use natural signs, the conventions of their language—diligently pursued by students of divination—would be empty. Given this set of circumstances, we utterly compromise the idea that "nature" on its own plays the role of semantic stabilizer, or that "convention" by itself makes for instability. On the contrary, nature only guarantees a link between one thing and another. Considered from a strictly "natural" perspective, such links are mere "chance meetings," two things that we can "put together." They fit, yes, but so what? They have *semantic* stability only insofar as they reflect an intentionality, human or divine, that remains stable, a will that endures, embodied in a code of symbols.

The omen provides our earliest secure attestation of a symbol that is an interpretable enigma. We will see in chapter 5 that a connection with αἴνιγμα is explicit in the omen, just as it is in allegory. Many witnesses attest that divinatory signs are precisely "enigmatic." In fact, the area of divine signs is among the most important regions of the semantic field of αἴνιγμα (in addition to its connection with allegorical poetics). Such similarities will make the structure of divinatory semantics especially relevant to allegorical semantics. This point awaits our fuller consideration, but first we look at a final, perhaps even more relevant, classical symbol, which also anchors the symbolic in an eminently interpretable semantic system.

The Symbol as Interpretable Riddle II: Pythagoras and the Mysteries

Pythagoras, a storied figure of the sixth century B.C.E., is perhaps most widely known today for his mathematical theorem that the square of the hypotenuse of a right triangle is equal to the sum of the squares of the two remaining sides. This observation, glaring in its insight, universal in its application, and expressible in a short burst, carries the typical characteristics of the sort of philosophy for which the ancients knew him best. Much more than for this theorem, Pythagoras was famous in antiquity for a different set of insights, for example, that the number five is justice, that the sea is the tear of Kronos, and that one ought never to stir fire with a knife. These sayings are part of a large body of traditional Pythagorean wisdom, expressed through enigmatic epigrams concerning ethics, cosmology, ritual, and the nature of gods and humans. From very early on and consistently, Pythagoras's followers considered these sayings to be the most important and most characteristic of the master's teachings. From at least the time of the younger Anaximander of Miletus (c. 400 B.C.E.) and down through late antiquity, they were known collectively as the "Πυθαγόρεια σύμβολα," the Pythagorean symbols.

Many of the sayings take the form of proscriptive cultic rules.[38] In addition to warning his followers never to stir fire with a knife, Pythagoras supposedly told them not to step over a yoke or to let a swallow into the house. They should not eat beans, urinate into sunlight, pare their nails when sacrificing, travel by the main roads, use public baths, or speak in the dark. They should not wear rings that depict the gods, sacrifice a white cock, make a detour on the way to the temple, sacrifice or enter the temple barefoot, pick up food that falls from the table, eat various kinds of fish, break bread, or look at themselves in a mirror with the help of artificial light. Iamblichus, working from Aristotle's lost work *On the Pythagoreans*,[39] tells us that, in addition to the rules governing cultic prohibitions, there were two other types of Pythagorean sayings: the "what is it?" sort and the "what is the most?" sort:

> Examples of the "what is it?" sort are: What are the isles of the blessed? Sun and moon. What is the oracle at Delphi? The *tetractys*: which is the harmony in which the Sirens sing. Examples of the "what is the most . . . ?" sort are: What is the most just thing? To sacrifice. What is the wisest? Number; but second, the man who assigned names to things. What is the wisest of the things in our power? Medicine. What is the finest? Harmony. What is the most powerful? Knowledge. What is the best? Happiness. What is the truest thing said? That men are wicked.[40]

Another fragment of Aristotle's work on the Pythagoreans adds a few more examples of the "what is it?" type: The sea is the tear of Kronos; the constellations of the Great Bear and the Little Bear are the hands of

[38] This list is assembled mainly from Iamblichus's *Life of Pythagoras* (*V.P.*) and *Exhortation to Philosophy* (*Protrepticus*), along with Porphyry's *Life of Pythagoras*.

[39] Cf. Porphyry *V.P.* 41 (= Aristotle frag. 196; = D-K 58c2), cited below, which tells us that "Aristotle has recorded most of these."

[40] *V.P.* 82 (= D-K 58c4); translation from *The Presocratic Philosophers: A Critical History with a Selection of Texts*, ed. G. S. Kirk, J. E. Raven, and M. Schofield (Cambridge: Cambridge University Press, 1983), frags. 277, 232.

Rhea; the Pleiades is the lyre of the Muses; the planets are the dogs of Persephone; and the sound of bronze when struck is the voice of a daemon trapped inside it, crying to get out (from Porph., *V.P.* 41).[41]

Though a great deal of legend surrounds the figure of Pythagoras, we can be sure that he was a charismatic philosopher who was a part of the Greek migrations westward into the southern tip of Italy. He set up several societies in the region, with followers devoted to his various teachings and to asceticism. This organizing activity got him into trouble with other regional authorities, and he and a large number of his followers died in dubious circumstances, perhaps in a great fire. He speculated widely in many areas of knowledge and had a particular fondness for mathematics, which for him contained a large component concerning the philosophy of number. We are not sure whether Pythagoras actually wrote anything; some later figures claim he did not. Many texts that bear his name are certainly pseudepigraphical, written during the Hellenistic period. It is possible that Pythagoras's well-known *Golden Verses*, a poem of about seventy lines that lays out a Pythagorean way of life and remained popular into the Renaissance, was composed, or at least compiled, during the Hellenistic period as well.[42] We can be reasonably sure, though, that Pythagoras himself handed down, whether in written or oral form, a number of his aphoristic symbols.[43]

Whether Pythagoras used the term symbol is difficult to decide conclusively. We do not have direct evidence that he did, but this proves nothing, since the early record is so fragmentary. The term is documented in Pythagorean literature from about 400 B.C.E., when the younger Anaximander of Miletus wrote an *Interpretation* [ἐξήγησις] *of the Pythagorean Symbols*, which does not survive.[44] From its first appearance in our records, then, the notion of a Pythagorean symbol is linked with the notion of interpretation. Anaximander wrote in what turned out to be a long tradition of exegeses of the symbols. The fragments of Aristotle's work on the Pythagoreans nicely fit the genre. He was followed on this topic by Philochorus (b. before 340, d. after

[41] Clement of Alexandria also testifies that the sea is the tear of Kronos and that the planets are the dogs of Persephone (*Stromata* 5.8).

[42] See Johan Carl Thom, introduction to *The Golden Verses of Pythagoras: Its Literary Composition and Religio-Historical Significance* (diss., University of Chicago, 1990).

[43] Burkert proposes a helpful stemma of many of the known Pythagorean *symbola*, attributing some to pre-Aristotelian tradition, some to the tradition that follows from Aristotle, some to Androcydes (Walter Burkert, *Lore and Science in Ancient Pythagoreanism*, trans. Edwin L. Minar, Jr. [Cambridge: Harvard University Press, 1972], 166–73). He also makes the point that a significant portion of the wisdom to which Pythagoras's name is attached dates back to pre-Pythagorean cult practice and folk tradition (Burkert, 176–78).

[44] Suda, "Anaximandros," alpha entry 1987.

261/60 B.C.E.), in *On Symbols*, a lost work that presents tantalizing possibilities, to which we will return below. Of the next figure in the tradition, Androcydes (who lived before the first century B.C.E. and perhaps as early as the fourth century), we know very little, but we do know that he wrote a work on the Pythagorean symbols.[45] His work survives only in scant fragments, but because of the frequency with which he is mentioned in later works, we know that he was a principal source of the later tradition.[46] He is followed by Alexander Polyhistor (b. Miletus, d. Laurentum c. 35 B.C.E). Some sections of works by Plutarch, Clement of Alexandria, and Iamblichus carry the tradition into late antiquity.[47] The surviving pieces of Aristotle present short equations between certain symbols and some hidden answers to them. For example, the question, "What is the sea?" provoked the interpretive answer, "the tear of Kronos." Androcydes' surviving paraphrases provide us with our earliest glimpse of how Pythagorean symbols having to do with cultic prohibitions could be interpreted. One summary tells us that the symbol "Do not step over a yoke" means "Do not transgress justice." The saying that marks out the cultic prohibition is seen to carry a hidden philosophical significance, and this particular interpretation seems plausible enough. The yoke is a sort of leveling balance, an item that has a broad resonance with the notion of justice, while overstepping has the same transgressive connotation in Greek as it does in English. Though only short paraphrases survive, presumably commentators made more expansive types of interpretations also.[48] If someone devotes a full work to the interpretation of symbols, it is unlikely that he or she would stop at mere equivalences. There are many variant readings (as we would expect), from the beginning of the tradition onward, but the symbols are

[45] For a summary of the scholarship, see Burkert, 169, nn. 8–10.

[46] Burkert, 167.

[47] Plutarch *Quaest. Conv.* 727b–730f. Clement devotes all of chap. 5 of bk. 5 of the *Stromata* to interpreting Pythagorean symbols, using biblical citations as prooftexts. His interpretations are as extensive and careful as those of Iamblichus.

[48] The later material provides relevant comparanda. Iamblichus, in his *Exhortation to Philosophy*, gives us more elaborated readings, of between ten and twenty lines, with justifications. For example, he reads the "Do not step over a balance" symbol this way:

> "Don't step over a balance" encourages us to act justly, to honor with great admiration equality and moderation, and to know justice as the most perfect virtue, to which the other virtues give completion, and without which none of the virtues are any help. Also it says that it is right to know this virtue not in a cursory way, but through theorems and scientific demonstrations. But this knowledge is the work of no other art and science than the Pythagorean philosophy alone, which especially honors the learned sayings before everything else. (*Iamblichi Protrepticus*, ed. Pistelli (Stuttgart: Teubner, 1967), 114.20–28; cf. Iamblichus *Theologoumena arithmeticae* 40.8).

consistently considered to require explanations. Every hundred years or so, we find another scholar trying his hand at them.

Pythagorean "Symbols"?

At this point, it behooves us to pose a question that has remained open up to this point. How does the term symbol come to mean enigmatic speech with hidden messages? Given what we know of the classical context for the term, how do the Pythagoreans come to use it as they do? The answer here is not far afield. The evidence suggests that from the earliest times the Pythagoreans use the "symbols" as a proof of membership in their circle. Knowledge of the symbols establishes one's identity as a Pythagorean initiate, thereby entitling the "holder" to certain privileges and opening access to various levels of the Pythagorean cult of wisdom. Like the "symbolic" token we have seen in the classical period, which is a proof of one's identity or status, or a password for entry, the Pythagorean symbol serves as a token of identity for the followers of Pythagoras's tenets. Aristoxenus (b. Tarentum between 375 and 360 B.C.E.) relates that Pythagoras himself was able to identify those who were sympathetic to his way of life by their knowledge of his sayings: "Whenever he heard a person who was making use of his symbols, he immediately took him into his circle, and made him a friend."[49] Much later Iamblichus tells us that the symbols were a kind of secret code: "If outsiders, the profane, so to speak, were present, the Pythagoreans spoke to each other in enigmatic symbols. Familiar phrases still bear a trace of this: 'don't poke fire with a knife,' and other such."[50] Iamblichus also relates what is probably an old tale about a Pythagorean who died, leaving an innkeeper with an unpaid bill. The dying man asked the innkeeper to post a particular "symbol" outside his inn. Some days after his death a Pythagorean happened by and on seeing the symbol presented himself to the innkeeper to settle the account on behalf of his fellow Pythagorean.[51] So the symbol, as an enigmatic saying or a displayable marker, welcomes a person into the Pythagorean circle, distinguishes a Pythagorean from those outside the cult, and entitles him or her to special treatment by peers.

The general power of secrecy, present in all kinds of societies, cultic and otherwise, would certainly have been attractive to Pythagoreans. The symbols function like a secret handshake, or a creed, that is known only by those who genuinely belong to the group. They bind the group

[49] Aristoxenus *Frag.* 43.10, from Diogenes Laertius 8.15–16.

[50] Iamblichus *V.P.* 227.

[51] Cf. *Schol. in Lucianum* (*scholia vetera et recentiora Arethae*), on *Pro lapsu* 5. A symbol, here the pentagram, is said to be a means by which Pythagoreans identify one another.

together and draw distinctions between them and the outside world. The symbols are a kind of proprietary knowledge that secures and even constitutes one's membership in the Pythagorean club.[52] But there may also be reasons for secrecy that are specific to the Pythagoreans. We can be relatively confident that at some point the Pythagoreans got into trouble with local authorities, and that they were ultimately suppressed. The legend (as it most surely soon became) of political oppression makes the symbols a necessary code, a secret language by which members of an outlawed society identify each other.[53] Iamblichus places their secretive tendencies in the context of a legend of persecution. Citing Nicomachus (of Gerasa), he describes the aftermath of the catastrophe, which he says was a deliberate fire in which many of the original Pythagoreans died:

> And these people [the few survivors], left solitary and totally dispirited by what had happened, scattered here and there and could bear not at all to share their doctrine with any human being. . . . But, fearing that the name of philosophy might be utterly effaced from humanity, and that they would be hated by the gods if they brought such a venerable gift to nothing, they composed brief, symbolic commentaries [ὑπομνήματά τινα κεφαλαιώδη καὶ συμβολικά], collecting the writings of older men and the things they themselves remembered, and then each left this in the place where he happened to die, charging sons or daughters or wives not to give it to anyone outside the household.[54]

So it is part of Pythagorean legend that the early adherents went underground, as it were. They spoke to each other through secret code because they were afraid of suffering the fate of their founding comrades.

[52] See Burkert, 176–80.

[53] There is little evidence that the political oppression continued beyond the original infamous fire, but such a cataclysm would surely have a chilling effect for some time. The complex motivations of Iamblichus, who was in all likelihood involved in a polemic against the Christians, complicates our evidence a great deal. Iamblichus would have had an interest in playing up the legend of oppression, in order to gain sympathy and present a martyrology to compete with the emerging Christian narrative.

[54] *V.P.* 35.253. The same reasoning seems also to appear in the work of Asclepius, a late Aristotelian commentator (though the sense of the passage is difficult):

> For the Pythagoreans did not use myths but symbols, in order that those overhearing them might remain just short of a clear understanding, lest they be wronged, just as [it once happened?] against the Pythagoreans. In addition, they did not wish to set out in clear view their wisdom even to shoemakers, since things are not clear. [cf. Plato *Theaetetus* 180d]
>
> οἱ γὰρ Πυθαγόρειοι μύθοις μὲν οὐκ ἐκέχρηντο, ἀλλὰ συμβόλοις, ἵνα κἂν μείνωσιν οἱ ἀκούοντες μέχρι τοῦ φαινομένου, μὴ ἀδικηθῶσιν ὥσπερ ἐπὶ τῶν Πυθαγορείων. πρὸς τούτοις δὲ σαφῶς οὐκ ἐβούλοντο ἐκθέσθαι διὰ τὸ μὴ καταφανῆ γενέσθαι τὴν ἑαυτῶν σοφίαν καὶ σκυτεῦσι. (*In Aristotelis metaphysicorum libros A–Z commentaria* 44.13–17)

In later generations, the tradition of secrecy and the esoteric power it accrues simply became part of the Pythagorean inheritance.

Our evidence, then, suggests that the Pythagoreans coined the term symbol not out of an association with figurative language, which sense, as we have seen, is not attested until Demosthenes. Rather, they call their master's famously obscure sayings "symbols" because they function as identity tokens for those in his cult.[55] Whereas the symbol as omen grows out of a chance meeting, the symbol in a Pythagorean context grows from its well-attested function as a marker of identity, and therefore as an authenticating password. The allegorical symbol shares the characteristic of interpretability with both the divinatory and Pythagorean ones, but the parallel is even closer in the Pythagorean case. Unique among early symbols, those of the Pythagoreans are enigmatic language, spoken by a venerated wise man and used to carry weighty truths about the cosmos, humans, and gods. The proximity of this use to the allegorical one is provocative indeed. Oddly enough, then, the extant evidence suggests no other conclusion than this: we owe to the Pythagorean tradition (and to parallel traditions to which we will turn in a moment) the symbol's *specific* association with enigmatic language. The Pythagorean context (and others like it) pulls the term from its strict classical role of authentication over into its role as a label for enigmatic language that carries a hidden significance. It appears that the symbol's long and storied history as a mode of obscure and hinting discourse is in no small part initiated because certain ancient identity tokens just happened to be enigmatic riddles. This genealogy clinches the importance of the Pythagorean tradition for our understanding of the formation of ancient forms of symbolic discourse. Such a legacy works in tandem with the meaningful coincidence of the divinatory tradition to broaden the notion of what symbols can do. These symbolic visions form the ground of possibility of a new theory of poetic symbols, one that labels poetry as carrying a surplus of signification, a density of meaning reserved for the speech of ancient wise men and gods. The power of the symbol is born out of the power of the secret.

Pythagorean Ties to Allegorical Traditions

Marcel Detienne reopened the question of explicit ties between the Pythagoreans and allegorists after Buffière's early suggestion that what he called "mystical" allegory was solely a product of the much later

[55] Burkert suggests that the notion of "symbolic" interpretation plays a principal role in the adoption of this term (166), but we have already seen the evidence that the identification-token meaning predominates entirely.

Pythagorean Numenius.[56] Robert Lamberton has produced a careful summary and reconsideration of the possible early ties between Pythagoreans and allegorical readers of Homer and Hesiod.[57] Both Detienne and Lamberton make a strong case for considering that allegorical interpretation of the poets may have been part of early Pythagorean tradition. That the two traditions share an idiosyncratic notion of the symbol as interpretable nugget of wisdom is a concrete link between them. I will be adding a few points here. Both Pythagoreans and allegorists make use of a similar notion of enigma. From at least Androcydes' time, Pythagoras's σύμβολα are also αἰνίγματα, or they αἰνίττονται some hidden meaning, or they indicate enigmatically [αἰνιγματικῶς] some other meaning. The enigma remains a prominent feature of the vocabulary of many later Pythagorean interpreters and observers of the tradition, including Androcydes, Trypho, Philo, Plutarch, Clement of Alexandria, Athenaeus, Porphyry, Iamblichus, Theodoretus, and Philoponus.[58]

Ancient observers from many periods posit (or embody) links between allegorism and Pythagoreanism. Anaximander, at the very head of the interpretive Pythagorean tradition, was in addition a literary critic who was skilled at reading Homer's "undermeanings."[59] Xenophon compares Anaximander to another early critic, Stesimbrotus, whom we know from other contexts to be an allegorist.[60] The grammarian Trypho (first century B.C.E.) gives us our earliest testimony of Androcydes' book interpreting the Pythagorean symbols. Significantly, Trypho includes the notice in a section on specifically *literary* αἰνίγματα. Trypho defines αἰνίγματα as darkened or obscured [ἀμαυροῦνται] allegories[61] and brings Pythagorean symbols into the discussion immediately after a section on literary ἀλληγορία. He gives an account of various species of αἰνίγματα, and several examples from Homer, Pythagoras (via Androcydes), and

[56] Marcel Detienne, *Homère, Hésiode et Pythagore: Poésie et philosophie dans le pythagorisme ancien* (Bruxelles-Berchem: Latomus, 1962), 94–99.

[57] Lamberton, *Homer the Theologian*, 31–43.

[58] For Androcydes, see Burkert, 174; Trypho *RhGr* 3.193f. Philo *Quod omnis probus liber sit* 2; Plutarch *Quaest. conv.* 727A, *De Is. et. Os.* 354E, *De edu. puer.* 12d–e; Clement *Stromata* 5.5.27, 5.5.28; Athenaeus 10.452d–e (citing Demetrius of Byzantium); Porphyry *V.P.* 12; Iamblichus *V.P.* 23 (103), 34 (247), *Protrep.* 112.20, 123.16, 125.13, 127.6, 129.20; Theodoretus *Graecarum affectionum curatio* 8.1.7; Philoponus *In Aristotelis de anima libros commentaria*, ed. Hayduck, *Commentaria in Aristotelem Graeca* (Berlin: Reimer, 1897), 15: 74.3 and 117.24.

[59] Of this fact, Burkert says that we could hardly find more apposite confirmation that the work "On symbols" cited in later sources is indeed by Anaximander. Other scholars have claimed that the citation is a corruption from Alexander (Polyhistor), whom we know from other sources to have written commentaries on Pythagorean symbols.

[60] Xenophon *Symposium* 3.6. See also Plato *Ion* 530d; Tatian *Address to the Greeks* 31.

[61] See below, chap. 3. The characterization of enigmas as even more obscure forms of allegory is common in the rhetorical tradition of criticism.

Hesiod. Trypho feels no need to distinguish between the poets and Pythagoras and seems to have expected his audience to share this view. His text further suggests that Androcydes himself (again perhaps as early as the fourth century B.C.E.) included citations of Hesiod in his interpretations of the Pythagorean symbols, indicating that any strong division between poetic and philosophical modes of discourse was also elided for Androcydes.

It is easy to understand why Trypho and Androcydes note a connection to Hesiod. Several Pythagorean symbols mirror, in form and content, passages from a gnomic section (lines 705–65) of the *Works and Days*, with even some verbatim repetitions.[62] For example, Hesiod tells us, "Never put the ladle upon the mixing-bowl at a wine party, for harmful bad luck comes with it." Plutarch attributes precisely the same counsel to Pythagoras.[63] The similarities between Hesiod's gnomic poetry and Pythagoras's apothegms did not escape Hesiod's ancient commentators. Two Hesiodic scholia, one on this passage, another at *W.D.* 722, point out explicitly the similarity of the Hesiodic passages to the Pythagorean sayings and label both of them "symbolic." Yet another scholiast further equates the symbolic passages of Hesiod and Pythagoras with literary allegory.[64] Given such testimonia, it is not too difficult to see how, under the influence of the Pythagoreans, these Hesiodic commentators might have come to find "symbols" in poetry as well. It is, of course, impossible to date the scholia, but Pythagoras's echoes of Hesiod indicate a very old and diffuse tradition of wisdom sayings—handled equally by poets and by philosophers. The Pythagoreans put a decisive name on an old tradition, gathering a number of early wisdom sayings under the heading of "symbols."[65]

The Symbols of the Mysteries

The theory that the Pythagorean symbol bridged the "password" sense of the classical symbol and the later allegorical use of the term to mean an enigmatic nugget of poetry faces an impediment. While Pythagoras surely had his followers, it is not clear that their numbers were sufficient to have enacted such a shift in literary-critical vocabulary—their ob-

[62] The most useful summary of the connections between particular passages is M. L. West's commentary on lines 727, 742–43, 744–45, and 748 of the *Works and Days* (New York: Oxford University Press, 1978).

[63] Plutarch frag. 93.5.

[64] Scholia in *Opera et Dies* (Pertusi, ed.) at lines 744–45 πολλὰ τοιαῦτα καὶ τοῖς Πυθαγορείοις ἐλέγετο; (Gaisford, ed.) at line 722 τὸ δ' ἀλληγορικώτερόν ἐστι, συμβολικὴ παραίνεσις Πυθαγόρειος.

[65] See Burkert, 176–78.

servable connections to allegorism not withstanding. Perhaps even more attractive, then, is a tradition that, while not as well documented as the Pythagorean one, is surely widely current in the classical period and makes a nearly identical use of the notion of the symbol. Burkert has rightly suggested a connection between Pythagorean symbols and the symbols of the mystery religions.[66] Burkert has remarked on the multiple similarities between the Pythagorean symbols and ancient magical-ritual prohibitions, of the sort adhered to by initiates into the mysteries. The Pythagorean symbols recapitulate rules for worshipers at Eleusis, Haloa, Delos, and Lycosura, and in the Trophonius cult, at the temple of Asclepius, and in the Hippocratic corpus. The abundant similarities lead Burkert to the conclusion that the symbols are, "rather than simple, commonsense wisdom in abstruse form, ancient magical-ritual commandments."[67] In the mysteries, particular sayings or tokens, specifically called symbols, are given to new initiates as a guarantee that other members of the cult, and especially the gods, will recognize their new status. We see these from the classical period forward, among the Eleusinian, Orphic, and Dionysian initiates.[68] Aristophanes confirms this sense (in passages that were included in our tally of classical uses of the symbol):[69] the token that Charon gives one for passage into the next world is called a symbol, as is the token that a guard in the *Birds* demands for entrance into the mock-heavenly realm of Cloudcuckooland.[70] (Lucian's satire indicates that the Pythagorean symbols were still famous for serving a similar function in the second century C.E.).[71] These texts equate symbols with ἐπῳδαί (magic spells) and συνθήματα (tokens)—a term that will become increasingly important among the Neoplatonists. We will see σύμβολα as συνθήματα in other magical-ritual traditions below.

A find at Pherai supports the evidence of the symbol as a password for entry into extraordinary realms. A recently uncovered gold tablet (late fourth-century B.C.E.?) bears the following inscription:

Symbols: Andrike-
paidothurson - Andrikepai-

[66] To investigate the background of the term in the mysteries, for which the corpus of evidence is notoriously difficult, Müri also used the better-documented Pythagorean tradition as the most proximate analogue (37).

[67] Burkert, 177.

[68] For the Orphics, see D-K 1 B23, cited in Burkert, 176; for Eleusis, see Burkert, 176; for the Dionysian tradition, see Albert Henrichs, "Changing Dionysiac Identities," in *Jewish and Christian Self-Definition*, ed. Ben F. Meyer and E. Sanders (Philadelphia: Fortress Press, 1982), 3: 156–57. Henrichs here considers the symbols as strictly tangible objects, but oral formulas were used interchangeably; see the Pherai text below.

[69] These appeared under the category of the symbol as a token of entry.

[70] Aristophanes *Plutus* 278; *Birds* 1214.

[71] Lucian *Pro lapsu* 5.

dothurson. (Manly boy give the thursus)
Brimo - Brimo. Enter
the sacred meadow: for
the initiate is sober [or, has paid the atonement?]

Σύμβολα· Ἀν<δ>ρικε-
παιδόθυρσον - Ἀνδρικεπαι-
[ι]δόθυρσον. Βριμώ - Βριμώ. εἴσιθ<ι>
ἱερὸν λειμῶνα· ἄποινος
γὰρ ὁ μύστησ.[72]

Here the symbol functions as a word that gives one access to the fields of the blessed. It seems clear here that it is a formula that the initiate utters to the guard. The guard then repeats the word back in confirmation, like the second half of a split token, completing the transaction. This symbol allows one entrance to the holy fields, perhaps between Pythagorean reincarnations.[73] We will see in a later chapter that the σύμβολον is especially called a σύνθημα when it is used in this context. In this particular case, the symbols are divine cultic epithets. "Brimo" is attested in several places as one of the names of Hecate, Persephone, or Artemis of Pherai.[74] "Andrikepaidothurson" indicates Dionysus, either the "manly boy" who gives the "thursus" or a transformation of Ἠρικεπαῖος, attested elsewhere, plus "thursus."[75] Whatever we make of it, in this context the symbol is a token, a god's secret name or perhaps another formula, that allows one to pass into extraordinary planes of reality—into the otherworlds of the gods, the afterlife, or divine levels of wisdom.

This rather exotic background, which uses secret knowledge to mark the boundaries of a philosophico-religious sect, then, paves the way for the symbol to expand from its limited classical sense of an authenticating credential into a broader and more enduring use in the discourse of

[72] Pavlos Ch. Chrysostomou, *Ἡ Θεσσαλικὴ θεὰ Εν(ν)οδία ἤ φεραία θεά* (diss., Thessaloniki, University of Thessalonica, 1992), 375–98. I thank K. Tsantsanoglou for the reference and the text, sent in correspondence.

[73] I am grateful to Walter Burkert for this suggestion.

[74] The epithet usually refers to Artemis of Pherai in the *Papyri Graecae Magicae* (4.2270, 2291, 2611, 2964; 7.692) (cf. O. Kern, "Brimo," in Pauly-Wissowa, *Real-Encyclopädie* 3: 853–54). Given the location of the find, this is the logical reference. Interestingly, at *PGM* 2291, the epithet appears in a magical formula called a "symbol," and at *PGM* 7.692, Brimo is a holy name which the goddess is not able to ignore. For "Brimo" as an epithet of Hecate and Persephone, see *A.R.* 3.861, *Orph. Fr.* 31, Lucian *Necyomantia* 20, and *PGM* 70.20.

[75] This reading of the Dionysus epithet was suggested to me by K. Tsantsanoglou, drawing on the work of Chrysostomou. Ἠρικεπαῖος is the name of a bisexual Orphic divinity, *Orph. Fr.* 167a.1, cf. *Orphic Hymns* 6.4, and *Orph. Fr.* 60. The term is an epithet of Dionysus in Hesychius.

literary criticism.[76] We will find corroboration of this lineage in that of the symbol's closest cousin, the enigma. Gregory Nagy has shown that an "ideology of exclusiveness" also gives birth to the literary αἴνιγμα,[77] and the true genealogy of the symbolic lies in this same direction—an interpretable riddle, like an omen or shibboleth, that joined one sense to another but also and more importantly cleaved its audience into those who knew and those who did not. We can find a *terminus ante quem* for this development in Demosthenes' claim in his law court address, which we considered above, that the ancient lawgivers had included in their language a "symbol" with a hidden meaning.

Philochorus and the Emergence of the Symbol

In our survey of the Pythagorean commentaries above, we mentioned a work that the Suda attributes to the historian Philochorus (b. before 340, d. after 261/60 B.C.E.), the *Περὶ συμβόλων*, or *On Symbols*. Both Burkert and Jacoby claim that it must have been written with reference to specifically Pythagorean symbols, and their case is supported by the title of another work by Philochorus, *Collection of Heroines, or Pythagorean Women*, which indicates an interest in Pythagorean matters. It is certainly reasonable to consider that this work should be included in the long series of Pythagorean symbol interpretations. However, before making a final judgment, we might also examine three additional texts.

[76] Müri has suggested the less satisfying, though still possible, explanation that the interpretable symbol arose from an altogether different sense of the verb συμβάλλειν (17–18). From the notion of "putting together" the term also came to mean bring together, tally together, compare, conjecture, understand, and eventually to interpret. Müri suggests that the use of the verb to mean "interpret" stands behind a more general category of symbol as sign [σημεῖον], a use which Müri admits has the other more specialized senses of the term "nearly always beside it" (20) and which is "very rare" (22–23). Two factors argue against this. First, on philological grounds, Müri himself has shown that omicron forms in the neuter from -βάλλειν verbs act as *nomen rei qua agitur*. A σύμβολον derived from a verbal notion of "interpret," then, would be that by which an interpretation is carried out and not the thing interpreted. Second, and more compelling, we simply have no need for such a broader notion of a generally interpretable thing, when the surviving evidence is entirely subsumable under a noun formed from a verbal idea of "to reach agreement." All senses of authentication and proof are traceable to this sense. The only odd fit is the case of the divine sign or omen, but here there is no reason to quarrel with Müri's suggestion that we have a properly masculine noun (σύμβολος, "that which one meets") from the verbal sense of "to meet," which, in a quirk, became assimilated to the neuter form. This history would place the symbol as omen and as cultic formula as antecedent to the verbal sense of "to interpret."

[77] See below, chap. 5.

A scholion on Pindar's *Olympian Ode* 12.7 glosses the word σύμβολον this way:

> Masculine and neuter. We call sneezes, prophetic utterances, or chance replies [ἀπαντήσεις] symbols [συμβόλους]. Thus Archilochus says: "I approach you and make a symbol" [μετέρχομαί σε σύμβολον ποιούμενος]. Accordingly, he [Pindar] says, no man would discover an omen [τεκμήριον] or a sign [σημεῖον] from god capable of being trusted concerning what might happen. Philochorus says that divinations from speech, that is to say, chance utterances and sneezes, are called symbols. Demeter was the first to use them.

A scholion on Aristophanes' *Birds* 721 glosses Aristophanes' mention of a "bird symbol" as one among many divinatory arts:

> For these things they used to deem symbols, the first things one meets, and from the meeting something is foretold, and all these things used to be dedicated to Demeter, as Philochorus says.

Lastly, in his entry for the form ξυμβόλους, Hesychius tells us this:

> They used to call "symbols" prophecies through sneezes, and these were dedicated to Demeter, and certain prophecies that arise from utterance, which Philochorus says Demeter invented.

These texts show that Philochorus's name was also attached to the notion of the "symbol" in divinatory contexts. When a scholiast or lexicographer needed an authority on divinatory symbols, his name was ready at hand. One would expect, then, his work *On Symbols* to include some reference to symbols in a divinatory context. After all, Philochorus held the positions of μάντις and ἱεροσκόπος in Athens in 306, indicating a professional interest in divinatory matters, and also wrote a work *Περὶ μαντικῆς*. Does this mean that Jacoby and Burkert are mistaken to see this work as dealing with Pythagorean symbols? I don't think so. Just as it is doubtful that Philochorus would have written a work on the more arcane topic of "Pythagorean Women" unless he was also familiar with the more famous Pythagorean teachings, we may also assume that a work *On Symbols* written by a person with a more than passing knowledge of the Pythagoreans would likely have included reference to the Πυθαγόρεια σύμβολα. This evidence taken together indicates that Philochorus's work had multiple foci. As further evidence, we might also enlist the vagueness of the traditional title. Both Anaximander's and Androcydes' commentaries were passed down under the more specific titles *On Pythagorean Symbols*. Philochorus's work, *On Symbols*, then, was likely a more general treatment of symbols in various manifestations.

Whatever Philochorus said about them, it is most significant that he considered symbols to be a subject worthy of a complete treatise. The traces of this lost work, written at the threshold of the Hellenistic era, are our earliest evidence that the symbol has begun to have an identity of its own and to assume a certain prominence. Its import has changed a great deal from the days when it was rarely more than a receipt. The symbol's uses in divination, the mysteries, and Pythagoreanism create a much more interesting form of figuration. Philochorus's work on symbols may have codified the developments we have traced in these traditions, marking a turning point in the evolution of this once narrow term.

Philochorus and Literary Symbols?

Aristotle raised the status of "metaphor" to that of a master literary trope and set it up as the touchstone for all the others. In discussions of figured language, later critics in the rhetorical tradition of literary commentary gave metaphor pride of place. Is it possible that Philochorus did something similar for the symbol among later allegorical commentators, most of whom make prominent use of the term? Here we walk on speculative ground, but such a development is possible. We could only confirm this if we had evidence that his work *On Symbols* made explicit mention of literary symbols, and we do not. Philochorus certainly had an interest in literary matters. In addition to his historical writings, and his works on Pythagoreanism and divination, he wrote *On Tragedy*, *On the Myths of Sophocles*, and *On Euripides*. Scholiasts on the dramatists and lyric poets preserve dozens of his individual comments on lines from the poets.

Since it was especially allegorical readers that developed the symbol as a conceptual category and put it to use, we would expect from this later history that the symbol as a term of literary study was coined by a commentator who worked in an allegorical mode. And since the language of allegorism, as we have already seen and will see in more detail, is marked in the early periods especially by cognates of αἰνίττομαι, we would expect to see Philochorus put such language to use in his reading. One of the fragments of Philochorus suggests that he referenced the poetics of the enigma in commenting on literature. Diogenes Laertius reports that:

> Philochorus says that when he [Protagoras] was sailing to Sicily, the ship capsized, and that Euripides riddles [αἰνίττεσθαι] this in the *Ixion*.

The syntax of the passage indicates that Philochorus himself used the most characteristic term of allegorism (αἰνίττεσθαι) to describe this poetic scene, though without more knowledge of the *Ixion* and its contents, we cannot be much more than intrigued by this short passage. Did Philochorus make the step of applying the category of the symbol to his strategies for reading the poets? This evidence is inconclusive. We have no firm textual evidence of the symbol used in a literary context until a generation after Philochorus, in the work of one of the formative thinkers in the Stoic tradition, Chrysippus (c. 280–207 B.C.E.).

3

FROM THE HEAD OF ZEUS: THE BIRTH OF THE LITERARY SYMBOL

IN THE CENTURIES between the death of Aristotle and the birth of the Roman Empire, the Stoic vision of the world came to dominate the Mediterranean. When one of the major Stoic thinkers of the school's middle period, Panaetius, befriended Scipio the younger at Rome, the ideas of the Stoics, especially their ethics, started to be tailored to meet the needs of statesmen and soldiers and so assumed an important place in the minds of the emerging elite of what was to become the largest empire yet seen. Given the diffusion and endurance of their ideas, it is a curious misfortune that nearly the entire corpus of the formative figures of Stoicism—Zeno, Cleanthes, and Chrysippus—has completely perished. From the shards that remain of their thinking, however, in their opponents, in later Stoics, and especially in Cicero's philosophical works, we are able to form a reliable general picture. (As to the details we will always be left with some element of speculation.) Two conclusions we can draw with confidence from the sources are that the allegorical interpretation of poetic texts occupied an important place in Stoic thought, and that the notion of the symbol, which they are the first to attest securely as a conceptual category for reading literature, was a noteworthy feature of the intellectual terrain.[1]

As we will see, the Stoics' innovative views in the areas of ontology and cosmology form uniquely productive resources for the development of their interpretive theories. The Presocratics had formed theories of the world as a unity, whether monistic, or, like Heraclitus, a world suffused by a single principle. In chapter 1, we saw that such views had some part in guiding the poetics of the enigma, which sets the stage for the development of the symbol. But the Stoics introduced detailed thinking into the linguistic aspects of a universalist ontology such as had never been seen. With the Stoics, *les mots et les choses* are now

[1] The sources attest to nine comments that Chrysippus proposed on Homer's text, most in an Aristarchan mode. Some cite this as evidence that he could not therefore be an allegorist. But we noted in chapter 1 that it is actually more the norm than the exception for allegorical critics to be interested in textual issues.

bound together ontologically, linked in their very substance. In a material way, the Stoic *logos/pneuma*, which we will examine below, serves as the underlying bridge between what may appear on the surface to be one thing but really indicates another. The relationship between word, surface meaning, and underlying referent becomes something like a synecdoche.[2] Here, I will trace the ways in which Stoic theories of being inform their theories of language and their interpretation of literary texts, with special reference to Chrysippus's adoption of the symbol as a conceptual tool for reading the poets. These other areas of thought will give new theoretical heft to the traditions of reading that the Stoics inherit and pass on, and give us some sense of the philosophical and linguistic contexts in which the notion of the symbol enters literary commentary.

As we saw in the last chapter, we have no attestation of the term σύμβολον used as a label for figurative literary constructions before the time Chrysippus was writing, in the third century. Among its senses in the fifth and fourth centuries, the notion of an authenticating token is by far the dominant one. Two specialized uses comprise an undercurrent for the development of the literary idea: the symbol as a divine omen (a meaningful coincidence) and as a special kind of identity token among Pythagoreans and devotees of the mysteries, for whom it was an enigmatic epigram or divine name that carried a hidden message. These cases speak directly to a hidden surplus of meaning that can be decoded by an interpreter skilled in a special language. The Stoics show no special affiliation with the Pythagoreans, and so it is unlikely that they would have developed a literary concept under the influence of this ancient school of thought. They do, however, display a deep and abiding interest in divination, which makes a more likely allied field in their case. However, as we saw in the previous chapter, the evidence suggests that the symbol may already have been in use to mark figurative language by the middle of the fourth century and that it may well have entered the language of allegorism some time before that, so Chrysippus may be employing an allegorical terminology that was already standard at the time he is writing. But Stoics have their own unique set of interests, which we should look at first with some general remarks about Stoic allegorism.[3] Here we will attempt to reconstruct the unique re-

[2] Later Neoplatonic proponents of the talismanic theory of indication will pursue this position with more vigor. Their theory becomes more self-consciously synecdochic in character.

[3] The most important guideposts for understanding Stoic allegorism are set out in Phillip DeLacy, "Stoic Views of Poetry," *AJP* 69: 241–71; Rudolph Pfeiffer, *History of Classical Scholarship* (Oxford: Clarendon Press, 1968–76), 234–51; Glenn Most, "Cornutus and Stoic Allegoresis," *ANRW* 2.36.3 (1989); David Dawson, *Allegorical Readers and*

sources for reading the poets that were at the disposal of a Stoic thinker like Chrysippus. Given the fragmentary state of the record, this is a difficult task. Our best bet is to follow a somewhat circuitous path through some basic propositions of Stoic thought.

The Nature of the Evidence

We should keep in mind, first of all, that we derive much of our sense of Stoic thinking on the poets from summaries, often reductive, of their interpretations put together by the Stoics' opponents. Such strong polemics have led the great scholar of Stoicism, A. A. Long, to claim that Stoic reading should not be considered under the heading of allegory at all.[4] His most strenuous objections involve refuting a reductive characterization of Chrysippus's literary commentary, which is very old indeed, as simply forcing his own views on the poets, or systematically twisting the text to ventriloquize Stoic ideas through the poets. This is a welcome advance in our understanding of Chrysippus and presents a more sympathetic view of his interpretive methods than one is able to find elsewhere. However, I am more comfortable with Long's claim that Stoic readings of the poets are not adequately described by the traditional, reductive definition of allegory than I am with his claim that the Stoics are not allegorists. Within the current scholarly vocabulary, the latter claim is equivalent to saying that they do not have anything to do with a rather long tradition of poetic interpretation. From one perspective, my investigation of the symbol has led me to extend precisely Long's more sympathetic approach to a larger range of the ancient allegorical evidence. In describing Chrysippus's reading, Long opts for the term "interpretation" as a better one to characterize it.[5] In this he is in line with Gerald Bruns, who suggests that we rename the whole allegorical tradition the interpretive tradition.[6] Such a move is attractive, provided that one not lose sight of the extended tradition of such reading—whatever we call it.

Among Stoic readers, Chrysippus (c. 280–207 B.C.E.) was especially notorious for manipulating a poet's words to mean things other than

Cultural Revision in Ancient Alexandria (Berkeley: University of California Press, 1992), 23–72; and A. A. Long, "Stoic Readings of Homer," in *Homer's Ancient Readers*, ed. Robert Lamberton and John J. Keaney (Princeton: Princeton University Press, 1992), 41–66.

[4] Long, 1992.

[5] Ibid., 59.

[6] Gerald Bruns, "The Hermeneutics of Allegory and the History of Interpretation" (review of Robert Lamberton and Jon Whitman), *Comparative Literature* 40 (Fall 1988): 384–95.

what they really meant. Plutarch, Cicero, and Seneca all characterize Chrysippus as a master manipulator of words, who reads into a poem what does not belong.[7] In ridiculing Stoic methods, Cicero has Velleius, the Epicurean spokesman in his *De natura deorum*, level perhaps the single most enduring criticism against such reading. He claims that in the hands of the Stoics, "even the earliest poets of antiquity, who had no notion of these doctrines, seem to be Stoics" [etiam veterrimi poetae, qui haec ne suspicati quidem sint, Stoici fuisse videantur] (1.41). Someone more sympathetic to Stoic views, like Cicero's Balbus in the same dialogue, is more likely to say that Chrysippus believed that ancient poets are keen observers of the world, that they handed down many stunning insights about it, and that some of these are in line with contemporary thinking (*De nat. deor.* 2.63–72). These competing views, neither of which is definitive, serve as guides for recovering Chrysippus's own approach. While we ought to keep a critical eye on interpretive overreaching among the Stoics, we should also reserve some of our skepticism for Stoic detractors. Balbus certainly suggests that Chrysippus had reasons other than hermeneutical mischief to read the way he did, that he was not simply grabbing at the poets' authority for his own views. We may better understand Stoic allegory and its influential legacy if we aim for a fuller picture of what, precisely, moved Stoic critics to such extensive rebuttals. If we step into Balbus's sandals for a moment, we are better able to identify the distinctive innovations of Stoic reading within the traditions of allegorism and broaden the simple understanding of allegory that their critics pass on to us. In short, following A. A. Long's suggestion, we can see that there is more here than "forced" or "twisted" reading.

Stoic Reading in Cicero's *De natura deorum*

In his dialogue *On the Nature of the Gods*, Cicero stages a three-way debate. The Epicurean Velleius and the Stoic Balbus lay out their opposed positions, and the Academic Cotta levels criticisms against both sides while not endorsing any particular positions. Balbus speaks for the Stoics under four headings: the existence of the gods, their nature, their providential involvement in the world, and their specific concern for

[7] It is also worthwhile to note that Plutarch and Seneca, though detractors of some allegorical approaches, made use of allegorical methods for their own purposes. In *On How to Read the Poets*, Plutarch appears to reject physicalist allegorical readings (19F), but he seems comfortable replacing them with moral ones (e.g., 20A). In *Isis and Osiris*, Plutarch has fewer compunctions about all kinds of allegorical and etymological reading, including physical, moral, and theological (351f, 352a, 355b–d, 361e, 362b–e, 363d, 365b–d). See also Seneca *Natural Questions* 2.45.

humans. His explanation of Stoic myth interpretation stands as the capstone of his treatment of the nature of the gods. After arguing that the gods' true natures can be deduced from the perfection of the sphere, from the observation of heavenly bodies, and from observation of the rest of created nature, Balbus suggests that we may gain information on the divine from the traditional myths concerning the gods and the cultic practices by which they are worshiped. The bulk of this section treats the theory, which he attributes to Zeno, Cleanthes, and Chrysippus, that the traditional myths [*fabulae*] convey information about the divine structure of the cosmos (*De nat. deor.* 2.63–71). "A not inelegant natural principle is enclosed in the vulgar myths" [physica ratio non inelegans inclusa est in impias fabulas] (2.64.1–2; cf. 2.70.2–3), Balbus claims. The myths Balbus mentions most prominently are the castration of Ouranos/Caelus, the binding of Kronos/Saturn, and Kronos/Saturn swallowing his children—all perennial problems for poetry's ancient defenders.[8] Balbus produces interpretations that are standard among allegorical commentators, as we will see in subsequent chapters. He claims that the castration of Ouranos indicates that the highest divine principles have no need of the physical organs of generation but engage in creation free of the human need for sex to produce offspring. That Kronos/Saturn swallows his children indicates that "time" devours all things, playing off a traditional pun between Kronos [Κρόνος] and the Greek word for time, χρόνος.[9] The binding of Kronos indicates Jupiter's limitations on the reign of time.

While Balbus never abandons his view that the mythic shells contain philosophic nuts, it becomes clear from his continuing exposition that the Stoics had considerable doubt about how well the poets handled the hidden messages that underlay their own poems. In a speech that sounds like it might have come from his opponent's mouth, the Stoic Balbus says:

> Do you see, therefore, how from a true and valuable philosophy of nature has been evolved this imaginary and fanciful pantheon? The perversion has been a fruitful source of false beliefs, crazy errors, and superstitions hardly above the level of old wives' tales. We know what the gods look like and how old they are, their dress and their equipment, and also their genealogies, marriages, and relationships, and everything about them is distorted into the likeness of human frailty. They are actually represented as liable to passions and emotions. We hear of their being in love, sorrowful, angry; according to the myths they even engage in wars and battles . . . for

[8] Plato threw down these gauntlets at *Rep.* 377e–378a.

[9] On my characterization of these readings as puns rather than false etymologies, see below.

instance, with the Titans and with the Giants. These stories and these beliefs are utterly foolish; they are stuffed with nonsense and absurdity of all sorts.

Videtisne igitur ut a physicis rebus bene atque utiliter inventis tracta ratio sit ad commenticios et fictos deos? Quae res genuit falsas opiniones erroresque turbulentos et superstitiones paene aniles. Et formae enim nobis deorum et aetates et vestitus ornatusque noti sunt, genera praeterea, coniugia, cognationes omniaque traducta ad similitudinem inbecillitatis humanae. Nam et perturbatis animis inducuntur. Accepimus enim deorum cupiditates, aegritudines, iracundias. Nec vero, ut fabulae ferunt, bellis proeliisque caruerunt . . . ut cum Titanis, ut cum Gigantibus, sua propria bella gesserunt. Haec et dicuntur et creduntur stultissime et plena sunt futtilitatis summaeque levitatis. (*De nat. deor.* 2.70)[10]

And yet, beneath the fanciful poetic accretions of the poets, one finds certain core truths:

But though these myths are repudiated with contempt, nevertheless a god is diffused through the nature of each thing. Through the earth is Ceres, through the sea is Neptune, and others have their own elements. We can understand who they are and what sort they are, and by the customary name by which the gods are known we ought to worship and revere them.

Sed tamen his fabulis spretis ac repudiatis deus pertinens per naturam cuiusque rei, per terras Ceres, per maria Neptunus, alii per alia, poterant intellegi qui qualesque sunt quoque eos nomine consuetudo nuncupaverit, quos deos et venerari et colere debemus. (*De nat. deor.* 2.71)

Balbus's evidence suggests that the Stoics had no grand visions of the poets as anachronistic channels of proto-Stoicism, as Velleius would have it, or as fonts of divine wisdom, as is assumed by the Derveni commentator and by a few other allegorists who emerge in late antiquity. Rather, the poets engage in a kind of embellishing process. Ancient mythmakers observe principles at work in the natural world; then generations of poets proliferate fanciful stories based on these core observations. The reader's task, then, is to sift through the myth's imaginary accretions to find the core truth that underlies it. Myth is a kind of degenerated form of scientific observation. Given Balbus's position, we would be naïve to accept Velleius's characterization of Stoic interpretation uncritically. Balbus's view is, after all, very close to one that in various forms held currency through the nineteenth century and even

[10] Text from *Cicéron. De natura deorum*, ed. M. van den Bruwaene, 3 vols. (Brussells: Latomus, 1970–81). Translation based on Cicero, *De natura deorum*, ed. H. Rackham, Loeb Classical Library (1933; reprint, Cambridge: Harvard University Press, 1979).

into the twentieth. While the "Nature Myth" school of Max Müller and his followers has been discredited, it deserves quite a bit more consideration than Velleius accords the somewhat similar views of the Stoics.[11]

According to Balbus, the Stoics are duty-bound (*debemus*) to examine closely traditional cult practices and the traditional forms and names of the gods handed down in the myths. Reading the myths properly, on this view, verges toward an act of piety. The bulk of a pious Stoic's information on traditional divinities would have come from the poets. In addition, Balbus suggests we supplement the textual poetic sources by reading messages passed down through cultic worship. He tells us that a truly religious person "retraces" or "rereads" [*relegere*] *everything* that has to do with the gods and makes what sense he or she can from it (*De nat. deor.* 2.72). Balbus stresses the literate nature of true piety, characterizing the study of the gods with terms that self-consciously repeat forms of the verb "to read." True religion is selective [from *e-ligere*], diligent [*di-ligere*], and demands understanding [*intellegere*]. He contrasts this sincere devotion with the superstitious person, who takes up the whole day pleading through prayer and sacrifice for a particular outcome. In fact, the Stoics from the early period through Cornutus (first century C.E.) make careful reading of the poets, specifically as contrasted with the "superstition" [*superstitio*, δεισιδαιμονία] of prayer and cult directed toward specific outcomes, central to piety, and this contrast endures in the works of later figures like Cornutus, Plutarch, and Persius.[12] We see here developing a notion of what we might call religion as a form of study and intellectual discipline, in which the reading of the poets occupies an important place.[13]

Following Balbus's logic, a superficial reading (as the Stoics would characterize it) of a myth might bring one to the simple conclusion that a poet has produced a mere fiction, a tall tale, perhaps even an obscene

[11] On Max Müller's "nature myth" school and its debt to classical allegorism, see, most recently, Fritz Graf, *Greek Mythology* (Baltimore: Johns Hopkins University Press, 1996), 25, 197.

[12] Plutarch separates true piety based on careful readings of the myths from superstition based on sacrifice (*On Isis and Osiris* 355d; cf. *De superstitione*). Cornutus also insists that proper reading of the myths recounted by the poets is crucial to true piety (*Compendium* 35). That Cornutus distinguished between true piety, based on reading the myths, and superstition, based on cultic sacrifice, is suggested in the fifth *Satire* of his student Persius. Persius dedicated the work, in which he contrasts true (studious) piety with superstitious cultic practice (120–23), to Cornutus.

[13] Glenn Most positions Cornutus's allegoresis similarly (2024–25). Further evidence for the relative importance of the different sources to which a Stoic might turn for evidence on the nature of the gods can be found in Cleanthes' commentaries on the gods, as Most has shown. Cleanthes draws from: poetry (*Stoicorum veterum fragmenta*, ed. J. Von Arnim, 4 vols. [Stuttgart: Teubner, 1964], hereafter *SVF*, 1.526, 535, 539, 549), cult (*SVF* 1.543–45), and divine names and epithets (*SVF* 1.540–42, 546–47).

or offensive one, and one might therefore miss entirely the recoverable wisdom that underlies it. This sort of stance toward the text, of course, stands in sharp contrast to that of the rhetorical critics and carries forward an entirely different view of what poetry is and how one should go about reading it. The Stoics insist that the purpose of poetry is to teach, not just to provide cathartic experience and not just to delight. Only the wise man can be a poet, according to the Stoics.[14] As we have already seen, one of the three formative figures of Stoicism, Cleanthes, thought poetry to be the vehicle uniquely suited for conveying philosophical ideas about the gods and men.[15] The sources tell us that Ariston and Diogenes of Babylon, both of the early Stoa, viewed poetry as primarily educational, not primarily for entertainment. Strabo (63/4 B.C.E.–at least 21 C.E.), who has Stoic affiliations, agrees with Polybius that "everybody" accepted that Homer conveyed allegorical knowledge in his poem and did not just entertain.[16] Strabo specifically associates poetry's transmission of knowledge (as opposed to its entertainment value) with allegorism.[17] These positions, insisting that poetry's primary and defining function is to convey knowledge about the world, hark back to the readers who found themselves mocked in Plato's *Ion* and will recur as a distinguishing characteristic in later allegorists.

Chrysippus and Allegorical Reading

The interpretation of the poets constituted a prominent part of Chrysippus's investigations, whatever the topic at hand. Book 2 of his *On the Nature of the Gods* is almost entirely lost. In Cicero's *De natura deorum*, Velleius says Chrysippus peppers his work with allegorical readings of the myths of Orpheus, Musaeus, Hesiod, and Homer. Galen spends the majority of his longish treatise, *On the Doctrines of Hippocrates and Plato*, saying that Chrysippus did precisely the same thing in his work *On the Soul*. Galen levels the charge, among others, that Chrysippus appealed to the authority of the poets to justify his scientific theories instead of conducting rigorous experiments. Galen scolds him

[14] *SVF* 3.654, 655.

[15] *SVF* 1.486. See introduction above.

[16] "Everybody considers the poetry of Homer to be a philosophic statement." [τὴν ἐκείνου [Ὁμήρου] ποίησιν φιλοσόφημα πάντας νομίζειν] (Strabo 1.2.17 = Polyb. 34.4.4). *LSJ* translates the term φιλοσόφημα in this context as bound up with allegory. Cf. Cornutus 53 for the use of the term φιλοσόφημα in a clearly allegorical context. Strabo 1.2.7 (see next note) also supports the position that allegory was understood in terms of the production of *knowledge*, considered to be of a philosophical sort.

[17] οὐ πάντα τερατευόμενος [Ὅμηρος], ἀλλὰ καὶ πρὸς ἐπιστήμην ἀλληγορῶν (Strabo 1.2.7).

for his overreliance on interpretation of the poets, saying at one point, "you should not have filled your book with lines from the poets, which you quote one after another" (*De plac.* 3.2.1). He then lists fully dozens of citations, mostly of Homer and Hesiod, though also of the tragedians and other writers, that Chrysippus made in articulating his theories concerning the soul. Galen characterizes Chrysippus's readings as allegorical.[18] While such literary interpretations may have made for shoddy science, they made pivotal contributions to the history of literary commentary.

Chrysippus on Hesiod

In his citation from Chrysippus's lengthy reading of Hesiod's account of the birth of Athena, Galen preserves the most important example of early Stoic allegorical reading and, as it happens, our earliest evidence of someone calling a literary construction a "symbol." He cites Chrysippus speaking in his own voice.

> I hear that some people speak in support of the view that the governing part of the soul is in the head. For, they say, the birth of Athena—who is wisdom and, as it were, thought—from the head of Zeus is a symbol [σύμβολον] that the governing part is there. . . . Although their argument has a certain plausibility, they are mistaken, as it seems to me, and they are unaware of the details of the story. A fuller account of these matters is not irrelevant to the present inquiries. Some simply say in this way that she was born from the head of Zeus, and they do not go on to recount the manner of her birth or the reason for it. Some write in their theogonies that her birth took place after Zeus lay first with Metis and second with Themis, and others write of it differently in other works.

> ἀκούω δέ τινας λέγειν παραμυθουμένους πρὸς τὸ ἐν τῇ κεφαλῇ εἶναι τὸ ἡγεμονικὸν τῆς ψυχῆς μέρος. τὸ γὰρ τὴν 'Αθηνᾶν, μῆτιν οὖσαν καὶ οἷον φρόνησιν, ἐκ τῆς κεφαλῆς γενέσθαι τοῦ Διὸς σύμβολόν φασιν εἶναι τοῦ ταύτῃ τὸ ἡγεμονικὸν εἶναι . . . πιθανοῦ μέν τινος ἐχόμενοι, διαμαρτάνοντες δ' ὡς ἐμοὶ φαίνεται καὶ ἀγνοοῦντες τὰ περὶ τούτων ἱστορούμενα, περὶ ὧν οὐ χεῖρόν ἐστιν ἐπὶ πλέον εἰπεῖν τοῖς ἐνεστῶσι ζητήμασι. φασὶ δ' οἱ μὲν οὕτως ἁπλῶς ἐκ τῆς τοῦ Διὸς κεφαλῆς αὐτὴν γενέσθαι οὐδὲ προσιστοροῦντες τὸ πῶς ἢ κατὰ τίνα λόγον, τινῶν μὲν ἐν ταῖς θεογονίαις γραφόντων τὴν γένεσιν αὐτῆς

[18] ἐξηγούμενον αὐτῶν τὰς ὑπονοίας (*De plac. Hipp. et Plat.* 3.8.34). Long objects to the characterization and holds that Galen is purposefully misrepresenting Chrysippus as a reader of *huponoiai* in order to smear him. This is a something of a stretch, since it is far from obvious that reading for *huponoiai* was considered a scandalous activity among Galen's contemporaries.

πρῶτον μὲν Μήτιδι συγγενομένου τοῦ Διός, δεύτερον δὲ Θέμιδι, τινῶν δὲ ἐν ἑτέροις ἄλλως γραφόντων τὴν γένεσιν αὐτῆς· (Galen, *De plac.* 3.8.3–5)[19]

Chrysippus's opponents read the tale as evidence that reason (or the ruling part of the soul, in Stoic parlance) is located in the head. Chrysippus had a different interpretation of the story. He chastises his opponents for not consulting any particular authority in the matter and simply relying on the traditional account that she emerged from Zeus's head. But there are many versions of the story, he says, and he proposes what he sees as a more nuanced reading based on the more detailed account in Hesiod. He then quotes Hesiod at length, who claims that Zeus first has sex with Metis, then swallows her.[20] In the version Chrysippus knows, Metis births Athena inside Zeus, and only then is she born from his head. Chrysippus follows this long citation of Hesiod with his own exegesis of the literary symbol, paying careful attention to Hesiod's precise language, to the notions of "swallowing" and "giving birth," and to the fact that Hesiod once says Athena is born from Zeus's "head" [ἐκ κεφαλῆς] and once that she is born from the "crown" [πὰρ κορυφήν] of Zeus's head. Rather than seeing the passage as suggesting that reason is located in the head, Chrysippus preferred the view that the text indicates that the reasoning part of the soul is located in the chest and that it sends out the products of reason up through the head and out of the mouth (in the form of speech).

> Such, then, are the things which were said concerning Athena, giving the appearance of a symbol of something else [ἄλλου τινὸς συμβόλου ποιοῦντ' ἔμφασιν]. For first, on the one hand, Metis is said to be, as it were, a certain wisdom [φρόνησις] and a craft in practical matters, and in this sense it is necessary that the arts be swallowed down [καταπίνεσθαι][21] and be stored up inside. By this reasoning [λόγον] we also say that some people "absorb" [lit. swallow, καταπίνειν] things that are said; and on account of the "absorbing," we say by way of consequence that they are also stored in the belly. After this, it is reasonable that such an art, which has been swallowed in them, gives birth, since an art resembles a mother that gives birth,[22] and

[19] Texts are from Galen, *On the Doctrines of Hippocrates and Plato*, part 1, books 1–4, ed., trans., and comm. Philip De Lacy, *Corpus Medicorum Graecorum* 5.4.1.2 (Berlin: Akademie-Verlag, 1978), 227–29. I have based my translations on De Lacy's.

[20] He cites *Theog.* 886–90, 900, 924–26, 929; and lines that Merkelbach and West include as Hes. frag. dub. 343.

[21] Proclus will follow Chrysippus's interpretation of this word to explain the eating of children in general. See *In Tim.* 2.93.16; 2.99.7.

[22] M. C. Howatson, in the *Oxford Companion to Classical Literature*, 2d ed. (New York: Oxford University Press, 1989) is in general agreement with Chrysippus's reading of the myth: "By swallowing Metis, Zeus also acquired her practical wisdom." See "Metis," 358. A. A. Long also finds Chrysippus's reading plausible.

> in addition to these things there are things birthed in them by the scientific arts. It is possible to examine how they might emerge, and especially by what route. It is evident that they are brought out by the faculty of language [λόγῳ] through the mouth in the region of the head [κατὰ τὴν κεφαλήν]. The word "head" is here spoken in the same manner in which a sheep's head is talked about and in which they cut off the "heads" of certain people. According to similar language [λόγῳ], Metis is said to be born from the "crown," since very many of such shifts of meaning arise according to a symbol [τῶν τοιούτων παραλλαγῶν κατὰ σύμβολον γινομένων πλειόνων]. And quite apart from this account, a person could give a similar explanation from the mere circumstance of her being born by way of his head [κατὰ τὴν κεφαλήν]. For the poet does not say that she came to be inside his head, unless some people distort or alter the story, and say erroneously that she emerged after she came into being there. Therefore this is a better symbol in relation to the fuller account [ὥστε μᾶλλον καὶ τοῦτο σύμβολον πρὸς τὸν ἕτερον εἶναι], as I said. For the best meaning for the fuller narrative is that things pertaining to the arts and sciences first come into being inside them and then come out in the region of the head. (Galen, *De plac.* 3.8.15–20)

Even for a native speaker, Chrysippus's Greek is difficult. Galen joins the ranks of those who chide him for his opaque writing and spends several pages trying to unravel it. But we are able to make out the major points, with some help from Galen's glosses. Chrysippus is concerned to explain why, when Hesiod is being precise about where Athena emerges from Zeus, he uses a term for the very top, or crown, of the head [κορυφή] or just the part of the head where the hair grows. But if Chrysippus's reading is to be correct, he would have much preferred to hear Hesiod describe her as born from Zeus's mouth. He understands Hesiod to mean that Athena emerged from the head in general. He opts to emphasize the more general term that Hesiod uses, when he says that Athena emerges from his "head" [κεφαλή] and, according to Galen's explanation, glosses this term with common phrases (the mention of a sheep's head and a beheading) in which "head" means everything above the neck. More interesting, perhaps, Chrysippus is keen to emphasize the whole process of Athena's birth as told by Hesiod and argues against those who concentrate only on the end of the story, which is, to some extent, to pull it out of its context. The strange spectacle of birth from the head is preceded by the other strange action of swallowing. Zeus has sex with Metis and then swallows her. The chest cavity, Chrysippus tells us, is where Athena/reason gestates and comes to be, meaning that the chest is the seat of reason. Chrysippus then rummages through the Greek language, seeking support for this aspect of the myth (and his own anatomy of the soul) from commonly used turns of phrase. When we (Greeks) comprehend things that are spoken, we are said to "swallow" (in the sense of absorb) them, he tells us. In his own use of language, Chrysippus also emphasizes that the Greeks had a common word, φρόνησις, meaning right reason, that derived from the word for heart and chest [φρήν]. Here Chrysippus relies, interestingly enough, on a common Aristotelian strategy, the appeal to common linguistic usage.[23] He makes the case that reason is inextricably bound, in poetic myth and common language, with the chest. In this particular case, it is difficult to agree with Velleius that *all* we have here is a hamhanded attempt by Chrysippus to force Hesiod to speak Stoicism for him. For that matter, we might also wonder whether the reading of the story that Chrysippus opposes, which forwards it as proof for the belief that reason lies in the head, might also have been tendentious. Such a reading cannot account for the first half of Hesiod's version. In order to say that one reading is more motivated than another we need to be comfortable with some claim of primacy for one half of the story over the other. Given the nature of Hesiod's text, I think this is difficult. In short, as A. A. Long has already suggested, Chrysippus has a point. In any case, this single issue—whether Chrysippus's reading is fair to the text of Hesiod—does not exhaust the questions we can ask of him.

We can continue by noting that Chrysippus did not think of himself as foisting ideas onto the text that did not belong. He believed the text would bear his interpretation. He also believed, along with those who opposed this reading, that a right interpretation of it promised to yield knowledge of no simple kind, but of such heady aspects of reality as human reason and the divine itself. A closer look at Chrysippus's views of this text and of poetic language in general illuminates a broader context for his conviction that Hesiod's account carried enigmatic philosophical messages about the nature of souls and for the way Chrysippus thought such messages were conveyed. Such an investigation will offer up insights into the central conceptual category of the passage: the notion of the σύμβολον. At one point Galen rightly notes that Chrysippus all too quickly glosses over the essential point in his argument, that "many such shifts of meaning arise in a symbol."[24] Though we must share Galen's disappointment that Chrysippus did not expand further on this point, Chrysippus does give us some clues. Keeping in mind Long and Sedley's observation that "Of all ancient philosophies, Stoicism makes the greatest claim to being utterly systematic,"[25] these clues

[23] Galen testifies that Chrysippus typically appeals to common usage, citing him as saying, "We shall next inquire about these (matters), starting out in the same way from the common tendency and the expressions that are in accord with it" (*De plac.* 3.1.22).

[24] *De plac.* 3.8.27.

[25] A. A. Long and D. N. Sedley, *The Hellenistic Philosophers* (New York: Cambridge University Press, 1987), 1:160 (hereafter *HP*).

make up only small patches of what was surely a synthetic picture for Chrysippus. It seems reasonable, then, to try to reconstruct the place of symbolic interpretation in the larger context of Stoic thought.

Stoic Language Theory and Stoic Ontology

We will approach Chrysippus's symbol through Stoic language theory, a topic on which they had well-developed ideas. But to understand their theories of language and to see how these theories contribute to a strategy of reading, we will need to dig further into some basic propositions of Stoic ontology, propositions that defy Aristotelian or Platonic common sense. Speaking of Chrysippus, Plutarch describes the Stoic proclivity to confound in colorful terms.

> This man seems to me to put all his efforts and ingenuity into overturning and wrecking common sense. . . . They say that the octopus gnaws off its own tentacles in winter. Well, Chrysippus's dialectic destroys by amputation its own vital parts and principles. So which of our other conceptions has he left free from suspicion?

> ἐμοὶ δοκεῖ μετὰ πλείστης ἐπιμελείας καὶ δεινότητος οὗτος ὁ ἀνὴρ ἀνατρέπειν καὶ καταβάλλειν τὴν συνήθειαν . . . τὸν μέν γε πολύποδά φασι τὰς πλεκτάνας αὑτοῦ περιβιβρώσκειν ὥρᾳ χειμῶνος, ἡ δὲ Χρυσίππου διαλεκτικὴ τὰ κυριώτατα μέρη καὶ τὰς ἀρχὰς αὑτῆς ἀναιροῦσα καὶ περικόπτουσα τίνα τῶν ἄλλων ἐννοιῶν ἀπολέλοιπεν ἀνύποπτον; (*HP* 37I)[26]

Plutarch's image will be useful to keep in mind: the Stoics aim systematically to overturn our common sense. They also attempt to replace it with a new one. They proceed by holding unshakably to a number of foundational tenets, making scrupulously rigorous deductions based on these, and remaining undeterred by contradictions that may appear to outsiders to be self-consuming. As we will see, Chrysippus's innovative theories in physics, ontology, and anthropology offer him ways of understanding language and poetic figuration that were simply unavailable to his predecessors.

Naturalism and Ambiguity

It is well known that the Stoics thought a word had a "natural" connection to its meaning (*SVF* 2.146). Perhaps less well known, though equally well attested, is their vision that language is inherently ambig-

[26] Unless otherwise noted, translations of the Stoic material are taken from Long and Sedley, with only slight modifications. Texts from Long and Sedley.

uous and multilayered in its meanings (*HP* 37N).[27] Naturalism and ambiguity appear to be in conflict. If a word naturally indicates its meaning, it does not seem possible that the meaning could shift. Prior to the Stoics, the most serious extant look at naturalism is to be found in Plato's *Cratylus*. As we saw in chapter 1, Plato experimented with the position as a means to promote semantic stability, as opposed to the instability he considered inherent in a conventionalist model. Plato's main concerns are epistemological and depend upon his distinctive ontological scheme. If the real truth of things lies in a stable region of existing Forms, as it manifestly does for Plato, then language, in order to reflect reality adequately, must also be stable (439d–440d). Conventionalism allows too many variations to enter into language. If we are to have any true knowledge, we must take extra care that words themselves have some connection to the world; otherwise we build up the edifice of dialectic on faulty foundations (385c, 430d, 436d–e). These concerns drive Plato's exploration of natural-language theory, though in the end he does not subscribe to it. For the Stoics, the situation is quite different. I will explore ways in which naturalism and ambiguity could be compatible when contextualized within Stoic thinking.

A few points present themselves in relation to the larger investigation. First, though it seems paradoxical, we have seen (and will continue to see) that the history of the symbol testifies to the following proposition: Theories of linguistic naturalism tend to generate semantic *instability*. Such a notion is actually not so counterintuitive when we consider a rather simple fact. When the locus of meaning rests in words themselves, meaning is by definition no longer in the full control of a given set of language users. Conventionalist models of language put language itself precisely at the service of a group of speakers, who have full control over what meanings it might convey, by means of their sovereign agreement. But in theories of linguistic naturalism, words cease to be mere vessels for whatever content their users fill them with and begin instead to assert themselves, making a claim on the formation of meaning and usurping a position for themselves in the process of signification. As we saw in chapter 2, precisely such a difficulty haunted the economy of meaning governed by the "symbol" in the classical period. The broken token that served to mark a business or social arrangement

[27] Long and Sedley (37N, notes) suggest that the Stoics may have considered ambiguity to mean simply that each word designates some thing and also itself as a word. But 37N suggests something more is at stake than this, and Diogenes Laertius treats ambiguity in a more substantive way (7.62 = *HP* 37P). Dawson mentions this tension (34). Also, such a characterization makes one wonder why Chrysippus would have written several entire tracts on the question (D.L. 7.193). Catherine Atherton has written the most thorough treatment of the topic, *The Stoics on Ambiguity* (New York: Cambridge University Press, 1993).

matched its other half by its very nature and in that sense functioned as a "natural" signifier. However, the threat that this natural sign might fall into the wrong hands always held out the possibility of abuse and confusion—in the end, the attempt to do away with ambiguity through naturalism founders. Securing meaning "naturally" within a particular linguistic sign does not resolve ambiguity but merely delays it to a later moment, the moment when that meaning is redeemed by the receiver of the message. The naturally signifying chit, precisely because it has autonomous signifying power, can always misplace its "payoff." I will be suggesting here that a situation such as this is operative in Stoic language theory as well. When we later turn to the Neoplatonists, naturalism and ambiguity (understood in the sense of polyvalence) will again be paired. These observations raise the question of different types of stability, ontological and semantic. At this point we might only suggest that a system that concentrates and guarantees the former in a single transcendent principle tends to be less successful at guaranteeing the latter. For our present purposes, understanding the dialectic between semantic and ontological stability will be crucial for making sense of the "shifts" that Chrysippus tells us are typical of a literary symbol.

Naturalism

Naturalism in theories of language is a deceptively complex notion. Of the various thinkers who explore the idea in the ancient world, each takes an individual approach to the topic. As we have noted, Socrates investigates an onomatopoetic naturalism, where the sounds and actions of the mouth mimic or reproduce some essential aspect of the term's meaning. The Neoplatonists of late antiquity, as we will see later, have something more radical in mind. The Stoics also have their own views on the matter of linguistic naturalism. A longish summary of Stoic thinking from Augustine's *De dialectica* is a useful place to begin. After looking at cases of onomatopoetic imitations of words for "clanging," "whinnying," and the like, he moves on to other forms of "naturalism":

> But since there are things that do not make a sound, in these cases the similarity of touch applies; thus, if [things] touch the sense smoothly or roughly, just as the smoothness or roughness of letters touches the hearing, so it has produced names for them. For example, when we say "smooth" [*lene*] the word itself sounds smoothly. Likewise, who would not judge roughness [*asperitatem*] rough in its very name? . . . Things themselves affect us in the same way as words are perceived. In the case of honey [*mel*], as sweetly as the thing itself touches the taste, so smoothly does it touch the hearing with its name. "Harsh" [*acre*] is rough in both ways They believed

that this is, as it were, the cradle of words, when the sensory perceptions of things agree with [*concordarent*] the sensory perception of the sound.

Sed quia sunt res quae non sonant, in his similitudinem tactus valere, ut, si leniter vel aspere sensum tangunt, lenitas vel asperitas litterarum ut tangit auditum sic eis nomina pepererit: ut ipsum "lene" cum dicimus leniter sonat. Quis item "asperitatem" non et ipso nomine asperam iudicet? Lene est auribus cum dicimus "voluptas," asperum cum dicimus "crux." Ita res ipsae afficiunt, ut verba sentiuntur. Mel, quam suaviter gustum res ipsa, tam leniter nomine tangit auditum. "Acre" in utroque asperum est. "Lana" et "vepres," ut audiuntur verba, sic illa tanguntur. Haec quasi cunabula verborum esse crediderunt, ubi sensus rerum cum sonorum sensu concordarent. (Augustine, *De dialectica* 6)[28]

This summary suggests a deeper level of natural affiliation between word and thing than Plato had experimented with in the *Cratylus*. The Stoics clearly thought they could make meaningful translations between the various senses of sound, touch, taste, etcetera. Not only that, but things in nature "affect" us in the same way words are perceived [res ipsae afficiunt, ut verba sentiuntur]. And the sensory perceptions of "things" and "sounds" can be in harmony [sensus rerum cum sonorum sensu concordarent]. This degree of transparency between the spheres of "nature" and "sense" (including both the notion of perception and semantic content, as we will see) is most provocative and pushes us further back into Stoic ontology, epistemology, and perception theory. All these considerations advance us toward understanding just what the "thing itself" is that the Stoics think a word is able to capture in a natural way. The compressed survey to follow owes much to Long and Sedley's indispensable texts and commentaries in *The Hellenistic Philosophers*.

The Stoics inhabit a relentlessly material world. The two major features of the Stoic cosmos are both thoroughly material: unqualified matter and the divine breath, or "pneuma" [πνεῦμα], that permeates, guides, and controls it (*HP* 47).[29] The Stoics understand even attributes, such as colors and qualities, and mental entities, such as perceptions and conceptions, to be bodies. This rather extreme position is attributable to their insistence that immaterial causes (like, traditionally, souls and thoughts) could not affect material things (*HP* 45A–E). Earlier thinkers never really developed a clear solution for this problem either,

[28] I thank Elizabeth Asmis for the citation. Text and translation (adapted) from B. Darrell Jackson, *Augustine, De dialectica*, Synthese Historical Library, vol. 16 (Boston: D. Reidel, 1975).

[29] Long and Sedley's volume on Hellenistic philosophy will be cited by section number. This is meant to refer to notes as well.

but the Stoics seem to have been bothered enough about it to propose their unique and radical solution. They materialize everything that can properly be said to exist.[30] In order to maintain this counterintuitive position, they redefine most of the items that previous thinkers had considered incorporeal as being material configurations or dispositions of the highly rarefied, but nevertheless material, pneuma. For example, the divine breath, molded into a certain shape, produces the color red; into another, the conception of a "horse" in a person's mind. In Stoic thinking, such configurations are not abstractions or general visions of some informing principle, they are specific, material, concrete shapes of the divine breath, located in space and time.

Of the four traditional elements, air and fire combine to make the pneuma, an evanescent, exceedingly light material (*SVF* 2.442, part). The pneuma then utterly permeates the rest of matter to make the existing things that populate the cosmos. It stabilizes and controls the world by penetrating and qualifying wholly unqualified matter. They coin a new term for the process by which the pneuma mixes with the unqualified matter it holds together, calling it blending [κρᾶσις; see *HP* 48]. The pneuma in every individual thing operates like an interior twin, a body that coexists within, binding a thing together and making it what it is. The Stoics assign the name of "tenor" [ἕξις] to the configuration of pneuma that holds together inanimate objects like stones and logs. Something called φύσις,[31] which is the pneuma in a slightly more rarefied state, holds together plants and the human fetus between conception and birth. Soul [ψυχή], an even more rarefied pneuma, holds together the matter of which an animal is made up. Primarily, soul has the powers of sensation and movement. The logical soul [λογικὴ ψυχή], which is rarefied further still, holds together the inert matter that makes up the human body and uniquely manifests the characteristic of *logos*, or speech and reason.[32] Though the various grades of pneuma impart different characteristics to different things, they are all portions of a single entity, the divine, and constitute an unbroken material connection of all things to all things in the cosmos. The Stoics often call the cosmos a single organism, and the divine pneuma its soul (*HP* 54). The various configurations of pneuma that hypostasize the things we see are no more different from one another than different aspects of a single soul. I will suggest in a moment that this position, a universalist materialism,

[30] Some things, though, were beyond their ingenuity. The Stoics posit four immaterial features of the universe: time, place, void, and the sayables [λεκτά]. The ontological status of these incorporeals is somewhat difficult to determine. Since they are not bodies, the Stoics will insist that they do not properly exist.

[31] A specialized use of the general term.

[32] On this hierarchy of pneumatic configurations, see *HP* 47O–Q, 53A–B and notes.

forms the ontological background for their powerful version of the theory of linguistic naturalism and informs what likely was a sophisticated theory of allegorical reading.

The Stoic pneuma not only serves as the ontological basis of every existing thing but also provides the basis of all intellectual reality. The sources tell us that the Stoics equate the divine pneuma with the logos.[33] In its capacity as logos, the pneuma is the power of reason broadly construed, the (material) principle that underlies, stabilizes, and coordinates all things in the cosmos. But this is no abstract set of principles. Like all other existents in the Stoic world, the intellectual aspects of the cosmos, embodied and passed down through the pneumatic logos, are fully material. In sharp contrast to the theories of Plato and Aristotle, Stoicism did not position ideas or conceptual categories on an abstract plane of reality, somewhere above or within existing things. For the Stoics, the sum total of intellectual reality is identical with the evanescent, though still material, logos.[34] Since a configuration of pneuma dwells at the ontological core of every existing thing, a share of divine reason, logos, does also. The structuring principle of each thing, then, is at the same time an embodied portion of the whole synthetic intellectual reality. Of course, the power to use the logos, to use reason, does not manifest itself in pneumatic configurations below the level of the logical human soul (sticks and stones can neither reason nor speak). Nevertheless, *all* things, from the highest human to the lowest stone, have an *indwelling noetic content.*

The Stoics define thoughts or "conceptions" [ἔννοιαι], as they exist in a person's rational soul, in a way that very much fits with their pneumatic view of intellectual content (*HP* 39E–F). Thoughts are configurations of pneuma, stored in the mind of the one who thinks them. A logical soul (which, we remember, is itself a portion of breath) forms thoughts such as "human" or "horse" from perceptions that the soul collects and compares. The sense organs, all of which work pneumatically in Stoic physiology, receive data from objects and send percep-

[33] Both the pneuma and logos are the divine principle suffusing the universe. See, e.g., *SVF* 2.300, part; 2.299 ("They [the Stoics] think that there are two principles of the universe, that which acts and that which is acted upon. That which is acted upon is unqualified substance, i.e., matter; that which acts is the *logos* in it, i.e., god") and *HP* 46A ("The Stoics made god out to be intelligent, a designing fire which methodically proceeds toward creation of the world, and encompasses all the seminal principles [σπερματικοὺς λόγους] . . . , and a breath [πνεῦμα] pervading the whole world"). Long and Sedley call pneuma the "vehicle" of logos. "'Breath' is the vehicle of god, the active principle or *logos*" (*HP*, 1: 292).

[34] See A. A. Long, "Dialectic and the Stoic Sage," in *The Stoics*, ed. John M. Rist (Berkeley: University of California Press, 1978), 116.

tions, in the form once again of configurations of pneuma, back to the ruling part [ἡγεμονικόν] of the soul. Aetius describes this process:

> From the commanding faculty [ἀπὸ τοῦ ἡγεμονικοῦ] there are seven parts of the soul [τῆς ψυχῆς] which grow out and stretch out into the body like the tentacles of an octopus. Five of these are the senses of sight, smell, hearing, taste, and touch. Sight is breath [πνεῦμα] which extends from the commanding faculty to the eyes, hearing is breath which extends from the commanding faculty to the ears. . . . Of the remainder, one is called seed [σπέρμα], which also is this very breath extending from the commanding faculty to the genitals. The other . . . which they call utterance [φωνή], is breath extending from the commanding faculty to the pharynx, tongue, and appropriate organs. The ruling part itself rests in our spherical head, just as in the cosmos. (*HP* 53H)[35]

Aetius's description of utterance, in particular, is highly suggestive, and we will consider it in a moment. In the reasoning process, the ruling part identifies and categorizes certain familiar pneumatic shapes and then stores them away, like tiny stamps on its breathy substance (*HP* 53U).[36] (Aetius gives the more general Stoic position, that the ruling part of the soul is in the head. Chrysippus, as we learned from his reading of the Hesiod passage above, insisted that it was located in the chest, at the seat of the respiratory function. Perhaps he took this position to emphasize more strongly the pneumatic dimension of thought.)

The Stoics' understanding of the word is no less material than the rest of their cosmos. They define an uttered word [φωνή], straightforwardly enough, as a corporeal shape of air in motion (*SVF* 2.135, 139–42). Like all existing things, the word consists of two parts: inert matter—in this case the dense air that we breathe—and the evanescent pneuma that gives it its shape. The similarity between the Stoics' notions of word and thought is plain enough. In fact, I read the sources to suggest that the Stoics understood the foundations of individual words and thoughts to be materially identical. A word is merely a thought that has been exhaled; it is a configuration of pneuma transferred from the medium of the soul, a certain kind of breathy substance itself, on which it has been stored, to the medium of the dense air by the organs of speech (*SVF* 2.135). The same highly rarefied shape of pneuma constitutes and holds together both these entities. Such a theory has a precursor in Plato who suggests that thought is simply internalized speech (*Theaet.* 189e and *Soph.* 263e). But the Stoics have something characteristically more

[35] Galen gives an identical account and attributes it to Chrysippus (*SVF* 238–39). The last sentence refers to the opinion of Zeno, with which Chrysippus disagrees.

[36] See *HP* 1: 182, including reference to *HP* 29.

concrete in mind. Galen describes, for example, the view of Chrysippus, who once again argues for a respiratory seat of intellection:

> Meaningful language [λόγος] and utterance [φωνή] have the same source. But the source of utterance is not the region of the head, but evidently somewhere lower down; for it is obvious that utterance passes out through the windpipe. Therefore language too does not have its source in the head, but lower down. But that too is certainly true, viz. that language has its source in thought [ἐκ τῆς διανοίας]; for some people actually define language as meaningful utterance sent out from thought [φωνὴν σημαίνουσαν ἀπὸ διανοίας ἐκπεμπομένην]. It is also credible that language is sent out imprinted [ἐνσεσημασμένον], and stamped as it were [οἷον ἐκτετυπωμένον], by the conceptions [ὑπὸ τῶν ἐννοιῶν] present in thought, and that it is temporally coextensive with both the act of thinking and with the act of speaking. Therefore thought too is not in the head but in the lower regions, principally no doubt around the heart. (*HP* 53U)

Now, keeping in mind the Stoic's expansive vision of the ontological, noetic, and linguistic capacities of configurations of pneuma, we are able to gain a fuller understanding of what the Stoics might have had in mind when they proposed that a word had a "natural" meaning. Subtle, evanescent shapes of the divine breath suffuse every object in the Stoic cosmos. These pneumatic configurations are not materially different from the shapes of rarefied divine breath that stamp themselves onto the human soul as stored thoughts and in turn shape the denser human breath into words that the mouth, lips, pharynx, and tongue impart to the air. This suggests that the underlying principles that shape a concrete thing, a thought, and a word are not materially different from one another, they differ only in location. In further confirmation of this view, we return to Aetius's explanation of the sensory system. The Stoics see the production of significant speech as analogous to a sensory activity. It is just another tentacle of the octopus that makes up a Stoic soul. On this evidence, we might draw a useful analogy to the realm of current perception and neurological theory: The fact that a word has natural content will be just as obvious to Chrysippus as it is to a modern observer that a particular electrical impulse has a natural connection with the perception it relays to the brain.

Given the Stoics' universalist materialism, the notion of "natural" language takes on a far-reaching and deeply ontological character. This is a far cry from Socrates' experimentations with the sounds we produce having some mimetic relation to the ideas they convey. The Stoics are proposing an entirely new understanding of naturalism in language. For them the word is not a sound to which we might attach one meaning or another, whether by nature or convention. Rather, simply by being a configuration of dense air, formed by an underlying shape of divine pneuma, it already has a real link to the very stuff of intellectual and physical reality itself, and in that sense, already has a meaning.[37]

Ambiguity

The naturalism of the Stoics is complicated by their vision of language as inherently ambiguous. For Chrysippus, the notion that a word has natural intellectual content does not guarantee linguistic stability. The sources testify (just as clearly as they testify to naturalism) that Chrysippus thought of language as ambiguous at its very core. As a matter of fact, Chrysippus thought that words were ambiguous *by nature*, as is evident in this exerpt from Aulus Gellius:

> Chrysippus said that every word is ambiguous by nature, since two or more meanings can be understood from it. But Diodorus Cronus[38] said: "No word is ambiguous, and no one says or thinks anything ambiguous, and nothing should be held to be being said beyond what the speaker thinks he

[37] This discussion has omitted consideration of Stoic semantics and their vision of the *lekta*. This category would be crucial for a wider discussion of Stoic theories of meaning in larger, syntactic structures. But for the purposes of understanding Stoic allegorism, such consideration of syntactic units is less promising. When the Stoics interpret allegorically, their object of interpretation is nearly always nominalized: a state of affairs is reduced to a "thing," whether a noun or an abstract verbal idea, that is read as having some connection to another thing. In Stoic understanding, it is not so much a *lekton* they are reading but rather a common quality. For example, the statement "Zeus swallows Metis" is a completed thought that is analyzable in Stoic semantics into a threefold schema: the physical sounds of the words, the "signifying thing" [σημαῖνον]; the state of affairs to which they refer, the "name bearer" [τυγχάνον—for this translation, see *HP* 2: 197]; and a third thing, which is the state of affairs revealed by the utterance, the "thing signified" [σημαινόμενον] or "lekton." But this threefold analysis is only applicable to complete thoughts (see *HP* 1: 199–201). Single nouns and verbs on their own do not qualify as having *lekta*. If we look back at the example from Chrysippus, when he sets out to track the shifts of his symbol, he does not interpret "Zeus swallows Metis and gives birth to Athena from his head" all at once as a single unit. Instead he atomizes the parts of the statement into nominalized components and interprets each of them as standing separately for another thing ("Metis" for "practical wisdom," the idea of "swallowing" for "absorbing," and the "head" for the "crown of the head"). He then reassembles them. Recalling the Derveni commentator's readings, this tendency holds there as well. "Genitals" shifts to "sun" and "procreative power." In the actual practice of allegorical reading, in fact, shifts of meaning in larger syntactic structures are far overshadowed by shifts of meaning in individual elements inside of sentences. For treatments of the *lekta* (of which there are many), see *HP* 33 and bibliography in *HP*, vol. 2. See also the intelligent and lucid discussion of Giovanni Manetti, *Theories of the Sign in Classical Antiquity*, trans. Christine Richardson (Bloomington: University of Indiana Press, 1993), 92–110.

[38] He was a man who named one of his slaves "However."

is saying. When you have understood something other than what I had in mind, I should be held to have spoken obscurely, rather than ambiguously. For the characteristic of an ambiguous word would have had to be that whoever said it was saying two or more things. But no one is saying two or more things if he thinks he is saying one."

Chrysippus ait omne uerbum ambiguum natura esse, quoniam ex eodem duo uel plura accipi possunt. Diodorus autem, cui Crono cognomentum fuit, "nullum" inquit "uerbum est ambiguum, nec quisquam ambiguum dicit aut sentit, nec aliud dici uideri debet, quam quod se dicere sentit is qui dicit. at cum ego" inquit "aliud sensi, tu aliud accepisti, obscure magis dictum uideri potest quam ambigue; ambigui enim uerbi natura illa esse debuit, ut, qui id diceret, duo uel plura diceret. nemo autem duo uel plura dicit, qui se sensit unum dicere." (*HP* 37N)

According to this testimony, Chrysippus thinks that words have a capacity, and even a *natural* one, to convey more than one meaning, and that the meaning they convey is not fully under the control of the speaker. Gellius contrasts Chrysippus's position with that of a person claiming that the speaker has complete power to stabilize the meaning of his or her words. Apparently, Chrysippus is not so sure. For him, it appears, the word itself becomes empowered again, as it was for Gorgias and Plato (though in different ways), and it saps some of the sovereignty of the speaker that Aristotle had maintained. In this aspect of Stoic thinking, language begins to take on a life of its own again.

Catherine Atherton has considered this text from Aulus Gellius in her work on Stoic concepts of ambiguity. She calls Gellius's claim of ambiguity by nature "apparently bizarre."[39] Atherton is here operating from the premise that naturalism and ambiguity are simply irreconcilable. In the end she suggests that the sense of "ambiguum" in Gellius's text is limited to the case of a word indicating both itself as word and its referent.[40] I will here present an argument for a broader reading of "ambiguum" in this text, based on evidence from Stoic theories of ontology and reading. In introducing her study, Atherton has rightly pointed out that ambiguity was standardly viewed among ancient teachers of style and composition, logicians, and rhetoricians as a difficulty and a defect. She has also shown conclusively that the Stoics, when engaged in such fields of inquiry, also "considered ambiguity a bad thing" (26). Her main focus is on illuminating difficult and (before Atherton) ill-understood passages from Galen, Theon, and Diogenes Laertius, which set ambiguity within these contexts. But in her otherwise encyclopedic

[39] Atherton, 156, n. 18.
[40] Atherton, 298–310.

treatment of the subject, Atherton does not consider Stoic readings of the poets to be relevant to the topic. This view is partly generated by her assessment of literary criticism in the ancient period. Following Russell, she claims that it carried the fundamental defect of a certain tone-deafness to the creative possibilities of ambiguity in a poetic context. "This fundamental defect in ancient literary criticism is associated by Russell with the immense influence of rhetorical training, whose explicit aim is to teach ways of clothing a predetermined meaning in the, or the most, appropriate words."[41] This orientation, she says, encouraged "rigid and unsubtle literary critical methods."[42] Inarguably true—if we look only at rhetorical criticism. But in my estimation, in their readings of the poets—as opposed to in rhetoric and logic—the Stoics are prominent among those ancient critics who did *not* consider ambiguity a defect. Atherton is surely right in pointing out the sad fact that "the arguments with which Chrysippus must have supported his thesis have not survived," and that we are to some extent left to our own devices to figure out what he had in mind. To that end, and with that proviso, we turn to the difficult task of rebuilding a context for understanding Aulus Gellius's claim of a "natural ambiguity," but here within Stoic ontological, linguistic, and literary theories.

If Stoic conceptions have a thoroughly material existence, as pneumatic configurations inside the soul, the concept, the abstract entity that supposedly underlies the intellectual entity, does not. For example, when we look at a person, the conception [ἔννοια] "human" that enters our minds is a material object, a disposition of the pneuma that our senses send to the soul's ruling part. But for the Stoics the corresponding concept [ἐννόημα] "humanness" does not exist as an autonomous entity at all. The object of our thought, that is, the thing that we think *about* when we think "human" in a universal sense, is a concoction of our own. In sharp contrast to their predecessors, especially Plato, the Stoics denied an autonomous stratum of intellectual reality against which we might measure and authenticate our thoughts and the natures of material things in the world. Long and Sedley have emphasized that this has to do with the Stoics' objection to a class of abstract entities that are supposed to exist on some disembodied, immaterial plane (see *HP* 30, notes). The Stoics pointedly redefine Plato's anchor of reality, the Form, as a figment of the imagination. Plato's ἰδέα is called an ἐννόημα, an item that the Stoics classify as a nonexistent product of the

[41] Atherton, 25, n. 13. Atherton cites D. A. Russell, *Criticism in Antiquity* (Berkeley: University of California Press, 1981), 4.

[42] Atherton, 25.

imagination (*HP* 30A). To push their point against Plato even more colorfully, they put our concepts on a par with the phantoms that appear to dreamers and madmen (see *HP* 30, notes).

We fabricate these "concepts," the Stoics say explicitly, for *linguistic* convenience (*HP* 30H). Reason constructs the phantom concept in order that we may use words and speak of things. We hypostasize certain common qualities [αἱ κοιναὶ ποιότηται], which in Stoic ontology are *aspects* of concrete things, into a quasi-existence.[43] We pretend that there is such a thing as "humanness," for example, in order that we might discuss as a group those things that display the common quality "human." We do this because it is linguistically useful to discuss as a group the many individuals in which we see the common quality "human." But the Stoics insist that such a bizarre, unidimensional creature as "humanness" does not exist on its own. "The Stoics of Zeno's school said that the Ideas were our own concepts" [οἱ ἀπὸ Ζήνωνος Στωικοὶ ἐννοήματα ἡμέτερα τὰς ἰδέας ἔφασαν (*HP* 30B)]. This is not to suggest that the recognition of such a common quality is not important, the Stoics show a keen interest in asserting that knowledge of the pieces of the world through cognitive impressions of them is attainable (*HP* 40). This knowledge is expressed in the common conceptions assembled by humans collectively in acts of reason drawn from cognitive impressions. However, these discrete categories of being have no priority, ontological or otherwise, over the myriad existing things that present themselves to us. In fact, they are parasites on them. Such radical innovations in ontology greatly deemphasize the importance of discrete abstract units of being, that is, essentialist categories by which things are what they are.[44] Rather than granting ontological priority to some set of Aristotelian essences or Platonic Forms, the Stoics understand all things to be at root the divine pneuma, which they see as a totality. Under a universalist materialism such as this, each particular, while surely knowable as one or another kind of thing in the world, is not *in essence* one kind of thing or another. If we ask after the fundamental reality of any existing thing, the answer will always be the same: the divine pneuma. To put it into Aristotelian terms, all its other qualities become "attributes" or "accidents."[45]

[43] ὡσανεί is the term often used in the Greek sources; *quasi* in Latin.

[44] See Gerard Watson, *The Stoic Theory of Knowledge* (Belfast: Queen's University, 1966); and Andreas Graeser, "The Stoic Theory of Meaning," in *The Stoics*, ed. John M. Rist (Berkeley: University of California Press, 1978), 77–99.

[45] I.e., those qualities that are discussed under the heading of συμβεβηκός in the sense it is given in *Metaphysics* 1025a30–35. The stress that the Stoic understanding places on the scheme of essence and accident is brought to light in Plutarch, *On Common Conceptions* 1085e–1086b, and Galen *Quod qualitates incorporeae sint* 9.

Naturally enough, knowledge of the logos, or the pneuma, becomes the ultimate concern for all Stoic inquiry. In their ethics, the Stoics make "living in accordance" with nature and the logos that sustains it the *telos* of all human existence (*HP* 63). To do this, one must know what the logos "wants" one to do. This means knowledge of *it*. The object of Stoic scrutiny is, then, primarily a synthetic whole, and the study of particulars a means to this end. At one point in Cicero's *De natura deorum*, Velleius (a detractor of the Stoics) characterizes Chrysippus's thinking in a way that assumes such a physics as this:

> Chrysippus [in book 1 of his *On the Nature of the Gods*] . . . musters an enormous mob of unknown gods—so utterly unknown that even imagination cannot guess at their form and nature. . . . For he says that divine power resides in reason, and in the soul and mind of the natural world; he calls the world itself a god, and also the all-pervading world-soul, and again the guiding principle of that soul, which operates in the intellect and reason, and the common and all-embracing nature of things; besides this, the fire that I previously termed aether; and also the shadow of Fate, and the Necessity that governs future events; and also all fluid and soluble substances, such as water, earth, air, the sun, moon and stars, and the all-embracing unity of things.
>
> Iam vero Chrysippus . . . magnam turbam congregat ignotorum deorum atque ita ignotorum ut eos ne coniectura quidem informare possimus. . . . Ait enim vim divinam in ratione esse positam et in universae naturae animo atque mente ipsumque mundum deum dicit esse et eius animi fusionem universam, tum eius ipsius principatum qui in mente et ratione versetur communemque rerum naturam universam atque omnia continentem, tum fatalem umbram et necessitatem rerum futurarum, ignem praeterea et eum quem ante dixi aethera, tum ea quae natura fluerent atque manarent ut et aquam et terram et aera, solem, lunam, sidera universitatemque rerum qua omnia continerentur. (*De nat. deor.* 1.39)

Velleius's polemic, however overblown, suggests a Chrysippean position that the divine pneuma ultimately underlies all these things, and that therefore all things—from what we designate as "aether," "fate," and "intellect" all the way down to "water," "earth," and "air" (that is, to the inert elements that make up all things)—ultimately *are* the pneuma. Pushed to its logical conclusion, this theory suggests a certain provisionality in all things, since all things are really, *in essence* so to speak, manifestations of the divine. When we assign a name to some existing thing in the world, we are indicating what is in essence the divine pneuma insofar as it has adopted some particular shape and placed its stamp on some clump of inert matter.

Another well-attested and idiosyncratic component of Stoic cosmology further illuminates this basic provisionality of existing things. The Stoics believe that the world ends periodically, being consumed with divine fire. Over great spans of time, the fiery pneuma (considered in this role as the divine godhead, Zeus) advances as a movement of providence, pervades all things, and folds them into itself. During the conflagration all things lose their being and are consumed into the fire. They are no longer *co*extensive with Zeus/pneuma but actually become him. Zeus alone endures. This is a radically different, and more provisional, cosmos than Aristotle's or Plato's. Aristotle's cosmos is eternal, each thing tucked into its place in the grand taxonomy and pursuing its *telos*, and though Plato sometimes suggests cyclical destruction, there is no hint that intellectual reality, the Forms, would be subsumed. In the Stoic cosmos the pneuma becomes the ultimate and uniquely stable referent of *all* language.

This provisionalism, an inescapable feature of the Stoics' universalist materialism, has far-reaching implications for their theory of language. Words become secure and natural designations of aspects of what is essentially a provisional reality. The sources indicate that the Stoics spelled out explicitly such linguistic implications.

> The Stoics made god out to be intelligent, a designing fire which methodically proceeds toward creation of the world, and encompasses all the seminal principles [σπερματικοὺς λόγους] . . . and a breath [πνεῦμα] pervading the whole world, which takes on [μεταλαμβάνον] different names [προσηγορίας] owing to the shifts of the matter through which it passes [κατὰ τὰς τῆς ὕλης, δι' ἧς κεχώρηκε, παραλλάξεις]. (Aetius 1.7.33; *HP* 46A)[46]

The divine pneuma expands through the cosmos, hypostasizing individual entities according to its seminal principles. Words have as their ultimate referent this underlying synthetic unity, which simply adopts different names when it appears in different aspects. Another citation from Aetius suggests an identical consideration:

> The Stoics say that the whole pneuma is a rush of air, and that it alters its names by shifts of location [ταῖς τῶν τόπων παραλλαγαῖς τὰς ἐπωνυμίας παραλλάττουσαν]. For example, Zephyr is from the West [ζόφος] and the sun's setting-place [δύσις]; the Apeliotes is from the East [ἀνατολή] and the

[46] There is a general resonance here with Heraclitus, D-K 22 B67 (discussed in chap. 1). The Presocratic first tells us that god is all manner of things that we consider opposites: "God is day night, winter summer, war peace, satiety hunger." He then says that when god enters the things in the world, god is "transformed, just as when fire is mixed with incense, and it is named according to the flavor of each" [ὁ θεὸς ἡμέρη εὐφρόνη, χειμὼν θέρος, πόλεμος εἰρήνη, κόρος λιμός. . . . ἀλλοιοῦται δὲ ὥσπερ πῦρ, ὁπόταν συμμιγῇ θυώμασιν, ὀνομάζεται καθ' ἡδονὴν ἑκάστου].

sun [ἥλιος]; Boreas is from the north [ἄρκτος]; and the Lips is from the south [νότιος]. (*SVF* 2.697; not cited in *HP*)[47]

Here again, the pneuma is an underlying unity that changes its name due to variations in in its location. If we put these texts together with our earlier reconstruction of Stoic naturalism, we arrive at a more complete picture of how language is supposed to work. In the process of bringing an existent into being, the pneuma takes on a particular configuration and therefore has a perceivable common quality that is not materially different from an intellectual content. This intellectual content is equivalent to the pneuma, considered as logos, that dwells within it. It becomes naturally designated by the word whose logos is congruent with it. But this designation derives from and points back to the shape that the pneuma happens to take, and not to some essential quality of the thing itself. The word "egg," for example, is really a sort of shorthand for the pneuma insofar as it has formed a clump of matter into something with the common characteristic "egg." While Velleius's characterization of a "mob of unknown gods" suggests an ontological position that all things are at root manifestations of the divine, Aetius's two testimonia are evidence for a linguistic corollary: all things can be *named* only as manifestations of the divine.

This reading of the linguistic and ontological evidence also provides perhaps a more useful context for another of the Stoics' most characteristic forms of investigation: their reading of puns within the names of the traditional Greek gods. While such playing with words does not generate reliable etymological information, it is clear that the Stoics were after something slightly different than a philologically minded history of terms. The pun is closer in spirit to the Stoics' own goals than etymology as understood in a modern philological sense,[48] and the investigation of divine names is a well-attested feature of Stoic thinking.[49] As has been mentioned above, in Stoic reckoning, the stories of the Olympian gods were created by ancient mythmakers who through them transmitted (and sometimes corrupted) various truths about the cosmos. Testimony from Diogenes Laertius gives us a way to understand their investigations of divine names precisely within the context of the ontology of universalist materialism and its linguistic implications:

[47] Diogenes Laertius attests to this also, using the same vocabulary (7.152).

[48] M. L. West argues something similar in his treatment of Hesiod's etymological explanations of names (introduction to Hesiod, *Theogony and Works and Days* [New York: Oxford University Press, 1988], xviii).

[49] Many such readings of divine names can be found at *SVF* 2.1061–1100; Cicero *De nat. deor.* 1.41; Philodemus *De piet.* cols. 1–10, in Henrichs, "Die Kritik der stoischen Theologie im PHerc. 1428," *Cronache Ercolanesi* 4 (1974): 5–32.

> [God] is the creator of the whole and, as it were, the father of all, both generally and, in particular, that part of him which pervades all things, which is called by many descriptions [προσηγορίαις] according to his powers. For they call him Δία[50] as the cause [δι' ὃν] of all things; Ζῆνα[51] insofar as he is responsible for, or pervades, life [ζῆν]; Athena because his commanding faculty stretches into the aether; Hera because it stretches into the air; Hephaistos because it stretches to designing fire; Poseidon because it stretches to the sea; and Demeter because it stretches to the earth. And likewise also, did they assign the other names [προσηγορίας], holding to a certain kinship among them. (*HP* 54A = D. L. 7.147)

We see here a tendency to read behind names a single unified divine presence. One can see a similar position already implied in the epithet "many-named" [πολυώνυμε] that Cleanthes attributes to Zeus at the very earliest stages of Stoic thinking (*HP* 54I). Here Cleanthes transforms a traditional Greek invocation of a god as having many powers, and in that sense many names, into the Stoic push toward a consolidation of all the Greek gods as manifestations of a single logos. But the passage above does not differ materially from passages cited earlier in which the divine pneuma takes on different names owing to a difference in how it manifests itself. Also, the use of the term προσηγορία, which we saw in the passage from Aetius (*HP* 46A), is significant. Diogenes Laertius elsewhere tells us that this term specifically refers to that part of language that designates the Stoics' "common qualities," like "horse" or "man" (33M), reinforcing the idea that here the gods are no longer their traditional individual selves. This is further evidence for the suggestion that I made above: when we designate things like "Athena" or "Poseidon" or "horse" or "man," we are in reality saying "the divine pneuma insofar as it has taken on the quality this term names."

Semantic Possibilities in a Unified World: Naturalism without Essentialism

As opposed to the evidence from Galen, Theon, and Diogenes Laertius, which has logical and rhetorical concerns primarily in mind, these considerations and this evidence suggest precisely a "natural" ambiguity of language that goes farther than the notion of a name designating itself. When one approaches the issue from the Stoics' urge to interpret, whether by allegory, etymology, or both, each word aims at a thing that is always dual in nature. All existing things manifest the pneuma dwelling within them, and all words, therefore, have always *another* referent. Taking into

[50] One form of Zeus in the accusative case.

[51] A variant form of Zeus in the accusative.

account their unique ontology, then, we can find a way in which Stoic ideas of naturalism and ambiguity are compatible, for they are both attributable to what I have called their universalist materialism. The Stoics displace our sense of exhaustively capturing a thing through a designation of it either as an essence with provisional attributes attached to it or as some manifestation of an ontologically prior form. They propose in its place a naturalism without essentialism. Our words carry their intellectual content in their very nature as pneumatic configurations, but the indication of essence is something no single word can do. To do this the word would have to lay bare the collective logos itself, that is, the collective language that is the divine pneuma itself.[52]

The Symbol, the "Shift," and Chrysippus's Allegoresis

These considerations of Stoic theories of language and being give us a way to understand Chrysippus's method of reading and in particular his use of the σύμβολον as his central critical category to discuss Hesiod's story of the birth of Athena. Chrysippus's symbol is marked by changes in sense, but it is slightly more complicated than the substitutional logic of the enigma of classical allegory. Chrysippus classifies the story of Zeus swallowing Metis and giving birth to Athena through his head as symbolizing that the reasoning part of the soul lies in the chest, though his opponents mistakenly think it symbolizes that the reasoning part is in the head. Chrysippus leaves behind a thin reed of a comment: "very many of such shifts arise according to a symbol" [τῶν τοιούτων παραλλαγῶν κατὰ σύμβολον γινομένων πλειόνων]. Here the term παραλλαγή [shift] is the extent of Chrysippus's gloss on what he might mean by his literary term σύμβολον, but the background of Stoic linguistic and ontological thought that we just reconstructed puts us in a position to go somewhat further.

Our most illuminating evidence comes from the two passages in Aetius that we have already considered. These texts set Chrysippus's term for shift, παραλλαγή, and a cognate, παράλλαξις, right in the context of the larger Stoic vision of a language formed over the pneuma. Aetius told us that the rush of pneuma "alters its names by shifts of location" [ταῖς τῶν τόπων δὲ παραλλαγαῖς τὰς ἐπωνυμίας παραλλάττουσαν]. He elsewhere makes the same point more generally, discussing the pneuma which "takes on different names owing to the shifts of the matter through which it passes" [τὰς δὲ προσηγορίας μεταλαμβάνον κατὰ τὰς τῆς ὕλης, δι' ἧς κεχώρηκε, παραλλάξεις] (Aetius *Plac.* 1.7.33). These passages link Chrysippus's notion of the shifts of meaning that take place

[52] On this, see esp. Most, 2028.

in figurative literary constructions directly to Stoic views on the ontological unity that underlies the variety of manifested things, connecting things that might otherwise be thought of as distinct. When the symbol shifts its sense, it is retracing the normal path of language, by which different names are doled out as the pneuma makes its way from place to place. The symbol points back across these ontological subcurrents, making semantic connections in and through ontological ones.

Returning to the Chrysippus passage to test this hypothesis, we see that he provides evidence in his interpretation of Hesiod that accords with it. At several points in his interpretation, Chrysippus uses the common word *logos*. Twice Chrysippus says we use two different words "according to the same logos," for example, "swallowing" and "comprehending." It is possible to translate the logos in this context in a standard sense. We would arrive at something like "we say 'swallowing' by the same reasoning that we say 'comprehending.'" But given the central position the concept of logos holds in nearly all corners of Stoicism, especially in the context of their thinking on language and ontology, a more apposite technical sense is likely here. The same logos (as in one of the *spermatikoi logoi* that underlie existing things) manifests itself differently in different matter. Swallowing and comprehending, on this reading, would both be manifestations of the same logos, or divine underlying principle. When a particular logos (a material configuration of pneuma) manifests itself with respect to the mental faculty, it is a comprehension, when that same configuration manifests itself with respect to digestion, it is an act of swallowing. Shifts between related parts of the world, then, happen according to the logoi (which when taken collectively, Aetius tells us, are the divine pneuma)[53] that we know to underlie the various manifestations of reality. The trick for the reader, on this understanding, is to trace the logoi that tie things together. This project amounts to reading the suffusing immanence of the divine.

Within the context of his literary interpretation, Chrysippus would have insisted (we can assume) that the connection between the bare story of Athena's birth and its underlying meaning is not subject to the agreement of members of a language group but inheres naturally, buried in the order of things. For Chrysippus, it is true, the group of language users and myth readers came to a collective conclusion about the meanings of particular words and myths, but this is not a process of consensual agreement, where one thing could work just as well as another. The meanings that people find collectively are those revealed, by nature, through the logos. After all, the Stoics firmly trusted in our collective ability to recognize the true characteristics of things through our senses.

[53] *SVF* 2.1027, part.

Following this trust, language and myth would be good evidence to use in investigations of the true nature of the world, since traditional myths and language itself amount to a kind of distilled empiricism. They represent the collective observations of mythmakers and language users, accreted over time and handed down to the present. I have not found this opinion expressed explicitly in the sources, but it would have been available to Chrysippus if he were challenged. And his critics do not fault him for a lack of ingenuity.[54]

While it is difficult to claim these considerations make a definitive case for how to read Chrysippus's sense-shifting symbol, definitiveness is something of a fantasy when dealing with so fragmentary a record. Chrysippus surely had at his disposal a synthetic and powerful understanding for the way a literary "symbol" might indicate multiple referents. The pneuma within each thing has a material connection with the pneuma within other things and so forms an ontological basis for semantic links. It is also worthwhile to note that despite the vast expanses of time that separate them, such a theory is broadly consistent with the linguistic position that we saw in the Derveni commentator, and also with later developments in Neoplatonism, where the record is exponentially fuller. In all three of these critical clusters of allegorical texts, some hint of *ontological* linkage between surface referent and underlying referent forms the basis for a claim of polyvalence and a justification for expansive interpretive claims.

As we have seen, Aristotle had used the term "symbol" in a linguistic context, specifically to designate a word whose meaning is established by convention rather than by nature itself. Allegorical appropriation of the term in this context amounts to an attack (though likely an unintentional one) on the conventional theory of meaning in language. The subsequent history attests that the allegorical views of the symbol win this battle. Within two hundred years of Chrysippus, the σύμβολον becomes a common feature of the allegorists' critical vocabulary, but almost never appears in a substantive way in the work of literary critics in the Aristotelian rhetorical tradition.

[54] If indeed the Stoics made this valuation of language and myth as a whole—as a "text" in which we might read the deep meanings of the world and of human experience—it finds echoes in the contemporary approaches to myth of the Freudian, structuralist, and Eliadean schools.

4

SWALLOWED CHILDREN AND BOUND GODS: THE DIFFUSION OF THE LITERARY SYMBOL

When I began to write my history I was inclined to count these legends as foolishness, but on getting as far as Arcadia I grew to hold a more thoughtful view of them, which is this. In the days of old those Greeks who were considered wise spoke their sayings not straight out but in enigmas [δι᾽ αἰνιγμάτων], and so the legends about Kronos I conjectured to be one sort of Greek wisdom.

—Pausanias 8.8.3

IN THE first and second centuries C.E. we have abundant evidence of a broad diffusion of an allegorical approach to reading the poets. Writers as diverse as Pausanias, Maximus of Tyre, and Dio Chrysostom show that an allegorical understanding of the ancient tales was simply ready at hand during this period,[1] and several contemporary allegorical tracts survive as well. Cornutus, Heraclitus the Allegorist, and Pseudo-Plutarch (the *Life of Homer* author) show that different fields of inquiry were putting allegorical tools to use. They also all attest that the literary symbol, of which Chrysippus gives us our first direct testimony, has become a feature of the conceptual terrain, though the enigma still stands out as the dominant one. These writers represent a transition period in the life of the literary symbol, as it passes from one great philosophical movement, Stoicism, to another, Neoplatonism. Cornutus, who can be classified as a Stoic, writes a work that investigates the nature of the Greek gods. Heraclitus and Pseudo-Plutarch show no particular affiliation to a philosophical school. They both write tracts of literary commentary meant to demonstrate what they see as Homer's greatness. Both display some aspects of the literary-critical approach that grew out of the rhetorical tradition (Pseudo-Plutarch more promi-

[1] Specifics abound. For general characterizations see Dio Chrysostom (40–120 C.E.) *Orationes* 53.3–5; and Maximus of Tyre (125–85 C.E.) *Dissertationes* 4, 10, 26, 32, 37.

nently) and so testify to a continuing cross-fertilization of interpretive methods. The allegorical interpretation of this period owes a debt to the Stoics, and the symbol is a part of this inheritance.[2] A brief look at the work of these figures will testify to a diffuse tradition of symbolic reading in the early imperial period. The larger ontological positions that underwrite the symbol's grand signifying power in Chrysippus are likely only faint memories for these later thinkers. While Cornutus seems to have some familiarity with the details of Stoic physics, Heraclitus and Pseudo-Plutarch show only a gentleman's understanding. In these texts the Stoic symbol drifts away from the ontological positions within which it makes sense, but such intricacies matter little as a tradition of reading marches on, carried forward by a common sense that allows it. Great and sometimes counterintuitive shifts in meaning remain possible under the symbol's sway. The next major development awaits a later group of theorists, the Neoplatonists, who will reenergize the symbol within an entirely new ontological scheme.

Allegorical Sophistication in Later Stoics: Cornutus

Cornutus's full name, Lucius Annaeus Cornutus, suggests he was a freedman either of Seneca the Elder or of one of his relatives.[3] He was tutor to two eminent poets of the Silver Age, Lucan and the satirist Persius. Nero himself is said to have gone to him for literary advice (Dio Cassius 62.29.2). That Cornutus was reluctant to provide it may have provided

[2] The consensus remains that Apollodorus is the most important common figure behind these works. An Alexandrian and pupil of Aristarchus, Apollodorus later moves to Pergamum in 144 B.C.E. He wrote a treatise called *On the Gods,* which survives only in somewhat speculative fragments. Robert Münzel, *De Apollodori περὶ θεῶν libris* (Bonn, 1883) showed that several passages of Heraclitus, Macrobius, and Cornutus resemble the work of Apollodorus. Heraclitus's etymologies of Apollo are taken entirely from Apollodorus; Heraclitus himself says so in chap. 7 (Félix Buffière, introduction to Héraclite, *Allégories d'Homère* [Paris, 1962], xxix–xxxvii). For a summary of the scholarship, see C. L. Thompson, "Stoic Allegory of Homer: A Critical Analysis of Heraclitus' *Homeric Allegories*" (diss., Yale University, 1973), 10–13, 155–62. It is possible also to find links between these allegorists of the first two centuries C.E. and very early Stoic readings. For example, Cornutus recapitulates Cleanthes' textual emendation, made on allegorical grounds, of the description of Atlas at *Odyssey* 1.52. Cleanthes reads ὀλοόφρονος as though the initial omicron were rough. The resulting word, ὁλοόφρονος, makes Atlas "all-knowing" and not "with mischief in mind," a change consonant with Cleanthes' allegorization of Atlas as providence. Cornutus recapitulates this intricate reading (Cleanthes *SVF* 1.549; Cornutus chap. 26).

[3] See Robert Stephen Hays, "Lucius Annaeus Cornutus's 'Epidrome' (Introduction to the Traditions of Greek Theology): Introduction, Translation, and Notes" (diss., University of Texas at Austin, 1983), 30. Cornutus's text is referenced by several names in modern scholarship. I will be using *Compendium*, as this is becoming standard.

the grounds for his exile, in 63, 64, or 65, though his close relationships with Stoic anti-Neronians, like Lucan, probably had more to do with it. His *Compendium of Greek Theology* follows in the well-established Stoic tradition of using allegorical commentary on the poets to explore the nature of the gods. Written several centuries after the founding of the Stoic school, it is the only Stoic tract dealing with the interpretation of poetry that survives in toto. Cornutus's text is unique and most useful. He makes no pretense to being original, saying at one point that he is only summarizing the work of his predecessors (chap. 35; 76.6–9).[4] Furthermore, since his stated purpose is to provide his younger students with a handbook on the topic, the text assumes no expertise on the part of its reader.[5] We have fewer minutiae to sift through, and get rather straightforward statements of theory and interpretive method.

Cornutus as a Literary Commentator

Cornutus arranges his chapters into treatments of individual divinities. As others have stressed, he analyzes all the available sources on traditional divinities, including the visual arts, popular beliefs, cult epithets, and cult practices.[6] This is consonant with Balbus's prescription in Cicero's *De natura deorum* that the pious Stoic should study assiduously *all* traditional information on the gods, including lore and ritual. This practice of using interpretation to mine all sorts of cultural data will carry on into the Neoplatonists. Cornutus's readings of the cultic and iconographic elements of the gods demonstrate the basic approach. The vulture is characteristic of Ares because he is loud, scary, and affiliated with death (41.15), the swan is characteristic of Apollo, while the crow is alien to him (68.9–10); boxwood [πύξος] has an affiliation with Aphrodite because her devotees enjoy her posterior (πυγή) (46.18–47.1). Palm has meaningful characteristics too. It is appropriate to the Muses because it is delicate, productive, perennial, and hard to climb, and it bears sweet fruit (18.9–13). Olive oil has a resonance with virgin Athena because it does not mix with other things (38.20). Laurel, which is evergreen, combustible, and purifying, is appropriate for the purest and

[4] Page and line references to C. Lang, ed., *Cornuti Theologiae Graecae compendium* (Leipzig: Teubner, 1881). I give chapter references in addition when thematic issues are at stake as well as philogical ones.

[5] See chap. 35; 76.2. He addresses his reader as "my child" and follows a didactic course.

[6] Glenn Most, "Cornutus and Stoic Allegoresis," *ANRW* 2.36.3 (1989). See also Hays, 34. Plato is a precursor to Cornutus in reading religious cult allegorically. As we saw above (chap. 1), Socrates, without a trace of irony, tells us that the ancients who established the mysteries riddled a deeper message in the rites (*Phaedo* 69c).

most consuming god, Apollo (68.11). These examples from Cornutus attest to a new readability of the world: portions of it have meaning in and through their affinities with divinities. We will see this approach to the world recapitulated and deepened in various magical and ritual texts in the later periods. The greater part of Cornutus's information on the gods, however, and all of his textual evidence come from the traditional myths as passed on by the poets.[7] He refers to Homer and Hesiod fourteen times in his thirty-five chapters (eight by name, and Homer six times as "the poet"); direct quotations of these poets and others abound; and the only strictly theoretical section of the text (chap. 17), where Cornutus spells out his method, directly concerns the allegorical reading of the poets. As we will see, he prominently situates the symbol within his hermeneutical language.

Cornutus as Allegorist

Though Cornutus's vocabulary is relatively plain and direct, as befits his audience, it is marked by the standard concepts of allegorical reading. He makes use of αἴνιγμα cognates, which appear eleven times in his treatise, always in the sense of a poetic scene, name, or description that hints at a deeper meaning.[8] When Zeus overturns Kronos, for example, the poet is suggesting that order has triumphed over chaos in the cosmos (7.21). Though they have widely different philosophical and theological positions, Cornutus and the Derveni commentator both see αἰνίγματα as deeply resonant poetic images that carry hidden messages about the gods, the cosmos, or the place of humans in the world. The term ὑπόνοια makes only a single appearance in Cornutus (74.3). The term ἀλληγορία does not appear at all, but we should not necessarily have expected it, for Plutarch, two generations later, tells us that ἀλληγορία is a neologism.[9] More significant for our purposes, however, σύμβολον appears repeatedly. In this text a "symbol" seems especially to mark the accouterments of particular deities, which are interpretable codes of their qualities: the *skeptron* is a symbol of Zeus's reign (10.11); the serpents on Hermes' staff are a symbol that even beastly men are subdued by him (22.20); Asclepius's staff is a symbol of something like "caring" (70.13); each of Hercules' traditional emblems is a symbol of strength and noble birth (63.19). The more general characteristics of deities are also "symbols": Athena's virginity is a symbol of her purity

[7] Even the one philosopher he cites, Cleanthes, writes in verse (64.16).

[8] Cornutus *Compendium* 2.8, 7.21, 28.1, 28.1, 30.7, 32.14, 50.14, 55.1, 62.11, 65.4, 76.5.

[9] *On How to Read the Poets* 19f.

(36.9); that the Muses are female is a symbol of the fact that erudition comes from being indoors (15.11). We also find elements of ritual praxis called symbols: people place stones on a herm as a symbol that the world is made up of small parts (25.1); the collective attendants of Dionysus are a symbol of the playfulness and ecstasy of drink (59.7). The symbol as divine accouterment occupies a mediating position between the divine and human realms. It is a thing from this world that is affiliated with a being from beyond. This is in keeping with the older tradition we have seen, the symbol as divine omen, and is actually a precursor of later developments that are possible in the distinctive ontology of the Neoplatonists. Even more important, though, Cornutus makes the symbol, here right alongside αἴνιγμα, the centerpiece of his most explicit statement:

> And so, my child, it is my hope that you may be able in this same way to take the other things which have been handed down to us in mythical form, ostensibly about the gods, and may refer them to the elementary models that I have taught you, convinced that the men of antiquity were no common men,[10] but that they were competent to understand the nature of the cosmos and were inclined to make philosophical statements about it through symbols and riddles.
>
> Οὕτω δ' ἂν ἤδη καὶ τἆλλα τῶν μυθικῶς παραδεδόσθαι περὶ θεῶν δοκούντων ἀναγαγεῖν ἐπὶ τὰ παραδεδειγμένα στοιχεῖα, ὦ παῖ, δύναιο, πεισθεὶς ὅτι οὐχ οἱ τυχόντες ἐγένοντο οἱ παλαιοί, ἀλλὰ καὶ συνιέναι τὴν τοῦ κόσμου φύσιν ἱκανοὶ καὶ πρὸς τὸ διὰ συμβόλων καὶ αἰνιγμάτων φιλοσοφῆσαι[11] περὶ αὐτῆς εὐεπίφοροι. (chap. 35; 75.18–76.5)

These remarks appear as the closing, summary statement of the handbook. Cornutus equates σύμβολα and αἰνίγματα, the first explicit attestation of a relationship between the two terms that will endure in allegorical reading through late antiquity. We have seen that late classical testimony suggests that the two terms were perhaps synonyms as early as the mid-fourth century,[12] and we will find them paired again by later readers (like Porphyry). A common formulation will be that the poet riddles his meaning through symbols [αἰνίττεται διὰ συμβόλων].

[10] As Most ("Cornutus and Stoic Allegoresis") has pointed out, this is in direct contradiction to Aristotle *Pol.* 2.1269a4–8. It seems to be the doctrine of later Stoics and suggests an earlier age of greatness from which the current period has slipped. It is in tension with earlier Stoic meliorism that saw the advancing fire that periodically consumes the world as a good thing.

[11] Strabo also associates a cognate of this term with allegory (Strabo 1.2.17, cited above, p. 118, n. 16).

[12] Plato *Rep.* 1.322b, considered in tandem with Demosthenes *Against Aristocrates* 83. See above, chap. 2.

While almost all of the allegorical critics foreground some variation of the formula when they are stating their approach, it is utterly absent from the extant tracts of the rhetorical critics.

We will gain a better understanding of what Cornutus has in mind for symbols and riddles by taking a closer look at one representative example of his interpretation of poetry and cult, his treatment of Rhea and Kronos (chaps. 6 and 7). Following a reading that is documented from Plato's time (*Crat.* 402a), Cornutus says (on the basis of a pun) that Rhea suggests a kind of flow [ῥύσις], based on her association with rain.[13] In the cultic celebration of Rhea, drums, cymbals, horns, and torch processions create a racket and a flashing like thunder and lightning, further allying her with the flowing rain. The eponym "Ida" comes from the mountain, and Rhea is associated with mountains because the rain comes splashing down from there. They call her a mountain dweller and also associate the wild beasts of the mountains with her because storms have a rather wild look. She is similar to the Syrian goddess Atargatis, whom the people honor by abstaining from doves and fish, since things that fly or swim are especially flowing. The Syrian goddess is worshiped by the castrated priesthood of the Galli. Cornutus reads in these priests an explanation of the castration of Ouranos (though he does not give any detail). Kronos then eats up Rhea's children because, through a pun, Kronos is time [*chronos*], and the things that come into being through time are also consumed by it.[14] But Rhea gives him a stone to swallow instead of Zeus and this again is to be taken allegorically [ἄλλως εἴληπται]. For the myth truly concerns the beginning of the world, at which time the nature that governs it (Zeus) comes to maturity. This can take place only after the stone, meaning the earth, is swallowed and firmly fixed,[15] for all things come into being by being propped up on earth as a foundation. Next, Cornutus, out of

[13] Cornutus is fond of using etymological analysis to riddle out the hidden meanings in poetic texts and cultic practices. The allegorists' etymologies rarely stand up to modern scholarly standards, as modern scholars are fond of pointing out. But Stoic etymology springs logically from the Stoic theory of naturalism. (See above, p. 137.) If units of speech have natural meanings, then the sounds that make up proper names will be seen to have an indwelling intellectual content, and the pieces of which words are made up will as well. Rather than tracing a history of words, Stoic etymologies aim at a dissection of them and a determination of their nature.

[14] Balbus offers the same reading of the story a hundred years earlier in Cicero's *De natura deorum* (2.60–71).

[15] There is a resonance here with Orphic cosmogonies, like the one the Derveni Papyrus comments on. In these, Zeus swallows Phanes (or perhaps sometimes the genitals he has severed from Kronos), and the entire world gestates from inside Zeus's stomach/womb. The Derveni commentator also believes his cosmogony story is an enigma for a hidden meaning (see chap. 1).

sequence, takes up the castration of Ouranos. Since Ouranos kept descending to have sex with Earth, Kronos castrated him. But then Zeus binds Kronos and casts him down to Tartarus. Through these events, the poets hint enigmatically [αἰνίττονται] at deeper truths. In the castration of Ouranos, Kronos, who is the early order of the universe, stopped up the flow of the material surrounding the earth that (according to Stoic physics) condensed by pressing into it. In Cornutus's reckoning, Kronos initiates an outward flow of rarefied matter back from the dense earth into the air. The castration marks the beginning of the earth's "fighting back," as it were, against the pressure of the condensing material that surrounded it. After a time, Zeus intervenes to put a stop to the earth's counterattacking outward flow. He puts it into bonds and thereby produces an equilibrium.

In relation to cultic practices, Cornutus repeats a sentiment we heard from Cicero's Stoic spokesman in the *De natura deorum*. Like Balbus, Cornutus feels the need to team his bold interpretations of cult with prohibitions against "superstition." The conclusion of his treatise seems to warn us not to misunderstand him as promoting an overly zealous approach to traditional cultic practices:

> As to the myths and the worship of the gods and the things that are properly honored, accept both the traditions of the fathers and the complete account of them in the following way only: that young men be introduced to piety but not to superstition and be taught to sacrifice, pray, worship, and take oaths in a proper manner and according to fitting moderation in whatever situation arises.
>
> περὶ δὲ ἐκείνων καὶ περὶ τῆς θεραπείας τῶν θεῶν καὶ τῶν οἰκείως εἰς τιμὴν αὐτῶν γινομένων καὶ τὰ πάτρια καὶ τὸν ἐντελῆ λήψῃ λόγον οὕτω μόνον ὡς εἰς τὸ εὐσεβεῖν ἀλλὰ μὴ εἰς τὸ δεισιδαιμονεῖν εἰσαγομένων τῶν νέων καὶ θύειν τε καὶ εὔχεσθαι καὶ προσκυνεῖν καὶ ὀμνύειν κατὰ τρόπον καὶ ἐν τοῖς ἐμβάλλουσι καιροῖς καθ' ἣν ἁρμόττει συμμετρίαν διδασκομένων. (chap. 35; 76.9–17)

Stoic allegorical approaches regularly exhibit such a concern to distinguish what is learned in reading the myths from superstition. We have seen it articulated already by Balbus in the *De natura deorum*.[16] These anxieties are perhaps further indication that such reading tends to take on a devotional character, which the scholarly Cornutus and his Stoic peers embrace but are careful to distinguish from mere ritualism. We have seen such a devotional character (contrasted with mere ritualism) in the Derveni commentator and will see it again in the Neoplatonists.

[16] See above, chap. 3.

An embrace of the sacramental dimension of allegorical reading comes out most strongly in late figures like Proclus and Pseudo-Dionysius.

Cornutus and Authorial Intention: The Invention of Mythic Truth

The sources leave us without much information on the early allegorists' approach to the question of authorial intention. Was it important to them? Did they think the poets had deeper truths in mind when they composed their stories? Did these truths originate with the poets, or did they retell myths in which a hidden meaning already resided? Or perhaps something more diffuse was at work. In the case of Chrysippus, perhaps the logos itself manifests the truths that come through the writings of the poets; that is, the total system of reason/language (logos) makes itself known through the poets as the deep structure of the cosmos. We are able to direct such questions more fruitfully to Cornutus than to earlier allegorists. Chapter 17, "On the Traditional Myths," his only explicitly theoretical chapter, concerns the interpretation of poetry and expands our understanding of what this later Stoic understood as the principles behind allegorism. Cornutus attests to the distinction between poetry and traditional mythology that Cicero also attributes to the Stoics (cf. *De nat. deor.* 2.70):

> One must not conflate the myths or transfer the names from one to another; nor ought the myths be considered irrational if something has been plastered onto the genealogies which have been handed down in the myths by people who do not understand the message they hint at enigmatically, but use them as if they were mere fabrications.
>
> Δεῖ δὲ μὴ συγχεῖν τοὺς μύθους μηδ' ἐξ ἑτέρου τὰ ὀνόματα ἐφ' ἕτερον μεταφέρειν μηδ' εἴ τι προσεπλάσθη ταῖς παραδεδομέναις κατ' αὐτοὺς γενεαλογίαις ὑπὸ τῶν μὴ συνιέντων ἃ αἰνίττονται, κεχρημένων δ' αὐτοῖς ὡς καὶ τοῖς πλάσμασιν, ἀλόγως τίθεσθαι. (chap. 17; 27.19–28.2)

The poets, he claims, worked with preexisting mythic materials. Ancient mythmakers saw the deep truths of the world and then transmitted them through stories that contained enigmas of the structure of the cosmos. Earlier in chapter 17, Cornutus labels as a "fragment" [ἀπόσπασμα] (26.17) the nugget of truth that the poet passes on in his reconfiguration of the myth. If the poets mishandle the myths, a possibility Cornutus is perfectly willing to allow,[17] we should not dismiss the

[17] He expresses differences with Hesiod at the end of chap. 17: "There might be a more perfect interpretation than Hesiod's. For I think that he has transmitted some things from

myths themselves. Cornutus suggests a complex understanding of myth as cultural artifact, which the poets transmit.

The poet, then, becomes a conduit for a truth that is anchored by an ancient mythmaker, and the poet may or may not have understood the hidden wisdom contained in his material. Two points should be made here. First, this vision of the poet radically differs from that of the Aristotelian tradition, where the poet is the sovereign master of the meaning in his text. Secondly, Cornutus introduces an innovative category of what we might call "mythic truth." That "ancient" was equated with "true" was not a radical idea among the Greeks. But that a primeval "μῦθος" (meaning a story, usually in the sense of a "tall tale"),[18] which existed before the age of Homer and Hesiod, was the favored vehicle for these truths—this was a radical idea.[19] From the (admittedly thin) evidence we have, it appears that the pre-Stoic allegorists identified and revered the genius poet as the font of truth.[20] But Cornutus attests to a different stance. Ancient and now nameless fonts of wisdom encoded their accurate knowledge of the world in μῦθοι, using the language of enigmas and symbols, which we receive through potentially garbled lines of transmission. The "mythic," for the first time in serious Greek thought, becomes a privileged source of true scientific insight, and the "symbol" is one of its privileged vehicles. This idea was certainly operative at some level in Chrysippus's work, but, as we saw in chapter 2, the sources do not tell us that he thought of the truths to be gleaned from poetry as belonging specifically to "myth," rather than, say, the accurate observations of a particular poet.

Cornutus alludes to an earlier time, accessible to the present only in broken pieces, when people saw things more clearly than they do today, but he does not tell us much about these ancient seers. What was their special access to the truths they riddled for posterity? Why do they communicate their messages in symbols and not straightforwardly? No clear

---

the ancients, but has added other things of a more mythical nature from his own imagination. In this fashion he corrupted a great deal of ancient theology" (31.12–18).

[18] See, for example, Plato *Gorgias* 523A: "Listen, then, as they say, to a beautiful story, which you will consider a myth [μῦθος], I think, but which I consider an actual account [λόγος], for the things which I am about to tell, I will tell as the truth [ὡς ἀληθῆ].

[19] We see it also at Theon Rhetor *Progymnasmata* 3 (first or second century C.E.). At *Metaphys*. 1074b1–15, Aristotle forwards a similar theory, which Tate suggests might be a precedent for the Stoics. But Aristotle only briefly considers the idea and does not follow it up in the rest of his work; further, it is not at all clear that Aristotle divides myth from poetry. He refers only to "the ancients."

[20] The Derveni commentator certainly does this, and the caricatured allegorists that Plato lampoons venerate Homer as a one-man encyclopedia, with guaranteed knowledge of everything. The fragments of the early allegorists are too scant to form a solid conclusion but they seem to indicate the poet as the source of his poems' *huponoiai*.

answers survive on these points. But, as I suggested with regard to Chrysippus, he may believe that myth, like language, is a kind of distilled empiricism, which encapsulates the wisdom of generations.[21] Cornutus (or the earlier Stoics whose works he summarizes) is our first attestation of an "originalist" theory of mythic meaning. This densely significant, mythic material was the special province of the poetic arts, but one can also see it refracted through cultic tradition. The Stoics appear to be the first in a long chain of advocates of this idea in the history of respectable philosophy.[22] The view provides a theoretical foundation for the allegorists' traditional claim that the poem is primarily a vehicle for profound truths about the cosmos and our place in it.[23] Furthermore, and most interestingly for the purposes of this study, Cornutus designates "symbols" as a mode of transmission.

Heraclitus the Allegorist

Heraclitus, the author of a tract called the *Homeric Allegories*, is difficult to attach to a single philosophical tradition. He mentions Platonists, Epicureans, and Stoics but does not include himself among any of these groups.[24] His most marked affiliation is with Homer. Unlike the more nuanced theory of Cornutus, and the Stoic tradition he represents, Heraclitus states that Homer intended globally to communicate hidden pieces of wisdom about the cosmos. Whereas Cornutus sometimes criticizes the poets for retelling a tale with a nugget of truth in a misguided manner, Heraclitus insists from the outset that *nothing* in Homer is to be considered misguided, because he is, at any of these questionable points, using allegory (chap. 1). Perhaps this means that Heraclitus was a credulous critic, but more likely it means that he was writing in a polemical climate. Overbold statements of this sort are commonplace in ancient literary debate. We have already mentioned Eratosthenes, who said that Homer could be expected to teach us *nothing*, and that his

[21] See chap. 3, p. 139, with reference to Most.

[22] One can find such a position rearticulated at many points in the literary and philosophical traditions of the West: we find it in Petrarch in the late Middle Ages, in Novalis during the Romantic period, and in Freud in modern times.

[23] In the end, Cornutus only pushes back to the "mythmakers" the question of the origin of this profound insight and the proclivity to transmit it enigmatically. But the theory is significant in that it *is* a theory, an explanation that the commentator felt the need to advance.

[24] Heraclitus levels his most flamboyant charges against Plato, Homer's sometime detractor. In wrapping up his treatise, he says Plato profaned the sacred and divine Muses when he invoked them in the *Phaedrus* (237a) to tell a story of pederasty rather than one of great heroes and deep philosophical truths, such as Homer tells.

entire purpose was to entertain us (p. 22, n.2). Similarly, Plato's strictness in banishing the poets from his ideal Republic is sometimes explained not as his final word on the matter but as a hyperbolic debating strategy.

Heraclitus makes consistent use (though less frequent than Cornutus) of the conceptual vocabulary cognate with αἴνιγμα and σύμβολον, both of which appear here as terms generally marking allegorical interpretation.[25] Heraclitus does not show Cornutus's preference for using symbol to refer to divine accouterments but instead deploys it in a variety of contexts. When Homer calls the aether Zeus and the lower air Hades, he is using symbolic names as an allegory (37.3). Heraclitus of Ephesus also theologized through symbols (37.7). Since the lower fire among us (Hephaistos) needs wood to burn, Homer symbolically describes it as "lame" (41.5). There are many signs that the cosmos is round in Homer, but the clearest is the symbol of the making of Achilles' shield (70.10). Each shape that Proteus takes is an allegory of something else—when he is a tree, he is symbolically the air (86.15). The move to Hades is a move to the invisible, but even here Homer philosophically uses symbols to allegorize (98.2). But ἀλληγορία and its cognates are by far Heraclitus's preferred terms, appearing on nearly every page of the treatise (over sixty times in all). He is the first of our critics to make extensive use of the term. That he does not use the term ὑπόνοια conforms with Plutarch's testimony that the term "allegory" had come to replace it. But the prefix *hupo-* has survived in one significant term, ὑποσημαίνω, a word that does not appear among the other allegorists of this period but occurs ten times in his work and always as a synonym for ἀλληγορέω.

Heraclitus recapitulates a standard line in the repertoire of allegorists. He makes a contrast between himself and those who see only the surface fiction, missing the deeper meaning. He says that the latter kind of readers see merely fabrications [πλάσματα] in passages where the poets have in reality buried enigmatic truths. This formula will become a popular polemical characterization of those who do not read allegorically, who, the allegorists claim, miss the point.[26] In its standard sense, πλάσμα (from the verb πλάττω) indicates the creations of the plastic and

[25] αἴνιγμα cognates (7.6, 37.13, 57.7, 60.7, 81.9, 86.17, 94.21); σύμβολον cognates (37.3, 37.7, 41.5, 70.10, 86.15, 98.2). Page and line citations to F. Oelmann, ed., *Heracliti Quaestiones Homericae* (Leipzig: Teubner, 1910). For a modern translation, see Buffière, *Allégories d' Homère*.

[26] Heraclitus chap. 26 (40.6). Compare Porphyry *De antr.* 4. Eratosthenes (c. 275–194 B.C.E.), who advocated the position that it was foolish to think Homer had any other purpose than entertainment, also shows πλάσμα to have been in the vocabulary of this debate (Strabo 1.2.3, 1.2.17).

literary arts, something that has been shaped or molded. The semantic field of the term also neatly captures the difficulties of artistic representation that Plato had made so pointedly clear in the *Republic.* The term carries an additional sense of "forgery" or "fake," which the English term "fabrication" preserves. The allegorists will latch onto this range of meanings for πλάσμα when they oppose their view that the poets make symbols, enigmas, and allegories to the view that poets make "fabrications." This antithesis is a precursor of the later allegorists' claim that literary creations are somehow more than mere representations and will find an echo in the later and more significant opposition between symbols and μιμήματα. It is also interesting to note that the notion of metaphor plays very little part in the commentary of either Cornutus or Heraclitus. Heraclitus only once claims that Homer has produced a transfer of meaning via metaphor (73.4), and Cornutus finds no metaphors at all. (Critics in the rhetorical tradition reverse these tendencies and have a fondness for metaphor but rarely for enigma or symbol.)

While they had different approaches, there is no doubt that Cornutus and Heraclitus drew from the same pool of ideas. They share interpretations of many poetic scenes. When we add Pseudo-Plutarch to the mix, as we will in a moment, we see a diffuse tradition of allegorical reading in the period of the early Roman Empire, a tradition in which the literary "symbol" plays an important supporting part. Heraclitus and Cornutus show substantial overlap in many of their readings:[27] they agree, for example, on their interpretation of Hera,[28] the Prayers,[29] the Graces,[30] Hermes as logos,[31] Hephaistos (specifically, his wooden cane,[32] his expulsion from the heavens,[33] his binding of Ares[34]), Athena (her nature, etymology, virginity, and diverse surnames),[35] Poseidon,[36] Aphrodite,[37] Heracles,[38] Apollo (as sun and plague, his rays as arrows),[39] Hades and

[27] The following list expands a similar one in Buffière's introduction to his edition of Heraclitus, xxxi; numbers given are chapter references.

[28] Cornutus 3; Heraclitus 15.

[29] Cornutus 12; Heraclitus 37.

[30] Cornutus 15; Heraclitus 43.

[31] Cornutus 16; Heraclitus 73.

[32] Cornutus 19; Heraclitus 26. Plutarch uses this as an adage in his *The Face on the Moon* 922; cf. E-scholion at *Odyssey* 8.300.

[33] Cornutus 19; Heraclitus 26.

[34] Cornutus 19; Heraclitus 69.

[35] Cornutus 20; Heraclitus 19. On the etymology of her name, see also Philodemus *De pietate* col. 16; Plato *Cratylus* 407b.

[36] Cornutus 4, 22; Heraclitus 7, 25, 41.

[37] Cornutus 24, 19; Heraclitus 28, 30, 69.

[38] Cornutus 31; Heraclitus 33; see also Seneca *Moral Essays* 2 (*De Constantia*) 2.1.

[39] Cornutus 32; Heraclitus 6, 8.

the rivers in Hades,[40] and the binding of Zeus.[41] In addition Heraclitus shares other allegorical interpretations with earlier Stoics; for example, he repeats Cleanthes' reading of the prophylactic herb "moly," Odysseus's antidote to Circe's magic charms, as reason.[42]

Allegory as a Trope: Rhetorical and Allegorical Views

In a significant departure from most allegorists, Heraclitus defines allegory as a trope, presumably like metaphor, synecdoche, metonymy, etcetera: "The trope which says one thing but means something other than what one says is rightly called allegory" [Ὁ γὰρ ἄλλα μὲν ἀγορεύων τρόπος, ἕτερα δὲ ὧν λέγει σημαίνων, ἐπωνύμως ἀλληγορία καλεῖται] (5.15–6.1). Since he uses symbol and enigma synonymously with allegory, he presumably thinks of them as tropes too. He is an exception that highlights a significant rule. Allegorical readers rarely classify ἀλληγορία, αἴνιγμα, σύμβολον, or ὑπόνοια as individual tropes within larger schemes of tropes.[43] On the contrary, these terms generally serve them as a vocabulary to articulate the always receding, and to an extent untamable, meaning of a great poetic text. They do not mark out an intellectual map by which to classify particular turns of phrase and usually do not explicitly define or differentiate them. By contrast, Heraclitus's definition of ἀλληγορία (though, interestingly, not his use of the term) shares more in common with critics in the rhetorical tradition than with the other allegorists. Heraclitus's short, formulaic statement mirrors the rather straightforward definition of Quintilian in book 8 of the *Institutio Oratoria*, where allegory is said to be extended metaphor. Also dissonant with the other allegorists and consonant with rhetorical critics, Heraclitus cites an example (from outside the text at hand) to illustrate his definition—the very lines from Alcaeus that Horace uses as a basis for his ship-of-state allegory (Odes 1.14), and that Quintilian also cites in his definition of allegory.

Where Heraclitus differs from the rhetorical critics, though, is in the valuation of the trope. They typically mark allegory down for unclarity. Quintilian and Demetrius, echoing Aristotle, use αἴνιγμα as a term of censure: it is an allegory that has gone the way allegories tend to go, in

[40] Cornutus 35; Heraclitus 41, 74.

[41] Cornutus 17; Heraclitus 21, 25.

[42] Cleanthes *SVF* 1.526 (moly = *logos*); Heraclitus 73 (moly = *phronesis*).

[43] We have not seen this in the Derveni commentator, Chrysippus, or Cornutus and will see it again only in the first part of Pseudo-Plutarch's *Life of Homer*. In general, the allegorists do not match the rhetorical critics' often unsatisfactory attempts to classify the figurative modes of the poets schematically. See Quintilian's vague treatment of a long list of tropes at 8.6.

their view, toward incomprehensibility. As we saw in chapter 1, since clarity is a primary virtue of poetry for Aristotelian critics, murky riddles are not the honored mode of poetic discourse that they are for the allegorists. Quintilian puts the matter clearly, "An enigma is in my opinion to be regarded as a blemish, in view of the fact that lucidity is a virtue" [(Aenigma) vitium meo quidem iudicio si quidem dicere dilucide virtus] (8.52). Among the rhetorical critics, Demetrius has the most generous view of allegory. He asserts that ἀλληγορία can be useful in the "forceful" style of poetic discourse.[44] But he warns us in the next sentence that "excess is to be guarded against, lest the language become an enigma for us" [φυλάττεσθαι μέντοι κἀπὶ ταύτης τὸ συνεχές, ὡς μὴ αἴνιγμα ὁ λόγος ἡμῖν γένηται] (*On Style* 102). For the rhetoricians, then, allegory is primarily a trope, troublesome for its lack of clarity, which the skilled poet generally avoids. From Aristotle onward, they tend to define the αἴνιγμα as the most excessive case. On the contrary, allegorical readers do not usually set such notions within a scheme of tropes but instead use them without much distinction to indicate that the texts they read harbor secret wisdom. Heraclitus shows certain aspects of both approaches. Like the rhetorical critics, he views allegory as an individual turn of phrase, one of which Homer appears to be particularly fond. Also like the rhetorical critics, Heraclitus believes in Homer's total control over the text's meaning, a position sometimes absent, or at least nuanced, in allegorical readers. But more important are the characteristics Heraclitus shares with allegorical critics. He does indeed see Homer's text as a repository of wisdom, and as we said above, the wisdom he finds there often looks very much like what others in the allegorical tradition found.

Heraclitus and the Justification for Allegory

Whereas Cornutus left us in the dark as to why his mythmakers communicated their messages so obliquely, Heraclitus felt a need to explain why the ancients would have used the indirect means of poetry to convey their hidden messages about the cosmos. This may indicate that Heraclitus faced a more polemical audience, which would probably have been the case were he affiliated with a rhetorical school. One can only imagine the look on the face of a teacher training young orators if he discovered that one of his students had produced a work like the

[44] Significantly, Demetrius (whose dates are uncertain) is also the only one among the rhetorical critics to find a substantial role for poetic "symbols," which he includes along with allegories as useful in producing the forceful style (Demetrius 243). This style, which Demetrius adds to the three levels of style distinguished by Aristotle, is his own contribution to poetics in the Aristotelian mode.

Homeric Allegories. To explain why the poets didn't just transmit their meanings straightforwardly, Heraclitus tells us that we ought to remember that the philosophers themselves used to speak in an enigmatic style: Heraclitus of Ephesus (as we noted above) spoke through symbols [διὰ συμβόλων], and everything he said about nature he allegorized enigmatically [ὅλον τε τὸ περὶ φύσεως αἰνιγματῶδες ἀλληγορεῖ] (37.12–13). So did Empedocles. So if these philosophers spoke this way, why should we be surprised if the poets did? This method of justification is most interesting and will be revived, though with Pythagoras as the main prooftext, in the later Neoplatonic allegorists. The implication is that certain topics, especially what we might call the "deep structure" of the cosmos, simply demand oblique modes of discourse. We will find other justifications as the allegorical tradition continues.

Pseudo-Plutarch

The unknown author, probably of the second century C.E., who wrote the *Life of Homer*, a work passed down under the name of Plutarch, combines the approaches of rhetorical and allegorical criticism in a more striking way than Heraclitus does. Like Heraclitus, Pseudo-Plutarch is more a Homerist than a Platonist, Stoic, Peripatetic, or Epicurean. He too mentions these schools without affiliating himself with them. Until recently, this text has received little of the attention it deserves.[45] The neglect may be due, at least partly, to the credulity of Pseudo-Plutarch's claim that Homer had an encyclopedic range of knowledge. Pseudo-Plutarch presents his text as a demonstration that Homer provides the seeds of *all* later forms of discourse, including skill in the use of language, as well as the major insights of the philosophers, rhetoricians, politicians, medical doctors, artisans, and others. As was the case with Heraclitus, we ought to place this grandiose introduction in the context of the time. That the *Life of Homer*, like Heraclitus's *Allegories*, begins from such a strong premise is likely polemical bluster.

However we evaluate his overall project, Pseudo-Plutarch adds to Heraclitus's testimony that allegorical commentary had mingled thoroughly with other approaches to reading poetry during the early Roman

[45] A text, with an English translation, introduction, and commentary, was published by J. J. Keaney and Robert Lamberton in 1996; [Plutarch], *Life of Homer*, American Philological Association, American Classical Studies, no. 40 (Atlanta: Scholars Press, 1996). This is a much welcomed development, and the first such translation to appear. The following discussion is indebted to their work. Specific chapter and section citations below are to *[Plutarchi] De Homero*, ed. J. F. Kindstrand (Leipzig: Teubner, 1990), whose excellent edition appeared as the Keaney and Lamberton text was being produced. All discussion below pertains to the longer *Life* [B].

Empire. Pseudo-Plutarch does not make use of the term symbol in its allegorical context,[46] and this, along with Heraclitus's clear preference for allegory, prevents any overbold statement about the literary symbol's general prominence in this period. But Pseudo-Plutarch does provide relevant information on several issues. First, he offers uniquely clear evidence of two approaches coexisting in a single critic's work. He uses both a poetics in the Aristotelian analytical mode and another that is more allegorical and focused on interpretation. Next, his arrangement of material gives an early example of the relation between these approaches that we will come upon later in Porphyry as well. And finally, he introduces new justifications for the allegorical approach to the literary text, which he attaches to the notion of enigma and which will reverberate through the later history of the literary symbol.

The *Life of Homer* text shows, with unique clarity, the distinctive (and, in Pseudo-Plutarch's understanding, complementary) characteristics of Aristotelian and allegorical criticism. The practice of producing "lives" of the poets was common among Peripatetics,[47] and he shows a clear mastery of the methods for analyzing poetry that they developed. In the first 90 of his 218 chapters, Pseudo-Plutarch puts on display his familiarity with the various aspects of Aristotle's approach. He covers these standard topics: classification of meter (7); Homer's use of diction from various dialects (8–12); classifications of tropes (16–26); classification of figures, like pleonasm, homoioteleuton, ellipsis, and (he here briefly mentions) allegory (27–71); Homer's levels of style (72); and his mode of evoking character, place, and time (passim). Interestingly, in this part of his commentary, Pseudo-Plutarch defines allegory as a figure among the other tropes and figures, as Heraclitus had. He also defines it, as Heraclitus did, with a short, self-contained example, citing *Odyssey* 22.195–96, where Eumaios binds up a suitor and then mocks him: "Now the whole night long, Melanthios, you shall keep watch wakefully, laid, as you deserve, to rest on a soft bed" (70). The example and this section of the treatise allies allegory closely with sarcasm and irony, circumscribing its relevance to particular turns of phrase. But when allegory and enigma are put to use as categories of interpretation in the second part of the treatise, they quickly outgrow these narrow boundaries.

At about the midpoint of the treatise, after chapter 90, the author

[46] He uses σύμβολον only as the name for divination from overhearing random sayings (which we discussed in chap. 2) and not as a tool of literary interpretation.

[47] On the Peripatetic biographical interest in the poets, see George A. Kennedy, "Hellenistic Literary and Philosophical Scholarship," in *The Cambridge History of Literary Criticism*, vol. 1, *Classical Criticism*, ed. George A. Kennedy (New York: Cambridge University Press, 1989), 205.

makes a change. He shifts from examining Homer's mastery of the various genera of "diction" (using Lamberton's schema), which I understand as the Aristotelian-inspired analysis, to demonstrating his mastery of various kinds of discourse: historical, contemplative, and political (74–199). The most weighty of these main divisions treats contemplative discourse [θεωρητικὸς λόγος] (92–160); here Pseudo-Plutarch shows that a whole range of important philosophical views on the nature of the cosmos, the gods, souls, and ethics are all anticipated by Homer. This change in subject matter is accompanied by a distinct change in approach, method, and analytical vocabulary. He moves stylistic concerns to the background, for the most part, and foregrounds questions of interpretation. Rather than classifying the techniques of Homer's art, our critic here devotes himself to riddling out what he understands to be the hidden meanings of the text. His allegoresis is put to use always in the service of his larger goal, which is to prove that Homer is the source of all knowledge. He uses the vocabulary and methods of allegorical criticism, entirely absent from the first part of the text.[48] He organizes his analysis by concepts derived from αἴνιγμα,[49] ἀλληγορία,[50] and ὑπόνοια,[51] and he uses an allegorical vocabulary in his broadest theoretical statements of his enterprise in the latter part of the work, when he is explaining the general orientation. Homer's contemplative discourse helps us to understand the nature of things and the affairs of gods and men, to distinguish what conduct is excellent and what is base, and to learn the rules of reasoning. From Homer, that is, we can learn physics, ethics, and dialectic. To speak of these deep matters, Homer speaks through enigmas and mythic language [δι' αἰνιγμάτων καὶ μυθικῶν λόγων τινῶν] and through undermeanings [δι' ὑπονοίας]. Furthermore, though the Pseudo-Plutarch of the first part of the treatise located quite a few metaphors in Homer's text, he does not find them in the allegorical section of his work; rather, he finds enigmas.

From chapter 92 down to chapter 160, he interprets scenes many of which come from the standard repertoire of the allegorical critics. Lam-

[48] The exception, which we noted above, is where he defines ἀλληγορία as a trope 70 and mentions ὑπόνοια in connection with the trope of 'ἔμφασις 26. ῎Εμφασις is part of the allegorical critic's terminology as well, where it is sometimes married with the "symbol." See Chrysippus *SVF* 2.909 (the Galen passage cited in chap. 2): ἔμφασιν συμβόλου. For a later reader, see Iamblichus *VP* 103: συμβόλων ἐμφάσεις.

[49] αἴνιγμα: *Life of Homer* 92.3; αἰνίττεται: *Life of Homer* 100.1, 101.1, 102.2, 126.1, 201.2.

[50] *Life of Homer* 96, 102; also at 70 in his definition of the rhetorical version of allegory.

[51] Prominently at 92.3, in his most general description of his approach for the allegorical portion of his commentary; also at 26.1.

berton has already made a careful accounting of these readings.[52] Pseudo-Pluturch advances particular readings that often match those of Cornutus, Heraclitus, or both. The authors' readings coincide down to their particulars, except where variations are indicated in footnotes below, in the following cases: the tryst of Zeus and Hera on Mount Ida as the coming together of air and aether;[53] Zeus's punishment of Hera by attaching anvils to her feet as the earth and water stretching the air down from the aether;[54] the tryst of Ares and Aphrodite and Hephaistos's binding of Ares;[55] the theomachy as a battle between forces of nature (e.g., Poseidon vs. Apollo = water vs. fire; Hera vs. Artemis = air vs. the moon) or between virtues and vices (e.g., Athena vs. Ares = good sense vs. irrationality);[56] the eating of the cattle of the sun;[57] the Circe episode as base desire overcoming reason;[58] the equation of Hermes with λόγος;[59] Athena's grabbing Achilles by the hair as reason restraining the passions;[60] Achilles' shield as a representation of the cosmos;[61] that the plague is Apollo (the sun) shooting arrows (rays) down on the battlefield;[62] that Odysseus's praising of Alcinous's feast table does not underwrite a theory of pleasure, as Epicurus thought.[63]

Several generations later, Porphyry gives us a clue as to how we might understand Pseudo-Plutarch's arrangement of his material. Porphyry tells us in the preface to his *Homeric Questions*, a mostly philological commentary on the text, that he engages in work necessary as a preliminary exercise [προγύμνασμα] to a consideration of the "greater matters" [τὰς μείζους πραγματείας] (281.8–10, Schrader, ed.). Perhaps this is a reference to the sort of criticism in which he engages in *On the Cave of the Nymphs*. Porphyry explicitly warns that this preliminary work is

[52] Keaney and Lamberton, 19–27.

[53] Pseudo-Plutarch 94–96; Heraclitus 39. References to parallel scenes in this note and following are made to chapters.

[54] Pseudo-Plutarch 97; Heraclitus 40; Cornutus 17.

[55] Pseudo-Plutarch 101 says that this scene hints enigmatically at the union of Love and Strife that produces Harmony, claiming that Homer adumbrates Empedocles; Cornutus 19 says this scene is the conquest of iron by fire in the art of the blacksmith; Heraclitus 69 says it can be either.

[56] Pseudo-Plutarch 102; Heraclitus 52–58.

[57] Pseudo-Plutarch 120 reads them as a fate that will befall only those who choose by their own free will to err; Heraclitus 70 reads them as temperance, which Odysseus's men devour.

[58] Pseudo-Plutarch 126; Heraclitus 72.

[59] Pseudo-Plutarch 126; Heraclitus 72; Cornutus 16.

[60] Pseudo-Plutarch 129; Heraclitus 20.

[61] Heraclitus 43; Cornutus 19; for which Crates of Mallos (second century B.C.E.) is their source.

[62] Pseudo-Plutarch 202; Heraclitus 8; Cornutus 32.

[63] Pseudo-Plutarch 150; Heraclitus 79.

not to be undervalued. He criticizes those who neglect it and misunderstand Homer's diction [φράσις] because they run off [ἐπιτρέχειν] to make explantions of the poem as a whole.[64] Pseudo-Plutarch's treament would enact just this sort of combination of approaches. The treatise first situates questions of interest to the Aristotelian tradition of poetics, followed by those of a more allegorical and interpretive bent.

Pseudo-Plutarch and the Justification of Allegorism

As Lamberton has pointed out, Pseudo-Plutarch lacks the defensive tone that is pervasive in Heraclitus, but he does offer justifications for an allegorical approach.[65] At the beginning of his allegorical section, Pseudo-Plutarch sets forth what become two popular explanations of why the poets would use an oblique method of communication, rather than plainer speech. He tells us that the poets hide their messages as a spur to knowledge and as a shield from the ignorant:

> And if ideas are expressed through enigmatic and mythic language [δι' αἰνιγμάτων καὶ μυθικῶν λόγων τινῶν], this should not be unexpected. The cause is the nature of poetry and the custom of the ancients. They did this so that on the one hand lovers of learning, delighted by a certain elegance, might more readily seek and find the truth, while on the other hand the ignorant would not scorn what they could not understand. For I suppose that which is couched in hidden meanings [δι' ὑπονοίας] is attractive, where that which is spoken explicitly is cheap. (*Life of Homer* 92)

The poet communicates in code in order that the wise may have the pleasure of cracking it, and be left wanting more, and the ignorant may be kept away from profundities that they would not understand and may ridicule. This tendency toward esotericism is present in Heraclitus the Allegorist too, who tells us near the beginning of his treatise that only those who are holy and pure will see the philosophical truths that the poet really intended to express. The uninitiated will be left in ignorance (*Homeric Allegories*, chap. 3). This esoteric tendency was present as early as the Derveni Papyrus, which quotes the Heraclitean sentiment that the profane should "close their doors" to the wisdom that is about to be unraveled, and it will endure into later allegorical theorists. The philological considerations raised in chapter 2 fit well with this general picture. The ideology of exclusiveness and secrecy proved to be the

[64] We might also point out that such an arrangement would be in line with what will become a standard Neoplatonic understanding that the study of Aristotelian questions serve as a preliminary course of study to the higher issues. In their understanding Plato's writings reveal the sort of profound truths allegorists expect to find in poetry.

[65] Keaney and Lamberton, 10.

most productive of the semantic engines behind the vocabulary of allegoresis. Again, allegorical reading in general, and the symbol in particular, produce always two groups, those who know and those who do not. The whole topic of offering justification for allegory is interesting in itself. From the extant testimony, before Heraclitus and Pseudo-Plutarch, the allegorical critics do not leave behind much in the way of explanation or defense of method. While the argument from silence is treacherous, it is possible that earlier readers simply did not face such vigorous criticism on this issue.

From this brief look at three different readers of literature, we can safely say that by the second century of the common era the notion of the symbol, along with that of enigma and allegory, had entered a new stage in its history as a conceptual tool for understanding the poets. Carried along by the Stoics' apparently convincing approach to the poets, Chrysippus's symbol had gone from obscurity to a concept that had an established place in the exegesis of poems. The symbol's rise to real prominence awaits the work of the Neoplatonic critics, but to fully appreciate the Neoplatonic "symbol," we must first resituate some broader themes on ancient symbol reading more generally within the evidence uncovered up to this point.

5

300 B.C.E.–200 C.E.: THE SYMBOL AS ONTOLOGICAL SIGNIFIER

AS WE SAW earlier, beginning in the third century B.C.E., about the time of Philochorus's *On Symbols* and sometime before Chrysippus forwards his reading of the swallowing of Metis, the term "symbol" takes on a new life. It expands from being a narrow term for a contract marker, with specialized senses in Pythagoreanism, the mysteries, and divination, to being an important category of literary commentary. As we have seen, the Stoics and their allegorical followers present the first definitive evidence of this shift, though it was likely in place before them. During the Hellenistic and Roman periods the "symbol" appears in scattered references to a broader context that is not delimited by the term's strict classical heritage of contract authentication. Callimachus knows the symbol as a trophy commemorating victory in a contest.[1] Epicurus calls the lawfulness [δίκαιον] of nature a "symbol" for an ethical imperative that humans benefit by neither perpetrating nor suffering mistreatment.[2] Sources that date from the early Roman Empire attest to several other uses: symbols are the language of cultic instructions,[3] a god's traditional accouterments,[4] an object that marks one's power or status,[5] and the method by which Socrates' daemon educates him.[6] These other uses attest to a certain breadth of the term, which develops just as it begins to be used within literary contexts.

[1] Callimachus, *Aetia* frag. 59.7, *Epigrams* 27.4.

[2] Epicurus *Ratae sententiae*, frag. 31.

[3] Diodorus Siculus *Historical Library* 17.51.2. (Diodorus tells us that an Egyptian priest of Ammon calls out in symbols instructions for how to move a statue of a god during Alexander's consultation of the oracle.)

[4] Strabo *Geography* 13.1.48 (mouse as a symbol for Apollo); Pseudo-Apollodorus *Library* 2.5.9 (Ares' belt). We saw this sense also in the work of Cornutus (see chap. 4).

[5] Diodorus Siculus *Historical Library* 16.87.2 (a crown that marks a victory parade); Strabo *Geography* 13.1.53 (a leopard skin marks Antenor's status as a guest-friend of Menelaus, so the marauding Greeks spare his house); Plutarch *Nicias* 19.4 (staff and robe are symbols of Spartan power).

[6] Plutarch *Nicias* 13.6.

However, it is worth reiterating what Müri has already pointed out: the general uses of the symbol as a synonym for σημεῖον are nearly always influenced by the earlier, more specific traditions. Cases such as those just mentioned, where the connection with early uses is attenuated, are very rare and are greatly outnumbered by instances of σημεῖον.[7] It is right, then, to say that during this period "symbol" is still a term whose importance in specialized contexts far outweighs its importance in general contexts.

We have seen some ways in which these specialized uses are germane to the term's literary history, especially in marking secrecy and chance. Its uses within the mystery cults, a similar and better-attested tradition among the Pythagoreans, and in divination, which we explored in chapter 2 as a prelude to the Stoic symbol, deserve reconsideration in light of the developments in literary commentary that we have seen in chapters 3 and 4. In the term's pre-Stoic history these contexts catalyze the symbol's evolution from a token that authenticates social agreements into the role of literary signifier. When such parallels are reconsidered in light of what we have learned of allegorical techniques of reading, we begin to realize some significant gains in understanding the interpretive urge at the root of all these fields. As we will see, parallels among these fields where symbols are especially prominent are not only deducible from ancient evidence but directly observed by ancient witnesses, who testify to various affiliations between them. In addition, as we will begin to see here, the Neoplatonists resituate these histories, particularly the Pythagorean and divinatory ones, in pivotal later developments of the notion of the symbol. These later developments are quite separate from the earlier ones. As we saw earlier, the Stoics do not exhibit any special affiliation with Pythagorean ideas, and it is unlikely that they directly borrowed their literary symbol from them. The Neoplatonists, however, do show strong explicit connections with the Pythagoreans. As we will see below, the Neoplatonists place nearly the full expanse of mystified wisdom attributed to the ancient philosopher and his cult in the service of forming a new and now utterly dominant mode of symbolic literary language.

With respect to the earlier developments, though, there is still much to say. In the case of divination, I will attempt to evaluate and explore in more depth here a theme that I have only pointed out up to now: just as critics who follow in Aristotle's wake analyze literature by means of a critical apparatus held in common with the rhetoricians, the allegorically minded critics develop a set of analytical tools with its own affilia-

[7] See Walter Müri, "Symbolon," in *Griechische Studien* (Basel: Friedrich Reinhardt, 1976), 18–22.

tions to other ancient discourses, including the diviner's trade, the interpretation of esoteric philosophy, and the ritual use of cultic sayings. We begin here by considering links between allegorists and diviners; later we will turn to the other traditions. Andrew Ford, in his recent *Origins of Criticism*, is surely right to point to connections between allegoresis and the interpretation of divine signs.[8] As we saw in chapter 2, the fields use symbol terminology in near identical ways. Here we will see that the αἴνιγμα, the symbol's partner and twin and the earliest and best-attested conceptual engine of allegorical reading, is also an important organizing concept of divination. This sharing of a conceptual apparatus will provoke some further exploration of ties between the semantic systems by which the ancients organized the practices of divination and allegorical interpretation, and their relevance for understanding the (often implicit) assumptions of allegorical approaches. This is not to say that allegorists considered themselves to be doing divinatory activity when they interpreted Homer—any more than Aristotle thought he was analyzing public speeches when he read literary texts. It is rather to claim that these two interpretive discourses share common features, and that these reflect the assumptions and aspirations of the readers who situate themselves within these traditions of reading.

When we turn to the Neoplatonists in the following chapters we will see that they explicitly embrace such connections and adapt one of the semantic models on which divination had traditionally been based to their theory of the relationship between the literary symbol and the meanings it is understood to convey. The key for the later Neoplatonists is the idea of sympathy [συμπάθεια]. It will provide a well-established ground on which these figures will sometimes stand when they attempt to step away from imitation-based theories of poetry. Though the particular flight path of a bird may not obviously *imitate* a course of military action, a long-established tradition of divination nonetheless stipulated a meaningful connection between the two. The later allegorists will make use of precisely this paradigm, boldly suggesting that certain literary symbols are tied to their meanings not by economies of representation but rather by a mysterious system of ontological links between words and things. These later allegorists, while more extreme in this regard than earlier interpreters, are following in what is actually a very old tradition of mutual influence between allegorists and diviners—a body of shared assumptions about the proper approach to a certain kind of especially dense language. The Neoplatonists extend, rather than invent, an approach to reading that sees interpretive moves

[8] Andrew Ford, *Origins of Criticism: Literary Culture and Poetic Theory in Classical Greece* (Princeton: Princeton University Press, 2002), 80–85.

as being underwritten by hidden correspondences in the nature of things. We have seen that such a theory, based on various universalist ontologies, is observable in several earlier allegorical modes of reading.

In addition to reconsidering divination, I will spend some time revisiting Pythagorean notions of the symbol but now as they developed during the early and late Roman eras. As was the case with divination, direct evidence and testimony by ancient observers will give good reason to conclude that these lines of interpretive inquiry had much in common. This overlap becomes highly relevant among the Neoplatonic allegorists, who will find innovative uses for the new and powerful features of the symbolic that were now emerging. From our reconsideration of the divinatory, Pythagorean, and allegorical histories of the symbol, we will be able to deduce a broad general affiliation between these ancient forms of enigmatic language and suggest a common domain of enigmatic/symbolic discourse in the ancient world. Considered together, these ancient lines of thinking add up to a long-attested, and more or less continuously present, notion of a peculiar form of discourse—one marked by an overabundance of signification. Symbolic discourse consistently asks more of its audience than first appears. At root, it is a language in which words say (and sometimes do) more than they appear.

Poetry and Prophecy Revisited

Poetry and prophecy were mutually attracted from their earliest days. Plato's *Ion* gives us one of our most famous statements of this old view. He treats the poet and the prophet in perfect symmetry—clearly making light of both, but, as is often noted, we needn't ascribe sincerity to him to take him seriously as a witness to the commonsense notions of his contemporaries. This symmetry might lead us to ask, If a sizeable number of people in the ancient poet's audience were in the habit of viewing the poet as a mantic figure, might we not expect that at least some of them would have approached the poem with expectations and techniques of exposition that mirrored those with which they read an oracle? I will here suggest that the allegorists did just that. At every step, it will be difficult to say which of the fields is the source and which is the borrower, or whether the two drew from some third field. It seems likely that the two fields grew up together, one developing a new theory or conceptual tool, the other borrowing it. In any case it is beyond doubt that the two fields shared a great deal.

Divination had a long and healthy life in Greece and Rome.[9] In just

[9] The most important comprehensive work on the topic remains Auguste Bouché-

about every age, it seems, practitioners ranged from disrespected charlatans to highly esteemed advisors in matters of state. Cicero's *De divinatione*, our only completely surviving ancient survey of the subject, is generally taken as an authoritative, if rough, guide to the subject in the Greek and Roman worlds. Though Cicero's Stoic, Epicurean, and Academic characters disagree over whether divination actually works, they all attest that its traditional practices fall under two main headings: those that rely on a technique or an art and those that are artless and arise naturally (1.11, 34; 2.34).[10] In the artless type, a person becomes a conduit for the language of the gods. The two most common varieties are oracles given in a divine furor and dreams. Divination by art analyzes external omens or portents: for example, strange births (prodigies), lightning, entrails of sacrificial animals (haruspicy), the flights of birds (augury), celestial events (astrology), and the drawing of lots. In both the technical and the nontechnical forms of divination, the omen or mantic utterance, as it is traditionally portrayed in the literature, was understood to *require* interpretation.[11] For the technical variety of

Leclercq, *Histoire de la divination dans l'antiquité*, 2 vols. (Paris: E. Leroux, 1879–82). The body of literature has been growing fast in recent decades, however. See, for example, H. W. Parke and D.E.W. Wormell, *The Delphic Oracle* (Oxford: Blackwell, 1956); Hugh Lloyd-Jones, "The Delphic Oracle," *Greece and Rome* 23 (1976): 60–73; Joseph Fontenrose, *The Delphic Oracle* (Berkeley: University of California Press, 1978); W. K. Pritchett, *The Greek State at War* (Berkeley: University of California Press, 1979), 3: 47–90; J. Linderski, "Cicero and Roman Divination," *Past and Present* 36 (1982): 12–38 and "Watching the Birds: Cicero the Augur and the Augural Templa," *Classical Philology* 81 (1986): 330–40; Walter Burkert, *Die orientalisierende Epoche in der griechischen Religion und Literatur*, Sitzungsberichte der Akademie der Wissenschaften in Heidelberg, no. 1 (Heidelberg: C. Winter, 1984), 43–55, *Oedipus, Oracles, and Meaning: From Sophocles to Umberto Eco*, Samuel James Stubbs Lecture Series (Toronto: University of Toronto Press, 1991) and *Creation of the Sacred* (Cambridge, Mass.: Harvard University Press, 1996), 156–76; Ilse Becher, "Tiberüberschwemmungen: Die Interpretation von Prodigien in Augusteischer Zeit," *Klio* 67 (1985): 471–79; Mary Beard, "Cicero and Divination: The Formation of a Latin Discourse," *Journal of Roman Studies* 76 (1986): 33–46; Malcolm Schofield, "Cicero for and against Divination," *Journal of Roman Studies* 76 (1986): 47–65; Mark Riley, "Theoretical and Practical Astrology: Ptolemy and His Colleagues," *TAPA* 117 (1987): 235–56; Nicholas D. Smith, "Diviners and Divination in Aristophanic Comedy," *Classical Antiquity* 8 (1989): 140–58; Louise Pratt, "*Odyssey* 19.535–50: On the Interpretation of Dreams and Signs in Homer," *Classical Philology* 89 (1994): 147–52; Ineke Sluiter, "The Greek Tradition," in *The Emergence of Semantics in Four Linguistic Traditions* (Amsterdam/Philadelphia: John Benjamins, 1997).

[10] This distinction is confirmed by Pausanias 1.34.4; Plato *Phaedr*. 244; Pseudo-Plutarch 212.

[11] Fontenrose, in his search for scientific criteria of authenticity, has come up with rather different results by focusing on the epigraphical evidence (Fontenrose, 11–12). Of his list of seventy-five "genuine" oracles, forty-seven of them, or 63 percent, are secured by inscriptions. For a reevaluation of such a reliance on epigraphical texts in this case, see Pritchett, 301–2, n. 22.

divination, the interpreter—the haruspex or the augur, for example—is the one who observes and reads the sign. In artless divination, the situation is a little more complex. Several authors tell us that the one who interprets the oracle is separate from the mantic seer who pronounces it. Plato states this most plainly. In the *Timaeus* he speaks of the prophet [προφήτης] who makes judgments on the words that the mantic oracle [μάντις] utters in a divine frenzy. Plato says that the προφῆται are not diviners but interpreters of the apparitions and enigmas (Plato uses a rare masculine form, αἰνιγμοί) that appear to the μάντις (*Tim.* 72a–b). Euripides, Antiphon, Plutarch, and others testify to the split between interpreter and inspired speaker, and the *quindecemviri*, whose office was to interpret the sayings of the Sibyl, give us institutional evidence of the division of labor in producing natural divination.[12]

Especially in the case of artless divination, the superficial similarities to allegorism are striking. Even at first glance, three rather obvious points are already worth making. First, and most generally, both allegorists and diviners are at root interpreters. They see their respective texts primarily as sources of hidden meanings, which need to be decoded, brought into the light of day. As we saw in detail above,[13] this assumption separates allegorists from rhetorically minded readers of poetry and brings them into closer proximity to diviners. The rhetorical critic is less likely to focus on interpretation than on analysis. If the allegorist sees the poem as a riddle to be solved, we might say the rhetorical critics see it as a machine to be reverse-engineered: the strategy is typically one of isolating and investigating the methods by which a poet produces one effect or another. Allegoresis does not concern itself with this. Instead, more like diviners, allegorists see their task as primarily one of decoding. In both divination and allegorism the coded message typically contains some truth about the world, the way things really are. Second, both allegorists and an important class of diviners (that is, oracle readers) read texts that followed the same metrical constraints. The surviving evidence suggests that the lens of allegorism in its formative period was typically turned on the hexametric lines of Homer, Hesiod, and Orpheus. Those who tried to decode pronouncements from Delphi would have worked from a hexameter text as well. This means that the object of scrutiny for both interpreters was equally classifiable under the

[12] Euripides *Ion* 408–417, and elsewhere in the play, where Euripides mentions the oracles' interpreters. These figures are distinct from the Delphic priestess. The split between the interpreters and the prophets has been questioned by Lisa Maurizio, "Anthropology and Spirit Possession: A Reconsideration of the Pythia's Role at Delphi," *Journal of Hellenic Studies* (1995): 69–86. Maurizio points to the gender and class biases behind the view that the Pythia, typically a peasant woman, could not compose hexameters.

[13] See chap. 1.

term ἔπος. Dactylic hexameter had only specialized uses, in archaic and classical Greece. Christopher Faraone has found that hexameters play a role in magical spells in the archaic period,[14] and Parmenides and some of his peers found the meter to be a proper mode of expressing their philosophical ideas. But for the most part hexameters were produced by oracles and epic poets.

The third obvious point has already been made. The poet/prophet axis was a central pillar in the traditional edifice of ancient views on poetry. To be sure, it was nuanced, modified, denatured into a literary trope, and even rejected by some, but it remained a notably durable view within the tradition. If people were in the habit of seeing their poets as *manteis*, even in only a vestigial way, it strikes me as entirely plausible that at least some might be inclined to approach the poets' words with a set of assumptions that was congruent to that which guided their approach to oracles. As has been said, this is not to claim that all ancient allegorists actually subscribed to the traditional poet/prophet association. Such a view seems operative in the Derveni text but not among the Stoics. Cornutus would have had little patience with it, but Heraclitus the Allegorist and Pseudo-Plutarch might have entertained it, and it becomes popular again among the Neoplatonists. But this mixed reception of the poet/prophet axis is not a deterrent to the claim that allegorism developed by drawing on this association, and by transposing conceptual categories from one field to the other. By the same token, it is doubtful that a rhetorical critic would have claimed the poet to be somehow coextensive with the orator. It is a different thing to claim that the poet is in certain limited respects *like* an orator, and that this affiliation suggests that the tools a person uses to investigate one would yield results in investigating the other. I suggest that the borrowing between divination and allegorism happened in a similar way. Allegorists were highly sensitive to the capacity of fictive literature to carry multiple layers of significance, they knew from Delphi a tradition of reading hexametric lines that was attuned to similar densities of meaning, and they used a similar approach in each case.[15] So allegorists

[14] Christopher Faraone, "Taking the Nestor's Cup Inscription Seriously: Conditional Curses and Erotic Magic in the Earliest Greek Hexameters," *Classical Antiquity* 15 (1996): 77–112.

[15] If we can speculate a little further, it is also likely that the poet/prophet association—which made out the poet to be a light and winged thing, radiant with divine energy—would have been especially attractive to poets themselves. Bacchylides suggests just such a divinatory structure for the production and interpretation of poetry (Bacchylides 8.3 [Jebb, 1905]). If this is the case, might not at least some poets have consciously modeled their writing on oracles and consciously built in layers of significance, through subtle modes of reference? For a parallel, one could look at the influence of modernism as a

and diviners are linked by the meter of their texts, traditional views about the people who produced those texts, and their understanding of their own role as readers.

Given the general similarities, it should not be too surprising, then, that in the *De divinatione*, our only extant text devoted to the topic, Cicero draws a comparison between literary and divinatory interpreters. In the dialogue, Cicero makes his brother Quintus a spokesman for the efficacy of divination. Near the beginning of his remarks, Quintus suggests a connection between the interpreters of divine signs and the interpreters of the poets:

> The interpreters of all these signs, like the commentators who are interpreters of the poets, seem to approach very near to the divine foresight of the gods whose wills they interpret.
>
> Quorum omnium [oraculorum] interpretes, ut grammatici poetarum, proxime ad eorum quos interpretantur divinationem videntur accedere. (*De div.* 1.34)[16]

It is possible that Cicero merely juxtaposed these modes of inquiry casually, for illustrative purposes, and meant to propose no deeper connection between them.[17] After all, his main point is to suggest that the power of insight required to solve an oracle is nearly as remarkable as the divine ability to know the future. But alongside Cicero's statement a few other scattered bits of evidence already begin to hint at a pattern. The Derveni commentator, an unknown figure separated from Cicero by some four centuries, tells us that in addition to being an allegorical

---

theoretical apparatus on the production of literary work during the early twentieth century. James Joyce shaped his own writing in full and ongoing conversation with a whole host of modernist notions. Of course, the particulars are everything, and one would need to locate and explore specific ancient works and authors where such modeling occurred. For many centuries it was uncritically assumed that Homer wrote as the allegorists claimed he did. Pseudo-Plutarch's *Life* was included as a standard preface to Homer up into the fifteenth century (see Keaney and Lamberton, *Homer's Ancient Readers*, 2). Later scrutiny rightly unsettled any such assumption. Two contemporary scholars, Michael Murrin and Robin Schlunk, have argued for the influence of allegorical theory on a later poet, Vergil, claiming that he intentionally built allegorical associations into the *Aeneid*. (See above, p. 11, fn.19.) They make a convincing case because we can locate traditional allegorical readings that predate Vergil and track them in Vergil's own work. No such record of allegorical readings predates Homer, of course, so we would need to produce some other method to move from speculation on Homer's intentions to something firmer.

[16] The same idea turns up at 1.116, but Arthur Pease casts doubt on the authenticity of the manuscripts. He suggests that "ut grammatici poetarum" at 1.116 is awkward and therefore an interpolation. Pease, ed., *M. Tulli Ciceronis De divinatione* (Darmstadt: Wissenschaftliche Buchgesellschaft, 1963).

[17] An example of such a comparison is Panaetius's calling Aristarchus (hardly a mystic) a *mantis* (Athenaeus 14.35.12).

reader of poetry he was a professional dream reader (P. Derv. col. V). The Stoics were deeply engaged not only in allegorical reading but also in theorizing the practice of divination. And looking forward, the Neoplatonists will also develop expertise in both fields. When we take the invitations that these very different observers give us and examine these ancient traditions in tandem, we can locate evidence that not only did poets and prophets share a common repertoire of characteristics in the Greek cultural imagination, but their professional interpreters reflect this sharing in their approaches to their texts.

Tools of Interpretation

The gods, alas, have never spoken very plainly. In the literary record, ancient Greeks are repeatedly frustrated in their attempts to understand what exactly their gods are trying to tell them. To express this opacity, ancient observers regularly resorted to precisely the same language that allegorists used to describe what they considered to be the highly allusive language in which great poets spoke. As we have seen, among the standard terms of art, αἴνιγμα and σύμβολον and their cognates stand out as the real conceptual engines of allegoresis—and not ἀλληγορία, which Plutarch says is a neologism in his time,[18] nor ὑπόνοια, which appears in a prominent location in Plato but not very prominently in the allegorical texts themselves. When allegorists make general descriptions of their views of poetry and their techniques of reading it, they reach for these terms more consistently and prominently than any others. This habit of thinking among ancient allegorists, which sees the poet primarily as a producer of enigmas and cryptic symbols that carry hidden significances, had little to do with rhetorical approaches to criticism (in fact, we found, the rhetorical value of clear language was installed by Aristotle precisely to denature such grand views of poetry) and is the distinctive conceptual schema of allegorical critics.

In chapter 2, the early history of the term σύμβολον was surveyed. We found there that in the classical period the noun had a limited range of meanings and was nearly always a contract marker of some sort. Among the exceptions to this limitation, we examined the symbol as a divine sign, where it especially labels a portentous coincidence, one that snatches meaning from the void of chance. By situating coincidences (which by definition are random and happenstance) within the vocabulary of the gods, the ancient diviners demonstrated a certain willful resistance to nonsense. As we saw, this divinatory "symbol" predates by several centuries the allegorical one. The author of the *Hymn to*

[18] *De aud. po.* 19e–f.

Hermes,[19] Aeschylus,[20] Pindar,[21] Aristophanes,[22] and Xenophon[23] all attest to the symbol as occupying the paradoxical position of "meaningful coincidence." This and broader divinatory senses reappear in the work of many later figures, including Philo, the historian Appian (95–165 C.E.), the second-century novelist Achilles Tatius, Galen (130–200 C.E.), Aelian, Origen, Porphyry, Eusebius, Proclus, and Eustathius, in a scholion on Aristophanes, and in the Suda.[24]

A similar survey of uses of αἴνιγμα and related terms in the classical period yields an interesting conceptual mapping. The first point of note is that such terms are actually quite rare. If we focus on the classical corpus, as approximated by Greek texts in the Perseus database, the verb αἰνίττομαι appears slightly more than once per 100,000 words (1.1/100,000).[25] For comparison, over the same σημαίνω appears

[19] *Hymn to Hermes* (30).

[20] *Prometheus Bound* 487 (where Prometheus mentions the "symbols of the highway" in a list of mantic signs that he established for humans; it is apparently a divine omen that appears in remote areas).

[21] Pindar *Olympian Ode* 12.7 (where the symbol is a generic divine sign).

[22] *Birds* 721; cf. scholia ad loc.

[23] *Memorabilia* 1.1.3 (those who are familiar with the mantic arts make use of birds, oracles, sacrifices, and symbols). A similar list appears at *Apology of Socrates* 13.3.

[24] For references to these texts, see above, chap. 2, nn. 26–37.

[25] The frequency per 100,000 words is given over the entire database, which as of January 2001 was made up of the following texts: Aeschines *Speeches*; Aeschylus *Agamemnon*, *Eumenides*, *Libation Bearers*, *Persians*, *Prometheus Bound*, *Seven against Thebes*, *Suppliant Women*; Andocides *Speeches*; Antiphon *Speeches*; Apollodorus *Library* and *Epitome*; Aristophanes *Acharnians*, *Birds*, *Clouds*, *Ecclesiazusae*, *Frogs*, *Knights*, *Lysistrata*, *Peace*, *Plutus*, *Thesmophoriazusae*, *Wasps*; Aristotle *Athenian Constitution*, *Economics*, *Eudemian Ethics*, *Metaphysics*, *Nicomachean Ethics*, *Poetics*, *Politics*, *Rhetoric*, *Virtues and Vices*; Bacchylides *Odes*; Demades *On the Twelve Years*; Demosthenes *Exordia*, *Letters*, *Speeches*; Dinarchus *Speeches*; Diodorus Siculus *Library*; Euclid *Elements*; Euripides *Alcestis*, *Andromache*, *Bacchae*, *Cyclops*, *Electra*, *Hecuba*, *Helen*, *Heraclidae*, *Heracles*, *Hippolytus*, *Ion*, *Iphigenia in Aulis*, *Iphigenia among the Taurians*, *Medea*, *Orestes*, *Phoenissae*, *Rhesus*, *Suppliants*, *Trojan Women*; Herodotus *Histories*; Hesiod *Shield of Heracles*, *Theogony*, *Works and Days*; Homer *Iliad*, *Odyssey*; *Homeric Hymns*; Hyperides *Speeches*; Isaeus *Speeches*; Isocrates *Speeches* and *Letters*; Josephus *Jewish Antiquities*, *Against Apion*, *Jewish War*, *Life*; Lycurgus *Speeches*; Lysias *Speeches*; New Testament; Pausanias *Description of Greece*; Pindar *Odes*; Plato *Alcibiades 1*, *Alcibiades 2*, *Hipparchus*, *Lovers*, *Theages*, *Charmides*, *Laches*, *Lysis*, *Cratylus*, *Theaetetus*, *Sophist*, *Statesman*, *Epistles*, *Euthydemus*, *Protagoras*, *Gorgias*, *Meno*, *Euthyphro*, *Apology*, *Crito*, *Phaedo*, *Hippias Major*, *Hippias Minor*, *Ion*, *Menexenus*, *Cleitophon*, *Timaeus*, *Critias*, *Minos*, *Epinomis*, *Laws*, *Parmenides*, *Philebus*, *Symposium*, *Phaedrus*, *Republic*; Plutarch *Lives*; Sophocles, *Ajax*, *Antigone*, *Electra*, *Ichneutae*, *Oedipus at Colonus*, *Oedipus Tyrannus*, *Philoctetes*, *Trachiniae*; Strabo *Geography*; Thucydides *Peloponnesian War*; Xenophon *Anabasis*, *Cyropaedia*, *Hellenica*, *Memorabilia*, *Minor Works*, *Apology*, *Economics*, *Symposium*. While the database is strongly weighted toward the classical period, it includes some later authors, like Apollodorus, Pausanias, and Jo-

18.2 times per 100,000 words, and a very common verb like λαμβάνω appears 170 times. The noun αἴνιγμα appears as often as the cognate verb. The various adverb and adjective forms (αἰνικτηρίως; αἰνιγματώδης, -ες; αἰνικτός, -ή, -όν) appear a few times in the corpus (collectively, about a third as often as either the verb or the noun) and the variant masculine form αἰνιγμός shows up with about the same frequency. Of the 66 appearances of enigma terms in classical texts,[26] about a third (21) have to do with oblique language in general.[27] Nearly half of these appear in the context of tragedy, where a character, usually a messenger, speaks obliquely to deliver a message that is hard to bear. The interlocutor complains that the person is speaking in enigmas and asks the messenger to clarify. The generality of application here argues that these uses are figurative and derived from one of the more specific meanings that are attested. Three distinct meanings come into view. One cluster of αἴνιγμα terms in the classical period refers to riddles, which are posed as intellectual challenges put to a protagonist who must produce a solution, traditionally on pain of death (13/66).[28] These references are highly concentrated, which should lead us to discount slightly the prominence of this context: the famous riddle of the Sphinx accounts for 8 of these 13 references, and all 8 come from two texts, *Oedipus Rex* and the *Phoenician Women*. We have already surveyed a second specialized use of αἴνιγμα in the surviving corpus. In chapter 1, we saw evidence from Aristophanes, Xenophon, spurious Platonic writings, and especially the genuine corpus of Plato, that confirmed what the Derveni text already makes plain. In the classical period, enigma terms are marked as terms of art in allegorical reading (14/66).[29] Lastly, the surviving classical

sephus, for example. The frequency numbers cited can only be a rough guide, but they can be trusted to point out general tendencies. The collection of specific references to enigma terms listed below excludes the later materials.

[26] This figure refers to enigma terms in the texts listed in n. 25, exluding postclassical references.

[27] Aeschines 2.108, 3.121; Aeschylus *Suppliant Women* 464, *Prometheus Bound* 611, *Libation Bearers* 887; Aristophanes *Frogs* 62; Aristotle *Rhetoric* 1394b; Euripides *Rhesus* 755, *Electra* 946, *Heracles* 1120, *Helen* 788, *Suppliants* 1064, *Iphigenia in Aulis* 1148; Plato *Theaetetus* 180a, *Gorgias* 495b, *Apology* 27a, *Charmides* 161c, 162b, *Epistles* 312d, 332d; Sophocles *Ajax* 1158.

[28] Aristotle *Rhetoric* 1412a; Demosthenes 14.24; Euripides *Phoenician Women* 48, 1049, 1353, 1688, 1731, 1759; Plato *Apology* 27d, *Republic* 479b (in both noun and verb forms); Sophocles *Oedipus Tyrannus* 393, 1525.

[29] Of course, this number does not include the Derveni Papyrus. It does, however, include three references in Aristotle (two from the *Poetics* 1458a and one from the *Rhetoric* 1405a) where both the riddle and allegorical senses are present. Chapter 1 explored the breadth of the poetics of the enigma at the time Aristotle was writing and, based on this, concluded that the more important context in these three circumstances is the allegorical

corpus also clearly attests to another specialized use for this cluster of terms: they appear with equally high frequency in the context of oracles (18/66).[30] Though the limitations of the sample prevent any broad general conclusions, the oracular context is a bit more broadly attested than the others, and the spread of cognate terms in the lexicon is more pronounced within it.[31] And if we discount slightly the αἴνιγμα as riddle, due to this concentration of references, the oracular context appears to predominate over other classical uses of the term. In the standard extant classical corpus, enigmas seem to come most properly from the mouths of oracles.

Pindar, for example, used αἴνιγμα to describe the cryptic prophecies of the seer Amphiaraus (*Pythian Ode* 8.40), while Herodotus suggests that a prophetic dream speaks in enigmas (*Histories* 5.56). Interestingly, this particular dream relates a hexametric couplet to the dreamer, which suggests a relation both to epic and to Delphi.[32] Aristophanes at *Knights* 196 tells us that an oracle speaks enigmatically. Euripides, at *Ion* 533 and *Suppliants* 138, says that oracles speak in enigmas. In Aeschylus's

---

one, against which Aristotle was surely arguing. An argument could, of course, be made for double counting these particular references and including them in both categories.

[30] Aeschylus *Agamemnon* 1112, 1183, *Prometheus Bound* 833, 949; Aristophanes *Birds* 970, *Knights* 197, 1085; Demosthenes *Speech* 19.328 (pun, given the Delphic context); Euripides *Ion* 536, *Suppliants* 138, *Trojan Women* 625 (Talthybius's message is compared to an oracle); Herodotus 5.56; Pindar *Pythian Odes* 8.38; Plato, *Apology* 21b; *Symposium* 192d, *Timaeus* 72b, *Charmides* 165a; Sophocles, *Oedipus Tyrannus* 439.

[31] The distribution results of the frequency search look like this:

	general	riddle	prophecy	poetry
αἰνιγμός	4	1	1	
αἰνιγματώδης, -ες;	3		1	1
αἰνικτηρίως			2	
αἰνικτός, -ή, -όν			1	
αἴνιγμα	8	9	6	3
αἰνίττομαι	6	3	7	10
TOTAL	21	13	18	14
Percentage	32%	20%	27%	21%

[32] The full citation from Herodotus runs this way:

> Now this was the vision that Hipparchus saw in a dream: in the night before the Panathenaea he thought that a tall and handsome man stood over him uttering these enigmatic verses:
>
> O lion, endure the unendurable with a lion's heart.
> No man on earth does wrong without paying the penalty.

Agamemnon the prophetic pronouncements of Cassandra are called enigmas (1112 and 1183).[33] In the *Timaeus* 72b Plato tells us that it is the job of the interpreter of oracles to solve their enigmas [αἰνιγμοί, a rare masculine form]. In the *Apology*, when Socrates tells how the Delphic oracle declared him the wisest of men, he says that the oracle must have spoken in an αἴνιγμα (21b). Two additional texts from Plato put a rather fine point on this information. Plato reveals that a prophetic style is *by definition* an enigmatic style. Speaking of the person, whoever it is, who set the famous inscription "Know thyself" at Delphi, Critias claims he has made an enigma that really means "Be temperate" [Σωφρόνει]:

> But he speaks in a rather riddling fashion, like a prophet; for "Know thyself" and "Be temperate" are the same, as the inscription and I declare, though one is likely enough to think them different.
>
> αἰνιγματωδέστερον δὲ δή, ὡς μάντις, λέγει· τὸ γὰρ "Γνῶθι σαυτόν" καὶ τὸ "Σωφρόνει" ἔστιν μὲν ταὐτόν, ὡς τὰ γράμματά φησιν καὶ ἐγώ, τάχα δ' ἄν τις οἰηθείη ἄλλο εἶναι. (*Charmides* 164e–165a)

Leaving no doubt on the special affiliation of enigma language and divination language, *Symposium* 192d places the verbs αἰνίττεται and μαντεύεται in apposition:

> But the soul of each one clearly desires something else, which it is unable to express, but it expresses it in oracular fashion, and enigmatically.
>
> ἀλλ' ἄλλο τι βουλομένη ἑκατέρου ἡ ψυχὴ δήλη ἐστίν, ὃ οὐ δύναται εἰπεῖν, ἀλλὰ μαντεύεται ὃ βούλεται, καὶ αἰνίττεται.

Taken together, these last two texts also provide a noteworthy parallel to the *Second Alcibiades* (147b) and *Republic* (332b–332c) passages that we examined in chapter 1. These texts showed that speaking in αἰνίγματα worked equally well as a definition of poetic speech. In addition, the *Symposium* passage adds something to our view of how an

---

> As soon as it was day, he imparted this to the interpreters of dreams, and presently putting the vision from his mind, he led the procession in which he met his death.
>
> ἡ μέν νυν ὄψις τοῦ Ἱππάρχου ἐνυπνίου ἦν ἥδε. ἐν τῇ προτέρῃ νυκτὶ τῶν Παναθηναίων ἐδόκεε ὁ Ἵππαρχος ἄνδρα οἱ ἐπιστάντα μέγαν καὶ εὐειδέα αἰνίσσεσθαι τάδε τὰ ἔπεα·
>
> τλῆθι λέων ἄτλητα παθὼν τετληότι θυμῷ·
> οὐδεὶς ἀνθρώπων ἀδικῶν τίσιν οὐκ ἀποτίσει.
>
> ταῦτα δέ, ὡς ἡμέρη ἐγένετο τάχιστα, φανερὸς ἦν ὑπερτιθέμενος ὀνειροπόλοισι· μετὰ δὲ ἀπειπάμενος τὴν ὄψιν ἔπεμπε τὴν πομπήν, ἐν τῇ δὴ τελευτᾷ. (*Histories* 5.56)

[33] Fraenkel's edition (Oxford: Oxford University Press, 1950) contains a useful discussion ad loc., of the "enigma" as a mantic utterance.

enigma functions: Plato says that it is able to say what people are incapable of saying in ordinary language [ὃ οὐ δύναται εἰπεῖν]; it is a mode of discourse that (somehow) goes beyond words.

But a final reference from Aristophanes is as relevant as it is funny and might serve as a suitable closing thought on this portion of the evidence. In the *Birds* (959–90), an oracle monger appears to Pisthetaerus as one in the long string of interlopers who intrude on the founding of Cloudcuckooland. He is depicted carrying a book of Bacis and reading out hexameters, which are given below in italics, the Greek text is given only at the most relevant part of the passage:

ORACLE-MONGER: Let not the goat be sacrificed.
PISTHETAERUS: Who are you?
ORACLE-MONGER: Who am I? An Oracle-Monger.
PISTHETAERUS: Get out!
ORACLE-MONGER: Wretched man, insult not sacred things. For there is an oracle of Bacis, which exactly applies to Cloudcuckooland.
PISTHETAERUS: Why did you not reveal it to me before I founded my city?
ORACLE-MONGER: The divine spirit was against it.
PISTHETAERUS: Well, I suppose there's nothing to do but hear the terms of the oracle.
ORACLE-MONGER:

But when the wolves and the white crows shall dwell
together between Corinth and Sicyon—

PISTHETAERUS: What do the Corinthians have to do with me?
ORACLE-MONGER: Bacis enigmatizes this to the air [ᾐνίξαθ' ὁ Βάκις τοῦτο πρὸς τὸν ἀέρα].

They must first sacrifice a white-fleeced goat to Pandora,
and give the prophet who first reveals my words
a good cloak and new sandals.

PISTHETAERUS: Does it say sandals there?
ORACLE-MONGER: Look at the book.

And besides this a goblet of wine and a good share of the
entrails of the victim.

PISTHETAERUS: Of the entrails—does it say that?
ORACLE-MONGER: Look at the book.

If you do as I command, divine youth,
you shall be an eagle among the clouds;
if not, you shall be neither turtle-dove, nor eagle, nor woodpecker.

PISTHETAERUS: Does it say all that?
ORACLE-MONGER: Look at the book.
PISTHETAERUS: This oracle in no sort of way resembles the one Apollo dictated to me:

If an impostor comes without invitation
to annoy you during the sacrifice and to demand a share of the victim,
apply a stout stick to his ribs.
ORACLE-MONGER: You are drivelling.
PISTHETAERUS: Look at the book.
And don't spare him, were he an eagle from out of the clouds,
were it Lampon himself or the great Diopithes.
ORACLE-MONGER: Does it say that?
PISTHETAERUS: Look at the book and go and hang yourself.[34]

Aristophanes here lampoons the professionals as being accustomed to finding oblique references in oracles that they can twist in whatever way is necessary to make them fit a given situation—and benefit themselves in the process. Corinth is interpreted to mean the ἀήρ, or the lower atmosphere in standard Greek understanding, and so the oracle is interpreted to apply to the new city in the clouds. The term that sets off this parody is precisely the verb αἰνίτεται that we have been mapping here. The oracle text "enigmatizes" and so produces meanings other than those which appear on the surface. This text provides a rather precise parallel to the passage from Aristophanes' *Peace*, in which a wise Ionian suggests that the poet uses the dung beetle as an enigma for Cleon, which we saw in chapter 1 in the context of literary allegory. The verb does precisely the same service in each passage:

PISTHETAERUS: What do the Corinthians have to do with me?
ORACLE-MONGER: Bacis enigmatized this to the *aêr*.
Πι. τί οὖν προσήκει δῆτ' ἐμοὶ Κορινθίων;
Χρ. ᾐνίξαθ' ὁ Βάκις τοῦτο πρὸς τὸν ἀέρα.

Birds 969–70

FIRST SERVANT: What does the dung beetle refer to? And then some Ionian man sitting next to him says:
I think he enigmatizes this to Cleon.
Οι. "ὁ κάνθαρος δὲ πρὸς τί;" κᾆτ' αὐτῷ γ' ἀνὴρ
Ἰωνικός τίς φησι παρακαθήμενος·
"δοκέω μέν, ἐς Κλέωνα τοῦτ' αἰνίσσεται."

Peace 45–47

The *Birds* text provides some clarification for the *Peace* text, which leaves the subject of αἰνίσσεται unclear. If we assume consistency, Aristophanes uses the verb as a transitive, where the speaker of the enigma,

[34] Based on Eugene O'Neill's translation of Aristophanes, *Birds*, in *The Complete Greek Dramas*, vol. 2 (New York: Random House, 1938).

the prophet or the poet, predicates one thing *to* [πρός or ἐς] another. Aristophanes satirizes in precisely the same way these two situations where surplus meanings are dug out by professionals. The interpretive situations are functionally identical, and the knife edge of his wit, in both these contexts, makes precisely the same cut—even though these two moments of satire are separated by seven years (*Peace*, 421 B.C.E.; *Birds*, 414 B.C.E.). The satirical edge should also rule out the possibility that we have here a simple coincidence of language. Had he chosen the term casually, in either context, it simply wouldn't have been as funny. More likely, he is mocking the professionals in their own terms.

The association of αἴνιγμα and oracular speech recurs in many later sources, including the writings of the Hellenistic poet Lycophron (before 320 B.C.E.),[35] the historian Diodorus Siculus (fl. 60–30 B.C.E.),[36] and in the sophist Philostratus (fl. 200 C.E.).[37] In the fifth century C.E. Stobaeus excerpts and disseminates the references above to Plato's *Charmides* 164e–165a and *Symposium* 192d, which link enigmatic language with prophets.[38] The association between αἴνιγμα and the language of prophetic dreams is equally well attested in the later material. It is in evidence in Philo,[39] the sophist Aelian (170–235 C.E.),[40] and Heliodorus (220–50 C.E.), where αἰνίττομαι serves as a predicate for both ἐνύπνιον and ὄνειρος.[41] Centuries later, Eustathius still assumes that the enigma is the natural language of the dream.[42] But the most important evidence in this regard is Artemidorus's dream book (second century C.E.), the sole survivor of a long ancient tradition of handbooks for dream interpretation.[43] It merits close attention, and we will turn to it as we move into the later material below. Artemidorus tells us that the type of prophetic dream on which he focuses in his text, significantly the one that he labels "allegorical," speaks in symbols and enigmas.

There is no doubt, then, that when allegorical readers turn their lenses on poetry and find a uniquely dense discourse marked by σύμβολα and αἰνίγματα, the specimen they see looks similar to what the Greeks tradi-

[35] *Alexandra* 10 (the prophecies of Cassandra are compared to what the Sphinx riddlingly said).

[36] *History* 32.10.2 (the oracle that Alexander consults in Cilicia speaks in riddles).

[37] *Heroicus* 15.5.

[38] Stobaeus 3.21.25 for *Charm.*; 4.20a.35 for *Symp.* To this list we can also add bk. 14 of the *Greek Anthology*, esp. 14.64; Eunapius *Lives of the Sophists* 6.7.6; Proclus *In remp.* (Kroll, ed.) 2: 8.4, and the *Suda* 386 (under the letter eta).

[39] *De somniis* 2.3–4.

[40] *Varia historia* 12.1. A dream of Aspasia is said to riddle [ὑπαινιττόμενος] the fortune that was about to come to her.

[41] *Aethiopica* 4.15.1; 10.3.1.

[42] *Commentarii ad Homeri Odysseam* 2: 219. 44–45.

[43] Bouché-Leclercq (1.291–98) discusses the tradition that leads up to Artemidorus.

tionally imagined an oracle to be. Just as Aristotle shared his resources for conceptualizing poetry with professional public speakers, so the allegorical readers share their apparatus with readers of divine signs and develop an approach to reading the poets that is driven not by a formalist urge but by an interpretive one. Because divination seems to be the older practice (attested for millennia in the Mediterranean), the first temptation is to think that divination was the source of these notions and that allegorical readers borrowed from them, but the question of origins is more complicated.

We have already raised the issue with regard to the symbol and saw that it was indeed likely that the divinatory symbol was antecedent to the literary one. We saw in chapter 2 that the symbol in the classical period nearly always meant something quite narrow and restricted. Formed from the verb συμβάλλω, which commonly means to bring or set things together—and thereby "to agree," to form contracts of various kinds—in nearly all contexts it serves as the marker of the contract. In only two contexts does it develop in any substantial way beyond the notion of proof and authentication and into something whose meanings are hidden and require decoding: the symbol as cultic formula (in the Pythagorean sect and the mysteries) and the symbol as omen. In both cases, the characteristic of interpretability became attached to the term σύμβολον as a secondary development. When the Pythagorean and mystery contexts were compared with symbols in the larger classical corpus, it was shown to be most likely that these traditions used the term to name their enigmatic cult formulas not out of an idea that one could interpret them but because of their function as identity tokens. The classical notion of symbol as omen, on the other hand, is traceable to the Greek habit of reading coincidence as a divine message. This noun sense grows out of a separate meaning of the verb συμβάλλω, "to meet." The masculine form σύμβολος marks "that which one meets." The masculine is assimilated to the neuter in short order because of the preponderance of neuter uses and because of a preference for neuter forms in the terminology of divine signs. From this survey of the evidence we were able to establish that these two traditions, especially when set against the simple lack of other apposite contexts, provide the fertile ground in which the literary symbol grows. In the absence of more evidence, it is difficult to make any final arbitration between the relative weights of these lines of influence or to insist on an exclusive lineage. Were Philochorus's missing treatise *On Symbols* to have survived, this question may have been resolved. But even without clarity in the details, we are able to say that in circumstances where the Greeks began to think of "symbols" as interpretable enigmas (as opposed to tokens that authenticate contracts) only three figures commonly spoke such a language: cult initiates, poets, and prophets. The literary symbol, then, emerged under the influence of both the symbol as omen and the symbol as the secret piece of wisdom possessed by members of esoteric sects. It grew, in other words, out of coincidence and secrecy.

The question of a stemma of ideas behind the literary αἴνιγμα is also intriguing, and has notable similarities. The philological grounds, as Gregory Nagy has traced, show the originating idea in αἶνος, meaning "praise," which through the verb formation αἰνίτετται produces αἴνιγμα.[44] But how do we get from praise, that most public and open of commodities in Archaic and Classical Greece, to the idea of hidden meanings? According to Nagy's analysis, a standard trope of epinician praise poetry was an "ideology of exclusiveness": the subject of the praise was not openly named but was expected to deduce that it was intended for him. This suggests that the enigma's sense of interpretable puzzle grew out of what might be termed a quirk of the epinician genre of praise poetry. Such a stemma is most intriguing. After all, the poet Simonides, who seems to have originated the epinician ode in 520 B.C.E., is precisely the poet of whom Plato says: "As it turns out, Simonides was speaking enigmatically, in a poetic manner, about what the just is" [ᾐνίξατο ἄρα, ἦν δ' ἐγώ, ὡς ἔοικεν, ὁ Σιμωνίδης ποιητικῶς τὸ δίκαιον ὃ εἴη] (*Rep.* 332b–332c). This expectation of hidden meaning was also present in another αἶνος tradition. As Ralph Rosen has found, αἶνος applies to the animal fable as well, where tales traditionally have other registers of meaning.[45] Rosen has suggested a link between the poetry of praise and blame and animal fable, which share common tropes. These insights lead to the conclusion that in the case of the enigma, a literary context generates the term, and the divinatory one is dependent on it. As was the case with the symbol, we also arrive at a very short list of those in the classical period who properly speak in αἰνίγματα: esoteric philosophers, poets, prophets, and the Sphinx. Finally, if we read Nagy's lineage for αἴνιγμα back through the symbol traditions, a clearer picture comes into view. An "ideology of exclusiveness" is shared in prominent ways in the traditions of *both* symbol and enigma. The consistency here is our strongest suggestion of a root concept behind this mode of discourse. We may now include the enigma in the formula we generated in chapter 2: symbolic/enigmatic discourse is born from the power of the secret.

[44] Nagy, *Best of the Achaeans*, 239.

[45] Ralph Rosen, "The Ionian at Aristophanes *Peace* 46," *Greek, Roman, and Byzantine Studies* 24 (1984): 389–96.

Other-Speaking

The evidence surveyed so far, then, shows that divination and allegorism share important governing ideas. We can also adduce several later witnesses to ties between allegorical interpretation and divination. First, we turn to Plutarch. He speaks to us both as a scholar and a priest of the Delphic oracle and as one familiar with the methods of allegorical literary commentary. In his *On the Oracles at Delphi* he attempts to explain why oracles are no longer given in the traditional style and in the process gives us our most detailed surviving description of that style, which he calls "poetic." Of course, most obviously, this meant that oracles used to be delivered in verse, whereas in his time prose is apparently the norm. But it is also true that when he fleshes out what in particular he means by "poetic," his assumptions about poetic language are much closer to those of the allegorists than to those of rhetorical critics. In his view and in that of his anticipated audience, it made perfect sense to describe the traditional *obscurity* of the Delphic oracle as being "poetic." This suggests a tie not just between poets and prophets but also between allegorical visions of poetry and traditional views of oracular language. Plutarch's specific language is suggestive in this regard. Toward the end of his essay, he says oracles were once characterized by enigmas, allegories, and undermeanings, among other things:

> In the days of old what was not familiar or common, but was expressed altogether murkily in undermeanings, the mass of people imputed to an assumed manifestation of divine power, and held it in awe and reverence; but in later times, being well satisfied to apprehend all these various things clearly and easily without the attendant grandiloquence and artificiality, they censured the poetic language with which the oracles were clothed, not only for obstructing the understanding of them in their true meaning and for combining vagueness and obscurity with the communication, but already they were coming to look with suspicion upon metaphors, enigmas, and ambiguous statements, feeling that these were secluded nooks of refuge devised for furtive withdrawal and retreat for him that should err in his prophecy.

> πάλαι μὲν τὸ μὴ σύνηθες μηδὲ κοινὸν ἀλλὰ λοξὸν ἀτεχνῶς καὶ περιπεφρασμένον εἰς ὑπόνοιαν θειότητος ἀνάγοντας ἐκπλήττεσθαι καὶ σέβεσθαι τοὺς πολλούς· ὕστερον δὲ τὸ σαφῶς καὶ ῥᾳδίως ἕκαστα καὶ μὴ σὺν ὄγκῳ μηδὲ πλάσματι μανθάνειν ἀγαπῶντες ᾐτιῶντο τὴν περικειμένην τοῖς χρησμοῖς ποίησιν, οὐ μόνον ὡς ἀντιπράττουσαν τῇ νοήσει πρὸς τὸ ἀληθὲς ἀσάφειάν τε καὶ σκιὰν τῷ φραζομένῳ μειγνύουσαν, ἀλλ' ἤδη καὶ τὰς μεταφορὰς καὶ τὰ

> αἰνίγματα καὶ τὰς ἀμφιβολίας, ὥσπερ μυχοὺς καὶ καταφυγὰς ἐνδύεσθαι καὶ ἀναχωρεῖν τῷ πταίοντι πεποιημένας τῆς μαντικῆς, ὑφεωρῶντο. (407a–b)[46]

And a few pages later, he gives his final summation, addressing those of his contemporaries who look down upon the oracle for being too clear and therefore cheapening its own message:

> But, just as in those days there were people who complained of the obscurity and vagueness of the oracles, so today there are people who make an unwarranted indictment against their extreme straightforwardness. Such an attitude of mind is altogether puerile and silly. It is a fact that children take more delight and satisfaction in seeing rainbows, haloes, and comets than in seeing the moon and sun; and so these persons yearn for enigmas, allegories, and metaphors which are but concessions of the prophetic art when faced with something mortal and dependent upon imagination.

> Ἀλλ' ὥσπερ ἐν τοῖς τότε χρόνοις ἦσαν οἱ τὴν λοξότητα τῶν χρησμῶν καὶ ἀσάφειαν αἰτιώμενοι, καὶ νῦν εἰσὶν οἱ τὸ λίαν ἁπλοῦν συκοφαντοῦντες. ὧν παιδικόν ἐστι κομιδῇ καὶ ἀβέλτερον τὸ πάθος· καὶ γὰρ οἱ παῖδες ἴριδας μᾶλλον καὶ ἅλως καὶ κομήτας ἢ σελήνην καὶ ἥλιον ὁρῶντες γεγήθασι καὶ ἀγαπῶσι, καὶ οὗτοι τὰ αἰνίγματα καὶ τὰς ἀλληγορίας καὶ τὰς μεταφορὰς τῆς μαντικῆς, ἀνακλάσεις οὔσας πρὸς τὸ θνητὸν καὶ φανταστικόν, ἐπιποθοῦσι· (409c–d)

In these two texts Plutarch gives us evidence of a certain readiness to transpose the conceptual templates used to understand prophetic and poetic speech. One can, of course, point to the Aristotelian category of metaphor and the tendency to see enigmas as the mystifications of unscrupulous *manteis*. Such an eclectic mix of attitudes is typical of Plutarch. However, in order for his contemporaries to understand what he meant by calling the traditional oracular style "poetic," there must have been a currency to the view that the poet's language was by definition an obscure repository of hidden messages. If most of Plutarch's contemporaries had viewed poetry according to the Aristotelian model, or the other models suggested by critics like Aristarchus or Quintilian, they would have expected clarity and precision in a "poetic" style. Plutarch assumes that his readers have an understanding of poetic language that is part and parcel of allegoresis (though without the notion of the symbol).[47] Plutarch also hints at another aspect of this enigmatic lan-

[46] Text and translation (modified slightly) from *Plutarch's Moralia*, ed. and trans. Frank Cole Babbitt (Cambridge: Harvard University Press, 1969).

[47] This should not surprise us too much; the term was coming into its own in allegorism more or less in Plutarch's time (c. 46–c. 120 C.E.). We have already seen in chap. 4 that roughly around this time some (though not all) of the allegorical commentators were following Chrysippus's lead and using the term "symbol" as a category of literary criticism.

guage spoken by both poets and prophets. The prophetic art, he says, uses such language as a necessary concession to the imperfection of human nature. Specifically he sees it as a concession to a childlike pleasure in refracted things that delight the mind's eye. Later allegorists will claim that symbolic language is a more substantial form of concession to human nature. They will say it clothes in material objects, which are perceptible to the human mind, immaterial truths that humans have no means to grasp without such aids. While this is mainly a development of Neoplatonism, we have already seen that Plato hints at such a view in relation to oracular language (*Symposium* 192d). A century after Plutarch, Clement of Alexandria repeats Plutarch's characterization but adds the notion of the σύμβολον:

> All then, in a word, who have spoken of divine things, both barbarians and Greeks, have veiled the first principles of things, and delivered the truth in enigmas [αἰνίγμασι], and symbols [συμβόλοις], and allegories [ἀλληγορίαις], and metaphors, and such tropes. Such also are the oracles among the Greeks.[48]

In these texts, the use of the notion of ἀλληγορία (other-speaking) in descriptions of oracles is suggestive. First, while the concepts of symbol and enigma are the real conceptual engines of allegoresis, and in literary contexts they are distinctively marked by allegorism, they were never used in an *exclusive* sense for either allegorical or divinatory language. We have seen that these terms appeared in other contexts, such as contracts, the mystery religions, esoteric philosophy, and riddles. The term ἀλληγορία is different in this respect. When it emerges in the first century C.E.,[49] Plutarch calls it a newfangled term for literary undermeanings.[50] That Plutarch would use such a term to describe the speech of the Delphic oracle argues for a certain equivalence in his mind between oracular and poetic speech.

The term ἀλληγορία almost never appears outside of literary contexts but remains quite narrow as a term of art in allegorical commentary—with one notable exception. In divination it regularly labels a certain class of prophetic dream, one that carries hidden messages and can be decoded to reveal truths about the dreamer. The Suda's entry for ἀλληγορία gives us these two definitions: it is either oblique literary signification or a dream that indicates one thing by another. Artemidorus is our most important witness to this quite striking parallel between allegorism and divination. Macrobius also testifies to it in a more indirect, but perhaps even more compelling, fashion.

[48] *Stromata* 5. 4.21.

[49] Or perhaps earlier, depending on how one dates Demetrius (*On Style* 99, 243).

[50] Plutarch *On How to Read the Poets* 19f.

Artemidorus

Though we have testimony of a good number of dream books in antiquity, only one of the genre survives, that of Artemidorus.[51] His work in five books, most likely written in the second century C.E., has only recently begun to receive the attention it deserves—even if, as Denniston points out, it represents an area of study "which attracted the attention of serious men, as well as anecdote-mongers."[52] Artemidorus preserves for us a fully articulated theory of divination through dreams. For the present purpose, the most relevant part of his exposition is his use of the designations "allegorical" and "symbolic" for those dreams that are at once significant and puzzling, that require interpretation to be properly understood. This is the category of dreams that Artemidorus spends the major portion of his work investigating. The other categories, that is, meaningless dreams that come from overeating or other indulgences or those that simply and straightforwardly show us what will happen, do not call for the services of the dream interpreter. Artemidorus was not the first to use the term "allegorical" in the vocabulary of dream interpretation. At least a century before, Philo, at *On Dreams* 2.8, tells us that ἀλληγορία is the very guide and foundation for divination by dream interpretation. Also, Artemidorus refers to others who divide the category of allegorical dreams into several subcategories, suggesting that at least the idea and perhaps the term was in use before his time. At the beginning of his treatise he specifically defines allegorical dreams as those that disclose their meaning through enigmas:

> Allegorical dreams [as opposed to the theorematic] are those that signify one thing by another, when the soul says something enigmatically by physical means.
>
> ἀλληγορικοὶ δὲ οἱ δι' ἄλλων ἄλλα σημαίνοντες, αἰνισσομένης ἐν αὐτοῖς φυσικῶς τι τῆς ψυχῆς. (1.2)

In book 4 he repeats this definition: "All dreams fall into two groups: some are called theorematic, others allegorical [ἀλληγορικοί]. Theorematic dreams are those which come true just as they are seen. Allegor-

[51] Bouché-Leclercq, 291–98.

[52] J. D. Denniston, "Divination," *Oxford Classical Dictionary* (New York: Oxford University Press, 1970). Several recent studies of Artemidorus have appeared, including Michel Foucault, *The Care of the Self*, vol. 3 of *History of Sexuality*, trans. R. Hurley (New York: Pantheon Books, 1986), chap. 1; and John J. Winkler, *The Constraints of Desire* (New York: Routledge, 1990), 17–44. For the text, see *Artemidori Daldiani onirocriticon libri v*, ed. R. A. Pack (Leipzig: Teubner, 1963). For an English translation, see Artemidorus, *The Interpretation of Dreams*, trans. and comm. Robert J. White (Park Ridge, N.J.: Noyes, 1975).

ical dreams are those that disclose their meanings through enigmas [αἰνίγματα]" (4.1).

Artemidorus not only uses "allegory" as his label for dreams that contain hidden messages but makes use of the technical vocabulary of allegorical commentators in his various investigations, and in ways that are broadly consistent with the interpretive discourse of the allegorical critics. The terms αἴνιγμα and σύμβολον and their cognates appear over a dozen times each in the *Dream Book*—these in addition to multiple uses of ἀλληγορία and words related to it. The various and sundry items and situations that appear in Artemidorus's catalogue of dreams can be either riddles or symbols that indicate their referent allegorically, including faulty singing, sexual positions, penises, and chains.[53]

Macrobius

A final example from late antiquity marks with unique clarity the overlap between divination and allegorism that we have seen suggested in earlier sources. Macrobius (who writes in Latin around 400 C.E.) hands down an allegorical tract on the *Dream of Scipio*, a section from the closing sixth book of Cicero's *De republica*. Cicero closes his work with the dream in much the same way that Plato finished off the *Republic*

[53] In the list below, citations are to the book, chapter, and line within the chapter in Pack's edition. The first element of the equivalence is said to be a symbol of the second. "Symbol" appears always as a noun in predicate position, with a genitive dependent on it. In many cases, Artemidorus's symbolic meanings are qualified, limited to certain types of people or situations, and sometimes brief explanatory notes are added. I have included only a bit of this additional information in the interests of compression.

The following are symbols in Artemidorus: penis = necessity (1.45.16); swimming = danger and disease (1.64.50); singing off-key = unemployment and poverty (1.76.47); wearing worn-out clothes during summer = good health (2.3.6); the cypress tree = patience and delay (2.25.16—because of its extent); box trees, myrtle, and rose laurels = futile labor (2.25.34); a stepmother and a stepfather = living abroad and traveling (3.26.9); flying, an earthquake, war, thunderbolt = travel (4.prologue.101—for people versed in dream interpretation, because they dream in a richer symbolic vocabulary than those ignorant of the art); poverty = many evils (4.7.8—when dreamed by a man who is newly wealthy); old woman = death (4.24.4—on the basis of a numerological reading of the letters of the Greek words for each); milk in a basin = loss (4.62.2); gymnasium = good health throughout the whole body (5.3.7); building a hearth in a country in exile = dying in that country (5.27.3); Aphrodite = marriage and producing children (5.39.5).

Citations to other relevant terms include: αἴνιγμα (2.12.177, 4.1.4, 4.22.38, 4.59.19, 4.63.1, 4.71.10, 4.71.11, 4.80.8; αἰνίττεται (1.2.12, 1.56.24, 1.64.56, 2.11.43, 4.22.40, 4.22.41, 4.71.7, 4.71.9, 5.62.3); ἀλληγορικός (1.2.1, 1.2.11, 1.2.46 [with discussion throughout], 4.1.2, 4.1.3, 4.1.9, 4.1.19 (adv.) [further discussion throughout 4.1]).

with the Myth of Er.[54] Both are imaginative literary expositions of speculative issues that appear not to fit neatly into the form of philosophical dialogue. The simple fact that Cicero had substituted a dream for a myth is already suggestive. Given that he is consciously rewriting Plato's work, it indicates a congruence between prophetic dream and mythic tale. Both subtly suggest things that rational argument cannot (perhaps) quite bring itself to say.

With preliminaries out of the way, Macrobius devotes the second chapter of his first book to laying the theoretical ground for an allegorical reading of a literary work. Philosophy, he tells us, occasionally and with discretion, makes use of *fabulae* ("tales," "narratives," or "myths"). Not just any story is allowed to enter into the philosophical conversation. All those that are meant merely to entertain and delight us are put away like children's nursery rhymes. The philosopher is more interested in stories that draw us toward certain kinds of virtue—but not all of these are appropriate either, Macrobius says. Some morally educative stories are completely fictitious, like the fables of Aesop; these the philosopher discards. But some rest on a solid foundation of truth, which is treated in a fictitious style. Macrobius calls these the *narrationes fabulosae*, a term that becomes important for medieval allegorical exegesis. Examples of stories that treat truth in the style of fiction, Macrobius says, are the poems of Hesiod and Orpheus as well as, interestingly enough, the mystic conceptions of the Pythagoreans (more about this in a moment). But not all of these are appropriate for deep philosophical treatment, only those that deal with inoffensive subject matter and do not include such things as divine adulteries or the castration or binding of gods (those episodes that caused so much trouble to ancient commentators of all affiliations). Furthermore, in Macrobius's scheme, the poet ought never to try to depict the highest principles of the universe.[55] The poet should only represent the lower gods, the soul, and nature. So, inoffensive narratives that tell us the truth in the style of fiction and refrain from speaking of the highest divine principles are acceptable to put under the lens of allegorical scrutiny. Why are these indirect and narrativized methods used to speak of deep truths about nature or souls? Because, Macrobius tells us (availing himself of a standard explanation among the allegorical critics), nature likes to conceal herself behind a modest veil, which spurs on those who are worthy of the truth to peel back her garments and shields her from the gaze of those who are not. The sexualized aspect of the description is explicit. As has been

[54] In the *Commentary on the Republic*, Proclus takes a similar approach to Plato's Myth of Er. He devotes nearly 270 pages of his 600-page work to an exposition of it.

[55] In his Neoplatonic conception, this means the perfectly transcendent One (the divine unity and font of the universe) or the Nous (the second-level divine mind).

pointed out by William Harris Stahl in his helpful introduction to Macrobius, the basic allegorical apparatus here and in many other places in the commentary is likely borrowed from the third-century Neoplatonic commentator Porphyry.[56]

After he has laid this groundwork in allegory, Macrobius turns to a consideration of the theory behind dream interpretation. Because of the subject matter of the particular *narratio fabulosa* he examines, it makes perfect sense for Macrobius to give specific consideration to the methods of divination through dreams in order to extract all the meaning he can from Cicero's text. Immediately after laying out his allegorical apparatus in chapter 2, then, Macrobius reproduces in his third chapter a theory of dream interpretation. As Stahl has shown, this theory mirrors that of Artemidorus, down to the details. Macrobius claims that the dream Cicero has portrayed for us in the *De republica* embraces all the various types of dreams, including the one that Artemidorus called allegorical, the kind that hints at its meaning through ambiguities. This dream is distinguished from meaningless ones that arise from bodily disturbances and from those that present their meaning to us in a clear manner. It is

> one that conceals with strange shapes and veils with ambiguity the true meaning of the information being offered, and requires an interpretation for its understanding. We need not explain further the nature of this dream since everyone knows from experience what it is.[57]

> [id] quod tegit figuris et velat ambagibus non nisi interpretatione intellegendam significationem rei quae demonstratur, quod quale sit non a nobis exponendum est, cum hoc unus quisque ex usu quid sit agnoscat. (1.3.10)

Scipio's dream counts as Artemidorus's enigmatic type, Macrobius goes on, "because the truths revealed to him were couched in words that hid their profound meaning and could not be comprehended without skillful interpretation" [quia rerum quae illi narratae sunt altitudo tecta profunditate prudentiae non potest nobis nisi scientia interpretationis aperiri] (1.3.12).

Now, at this point, Macrobius begins his commentary, never bothering to tell us whether he is employing the theoretical apparatus of allegorical literary interpretation that he lays out for us in book 1, chapter 2, or whether he has in mind the theory of dream interpretation that he articulated in book 1, chapter 3. In fact, as comes out naturally and without self-conscious discussion in Macrobius's commentary, the tools

[56] Introduction to Macrobius, *Commentary on the Dream of Scipio*, trans. William Harris Stahl (New York: Columbia University Press, 1952).

[57] Translations of Macrobius draw from Stahl.

and approaches of the two methods are so similar that any difference between them is completely elided. This elision could only pass unnoticed in a tradition where the difference between the allegorical reading of literature and divination by dreams is very slight indeed.

The Semantics of Oracles, Omens, and Dreams

All together, this evidence on the overlap between the organizing concepts of divination and allegorism prompts us to look more closely at the specifics of divinatory semantics. A close look here will enable us better to understand the expansive interpretive moves we have already seen in the work of some allegorists. Divinatory signs had resonated with mysterious meanings for many millennia in the Mediterranean, and if it is true that allegorism and divination shared organizing concepts, it would only make sense that some of the semantic potency of divine signs would seep over to poetic ones. In the late Roman period the Neoplatonists explicitly borrow power for poetic symbols from divine omens. Taking divinatory semantics into account, we will be better able to understand how the Neoplatonists could make the bold claim that the literary "symbol" has a strong ontological connection with its referent. Such a claim is slightly different from, and quite a bit stronger than, those of earlier allegorists. We have already seen that, from the very beginnings, the semantic connections on which allegory builds itself have been deeply implicated in ontological ones. Starting with the Derveni commentator and continuing through the Stoics, we have seen that one form or another of universalist ontology has served as a foundational concept for asserting connections between surface meanings and hidden ones. This movement from surface to hidden meaning takes place entirely in the world of things "out there," where one thing has some form of equivalence to another, due to their sharing some property in common (genitals and the sun both carry the power to generate life, for example); hence, there is a real connection between things in the underlying structure of the world. These theories rest on an ontological assertion that relationships exist, sometimes intuitive, often opaque, in the world of things. The Neoplatonists advance such thinking by an order of magnitude. We will see them claim that real ontological links exist not just between one thing and another but between words themselves and the things they indicate. In this way, language is actually connected to things, and has the power to invoke and manipulate them. This exotic idea, so characteristic of Romantic poetics,[58] and the Holy Grail of the representational artist who seeks to truly capture his or her

[58] See conclusion.

subject, is well attested in late antique literary theory. The Neoplatonists explicitly borrow on the "sympathy" that was traditionally understood to connect the divine sign and its message, as well as a magical talisman and its "referent," in order to claim for the poets the power actually to invoke, rather than just represent, the realities they treat. As we will see, the most prominent term under which this development takes place is the "symbol."

Divination and Divine Immanence: The Stoics Revisited

In *De divinatione* Cicero makes his brother, Quintus, divination's defender. Quintus is careful to concede that there are rarely obvious logical ties between the divinatory sign and its meaning (1.12–13).[59] For example, it does not simply stand to reason that the particular croak of a frog means a storm is on its way. On what basis, then, do Cicero's Stoic defenders of divination suggest that the portent indicates its referent? Quintus rules out that the gods intervene directly in each and every omen. The Epicureans had opposed divination by claiming that such involvement in minutiae was beneath the divine dignity, and Quintus agrees. He suggests rather that the gods just set up the world with significant connections. Some events consistently precede other events in the great order of things:

> The gods are not directly responsible for every fissure in the liver or for every song of a bird, since, manifestly, that would not be seemly or proper in a god and furthermore is impossible. But, in the beginning, the universe was so created that certain results would be preceded by certain signs, which are given sometimes by entrails and by birds, sometimes by lightning, by portents, and by stars, sometimes by dreams, and sometimes by utterances of persons in a frenzy. . . . Assuming the proposition to be conceded that there is a divine power which pervades the lives of men, it is not hard to understand the principle directing those premonitory signs which we see come to pass.

> Nam non placet Stoicis singulis iecorum fissis aut avium cantibus interesse deum; neque enim decorum est nec dis dignum nec fieri ullo pacto potest;

[59] Quintus does give two brief examples of a logical, causative link between sign and meaning, taking both from earlier thinkers, but he does not pursue this mode of justification very vigorously. We may speculate that on this turf, the defender of divination lost more arguments than he won. According to Posidonius, if the dog star appears fuzzy, prophesying that the year ahead will be pestilential, this may be due to a miasmic atmosphere. Democritus said that if the entrails of sacrificial animals appear sickly, indicating that the harvest will be poor that year, it may be due to the poor quality of grazing (*De div.* 1.130).

> sed ita a principio inchoatum esse mundum ut certis rebus certa signa praecurrerent, alia in extis, alia in avibus, alia in fulgoribus, alia in ostentis, alia in stellis, alia in somniantium visis, alia in furentium vocibus. . . . Hoc autem posito atque concesso, esse quandam vim divinam hominum vitam continentem non difficile est, quae fieri certe videmus, ea qua ratione fiant, suspicari. (1.118)

Quintus justifies the efficacy of divination by a belief in the immanence of the divine in the world (which we have seen to be good Stoic reasoning). The last line of the citation is especially telling. It is indeed "not hard to understand" the principle by which meaningful connections are maintained between things, *provided* we concede that a divine power suffuses the world. The universalist view of a single divine principle will underwrite semantic connections where none are apparent. Quintus here touches on the theological issues surrounding the ancient debate on divination. The Stoics had linked their arguments in favor of divination with the question of the very existence of the gods themselves. The Stoics proved the gods' existence by divination's effectiveness and vice versa. In fact, Balbus, Cicero's Stoic spokesman in the *De natura deorum*, offers the efficacy of divination as the "very strongest proof" for the gods' existence and beneficent providence toward humans (*De nat.* 162). The argument ran something like this: if the gods exist, they surely rule the universe by providence; if they have guiding foreknowledge of events and care for humans, they will give signs of the future to humans so that they may steer their lives according to the divine will.[60] A random world, where things do not follow other things meaningfully, amounts to a kind of sacrilege.

The Semantics of Omens: Sympathy between Sign and Meaning

The broadest concept of the force that underwrites the interrelatedness between divinatory signs and their meanings is divine sympathy [συμπάθεια], a notion to which the Stoics give extensive ontological significance. In Stoic parlance, "sympathy" labels the presence of the divine logos through all things, that is, the material basis of the connection of every part of the existing cosmos.[61] Now, according to divination's supporters, the notion of sympathy needs to be kept separate from an observable causative explanation of the interrelation between events. (Predicting rain from a rain cloud does not make one a diviner.) Quintus

[60] In the second book of the *De divinatione* Cicero himself makes the most comprehensive rebuttal of this position in the extant literature.

[61] Cicero *De div.* 2.33. See also, e.g., Alexander Aphrod. *De mixtione* 223.25, 226.34; Aetius *Plac.* 5.12.3; Plutarch *De fato* 574d.

specifically distinguishes the empirical pursuit of causative explanations, as in the natural sciences, from the practice of divination (*De div.* 1.112). Later in the *De divinatione*, Cicero, who casts himself as the opponent of divination, includes a list of traditional examples of "sympathy": the connection between the moon and tides (which before Newton had no known causative link);[62] or the winter solstice and the blooming of the dry pennyroyal; or the effect of the moon on the growth of oysters or the seasons on sap in a tree; or the fact that when certain strings on a lyre are plucked, other strings sound as well (*De div.* 2.33–34). The diviner is forced into the position of denying *any* logical or scientifically comprehensible connection between the parts of the world that he or she claims to be affiliated. For, if the force that ties a particular sign to its meaning can be fit into some other area of scientific understanding (like botany, astronomy, or meteorology, for example), the diviner's art becomes superfluous. Diviners, it seems, uniquely enforce a semantic system *founded and maintained* on mystification. For the art to survive, it must hide the semantic links between sign and meaning under clouds of mystery. Such links need to be situated by definition beyond the reach of the other arts, and therefore, in practice, beyond the reach of reason.

Once we have granted that there exists a stratum of otherwise inexplicable connections between things, Quintus's line of reasoning suggests, we should be ready to accept that there may be many other connections between things that appear to be logically and scientifically separated. The gods sustain these connections for our benefit and infuse meaning into what appear to the untrained eye as insignificant or mundane events. That is, the gods make things into signs.[63] In fact, at the limit of this thinking, no event is insignificant, because nothing happens outside the economy of the divine synthesis of the world. The providential care of the gods ensures a semantic dimension to all things, and the world becomes entirely readable.[64] The art of the diviner, then, takes on a quasi-empirical dimension: to observe and record the meanings of

[62] On theories regarding tides in antiquity, see Pomponius Mela 3.1 and Strabo 3.3.3 and 3.5.7. He records Posidonius's dispute with Aristotle. Aristotle had claimed the rough shoreline of Iberia sent back waves forcefully. Posidonius observed correctly, according to Strabo, that the coast was sandy and low.

[63] Augustine will use a version of this theory to justify his allegorical reading of the Hebrew Bible (*De doctrina christiana* 1).

[64] This vision, of course, lies at the extreme end of a world where divination works. We do not see evidence of full-blown adaptation of this view. In practice, the Romans' governing institutions of the *quindecemviri* and the augur, as well as the designated seers and oracles of the Greeks, put limits around what could count as truly significant events. These traditions mark out the domain of meaningful, readable happenings. Stoic theory develops in this context.

things. This is an insistently inductive process, since it must resist the possibility of deducing rational rules to explain the information gathered.

Of course, to divination's detractors this will seem like mere empty speculation. What reason have we to believe that one thing has to do with another? Quintus attempts an answer. He draws an analogy to the medical arts. Though we may not know the precise reasons why certain drugs lead to particular reactions in the body, we nevertheless observe that they do. Similarly, we do not know why the magnet attracts iron, but it does. (Again, Quintus must base his semantics on mystery.) Quintus invokes the authority of the long traditions of whole societies, indeed every known people, who have experienced significant connections between ominous signs and particular outcomes. Whether these connections are valid can only be determined through carefully recorded observations over time, and this stock of knowledge constitutes the domain of the diviner (1.109). It is a range of data as valuable as that which doctors draw upon in their practice of the medical arts. So, though the frog's croak may not have any obvious relation to the storm it predicts, the connection is there nonetheless, a manifestation of an invisible and purposeful divine logos. The logos cares for humans and therefore leaves clues for those who know how to interpret its will. The Stoics see these invisible ties as dwelling in the very sinews of existence. The crucial point here is the ontology of universalist materialism, which we also looked at in chapter 3. We saw that this ontology lent itself to allegorical reading by stipulating material connections between apparently separate things. The Stoics justified divination's effectiveness by explicitly invoking this same position (*De div.* 1.118). The Stoic pneuma, a widely accepted concept in the early days of the Roman Empire and one into which Paul breathes new life in forming the Christian idea of the Holy Spirit, provided the principle on which very broad semantic connections could be built, whether by diviners or allegorists.

Based on the points of contact between divination and allegorism that we examined above, we should consider seriously the notion that divinatory semantics, a field dominated (in intellectual circles at least) by Stoic theories for most of antiquity, would have had something to say to those allegorical readers who gave thought to how literary signs make their meanings. For those who rely on divination in their daily lives (that is, for most of the population at that time), the invisible links between things will simply be a matter of fact. A person with heightened sensibilities, one attuned to the hidden workings of the divine in the world, such as a mantic oracle or an inspired poet, would be able to see these secret patterns and make use of them. The structural similarities between the two fields are compelling. Neither the diviner nor the allegorist need explicitly subscribe to the specific intricacies of the ontologies that make such systems of meaning comprehensible. It seems more likely the case that their fields of practice take on lives of their own and continue as traditions of reading, carried forward by individuals sometimes interested in ontological questions but many times not.

Thinking Symbolically among the Later Pythagoreans

We have seen indications that ancient witnesses often specifically classify the poet's symbolic messages as "philosophical" in nature. For example, the first-century Stoic Cornutus thought that the ancient mythmakers were inclined "to make philosophical statements" [φιλοσοφῆσαι] about the nature of the cosmos "through symbols and riddles" [διὰ σύμβολα καὶ αἰνίγματα].[65] Pseudo-Plutarch's treatment of contemplative discourse, wherein he uses allegorical interpretation, concerns the unearthing of specifically philosophical wisdom in Homer. Reporting Polybius's view, Strabo tells us that "everybody" considers the poems of Homer to be "statements of philosophy" [φιλοσοφήματα]; that is to say, philosophical messages are hidden under the allegorical surface of his poems.[66] At the outset of his treatise, Heraclitus the Allegorist says that those who truly understand the hidden messages in Homer will see his poems in the proper way: philosophically.[67] As we have seen, various esoteric philosophies exhibit points of contact with allegorical exegesis. In examinations of the theoretical background to the symbol, one school in particular has come up. We saw in chapter 2 the formative importance of the Pythagorean symbols for the early development of the notion of literary symbols. As we considered there, the Pythagorean symbol tradition is the better-documented example of what were likely broadly similar uses of the symbol within the mystery religions. In these esoteric cult settings, as well as in allegorical traditions, a symbol is enigmatic language, with an overabundance of meaning, that carries hidden messages of a philosophical nature to those who are able to read the code, in a manner similar to an oracle. They are the tips of so many gnomic icebergs. In addition to reevaluating ties between divinatory and allegorical hermeneutics, we stand to benefit from extending also our examination of the ancient evidence that links the symbol traditions of esoteric cults with literary symbols. Several rele-

[65] Cornutus, chap. 35 (76.5).

[66] τὴν ἐκείνου [Ὁμήρου] ποίησιν φιλοσοφήμα πάντας νομίζειν (Strabo 1.2.17 = Polyb. 34.4.4). See above, p. 118, n.16.

[67] Heraclitus *Homeric Allegories* 3.

vant developments for the symbol take place as the Pythagorean tradition matures into the Roman imperial period.

We mentioned in chapter 2 a few witnesses who testified to links between the allegorical and Pythagorean traditions, including Anaximander, who was both an interpreter of Pythagorean symbols and a reader of Homer's "undermeanings," and the grammarian Tryphon (first century B.C.E.), who includes the Pythagorean "symbols" alongside texts from Homer and Hesiod, as examples of literary allegory. Such a tendency to elide differences between the Pythagorean tradition of interpretation and the allegorical one reappears in later texts as well. Macrobius, for example, in the text that we looked at earlier, cites only a few ancient authorities whose language is worthy of specifically allegorical interpretation, including Hesiod, Orpheus, and the Pythagoreans. Several other late commentators also explicitly draw the connection between Pythagoras's symbols and literary ones. Olympiodorus calls Pythagorean symbols "little myths" [μυθάρια].[68] Also relevant are comments by the late antique Aristotelian commentators. First, Asclepius:

> The Pythagoreans did not wish to lay bare their wisdom even to shoemakers [cf. *Theaet.* 180d]. On account of this, they handed down their teachings symbolically, just as the poets speak covertly.
>
> οἱ Πυθαγόρειοι οὐκ ἐβούλοντο κατάδηλον ποιῆσαι τὴν ἑαυτῶν σοφίαν καὶ σκυτεῦσι. τούτου χάριν συμβολικῶς παρεδίδοσαν τὰ μαθήματα, ὥσπερ οἱ ποιηταὶ περικεκαλυμμένως ἔλεγον.[69]

John Philoponus holds the same view:

> But we know that the teaching of the Pythagoreans was symbolic and they hid their dogmas, so that, as Plato says, they would not lay bare their wisdom, even for shoemakers. Just as in the poetic myths, as Plato himself once said, if someone should remain with the appearance, he will look upon them as ridiculous, if however he seeks out the hidden meaning in them, he will need an inspired soul. The same ought to be said concerning the teachings of the Pythagoreans.
>
> ἀλλ' ἴσμεν <ὅτι> συμβολικὴ ἦν ἡ τῶν Πυθαγορείων διδασκαλία ἀποκρυπτόντων τὰ δόγματα, ἵνα μή, ὥς φησιν ὁ Πλάτων, καὶ τοῖς σκυτοτόμοις κατάδηλον ποιῶσι τὴν ἑαυτῶν σοφίαν. ὥσπερ οὖν ἐπὶ τῶν ποιητικῶν μύθων, ὡς αὐτὸς πάλιν ὁ Πλάτων φησίν, εἰ μέν τις ἐμμένοι τῷ φαινομένῳ, καταγελάστους αὐτοὺς ὄψεται, ἐὰν μέντοι τὴν κεκρυμμένην ἐν αὐτοῖς ζητῇ διά-

[68] Olympiodorus *In Platonis Gorgiam commentaria* 29.4.

[69] Asclepius *In Aristotelis metaphysicorum libros A–Z commentaria*, 34.6–8.

νοιαν, ἐνθουσιώσης ψυχῆς δεήσεται, τὸ αὐτὸ καὶ ἐπὶ τῆς τῶν Πυθαγορείων διδασκαλίας λεκτέον·[70]

In the later periods, the Pythagorean symbols catalyze a second crucial moment of transition in the symbol's history. Even from the beginning, but especially in the Roman period, the Pythagoreans thought their symbols, like the divinatory symbols that we examined, generated power and meaning in registers beyond that of straightforward communicative language. Pythagorean symbols in the Roman period begin to be regarded, to some extent, as efficacious speech. They have the capacity not merely to communicate ideas but also to get things done. Their early function as identity tokens, already a kind of efficaciousness, here expands into broader regions and picks up affiliations with ritual and even magical power. In these contexts, then, the Pythagorean "symbol" acquires capacities similar to the symbol of the mystery religions and takes on an increasingly *performative* power. Its function outgrows the boundaries of semiotics and encroaches on the territory normally reserved for the priest and the magician.

Though Pythagoras enjoyed a strong reputation throughout the ancient period, his stature soars with the Neoplatonists. Most of the major Neoplatonists hold Pythagoras second only to Plato in their esteem. And one pivotal figure, Iamblichus, whose work will primarily occupy the following chapter, may have even given the palm to Pythagoras. His great work, a massive ten-volume series, lays out an entire philosophical program based on Pythagorean principles.[71] Since, throughout antiquity, "symbols" were considered the most characteristic and profound aspect of Pythagoras's teaching, the notion of "symbolic" discourse was bound to enter a new phase with the Neoplatonic thinkers. Proclus, to whose work we will turn after Iamblichus, will bring his strong interest in poetry to this trend, refashion an expanded notion of symbolic discourse for literary theory, and set the tone for understanding the unique powers of symbols for many centuries to come.

Pythagoras and the Peculiar Power of Symbolic Discourse

Esotericism and Ritual

As we saw, from early in the Pythagorean tradition, secrecy played an important part.[72] Knowledge of the symbols, and of their traditional

[70] John Philoponus *In Aristotelis de anima libros commentaria*, ed. Michael Hayduck, *Commentaria in Aristotelem Graeca*, (Berlin, 1847), 15: 69.27–70.2.

[71] On this reading of Iamblichus's corpus, see Dominic J. O'Meara, *Pythagoras Revived* (New York: Oxford University Press, 1989).

[72] See Burkert, 178–79.

interpretations, was the exclusive wisdom of the Pythagoreans, which separated them off from those not "in the know." The symbols form the demarcation between a privileged inner circle and the outside world. Furthermore, knowledge of the symbols was not to leave the circle of Pythagoreans. Clement relates that after a Pythagorean named Hipparchus wrote out his master's tenets in plain language, he was expelled from the school and a mock tombstone was erected for him.[73] We have seen similar, if less drastic, esoteric tendencies in the allegorical tradition.[74] Plutarch describes Pythagorean esotericism specifically in terms of the shadowy practices of the mystery rites:

> Moreover, nothing is so characteristic of Pythagorean philosophy as the symbolic, a type of instruction compounded of speech and silence, as in a mystery initiation, so that they say not, "To those with understanding I shall sing; but close your doors, all you who are profane," but their pronouncement is immediately a light and a token for those familiar with it, but dark and meaningless to the inexperienced. Just as the Lord who is at Delphi, "neither affirms nor conceals but signifies," according to Heraclitus, so with the Pythagorean symbols what seems to be made known is really being concealed, and what is concealed is understood.
>
> Καὶ μὴν οὐδέν ἐστιν οὕτω τῆς Πυθαγορικῆς φιλοσοφίας ἴδιον, ὡς τὸ συμβολικόν, οἷον ἐν τελετῇ μεμιγμένον φωνῇ καὶ σιωπῇ διδασκαλίας γένος· ὥστε μὴ λέγειν, "ἀείσω ξυνετοῖσι, θύρας δ' ἐπίθεσθε βεβήλοι," ἀλλ' αὐτόθεν ἔχειν φῶς καὶ χαρακτῆρα τοῖς συνήθεσι τὸ φραζόμενον, τυφλὸν δὲ καὶ ἄσημον εἶναι τοῖς ἀπείροις. ὡς γὰρ ὁ ἄναξ ὁ ἐν Δελφοῖς οὔτε λέγει οὔτε κρύπτει ἀλλὰ σημαίνει κατὰ τὸν Ἡράκλειτον (D-K 22 B93), οὕτω τῶν Πυθαγορικῶν συμβόλων καὶ τὸ φράζεσθαι δοκοῦν κρυπτόμενόν ἐστι καὶ τὸ κρύπτεσθαι νοούμενον. (Plut. frag. 202)[75]

Plutarch articulates his understanding of the Pythagoreans' famed secrecy within the mysteries' ritualized context.[76] He says their tradition refines a characteristic saying of the ancient mysteries (which orders those who are uninitiated to stay out of earshot). The Pythagoreans achieve the same effect by a concealed form of speech. Only those who are initiated into the cult will understand the symbols' significance. Their enigmatic form shuts out those who are unworthy to hear them. It is also surely worthy of note that all of this reminds Plutarch of the oracular speech heard at Delphi. Iamblichus fleshes out this rather gen-

[73] Clement *Stromata* 5.9.

[74] See above, chap. 4.

[75] Text from Plutarch, *Moralia*, vol. 15, ed. F. Sandbach (Cambridge: Harvard University Press, 1969).

[76] For an attestation of the "symbol" as a ritual instruction generally, see Diodorus Siculus *Historical Library* 17.51.2, cited above, n. 3.

eral comparison and tells us more specifically about the role symbols play within the ritualized ascesis of knowledge that in his view was internal to the cult:

> The Pythagoreans had the habit, before giving scientific instruction, of revealing the subjects under inquiry through similitudes and images [διὰ τῶν ὁμοίων καὶ τῶν εἰκόνων], and after this of introducing the secret revelation of the same subjects through symbols [διὰ τῶν συμβόλων], and then in this way, after the reactivation of the soul's ability to comprehend the intelligible realm and the purging of its vision, to bring on the complete knowledge of the subjects laid down for investigation.[77]

Iamblichus places the symbols within a tiered process of initiation into the various levels of the cult. A Pythagorean devotee was first taught by means of likenesses and images, next, through symbols. The symbolic stage of the process teaches the secret revelation to the initiate; it energizes the soul and purges the vision, preparing one for direct revelation of complete knowledge. These are the kinds of powers commonly associated with initiation rites. How far back this view of Pythagorean training extends is unknown. But there is no doubt that in Iamblichus's time the symbols are a sort of passageway between the mundane world of likenesses and the divine world of complete knowledge, opening access to the higher levels of cultic wisdom. In this sense they operate like the passwords used in the mysteries and in magical rites.

Pythagorean Symbols and Magic Formulas

Pythagoras's symbols are also compared with directly efficacious forms of speech. Sometime before the first century B.C.E., Androcydes, the principal source of the later Pythagorean tradition, compares the Pythagorean symbols with the Ephesian "letters," a widely renowned set of ancient magical formulas.[78] The Ephesian letters are a few words, perhaps no more than six: "Askion," "Kataskion," "Lix," "Tetrax," "Damnameneus," "Aisia." Pausanias tells us that they were carved in the feet, crown, and girdle of the great statue of Artemis inside her temple at Ephesus, one of the seven wonders of the ancient world. He further says that they signified obscurely and "enigmatically" [ἀσαφῶς

[77] Iamb. *In Tim.* (Dillon, ed.). bk. 1, frag. 5. Porphyry supports the general view that the Pythagoreans couched their educational process in the trappings of ritual (V.P. 20).

[78] Chester C. McCown, "The Ephesia Grammata in Popular Belief," *Transactions and Proceedings of the American Philological Association* 54 (1923): 128–40. See also Roy Kotansky, "Incantations and Prayers for Salvation on Inscribed Greek Amulets," in *Magika Hiera*, ed. Christopher Faraone and Dirk Obbink (New York: Oxford University Press, 1991), 110–12.

καὶ αἰνιγματωδῶς (frag. 35, Schwabe)] and that they had magical powers. As far back as the fourth century B.C.E. the Ephesian letters are written down on certain materials, which are then folded up and worn around the neck as a magic token.[79] The author of the book of Acts seems to know of them, as do the writers of the *Greek Magical Papyri*, Plutarch, Clement of Alexandria, Hesychius, the *Suda*, and Eustathius.[80] According to these witnesses, both the spoken and written forms of the magic words have various capacities: they can ward off evil, secure good blessings on a marriage, and guarantee victory in athletic contests. Clement, in discussing the Pythagorean symbols, preserves Androcydes' comparison with the famous magic spells:

> Androcydes, the Pythagorean, says that the so-called "Ephesian letters," much-talked-about among the many, were of the class of "symbols." He says that "Askion" [shadowless], for example, means darkness, for it has no shadow, and "Kataskion" [shadowy] is light, since it illuminates the shadow. And "Lix" is the earth according to its ancient designation and "Tetrax" is the year, in reference to the season; and "Damnameneus" is the sun which overpowers [δαμάζω]; and "Aisia" [auspicious things] is the true voice. And so the symbol means that divine things have been arranged in harmonious order—darkness to light, the sun to the year, and the earth to every sort of nature's genesis.

> Ἀνδροκύδης γοῦν ὁ Πυθαγορικὸς τὰ Ἐφέσια καλούμενα γράμματα ἐν πολλοῖς δὴ πολυθρύλητα ὄντα συμβόλων ἔχειν φησὶ τάξιν, σημαίνειν δὲ Ἄσκιον μὲν τὸ σκότος, μὴ γὰρ ἔχειν τοῦτο σκιάν· φῶς δὲ Κατάσκιον, ἐπεὶ καταυγάζει τὴν σκιάν· Λίξ τέ ἐστιν ἡ γῆ κατὰ ἀρχαίαν ἐπωνυμίαν καὶ Τετρὰξ ὁ ἐνιαυτὸς διὰ τὰς ὥρας, Δαμναμενεὺς δὲ ὁ ἥλιος ὁ δαμάζων, τὰ Αἴσιά τε ἡ ἀληθὴς φωνή. σημαίνει δ' ἄρα τὸ σύμβολον ὡς κεκόσμηται τὰ θεῖα, οἷον σκότος πρὸς φῶς καὶ ἥλιος πρὸς ἐνιαυτὸν καὶ γῆ πρὸς παντοίαν φύσεως γένεσιν.[81]

[79] Anaxilas *Com. Att. Frag.* (Kock, ed.) 2.1.268; 2.2.108. A Cretan lead tablet, folded in such a way as to indicate that it was to be worn around the neck, confirms the magical use of the Ephesian letters during roughly this time period: Ziebarth, *Nachrichten der Gesellschaft der Wissenschaften zu Göttingen* (1899): 129–33. See McCown's text, translation, and commentary in "The Ephesia Grammata in Popular Belief," 132–36. See Kotansky, 127, n. 27, and D. R. Jordan, "A Love Charm with Verses," *ZPE* 72 (1988): 256–58 for a Sicilian lead tablet of similar date and purpose.

[80] *Acts* 19.19; *PGM* 70.12–13; Plutarch *Quaestiones convivales* 706e; Clement of Alexandria *Stromata* 1.15.73.1 and 5.8.2.1; Hesychius *Lexicon* epsilon 7401; *Suda* epsilon 3864; Eustathius *Commentarii ad Homeri Odysseam* 2: 201.43. McCown has also shown that the names appear in the pseudepigraphical *Testament of Solomon*; see "The Ephesia Grammata" for further references.

[81] *Strom.* 5.8.45. Text from Clemens Alexandrinus, *Stromata Buch I–VI*, ed. Ludwig Früchtel and Otto Stählin (Berlin: Akademie-Verlag, 1960). Translations my own, though I have consulted the *Ante-Nicene Fathers* series.

This comparison, by a prominent Pythagorean, of the Pythagorean symbols with the Ephesian letters connects the former explicitly with magic formulas. It may be that Androcydes only meant that the magic words were, like Pythagoras's sayings, interpretable, but a comparison moving in one direction would also surely produce some flow the other way as well. Associated with this we will see a development in the symbol's power to which we will turn in the next chapter. The writers of the *Greek Magical Papyri* know the symbol as a magical amulet or saying. Like the symbol as a password, the symbol as magic spell and magical token takes over at the limits of the descriptive capacities of normal speech; it has an efficacious power and a mode of signification that escapes discursive language.

The Symbol as Hieroglyphic Writing

Pythagoras's followers often claim that he traveled widely and collected the wisdom of many different foreign cultures. Alexander Polyhistor, for example, tells us that Pythagoras studied under an Assyrian named Zaratos (probably meaning Zoroaster), and also among the Galatians and the Brahmans.[82] Iamblichus says that Pythagoras took over all the scientific traditions of the Egyptians, Phoenicians, and Chaldeans.[83] Such tales of travel are common in the biographical accounts of late antiquity: Plato and Moses were sometimes said to have studied with one another (though who taught whom depended largely on one's religious commitments). These stories ultimately tell us more about the mixing of cultures in late antiquity than about the figures they supposedly document. Interestingly, in these later accounts of Pythagoras and Pythagoreans, the symbolic mode of speech is commonly associated with what were for the Greeks foreign or exotic cultures, particularly with Egypt. We start with Porphyry. He tells us that Pythagoras had three ways of speaking, which he learned from the Egyptians:

> In Egypt he lived among the priests and learned the wisdom and language of the Egyptians, and three kinds of writing [γραμμάτων], epistolographic, hieroglyphic, and symbolic, of which some is ordinary speech according to mimesis, and some allegorizes according to certain enigmas. [ἐπιστολογραφικῶν τε καὶ ἱερογλυφικῶν καὶ συμβολικῶν, τῶν μὲν κυριολογουμένων κατὰ μίμησιν, τῶν δ' ἀλληγορουμένων κατά τινας αἰνιγμούς.][84]

[82] *Strom.* 1.15.70.

[83] Iamblichus *V.P.* 158.

[84] V. P. 11–12. Text from *Porphyrii Philosophi Platonici Opuscula Tria*, ed. August Nauk (Hildesheim: G. Olms, 1963).

For one so well steeped in allegorical reading, Porphyry's language is suggestive, making use of concepts with a distinct resonance in allegorism to describe Pythagoras's symbols. It is also worthy of note that Porphyry contrasts the idea of ordinary speech, which works via mimetic representation, with allegorical speech, which operates by the enigma. Both here are species of the symbolic. Later Neoplatonists will specifically repeat this contrast, marking out for the first time in language theory a specifically "nonmimetic" mode of discourse (though with a preference for calling the nonmimetic mode "symbolic"). We saw a similar contrast above when Iamblichus split the Pythagorean ascesis into teaching through likenesses and, only later, teaching through symbols. Clement of Alexandria supplements this picture with more detail. Though he does not mention Pythagoras, the context is clearly similar to Porphyry's, and Clement is here leading up to a discussion of the Pythagorean symbols. The minor variations between Clement and Porphyry indicate either that Porphyry summarized Clement or that they are drawing from the same source (Androcydes is a likely candidate):

> Now those educated among the Egyptians learned first that style of the Egyptian letters which is called epistolographic [ἐπιστολογραφική]; and second, the hieratic [ἱερατική], which the sacred scribes [ἱερογραμματεῖς] use; and finally, and last of all, the hieroglyphic. Of the hieroglyphic, one kind is literal [κυριολογική] and uses the alphabet, and the other symbolic [συμβολική]. Of the symbolic, one kind is written literally by imitation [κυριολογεῖται κατὰ μίμησιν], and the other is written figuratively [τροπικῶς], as it were, and still another allegorizes outright, according to certain enigmas [ἄντικρυς ἀλληγορεῖται κατά τινας αἰνιγμούς]. When they want to indicate the sun, for example, they make a circle, and the moon a crescent shape, according to the literal form [κατὰ τὸ κυριολογούμενον εἶδος]. Other things they engrave figuratively, according to what is most fitting [κατ' οἰκειότητα], and they transpose and alter their character; they change some things, others they recast entirely. Praises of their kings, for example, they hand down in theological myths and engrave them on reliefs. Let the following stand as a specimen of the third type, the enigmatic. The rest of the stars, on account of their wandering course, are represented by the bodies of snakes, but the sun by that of the beetle, because it makes a round shape of ox dung and rolls it in front of its face. They say also that this creature lives six months under ground, and the other division of the year above ground, and emits its seed into the ball and reproduces, and they say that the female beetle does not exist.[85]

[85] *Strom.* 5.4.20–21.

The symbolic here is a general description of the Egyptians' hieroglyphic writing, of which there are three subtypes: the literal, figurative, and enigmatic.[86] The Egyptian hieroglyphs have a special relevance in our reconstruction of later Greek understandings of the "symbolic." Many later sources draw a linkage between the two. Pseudo-Justin claims that Pythagoras's symbols befitted Egyptian ways of thought;[87] Plutarch says that Pythagoras copied his symbolic style from the Egyptians, explicitly identifying the symbols with hieroglyphs;[88] and Philostratus, in his *Life of Apollonius of Tyana*, a hagiographic biography of a Pythagorean hero, tells us that symbols were especially an Egyptian mode of representing the divine.[89]

What about the Egyptian language struck these early and late Roman observers as being especially "symbolic"? This is a difficult question to answer fully. Clement's description suggests that the pictorial nature of the hieroglyphs was enough to qualify them as symbolic, but the other witnesses impute to them a pronounced component of what Clement called the enigmatic symbolic—meaning that hieroglyphs had little representational connection with their meanings. Another fact needs to be taken into account: during this period knowledge of the hieroglyphs was extremely spotty. For the most part, they stood mute on the imposing edifices of age-old Egyptian temples. We might speculate that a widespread ignorance of their meaning greatly enhanced their stature as repositories of secret, ancient wisdom, and so also ushered in the connection with Pythagoras. Symbols here become a paradoxically mute language. Like the symbol as password or magic spell, the symbol as dead language stands outside the normal rules of communication. In fact the symbol as "hieroglyph" (literally, "divine inscription") lies precisely beyond human communication. Language becomes translinguistic and so evanesces into the rarefied airs of emptiness, where, against all rational indications, a deep well of untapped meaning is simply asserted to lie. How much can language tell us? When it is hieroglyphic/sym-

[86] On the topic of Egyptian writing systems during this period, see Alan K. Bowman, *Egypt after the Pharaohs* (Berkeley: University of California Press, 1986), 157–58, and especially J. Cerny, "Language and Writing," in J. R. Harris, ed., *The Legacy of Egypt* (Oxford: Clarendon Press, 1971), 197–219. I thank David Frankfurter for guidance and for the reference.

[87] Ps.-Just. *Cohortatio ad gentiles* 18B. Pseudo-Justin is difficult to date. It is possible that he is to be identified with Marcellus of Ankyra (280–374). See introduction to Christoph Riedweg, ed., *Ad Graecos de vera religione* (Basel: F. Reinhardt, 1994).

[88] Plutarch *Is. et Os.* 354E.

[89] Philostratus *Vita Apollonii* 6.19.41. Unlike other Pythagoreans, Philostratus does not value the symbolic as the highest mode. He here proposes a provocative theory that the "imagination" [*phantasia*] has the greatest power to capture the true essence of the gods. He says imaginative representations look at the true reality, whereas those based on imitation, or mimesis, only account for the appearance (cf. Plotinus *On Beauty* 1.6.3).

bolic, it can tell us more than we can possibly know. The symbol marks out a space outside the economy of language, where nonetheless language promises to take us. A section of Porphyry's *Life of Pythagoras* is instructive in this context. He precisely contrasts symbolic utterances with those that can be articulated by discursive reasoning: "Whatever he [Pythagoras] discussed with those who came to him, he counseled either discursively or symbolically" [Ὅσα γε μὴν τοῖς προσιοῦσι διελέγετο, ἢ διεξοδικῶς ἢ συμβολικῶς παρῄνει] (*V. P.* 36).[90] Once freed from the logic of representation, language grows greatly in its capacity to carry the fantasies and desires of its readers. Unfettered by a referent, the signifier can take on the abstract life of a free signifier, meaning only a certain inexhaustible surplus of meaning. As was the case in divinatory semantics, these later Pythagorean symbols, then, assert meaning precisely beyond the limit of meaning, of representation, or of rational account. The old axis of meaninglessness, which in the archaic and classical periods ran between the omen (based on the senselessness of coincidence and chance) and the esoteric (based on the nothingness of silence), extends into the later periods. Once again, Greeks assert a strong resistance to nonsense in the notion of the symbol and imbue the senseless with the highest order of significance.

Speaking Symbolically in the Late Roman Period

We have already seen ancient observers mark connections between allegorism and divination on the one hand and allegorism and Pythagorean symbols on the other. It is also true that several ancient observers note a connection between Pythagorean symbols and the language of oracles, filling in the last leg of a triangle of mutual influence and affiliation. When Cicero needs a translation of Πυθαγορεία σύμβολα into Latin, he renders it as the Pythagorean "omina" (*De div.* 1.102). Philo remarks that a Pythagorean saying "speaks enigmatically through a symbol" [αἰνίττεται διὰ συμβόλου], conveying a message equivalent to an oracle [χρησμῷ].[91] As we saw, Plutarch notes a connection between Pythagoraean and Delphic language as well. And Iamblichus similarly compares Pythagoras's symbolic teaching to the "enigmas" [αἰνίγμασι] of the Pythian oracle, which are difficult to interpret.[92] This evidence rounds out the other links we have examined between the symbols of allegorism, divination, and philosophico-religious cult.

The literary, divinatory, and Pythagorean symbols that we have seen so far point to a broad and diffuse notion of enigmatic discourse that

[90] For this reading of διεξοδικῶς, see *LSJ*, including parallel citations.

[91] Philo *Quod omnis probus liber sit* 2.4.

[92] *V. P.* 34.247.

was generated during the classical period, became regularly known also as "symbolic" from the Hellenistic period onward, and was in rather broad currency during the Roman period. This language was the special territory of poets, inspired philosophers, and gods sending divine messages. These figures overflow with divine wisdom and convey oblique messages that a few enlightened souls are able to decode. It is not necessary to claim that Pythagoreans, allegorists, and diviners had, in general, any special esteem for each other (though we already have seen examples where this is the case). The more relevant point is that all these theorists spoke the same language—both in the sense that they were speakers of Greek, and in the sense that they nurtured a common conceptual vocabulary (though always for idiosyncratic ends). For example, when a diviner told her or his audience that a bird sign was a symbol, or that an oracle spoke symbolically, she or he opened up one more semantic niche for the term, for all those within earshot. Some of these people, or others to whom they had spoken, would have read a tract on the Pythagorean symbols (which a few odd ascetics in their town held in high esteem) or would have been participants in traditional mystery religions, and would have already marked the symbolic mode as having peculiar resonance. And when this person, or yet someone else with whom he or she had had a conversation, read an allegorical commentator who used the term symbol to label a poet's strange image, the term begins to resonate within a set of affiliations that have accreted over time. And when, at any point in this process, any of these people, or their interlocutors, set their own hands to literary interpretation, or to describing the peculiar style of oracular pronouncements, or to discussing the enigmatic sayings of Pythagoras, they began to reach for the same vocabulary.

I do not suggest that these phenomena were the "same" in any substantive sense, or that their observers did not distinguish between them. To be sure, each interpreter had his or her own interests in and reasons for using and reshaping the notion of the symbolic. But it is also true that the idea of the symbolic itself, or perhaps better, the term itself, takes on a history of its own—not a bloodless, abstract one but one attached to specific thinkers and traditions. Considered this way, the notion of symbolic discourse has a genealogical history, of sorts. It presents options to its users, who, in their own times and for their own needs, appropriate and reshape the semantic reach and possibilities of symbolic signification. None of these thinkers has in mind a developmental vision. They do not see themselves as adding to a unified tradition that advances toward some final and full realization of the "true" symbolic. Rather, each participant in the tradition draws from a common stock of conceptual tools, borrowing from the resonances the term acquires in other contexts, reshaping them for the needs of the moment, and then bequeathing a modified set of possibilities to posterity. This process produces an accretion of senses in the critical vocabulary and nurtures an idea, which many find compelling, that there does indeed exist a category of discourse with curious powers of signification.

I will close here with the full citation of a passage that I mentioned briefly above, from the fifth book of Clement's *Stromata*. Clement catalogues the various oblique languages that the ancients use for discussing the gods (which he will reshape in making new modes of understanding Christian Scripture). After his discussion of symbolic Egyptian hieroglyphs, examined above, he moves on to a chapter explaining the Pythagorean symbols:

> Everybody then, as they say, who has studied the gods, both barbarian and Greek, has hidden the first principles of things, and handed down the truth in enigmas and symbols and allegories, and also in metaphors and these sorts of tropes [αἰνίγμασι καὶ συμβόλοις ἀλληγορίαις τε αὖ καὶ μεταφοραῖς καὶ τοιούτοις τισὶ τρόποις]. Such also are the oracles among the Greeks. Even the Pythian Apollo is called "Loxias" [crooked, or oblique]. Moreover the maxims of those among the Greeks called wise men in a few words present an explanation of a matter of great importance [e.g., "Know thyself"]. . . . But also the poets, taught theology by these prophets, philosophize many things through undermeanings [δι' ὑπονοίας πολλὰ φιλοσοφοῦσι]. I mean Orpheus, Linus, Musaeus, Homer, and Hesiod, and those wise in this way. Their poetic charm is for them a veil [παραπέτασμα] intended for the many. Dreams and symbols are all more or less obscure [ἀφανέστερα] to men, not from jealousy (for it is not right to conceive of God as subject to passions), but in order that, with a view to understanding the enigmas [αἰνιγμάτων], the investigation may trace back and penetrate to the discovery of the truth. Thus, you know, Sophocles the tragic poet somewhere says:
>
> > "And I know that the divine is this sort,
> > Always to the wise prophesying as a riddler [αἰνικτῆρα],
> > But to the sinister the divine is a simple and brief teacher."[93]

Clement, writing around the year 200, here expresses in a kernel what we have seen building in the preceding chapters. The symbolic mode is a language uniquely suited for conveying the most profound knowledge. It is the special language of oracles, dreams, poets, and certain philosophers. Its primary referent is always a certain surplus and inexhaustibility of meaning.

[93] *Strom.* 5.4.21–24.

6

IAMBLICHUS AND THE DEFENSE OF RITUAL: TALISMANIC SYMBOLS

THE FOLLOWERS of Pythagoras introduced us to a sacramental dimension of the ancient concept of the symbol. The secretive tradition that grew up around the Presocratic philosopher's legend employed his "symbols," the short epigrammatic sayings attributed to him, as tokens of true identity and as a kind of catechism in a ritualized ascent to knowledge. They also made comparisons between Pythagoras's symbols and the efficacious speech used in magical practices. But after the third century C.E., the idea that symbols have the power to *do* things and not just *say* them reaches a new and determining prominence with the Neoplatonists. In this sense, the symbol functions as what I am calling a "talisman." Since no cognates are in use by the ancients themselves, a few remarks on the term are perhaps appropriate.[1] Talisman has an etymology in the perfect passive participle of the Greek term *telein*, meaning "to complete, or consecrate." In medieval Greek, Turkish, and Arabic, the root evolves into words designating amulets that were consecrated through a ritual and became animated with numinous power. Though a noun form equivalent to "talisman" is not found in classical Greek, the way we use this term in English, to designate a token with some form of efficacious link to what it is supposed to represent, appropriately captures the new directions in which the Greek term "symbol" began to develop in the hands of the Neoplatonists.

This part of the symbol's story begins in the late third century, when two of Plotinus's successors engage in an argument that will determine the future of Platonic thinking down to at least Ficino's time.[2] Their struggle comes to a head in a uniquely accessible manner. Porphyry (233–c. 305), the immediate successor to Plotinus and the editor of his corpus, composed, probably late in life, a polemical letter to one Anebo,

[1] On this topic and for further references, see Christopher Faraone, *Talismans and Trojan Horses* (New York: Oxford University Press), 3–4. The material that follows draws from Faraone's work.

[2] For more on this debate, see Peter T. Struck, "Speech Acts and the Stakes of Hellenism in Iamblichus, *De mysteriis* 7," in *Magic and Ritual in the Ancient World*, ed. Paul Mirecki and Marvin Meyer, Religions of the Graeco-Roman World Series (Leiden: Brill, 2002), 289–303.

an Egyptian priest. He delivers to his addressee a meticulous series of pointed questions regarding supposedly Egyptian ritual, many of which are easily generalizable into a broad attack on ritual practice. Among many other things, Porphyry asks, If the gods are pure intellect, which Neoplatonists think they are, how could they be swayed by the sensible things (sacrifices, incense) offered up in sacred rites? Why would the highest gods answer to the bidding of the lowly priest? What good are ritual prognostications (a standard component of liturgy at the time) when knowing the future does not necessarily bring happiness?

Iamblichus (d. 330), a fellow devotee of Plotinus's work, decides to take up the questions that Porphyry posed in his letter to Anebo and answer them under the guise of Anebo's spiritual superior, Abammon.[3] The resulting book-length treatise, known since Ficino's day as the *De mysteriis Aegyptiorum*, delivers a point-by-point refutation of Porphyry's charges. Their exchange showcases a complicated philosophical debate over the efficacy and usefulness of rituals in the pursuit of spiritual ascent. In this debate, the capacities of "symbolic" speech take a critical turn. One of Porphyry's questions is of particular interest for us. It concerns a practice that had a broad currency in the late-antique Mediterranean world:

> Also, what do the meaningless names mean? And why are the foreign ones preferred to our own? For if one refers the thing heard to the thing it signifies, the conception itself remains the same, whatever word one may assign to it. For the god invoked, I suppose you would agree, is not of the Egyptian race. Even if he is Egyptian, at any rate he does not use Egyptian, nor, in short, any human language. For either all these are the artificial contrivances of magicians, and veils originating from our affections, which we attribute to a god; or unawares we hold conceptions concerning god that are the opposite of what is really the case.[4]
>
> Τί δὲ καὶ τὰ ἄσημα βούλεται ὀνόματα καὶ τῶν ἀσήμων τὰ βάρβαρα πρὸ τῶν ἑκάστῳ οἰκείων; εἰ γὰρ πρὸς τὸ σημαινόμενον ἀφορᾷ τὸ ἀκοῦον, αὐτάρκης ἡ αὐτὴ μένουσα ἔννοια δηλῶσαι, κἂν ὁποιονοῦν ὑπάρχῃ τοὔνομα. οὐ γάρ που καὶ ὁ καλούμενος Αἰγύπτιος ἦν τῷ γένει· εἰ δὲ καὶ Αἰγύπτιος, ἀλλ' οὔ τί γε Αἰγυπτίᾳ χρώμενος φωνῇ, οὐδ' ἀνθρωπείᾳ ὅλως χρώμενος. Ἢ γὰρ γοήτων ἦν ταῦτα πάντα τεχνάσματα καὶ προκαλύμματα διὰ τῶν ἐπιφημιζομένων τῷ θείῳ τῶν περὶ ἡμᾶς γινομένων παθῶν, ἢ λελήθαμεν ἐναντίας ἐννοίας ἔχοντες περὶ τοῦ θείου ἢ αὐτὸ τῷ ὄντι διάκειται.

[3] The best introduction to Iamblichus is John Dillon, "Iamblichus of Chalcis (c. 240–325 A.D.)," *ANRW* 2.36.2 (1987): 826–909.

[4] Porphyry *Letter to Anebo*, in Parthey's edition of Iamblichus, *De mysteriis* (Berlin, 1857), 33–34.

In Egypt and elsewhere in the Hellenized world, certain rites made use of what were called the *onomata barbara*, divine names that were nonsensical or imported from some exotic foreign language like Hebrew or Egyptian and were considered to have a special power to summon the gods. Porphyry lines up this practice for explicit censure. His charge relies on the vision of language that Aristotle articulates in the *De interpretatione* (a work that Porphyry and his colleagues knew well). As we discussed in chapter 1, according to Aristotle in this text, words are conventional signs of affections of the soul, which are impressions on the soul made by things out in the world. Languages differ from one race to another, but the affections themselves are the same, just as the reality that produces them is the same for all races. Therefore, Porphyry concludes, whether we call the divine by one name or another makes no difference, and there is no possibility that a certain name is more suited to the divine than another. This charge gives Iamblichus an opening to articulate his bold and, as it turns out, influential theory of symbolic speech. Iamblichus answers Porphyry by saying that words do not operate by convention but are suspended from [συναρτᾶσθαι] the very nature of things, so that some are more fitting to their objects than others. We remember the Stoic notion that words had "natural" meanings, but Iamblichus has something more drastic in mind. To understand it will require a foray into his complicated metaphysics, a detour we will take in a moment.

Furthermore, Iamblichus will maintain that certain races have a more accurate impression of reality and have names that are better suited to it. Wrapped up in this argument between two Greek-educated, prominent intellectuals in the late Roman Empire (both from Syria) is also a curious movement of cultural and intellectual transference. Plotinus's two most powerful heirs ventriloquize their debate through Egyptian holy men. This is odd. Though I will not be able to explore this question in depth here, several factors are of interest, including Egypt's prestige as an old and wise culture, the status of Syria at the time Iamblichus is writing, and the resemblance of some Egyptian ritual practices to those that Iamblichus wishes to institute.[5] Of special interest, though, is the controversial nature (from a traditional Platonic view) of Iamblichus's program. This final point suggests the possibility that the post-Iamblichean heirs of Plato take on Egyptian personae in order to express their own troubling admissions of, and forays beyond, the limits of rationalism. In other words, the keepers of Platonic wisdom make their exotic neighbors into spokesmen for ideas that, they knew well, would have been difficult for the master to swallow.[6]

[5] On this topic, see G. W. Bowersock, *Roman Arabia* (Cambridge: Harvard University Press, 1983), 110–37; and Struck, "Speech Acts."

[6] In so doing they were following a path already pointed out by Plato. He himself

Hierarchy and Emanation

Iamblichus and Porphyry rely on a relatively settled body of metaphysical thought. Since these positions would have passed for something like common sense among their fellow students of Plotinian metaphysics (which is to say, most philosophically educated young men of the day) and their theories of language are influenced by their metaphysics, it is necessary to lay down some of the most important features of the Neoplatonic cosmos. We will find out that Iamblichus means something quite specific when he claims that words are "suspended from" the things they name. In their elaborate and various metaphysical schemes, the Neoplatonists are notorious hairsplitters.[7] We will set out here only the most general picture, one that all of the major figures could embrace, though each of them refines and complicates it.

From Plotinus forward, the Neoplatonic cosmos was arranged hierarchically. This hierarchy is usually discussed in terms of "superior" [κρείττονα] and "inferior" [ὑποδεέστερα] beings or manifestations that dwell in tiered levels, or "hypostases." At the top rests the utterly transcendent One, the source of all that exists. Since it is the source even of being itself, the Neoplatonists claim that the One must be above being,[8] and certainly beyond all categories of thinking and all attempts to name or describe it. They often cite Plato himself for the belief, drawing from the reference in *Republic* 6 to a good "beyond being" (509b). The One radiates out from itself all that exists in the cosmos, in a process most commonly known as emanation. Like the sun giving off light, it is undiminished by the outflow and produces the world out of an overflowing superabundance. The rays of the One emanate, in a movement called "procession" [πρόοδος], and manifest (or hypostasize) the lower levels of reality. The lower hypostases are successive degradations into multiplicity, from the perfect and transcendent unity of the One.

The second major hypostasis, the first level that the One manifests below itself, is the divine Mind or *Nous*. This level contains intellectual

turned to Egypt in the *Phaedrus* (274c–275c), where he recounts a myth about the origins of writing; and in the *Timaeus* he portrays the Egyptians as an ancient and wise culture.

[7] The best synthetic treatment of Neoplatonic thought remains A. H. Armstrong's discussion of Plotinus and A. C. Lloyd's of Porphyry, Iamblichus, Proclus, and Damascius, in A. H. Armstrong, ed., *The Cambridge History of Later Greek and Early Medieval Philosophy* (Cambridge: Cambridge University Press, 1970), 195–325. The following discussion is indebted to them.

[8] Porphyry suggests at one point in his *Parmenides* commentary that the One is absolute being. This position puts him closer to the position of the Middle Platonist Numenius; see Pierre Hadot, "Fragments d'un commentaire de Porphyre sur le Parménide," *Revue des Études Grecques* 74.351–53 (1961): 410–38.

reality and is home to Plato's forms. The forms dwell here as a perfectly unified and interpenetrating whole. Plotinus uses the memorable image of light dwelling within light to describe their state, and Proclus will use the image of light within air.[9] The Nous is a purely intellectual reality, unsullied by matter, but not intellectual in the sense that we commonly know it, as discursively rational. The divine mind thinks without need for limits or categories or sequential strings of logic. It remains perfectly still; it thinks and knows everything all at once. The Nous manifests out of itself the hypostasis of Soul, a whole stratum of reality of which the individual soul partakes. Soul performs a mediating role between intellectual and material reality. Movement and true multiplicity and dividedness begin to take place at this level. The Soul is the source of all motion, from the growth of plants to the perambulations of humans. The operations of the principles of nature [φύσις] typically take place here. Beings that exist at the level of this hypostasis can only think of one thing at a time and must use chains of discursive reasoning to acquire knowledge. Soul covers the greatest ontological range of the hypostases. It can reach all the way up to the perfectly pure and unified intellect and all the way down to base, inert matter.

Below the hypostasis of the Soul exists the region of unformed, brute matter [ὕλη]. If Plato had problems with the material world, the Neoplatonists only deepened and systematized them. For Plotinus, matter does not even count as a hypostasis, since it is so far away from true reality that it cannot be said to exist in any proper manner. What then is matter's status? Plotinus stretches himself between two firmly held beliefs. Matter is a ghost-world of utter darkness and lack, incapable of acknowledging the good, and absolute evil (see *Ennead* 1.8.4). And yet, Plotinus also argues firmly against Gnostic dualism. Matter simply cannot be pure evil, he says in *Ennead* 2.9, since such a valuation would place a certain part of the cosmos outside the ken of the One, an ontological consequence that is simply absurd.

> If matter is really abandoned and isolated, then the divine will not be everywhere, but in a particular bounded place, walled off, so to speak; and if that is not possible, then matter must receive the divine light.
>
> Εἰ δὲ (ἡ ὕλη) μόνη καταλειφθήσεται, οὐ πανταχοῦ, ἀλλ' ἔν τινι τόπῳ ἀφωρισμένῳ τὰ θεῖα ἔσται καὶ οἷον ἀποτετειχισμένα· εἰ δὲ οὐχ οἷόν τε, ἐλλαμφθήσεται. (2.9.3)

The future most vivid constructions drive home his heartfelt horror at the prospect of a divine that is somehow separate from its creation. The tension is not resolved fully in his work, and it is difficult to judge whether it is a creative one or simply an aporetic paradox.

[9] Plotinus 5.8.4; Proclus *In Parm.* 755.1–5.

All the Neoplatonists pair the downward procession out from the One with an equally strong upward current: the aspiration of humans, and all other existing things, including the lowliest rock, to reach back up through the levels of being, to pure Soul, pure Intellect, and ultimately to the utterly transcendent One itself. Like salmon swimming upstream, humans, and all other existing things, make the One the *telos* of everything they do, though from varying states of ignorance. The study of philosophy plays the central role in the upward movement. The Neoplatonists reconceive philosophy as a soteriological discipline [ἄσκησις] of spiritual exercises meant to lead the soul to the One.

Iamblichus versus Porphyry

Both Iamblichus and Porphyry would have been able to agree with most of what we have said so far. The main point of disagreement between them can be summed up as a difference over the proper path for human beings in their upward journey back toward the One. At least later in his life, Porphyry thought, like Plotinus, that contemplation alone was sufficient, while Iamblichus considered that a program of ritual action was a necessary component of the upward reach. Their differing visions can be linked to their differing opinions on the nature of the individual human soul.[10] Porphyry tended to think more highly of its capacities, while Iamblichus was convinced it needed to ask for help. Porphyry shows a certain tendency to telescope the hypostases, which amounts to a hint that the highest, utterly transcendent divinity leaves a trace of itself within the human soul. The distinctions between the realms of Soul, Nous, and the One may not be so sharp after all.[11] Since both Porphyry and Plotinus can entertain the notion of a *scintilla* of the highest orders resting inside the soul, they prescribe, naturally enough, spiritual exercises in which the aspirant turns inward and reaches the One through contemplative reflection. As aspirants get closer and closer to the essences (and ultimately the hyperessence) underlying their own souls, they simultaneously approach the One itself.

But Iamblichus has a different psychology, one that calls for a different method of approach to the One. In contrast to his predecessors' tendency to collapse distinctions between the various levels of reality, Iamblichus insists on their separateness, and specifically on the inferior

[10] This has been pointed out by Gregory Shaw in *Theurgy and the Soul: The Neoplatonism of Iamblichus* (University Park: Pennsylvania State University Press, 1995), 72.

[11] Plotinus balances this position with equally weighted statements that insist on the separateness of reality's various levels. Porphyry shows a marked fondness for telescoping the levels into one (see Lloyd, 287–93). Cf. Proclus *Elements of Theology* prop. 103 and Iamblichus *Commentary on the* De anima (from Stob. 1.49.32.63–77 [Hense and Wachmuth, eds.]).

position of Soul, and especially the individual human soul. Consequently, he does not believe that contemplation alone has the power to bring a person face to face with god. He advertises this opinion as that of Plato himself, and, if one analyzes their writings with real knowledge, of Pythagoras, Aristotle, and all the ancients.[12] What led Iamblichus to draw the lines between the various levels of reality more sharply than his predecessors? He gives a clue as to his reasoning in his commentary on the *Timaeus*:

> But if, when the best part of us is perfect, then the whole of us is happy, what would prevent us all, the whole human race, from being happy at this moment, if the highest part of us is always enjoying intellection, and always turned towards the gods? If the Intellect is the highest part, that has nothing to do with the soul: if it is a part of the soul, then the rest of the soul also must be happy.[13]

Iamblichus makes an argument from his own experience of human souls in the world. Unlike Plotinus (in whom one does not detect a strong empirical interest), Iamblichus studies the embodied souls he sees day-to-day and, failing to observe a transcendent spark within them, takes a decidedly less sanguine view of the human condition. His observations lead him to question, in John Dillon's memorable paraphrase, "If this hidden generator . . . was continually humming away, how could we not feel its effects?"[14] Iamblichus therefore reasserts the distinctness of the ontological gaps between ourselves and the gods, and, naturally enough, it leads him to a position that the approach to the One, if it is to happen at all, must come from some power greater than the human soul, from some part of the higher orders that breaks through to the lower ones. Human contemplation, time-bound and limited to discursive modes of thought, cannot bring an aspirant to the real Truth without some form of outside help. In the *De mysteriis*, this help comes in the form of rituals, which sometimes employ mysterious, unspeakable, abundantly powerful "symbols."

Theurgy

In the intellectual and religious stir of late antiquity, Iamblichus attempts to focus the disparate cults of Hellenism into a coherent liturgi-

[12] See John M. Dillon, ed., *Iamblichi Chalcidensis in Platonis dialogos commentariorum fragmenta* (Leiden: E. J. Brill, 1973), 41.

[13] Iamblichus *Timaeus Commentary* frag. 87 (Dillon, ed.).

[14] Dillon, introduction to *Iamblichi Chalcidensis in Platonis dialogos commentariorum fragmenta*, 43.

cal program called "theurgy,"[15] which he describes most fully in his answers to Porphyry in the *De mysteriis*. The traditional theurgic rites center on the invocation of a god, who becomes mysteriously present to the celebrants in a votive statue, through a rite of consecration.[16] The key elements of the ritual are "symbols" (the term σύμβολα is used interchangeably with συνθήματα in this context), which are words or objects that have special connections with the divine. The material symbol is a bone, a gem, a stone, an herb, or other object from the natural world with which the divinity has an affiliation.[17] The celebrant inserts the symbol into a cavity, perhaps the mouth, in the devotional statue. The verbal "symbol" in Iamblichus usually takes the form of a secret divine name that is thought to have similar powers to invoke the gods. Like the password of the mysteries, it verifies a mortal's fitness to inhabit a higher plane of reality and to receive the divine. We will revisit the topic of the nature and function of these symbols after a more general consideration of theurgy and its antecedents.

Skeptical of the power of human reason to transcend itself, Iamblichus constructs a theology of the hyperrational in the *De mysteriis*. Dodds's description of the tract as a "manifesto of irrationalism" hardly does justice to it.[18] First of all, such a characterization obscures the fact that Plotinus, Porphyry, and Iamblichus shared a belief in the limited capacities of the strictly cognitive powers of human reason. Though many have rightly pointed to the elegance and force of Plotinus's insights (a power Iamblichus can rarely match), Plotinus speaks of the final movement of the soul toward the One as being beyond human

[15] For this characterization of theurgy, see Garth Fowden, *The Egyptian Hermes* (Princeton: Princeton University Press, 1986), 116–41. The term "theurgy" was a neologism a century or so before Iamblichus. In the second century C.E., a father-and-son team who claimed to be of "Chaldean" (Babylonian) extraction coined it as a contrast to "theology"—that is, in order to stress the importance of deeds (*erga*) and not just language or reason (*logos*) in one's spiritual ascent.

[16] For discussion of the principles behind this practice, see *De myst.* 5.23.35–45 and Shaw's discussion (162–69). On the practice itself, see esp. Proclus *On the Hieratic Art*, published in *Catalogue des manuscrits alchemiques grecs*, fasc. 6, ed. J. Bidez (Brussels, 1928) and translated by A. Bremond in "Notes et documents sur la religion néoplatonicienne," *Recherches de Science Religieuse* 23 (1933): 102–6. For a commentary, see H. Corbin in *Eranos-Jahrbuch* 24 (1955): 199–205 and 263–67. Cf. the Hermetic *Asclepius* 38a. See also the helpful commentary of A.D.R. Sheppard, *Studies on the 5th and 6th Essays of Proclus' Commentary on the Republic* (Göttingen: Vandenhoeck and Ruprecht, 1980), 145–61; on the differences between Iamblichean and Proclean theurgy, see Sheppard's "Proclus' Attitude to Theurgy," *Classical Quarterly* 32.1 (1982): 212–24. Further illustrations can be found at Proclus *In Parm.* 847; *In Tim.* 1.51.25; 3.6.8ff. and 155.18ff.

[17] Iamblichus *De myst.* 5.23.29–35; Proclus *On the Hieratic Art*.

[18] E. R. Dodds, *The Greeks and the Irrational* (Berkeley: University of California Press, 1951), 287.

reason, and beyond even undivided intellect. It is something like an intuition, or a dance, or a drunkenness, in other words a moment of rapture in which the divided, embodied human, subject to time and space, partakes of the utterly transcendent source of all existence.[19] One could just as easily label this "irrationalism," but we would lose much in our understanding.

Iamblichus differs with his predecessors on the type of discipline he envisions. Whereas Plotinus thought contemplation could bring us right up to the very doorstep of the One, Iamblichus insists that the One has to reach down to us. But the One will not descend haphazardly. Humans must invoke it, and demonstrate, by their actions, a readiness to receive it. In Iamblichus's thinking, the performance of theurgic rites is the clearest, most effective expression of this readiness. While the main function of the ritual is to promote spiritual union with the One, Iamblichus also speaks regularly of a divinatory component to the rituals (*De myst.* 3.15–17). He explains this as an outflow of the gods' inclination to benevolence and their interest in nurturing those who sincerely worship them. At some point, we know not where, in the rite, the divine lifted back the veil of the future and informed the devotee of how best to conduct his actions.

The distinction between "magic" and more properly "religious" ritual is often vague and nearly always under scrutiny, but since it is still operative in scholarly discussion of the late Neoplatonists, we need to consider it. We can hardly equate Iamblichus's ideas with "vulgar magic," as Dodds does,[20] for his theurgy does not include two central components of most traditional definitions of magic: he does not envision it as being coercive, and he does not have narrow, practical goals. First, Iamblichus says over and over that the divine is not forced into service by the theurgic rites. Rather, the god or goddess responds to a call for intervention out of his or her own overflowing goodness.[21] While this may appear to be a distinction without a difference, it is a standard trope in the rhetoric of ritual theory, both ancient and modern. Second, in contrast with, for example, the writers collected in the *Greek Magical Papyri*, Iamblichus expends most of his energy addressing phi-

[19] προσβολή (a "kiss" or "embrace"), 3.8.10; choral dance as movement of the soul within the cosmos, 4.4.8, 33, 35; drunkenness, 5.8.10, 6.7.35; on the linguistic issues raised by Neoplatonic spiritual ascent, see Sara Rappe, *Reading Neoplatonism* (New York: Cambridge University Press, 2000), 45–66, 91–114.

[20] Dodds, 288. For more recent evaluations of these categories, see Fritz Graf, "Prayer in Magic and Religious Ritual," in *Magika Hiera*, ed. Christopher Faraone and Dirk Obbink (New York: Oxford University Press, 1991), 188–213; and J. Z. Smith "Trading Places," 13–27, and Graf, "Excluding the Charming," 29–42, in *Ancient Magic and Ritual Power*, ed. M. Meyer and P. Mireki (Leiden: Brill, 1995).

[21] *De myst.* 1.12, 3.26, 4.9, 4.3, 5.7–9.

losophers' concerns with respect to rites in general, and not pursuing the limited goals—health, success in business, the torment of an enemy—that more often motivate the rites recorded on the *PGM*. There is no doubt that Iamblichus has in mind union with the divine through properly performed worship. Though I will not be able to treat all of them, several points in Iamblichus's program bear further scrutiny: the *De mysteriis* includes a sophisticated argument on the limits of human reason; a well-constructed (and enduring) philosophical justification of the role of ritual in the approach to the divine; a remaking of traditional Stoic arguments for divine involvement in the world, through a reevaluation of the concept of "sympathy"; and new theories of the power of language, based on a reconfiguration of several ancient traditions of the "symbol."[22] The last point will detain us at greatest length and will occasion less detailed investigations into the others.

The Talismanic Symbol

Iamblichus makes the "symbol" the central link between the divine and human realms. The symbol makes the impossible happen; it becomes the node on which the transcendent can meet the mundane. As we saw, according to Iamblichus's psychology, humans dwell on a plane of existence that is remote from the higher orders and have souls that have fully descended into material bodies. But he will not allow that humans have *no* access to transcendence, as, for example, the Epicureans before him had maintained. For a Neoplatonist, this would be a pessimistic vision indeed. Iamblichus makes the "symbol" his solution. Like the Pythagorean password or the mantic pronouncement of an oracle, the symbol becomes once again the crucial link between the mundane and the transcendent, between the daily world in which humans live and the divine mansions of the gods.

Antecedents to Iamblichus's Theurgic Symbol

Iamblichus would have recognized the senses of the "symbol" that we have traced out in earlier chapters. It is safe to assume that he had knowledge of Porphyry's treatise *On the Cave of the Nymphs* and would have understood "symbol" as a proper designation of an allegorical literary image that conveys a hidden message. It is certainly the case that Iamblichus was familiar with "symbols" as the oblique language by which the gods speak to humans in oracles, omens, and dreams. (This

[22] For more detail on these questions, see Struck, "Speech Acts."

sense appears in his own work.[23]) He would also have been familiar with "symbols" as the enigmatic sayings of Pythagoras and his followers, which contained the most profound hidden wisdom. As Dominic J. O'Meara has demonstrated, the entire Iamblichean corpus is arranged as an exposition of Pythagoreanism,[24] and his *Life of Pythagoras* contains explicit references to their "symbols" (see above, chap. 5).

But, in forming his vision of theurgic "symbols," Iamblichus knew and made use of traditions that we have not yet examined. Despite his greater theoretical sophistication, Iamblichus's program of theurgy bears a number of significant similarities to the rituals we see prescribed in the group of magical handbooks recovered in Egypt and now referred to under the name of the *Greek Magical Papyri*.[25] The papyri show a great range of magical practices, including binding rituals, divination rituals, erotic love charms to make a suitor irresistible, and foolproof methods of cursing one's enemies. As Dodds and others have shown, several of the magical rituals in the *PGM* refer to practices of statue animation that bear some similarity to theurgic practices.[26] Furthermore, the *PGM* authors and Iamblichus use the word "symbol" in somewhat similar ways. In the *PGM*, symbols are the magic names or accouterments or attendants of a god, such as animals, plants, stones, kinds of wood, kitchen utensils, and various and sundry other items, like coral, the blood of a turtledove, the hoof of a camel, the hair of a virgin cow, or a black sphinx's pierced vagina.[27] The magicians think that these objects and names have some sort of sympathetic connection with the god, that is, some invisible but nonetheless real and efficacious link with the divinity. When manipulated or recited, the magic accouterments and names give the devotee the power to coerce the god or demon associated with them. Imperative constructions are common, as

[23] *De myst.* 3.15.

[24] Dominic J. O'Meara, *Pythagoras Revived: Mathematics and Philosophy in Late Antiquity* (New York: Oxford University Press, 1989), 32–35.

[25] The question of Iamblichus's debt to the Egyptians is a subject of ongoing discussion in the scholarly literature. Hans Lewy was surely open to considering Egyptian antecedents (*The Chaldean Oracles and Theurgy: Mysticism, Magic, and Platonism in the Later Roman Empire*, ed. Michel Tardieu [Paris: Études Augustiniennes, 1978]). Dodds took at face value Iamblichus's claim of an Egyptian origin (Dodds, 283–99). This thesis was revised in a strong way by Dagron (*Travaux et mémoires du Centre de Recherches d'Histoire et Civilisation Byzantines* 3 [1968]: 155, n. 39), who claimed that "Egypt" here stood only as a mystified origin for irrationalist beliefs in which Hellenistic thinkers were dabbling. Garth Fowden has since been more open to reconsidering some actual Egyptian elements in the theurgic program (Fowden, 135).

[26] Dodds, 293 and notes.

[27] See, e.g., *PGM* 4.559; 7.786; 7.560; 4.2300–40; cf. *PGM* 8.13, where the term itself does not appear, but we get a nice recounting of the kinds of objects called "symbols" in other contexts.

are threats and demands (lacking in Iamblichus) directed at the divinities. In the *PGM*, the symbols also appear in a context similar to the Pythagorean one we saw in the last chapter. In the "Mithras Liturgy," the symbol is a magic formula that functions as a token of identity or a passport. Performance of the liturgy raises the devotee up to the level of the gods; but, the text warns, the divinities will then come rushing at the suspected intruder and glare menacingly. To satisfy the gods that he or she belongs in this exalted realm and to gain passage to the next levels, the devotee must utter a "symbol."[28]

The *Chaldean Oracles* are a more important precursor to Iamblichus than the practices of Greco-Egyptian magic.[29] These texts took on a great authority among the later Neoplatonists. According to the Byzantine writer Michael Psellus (who was probably drawing on Proclus), the "oracles" were extracted by Julian the Chaldean, perhaps using his son Julian the Theurgist as a medium.[30] The handiwork of this father-and-son team emerges in the late second century. It is possible that the elder Julian was actually a Chaldean (a Greco-Roman name for the Babylonian priests encountered for the first time by the Greeks during Alexander's expeditions and celebrated for their wisdom throughout the Greek and Roman world). Near the beginning of the first century, the emperor Trajan reached as far as the Persian gulf in his campaign against the Parthians, and the elder Julian may have been transplanted during the increased communications between East and West that ensued, but this is not much more than speculation. It is also possible that the Juliani adopted the identity of "Chaldeans" to take on some of the aura and authority of that faraway place. Two Syrian names, Ad and Adad, appear in the text, and the doctrine of the oracles resembles that of Numenius (a forerunner of the Neoplatonists), who lived at Apamea in Syria.[31] This evidence suggests a possible Syrian origin, a suspicion that Iamblichus's fondness for and familiarity with the oracles may confirm. He himself was born near Apamea and set up his school there after his education in Plotinian metaphysics. Furthermore, one fragment

[28] The text gives the password as a long string of letters, whose sense is not clear.

[29] The bibliography here is rather large. For those interested in pursuing the topic further, see Sarah Iles Johnston, *Hekate Soteira: A Study of Hekate's Roles in the Chaldean Oracles and Related Literature* (Atlanta: Scholars Press, 1990), chap. 7; Friedrich W. Cremer, *Die Chaldäischen Orakel und Jamblich De mysteriis* (Meisenheim am Glan: Hain, 1969); and Otto Geudtner, *Die Seelenlehre der Chaldäischen Orakel* (Meisenheim am Glan: Hain, 1971).

[30] See Dodds, 284. The scene is described in *Michaelis Pselli philosophica minora*, ed. J. M. Duffy (Leipzig: Teubner, 1992), 46.43–51.

[31] See Ruth Majercik, introduction to *The Chaldean Oracles: Text, Translation, and Commentary*, ed. Majercik (New York: E. J. Brill, 1989) for references to the scholarship on this point.

of the *Oracles* makes a claim that they agree with Assyrian theology (frag. 67), a rather parochial concern for someone from "Chaldea." Perhaps trumping any of these considerations, is the obvious point that the oracles are not set up to spread the cult or worship of any Eastern pantheon. Hecate and Apollo are the central figures throughout, and the philosophical positions inside of the texts can nearly all be found within Greek Middle Platonism, of the sort which thrived at learning centers like Apamea.[32]

As is common in the literature of this period, the *Chaldean Oracles* describe a Platonist hierarchical cosmology and the devotee's mystical ascent through it. The scant fragments that survive also clearly indicate that some form of ritual is involved in the mystical ascent. References are made to "sprinkling" (frag. 133), deep breathing (frag. 124), and to ritual implements, such as the mysterious *iunx*. These elements will sound familiar to readers of the *PGM*. According to the reconstruction of Hans Lewy, the Chaldean ritual also involved the use of "σύμβολα"—though the extant fragments do not specifically mention "symbols" in a ritual context. But there is one noteworthy use of the term: the *Oracles* tell us that the divine father of the universe, the Nous in the author's understanding, sowed [ἔσπειρεν] secret "symbols" [ἄφραστα σύμβολα] throughout the universe [κατὰ κόσμον].[33] Tracing back from later sources, Lewy concludes, rightly in my view, that the earliest theurgists saw themselves as gathering these divine seeds (in the form of certain stones, herbs, gems, plants, etc.) in theurgic ritual. As we mentioned above, Iamblichus will also tell us that certain words or spoken formulas are called "symbols," and have, like their material counterparts, real and efficacious connections with the higher orders. These developments in the symbolic imagination push the powers of the symbol in the direction of the talismanic, which proves to be of profound importance for Iamblichus and, through him, for the later history of the symbolic.

Another precursor to Iamblichus, this one also with a partially Egyptian pedigree, is the collection of texts known as the *Hermetica*. These texts were written in Hellenized Egypt probably between the first and third centuries C.E. (though parts are perhaps much older) and take the form of a collection of dialogues between Hermes the thrice-great ("Trismegistus") and a few other characters. They exhibit affinities with Middle Platonic, Gnostic, and pre-Hellenistic Egyptian traditions. The term "symbol" appears in this corpus only in the sense that we traced in chapters 2 and 5, as an omen (*Corpus Hermeticum* 12). Significantly,

[32] Johnston; Fowden, 135.

[33] From Procl. *In Crat.* (Pasquali, ed.), 20.31–21.2.

this Hermetic writer invokes the term in the context of establishing a continuity between the realms of the gods and humans. Symbols (in daytime) along with dreams (at night) are the means by which the gods communicate with humans. They are vehicles that bear messages through the sometimes porous barrier separating the divine from the mundane.

More important, the *Hermetica* also discuss specific practices of statue animation that bear a detailed resemblance to the theurgic rites. The Hermetic texts broaden still further the potential audience for rituals of statue divinization which the theurgists will later center on their notion of the symbol. References to statues as liturgical elements appear in the incomplete *Corp. Herm.* 17. More extended and significant references to the practice occur in the Latin *Asclepius*. Trismegistus minces no words about the actual presence of divine spirits (whether gods or demons) in the devotional statue. He tells his interlocutor, Asclepius, of the great powers of "man-made" gods: "Statues, Asclepius, yes . . . I mean statues ensouled and conscious, filled with spirit and doing great deeds; statues that foreknow the future . . . , statues that make people ill and cure them, bringing them pain and pleasure as each deserves" (23–24).[34] Hermes gives a clearer picture of these devices later in the dialogue. He says that the image makers "called up the souls of demons or angels and implanted them in likenesses through holy and divine mysteries" (37). Furthermore, these images have a "property" [*qualitas*], most likely a divine/magic power, that derives from certain "plants, stones and herbs . . . that have in them a natural power of the divinity" (38). These later clarifications are especially resonant with the theurgic rites as Iamblichus and his followers explain them.[35]

Finally, we need to look at another important, and often overlooked, precursor to Iamblichus's thoughts on the practice of theurgy and the power of symbols: Iamblichus's opponent in the struggle over the value of theurgy, Porphyry. In all likelihood, the zeal with which Porphyry attacks theurgic practices in his *Letter to Anebo* is the zeal of a lapsed believer. His earlier works, *On Philosophy from Oracles* and *On Statues*, show that he was familiar with theurgy and was not at all

[34] Translations modified slightly from Brian P. Copenhaver, *Hermetica* (New York: Cambridge University Press, 1992).

[35] Walter Scott acknowledges this link to the theurgic rites but dilutes some of the strength of the parallel by claiming that the "animated" statues might be references to live animals (Walter Scott, *Hermetica*, 4 vols. [Boston: Shambhala, 1985], note ad loc.). While this is possible, the similarities to the theurgic rites of the *Chaldean Oracles* and the later Neoplatonists make the theurgic interpretation much more likely. Jean-Pierre Mahé has especially explored the specifically theurgic context for these passages (*Hermès en haute-Égypte* (Quebec: Presses de l'Université Laval, 1978–82), 2: 98–102, 224, 315, 385; further citations in Copenhaver, 254.

critical of it at that time. In these works, he uses the term "symbol" in several different senses. Wax likenesses of the gods in their traditional appearances (328F);[36] the traditional accouterments of the various gods, like Hecate's torch and serpent (328F), or Silenus's head wreath (358F); apotropaic objects that avert evil demons (326F)—all of these he characterizes as "symbols." Sometimes the gods themselves are symbols, for example, Hera, Hades, Adonis, and Silenus are symbols, respectively, of the air, the unseen pole (of the earth), the cutting of perfect fruits, and the wind's motion (356F, 358F). In all these uses, symbols are either a material entity standing in for a divine one (like a wax statue for Hecate), or a divine thing standing for a natural entity (like Hera for the air). Once again the term symbol marks a point of intersection between divine and mundane realms. We would like to know more about how Porphyry viewed the mechanics of symbols. The fragments of Porphyry's earlier works that survive do not give us systematic answers to the question within larger schemes of Neoplatonic physics or metaphysics. Analogies to the statue worship that Iamblichus attempts to institute are also attested in certain less arcane sources, including Dio Chrysostom (*Or.* 12), Maximus of Tyre (*Or.* 2), and the Emperor Julian (*Frag. Epist.* 293A)—an admirer of Iamblichean Platonism. Of course, Iamblichus has his own symbolic visions, to which none of the parallel sources mentioned offers a precise parallel. But these texts do indicate that a statue-animation ritual (of whatever sort), within a context of Middle Platonic and emerging Neoplatonic philosophy, was rather broadly diffused through the Hellenized Mediterranean during the imperial period, and that notions of the "symbol" played an important role in it.

Symbol and Synthema *in Iamblichus*

In the *De mysteriis*, Iamblichus deepens and systematizes the role of the "symbol" in ritual actions. In his answers to Porphyry he at the same time hints that such symbolic powers might on occasion loose themselves from a strictly ritual function and infuse the representational arts, whether plastic or literary, more broadly. We might begin by recalling the passage from the *Chaldean Oracles* that claims that the divine father sowed "symbols" like seeds throughout the cosmos. Iamblichus picks up this line of thinking at the close of the first book of the *De mysteriis*:

[36] Citations are to *Porphyrii Philosophi Fragmenta*, ed. Andrew Smith (Stuttgart: Teubner, 1993).

> The sacred rites imitate the order of the gods, both the intelligible and heavenly orders. They contain the eternal measures of beings, and the amazing traces which are sent down here from the demiurge and the father of wholes, by which even inarticulable things are spoken aloud through unspeakable symbols, and the formless are ordered into forms, and things higher than every image are stamped out through images. All the rites are performed through a single divine cause, which, whatever it is, is separated so far away from the passions, that not even reason is able to grasp it.
>
> [ἡ ἁγιστεία] μιμεῖται δὲ τὴν τῶν θεῶν τάξιν, τήν τε νοητὴν καὶ τὴν ἐν οὐρανῷ. Ἔχει δὲ μέτρα τῶν ὄντων ἀίδια καὶ ἐνθήματα θαυμαστά, οἷα ἀπὸ τοῦ δημιουργοῦ καὶ πατρὸς τῶν ὅλων δεῦρο καταπεμφθέντα, οἷς καὶ τὰ μὲν ἄφθεγκτα διὰ συμβόλων ἀπορρήτων ἐκφωνεῖται, τὰ δὲ ἀνειδέα κρατεῖται ἐν εἴδεσι, τὰ δὲ πάσης εἰκόνος κρείττονα δι' εἰκόνων ἀποτυποῦται, πάντα δὲ διὰ θείας αἰτίας μόνης ἐπιτελεῖται, ἥτις τοσοῦτον κεχώρισται τῶν παθῶν, ὥστε μηδὲ λόγον αὐτῆς δυνατὸν εἶναι ἐφάπτεσθαι. (*De myst.* 1.21.10–20)[37]

Several components of this theory will repay close investigation. The general picture of a paternal Nous that sends down wonderful traces into the mundane world recapitulates the *Chaldean Oracles*. In Iamblichus's work, these traces are called συνθήματα and σύμβολα interchangeably—though here, in a *falsa lectio* (according to *LSJ*) they appear as ἐνθήματα. Iamblichus's text, as opposed to the fragmentary oracles, spells out for us that these very traces are harnessed in his sacred ritual. So the symbols of which the oracles speak make their powers available to the priest. What do these mysterious traces do? In the above passage and consistently in the work of the post-Iamblichean Neoplatonists, they do the impossible: they give voice to [ἐκφωνεῖται] things which cannot be voiced [ἄφθεγκτα, ἀπόρρητα, ἄρρητα]; they represent that which is above representation and put that which is beyond reason into terms accessible to humans. On four of the sixteen occasions that the "symbol" appears in Iamblichus's text, it shows up in the formula "the unspeakable symbols."[38] These constructions could mean simply "secret symbols," but as in the text above, they are often included in lists of paired opposites, like "forms for the formless" or "shapes for the shapeless." This argues for a translation along the lines of "speech for the unspeakable." The already well-developed Neo-

[37] Text from Iamblichus, *Les mystères d'Égytpe*, ed. and trans. É. des Places (Paris: Belles Lettres, 1966). An English translation is forthcoming from Emma C. Clarke, John Dillon, and Jackson P. Hershbell (Brill). For an introduction, translation and notes on selections from book 1, see Peter T. Struck, "Iamblichus, *De mysteriis*, book 1," in *Religions of Late Antiquity in Practice*, ed. Richard Valantasis (Princeton: Princeton University Press, 2000), 489–505.

[38] *De myst.* 1.21.14, 4.2.31, 6.6.9 (τὰ ἀπόρρητα σύμβολα); *De myst.* 2.11.23 (τὰ ἄφθεγκτα σύμβολα).

platonic position that the One is beyond all our categories of thought and language makes it clear that ἀπόρρητα are not just things that *should not* be spoken but things that *cannot* be spoken.

The symbols translate between ourselves and our gods by giving us a language of signs that (somehow) allows us to talk about (and thus to worship) that which by definition is beyond all our puny words and conceptions. This is no small feat. Internalizing an age-old quarrel between the Stoics (who insisted on divine immanence) and the Epicureans (who felt that putting god in, say, a worm, cheapened the divine transcendence),[39] the Neoplatonists simply insist on *both* immanence and transcendence. Beginning at least with Iamblichus, and perhaps as early as the *Chaldean Oracles*, the σύμβολα and the συνθήματα are a most productive means of addressing the issue, for the category of the symbol embraces and contains the paradox. Since a paradox can never actually be resolved, of course, to expect a convincing account would be to expect too much. But Iamblichus and his followers consistently favor a particular strategy in explaining their mysterious symbols: the symbols operate in a way that mirrors the deep structures of the cosmos. As Iamblichus says above, the sacred rites imitate the order of the gods. Three other passages in the *De mysteriis* help to explicate this position.[40] He tells us at one point that certain implements used in the theurgic rites operate "just like Nature, which has fabricated the world that comes to be and passes away, stamped out certain visible shapes of the invisible principles" [καθάπερ δὴ καὶ ἡ γενεσιουργὸς φύσις τῶν ἀφανῶν λόγων ἐμφανεῖς τινας μορφὰς ἀπετυπώσατο] (*De myst.* 1.11.7–9). Next, in discussing the divinatory aspects of his theurgic rites, he again compares the divine traces to cosmogony: "Just as the gods create everything by means of images, they also signify [that is, send portents of the future] in the same manner through traces" [καθάπερ οὖν δι' εἰκόνων [οἱ θεοὶ] γεννῶσι πάντα, καὶ σημαίνουσιν ὡσαύτως διὰ συνθημάτων] (*De myst.* 3.15.24–26). And finally, in a passage that we will revisit below, Iamblichus discusses his opinion of the Egyptians' acute understanding of the language of symbol:

> For they [the Egyptians] imitate the natural power of the universe and the demiurgic power of the gods, and themselves make appear certain images of mystic and hidden and invisible thoughts through symbols, just as also the power of nature stamped out, in a certain way, the invisible principles in visible forms by means of symbols.

[39] The clearest articulation of these positions appears in the quarrels between the Stoic Balbus and the Epicurean Velleius in Cicero's *De natura deorum*.

[40] See Shaw, 163.

> οὗτοι γὰρ τὴν φύσιν τοῦ παντὸς καὶ τὴν δημιουργίαν τῶν θεῶν μιμούμενοι καὶ αὐτοὶ τῶν μυστικῶν καὶ ἀποκεκρυμμένων καὶ ἀφανῶν νοήσεων εἰκόνας τινὰς διὰ συμβόλων ἐκφαίνουσιν, ὥσπερ καὶ ἡ φύσις τοῖς ἐμφανέσιν εἴδεσι τοὺς ἀφανεῖς λόγους διὰ συμβόλων τρόπον τινὰ ἀπετυπώσατο. (*De myst.* 7.1.4–9)

So according to Iamblichus, the use of "symbols" to depict that which is by definition beyond all depiction is no more transgressive or objectionable than the very process of creation itself. In Neoplatonic cosmogony, we remember, immaterial, invisible, and arcane principles manifest themselves in material form. The Neoplatonic One is the ultimate source of everything that exists; that which is beyond all form and shape manifests itself (by some mysterious process) in the forms and shapes that we see around us. The Neoplatonists sometimes illustrate the process by drawing on Plato's *Timaeus*, where a figure called the Demiurge uses the Forms as templates and stamps unformed matter into the entities that populate the cosmos we see around us. In Neoplatonic thinking, the Demiurge, a lower-order manifestation of the divine One, gets his hands dirty in the actual work of material fabrication. The *Timaeus* myth tells us, the Neoplatonists say, that the manifested universe is a whole collection of copies of the higher, true realm of the Forms, which, in turn, are representations of higher, more arcane principles that have their source, ultimately, in the utterly transcendent and utterly imageless One. How that which is utterly incapable of being imaged nevertheless produce images of itself is a mystery that Plotinus (one could even say Plato himself) left for his followers to answer.

We can detect in Iamblichus's statements a contrast developing between a "representational" scheme, where a Demiurge stamps out εἰκόνες and fabricates the material world, and a higher scheme that operates according to the συνθήματα/σύμβολα. This seems especially true in one of the passages cited above from book 3: "Just as [the gods] create everything by means of representations, they also signify in the same manner through traces" [καθάπερ οὖν δι' εἰκόνων [οἱ θεοὶ] γεννῶσι πάντα, καὶ σημαίνουσιν ὡσαύτως διὰ συνθημάτων]. Here the material world is fabricated by representations, but it is meaningful (that is, has a semantic dimension) through its being a σύνθημα/σύμβολον. The image [εἰκών] marks the material world in its status as a fainter reproduction of a higher principle, but the world seen as *symbol* indicates its status as a manifestation—that is, something that works according to the logic of the trace, with the capacity to point us back up to the higher orders that produced it.[41] The other passages cited above,

[41] On the specifically anagogic resonance of the symbol/*synthema*, see Andrew Smith,

though, contradict any firmly drawn distinction between the "representational" and the "symbolic" in Iamblichus. This difference—already intimated in Porphyry's contrast of "symbolic" speech with speech that operates "according to mimesis"[42]—will be sharper in Proclus.

Iamblichus insists that the power of his theurgic symbols to elevate the devotee rests in the symbols themselves. The symbols do not, in other words, awaken some power of the human mind or soul. They derive their power from an indwelling presence of the higher orders within them. In a passage that Dodds has made notorious, by claiming that it opens the door "to all those superstitions of the lower culture,"[43] Iamblichus states his case on this point:

> It is not thought that links the theurgist with the gods; else, what should hinder the contemplative philosopher from enjoying theurgic union with them? But, as it turns out, this is not the case. Theurgic union is attained only by the consecrating operation of the acts that cannot be spoken of correctly performed, acts which are beyond all understanding; and by the power of the unutterable symbols which are intelligible only to the gods. . . . For though we do not understand it, the symbols themselves, on their own, perform their proper work, and the unspeakable power itself of the gods, to whom these symbols belong, recognizes, by itself, its own images [εἰκονας], but not by being aroused by our intelligence.

> οὐδὲ γὰρ ἡ ἔννοια συνάπτει τοῖς θεοῖς τοὺς θεουργούς· επεὶ τί ἐκώλυε τοὺς θεωρητικῶς φιλοσοφοῦντας ἔχειν τὴν θεουργικὴν ἕνωσιν πρὸς τοὺς θεούς; νῦν δ' οὐκ ἔχει τό γε ἀληθὲς οὕτως· ἀλλ' ἡ τῶν ἔργων τῶν ἀρρήτων καὶ ὑπὲρ πᾶσαν νόησιν θεοπρεπῶς ἐνεργουμένων τελεσιουργία ἥ τε τῶν νοουμένων τοῖς θεοῖς μόνον συμβόλων ἀφθέγκτων δύναμις ἐντίθησι τὴν θεουργικὴν ἕνωσιν. . . . καὶ γὰρ μὴ νοούντων ἡμῶν αὐτὰ τὰ συνθήματα ἀφ' ἑαυτῶν δρᾷ τὸ οἰκεῖον ἔργον, καὶ ἡ τῶν θεῶν, πρὸς οὓς ἀνήκει ταῦτα, ἄρρητος δύναμις αὐτὴ ἀφ' ἑαυτῆς ἐπιγιγνώσκει τὰς οἰκείας εἰκόνας, ἀλλ' οὐ τῷ διεγείρεσθαι ὑπὸ τῆς ἡμετέρας νοήσεως. (*De myst.* 2.11.16–30)

Again, the empirical observation that even the wisest of men fail, through contemplation alone, to obtain union with the gods leads Iamblichus to a deep skepticism toward the power of human intellect to reach the real truth of the world. Such unions do happen, he says, but only because divine powers recognize and respond to their symbols, the traces of themselves that they have sown into the world out of their

Porphyry's Place in the Neoplatonic Tradition: A Study of Post-Plotinian Neoplatonism (The Hague: Martinus Nijhoff, 1974), 107, n. 11.

[42] See chap. 5.

[43] E. R. Dodds, introduction to *Proclus: The Elements of Theology*, 2d ed. (Oxford: Clarendon Press, 1963), xx.

overflowing goodness and care for the lower orders.[44] The uplifting powers dwell in the symbols themselves and in their connection with the divinity, not in any contemplative revelation we might reach. To claim otherwise would be an act of hubris and an affront to the god.[45]

Iamblichus articulates the connection he envisions between the symbol and its divine referent with some specificity. We recall that, with regard to the divinatory dimension of theurgy, he gives the designation of *synthêmata* to the divine signs in which we can read future events. Iamblichus tells us that these divine signs have a strong tie, in their very being, to the events to which they refer: "The art of divination somehow makes interpretations from the divine portents, according to the kinship of the events to the revealed signs" [ἀπὸ δὲ τῶν θείων τεκμηρίων κατὰ τὴν συγγένειαν τῶν πραγμάτων πρὸς τὰ δεικνύμενα σημεῖα συμβάλλει πως ἡ τέχνη] (*De myst.* 3.15.9–12).[46] The term συγγένεια refers to blood relations, those who are in the same family. The τὰ πράγματα is also suggestive. In ancient discussions of signs, πράγματα are usually (as here) the referents as opposed to the signs themselves. This suggests that Iamblichus is here displacing a traditional construal of some "resemblance" or "likeness" between a sign and its referent, with a stronger and more essential tie. We will see an even more definitive statement in this regard in Proclus. More than suggestive, though, is Iamblichus's claim that the divine *synthêmata* govern a theurgy that "attaches" [συνάπτω] the devotee to the higher powers (*De myst.* 4.2.25). The term has a dual use in the *De mysteriis*. As an expression of Iamblichus's emanationist ontology, it indicates the dependence of the products of emanation on those entities that produced them, while it also indicates the power of ritual actions to "join" the celebrant to the divine power.[47] Also, we recall, in discussing the secret names of the gods, which he calls "symbols," Iamblichus claims that they are "suspended from" [συναρτάω] the very nature of beings and are not simply conventional

[44] Cf. *Ch. Or.* 142, 143.

[45] Another passage (7.4.24–27) suggests that humans also have a divine symbol in their souls that gets awakened by the god: τὴν μυστικὴν καὶ ἀπόρρητον εἰκόνα τῶν θεῶν ἐν τῇ ψυχῇ διαφυλάττομεν, καὶ τὴν ψυχὴν δι' αὐτῶν ἀνάγομεν ἐπὶ τοὺς θεούς, καὶ ἀναχθεῖσαν κατὰ τὸ δυνατὸν τοῖς θεοῖς συνάπτομεν. Proclus agrees with this, as we will see in chap. 7.

[46] Two sentences later, Iamblichus says that these divine signs work "symbolically" [συμβολικῶς].

[47] In the first book of the *De myst.* this is already apparent. On the ontological side, see 1.5.28, 1.9.40, and to give a representative text, 1.19.2: Ἴθι δὴ οὖν κἀκεῖνο ἀποκρινώμεθα, τί τὸ συνάπτον ἐστὶ πρὸς τοῖς ἀσωμάτοις θεοῖς τοὺς ἔχοντας σῶμα ἐν τῷ οὐρανῷ. On the idea that ritual acts can lead to "attachment" to the higher orders, see 1.12.30 and 1.12.41, where the term is used to speak of the power of divine invocations to join the celebrant to the gods; and 1.15.25 and 1.15.71, where it marks the power of prayer to link the devotee to the god.

names arrived at through consensus.[48] Like συνάπτω, the term συναρτάω is also used in the context of emanation, specifically in discussing the connections of lower-order entities with their superiors.[49] So Iamblichus here begins to articulate the symbol's connection to its referent within the larger structures of Neoplatonic emanationist ontology, where things connect to their superiors in their very being. We will return to this in closing.

Iamblichus insists that symbols have a transformative power for the practitioner. They not only bring the devotee into the direct presence of the divine but raise the devotee to higher spiritual levels, which in the Neoplatonic scheme means to higher epistemological and ontological levels as well. The human being who practices theurgy is no longer simply a human being but is allowed to experience life on a higher plane. Iamblichus thus has an answer to Porphyry's question about why the theurgic rites use language that appears to give orders to the gods:

> The theurgist, through the power of the arcane *synthemata*, commands mundane natures, no longer as a man, nor as employing a human soul; but as existing superior to them in the order of the gods, he makes use of stronger orders than pertain to himself in his level of being. . . . He teaches us by such a use of words the magnitude and quality of the power which he possesses through a union with the gods, and which the knowledge of arcane symbols furnished.
>
> ὁ θεουργὸς διὰ τὴν δύναμιν τῶν ἀπορρήτων συνθημάτων οὐκέτι ὡς ἄνθρωπος οὐδ' ὡς ἀνθρωπίνῃ ψυχῇ χρώμενος ἐπιτάττει τοῖς κοσμικοῖς, ἀλλ' ὡς ἐν τῇ τῶν θεῶν τάξει προϋπάρχων μείζοσι τῆς καθ' ἑαυτὸν οὐσίας ἐπανατάσεσι χρῆται. . . . ἐν τῇ τοιαύτῃ τῶν λόγων χρήσει διδάσκων ὅσην καὶ ἡλίκην καὶ τίνα ἔχει τὴν δύναμιν διὰ τὴν πρὸς θεοὺς ἕνωσιν, ἣν παρέσχηκεν αὐτῷ τῶν ἀπορρήτων συμβόλων ἡ γνῶσις. (6.6)

Iamblichus expresses an identical opinion at *De myst.* 4.2. He tells us that the "unspeakable symbols" allow the theurgist to put on the very "cloak of the gods" [περιβάλλεταί πως διὰ τῶν ἀπορρήτων συμβόλων τὸ ἱερατικὸν τῶν θεῶν πρόσχημα]. These passages attest to the definitively transformative power of the symbols. Like other symbols in previous centuries, those of the theurgist function as the keys that unlock the doors to the divine realm.

[48] *De myst.* 7.5.8.

[49] See, for example, *De myst.* 8.8: "the generative power and the manifested universe are suspended from the intellectual essence" [τῇ νοερᾷ οὐσίᾳ ἡ γένεσις καὶ τὸ πᾶν τόδε συνήρτηται]; *De myst.* 6.1, where συναρτάω describes the connection between animals and the gods to whom they are allotted; *De myst.* 5.15, where Iamblichus contrasts συναρτάω with συνάπτω, the former being a connection that obtains between more corporeal entities, and the latter between more immaterial ones; *De myst.* 2.8, where Iamblichus speaks of the connection between soul and the air (a lower link in the chain of emanation).

Symbolic Speech in Iamblichus

Finally, we return to the topic of the so-called *onomata barbara.* The peculiar powers we have been discussing in Iamblichus's talismanic ritual symbols lend themselves to his somewhat odd and, as it turns out, pivotal, theory of the standard Mediterranean practice of invoking the gods by means of nonsensical divine names. These names contain amalgamations of semantic units from various languages, reputed to have a special affiliation with the god. The magicians in the *PGM* understood them as a means of controlling the god. They were a spell or a coercive incantation that made the god bend to the human will. In Iamblichus's reckoning, these names were a stylized form of incantation, whose very sounds were thought to have some spiritual power. They pleased the god, in accordance with Iamblichus's rule that "all superior beings rejoice in the similitude of inferior beings to them" [χαίροντα πάντα τὰ κρείττονα ὁμοιώσει τῶν ὑποδεεστέρων] (7.1.12), and prepared the devotee to receive the divine presence.

Porphyry casts a skeptical eye on the practice. He asks Anebo/Iamblichus, as we mentioned above, If words are conventional signs for things, created by human consensus, why would the gods prefer, or react to, some names rather than others? For surely they do not speak one language or another but are beyond such a feeble human device as language. Iamblichus begins his lengthy answer by stating that though the meanings of some of these names may be unknown to us, they are all significant [σημαντικά] to the gods, though not in an articulable mode [οὐ κατὰ ῥητὸν τρόπον] (*De myst.* 7.4.8–9). These divine names indicate their referents in a special way. We must, Iamblichus counsels, put away our pedestrian notions of the way language works. The divine names are beyond reason. We must remove every thought [ἐπίνοια] and rational account [λογικὴ διέξοδος] from our consideration of them. Furthermore, their link to their referents is not at all a simple "naturalism" such as Plato toyed with in the *Cratylus.* We should put away any notion of likeness between the sound of words and the nature of the things to which they refer [ἀφαιρεῖν τὰς συμφυομένας τῆς φωνῆς πρὸς τὰ ἐν τῇ φύσει πράγματα φυσικὰς ἀπεικασίας] (*De myst.* 7.4.13–16). "What is present" in the divine names, he says emphatically, "is an intellectual and divine symbolic mark of the divine likeness—this must dwell within the names" [ὅσπερ δέ ἐστι νοερὸς καὶ θεῖος τῆς θείας ὁμοιότητος συμβολικὸς χαρακτήρ, τοῦτον ὑποθετέον ἐν τοῖς ὀνόμασιν] (*De myst.* 7.4.16–18).

Iamblichus next tells us that we must disregard another common conception of language if we are truly to understand the divine names. As was mentioned at the outset of this chapter, Porphyry stated his position that certain names should not be preferred over others, and Iamblichus restates his position at this point in the text: "He who, you say, hears words looks to what they signify, so that it is sufficient that the conception remains the same, whatever the words may be that are used" [ὁ ἀκούων, φής, πρὸς τὰ σημαινόμενα ἀφορᾷ, ὥστε αὐτάρκης ἡ αὐτὴ μένουσα ἔννοια, κἂν ὁποιονοῦν ὑπάρχῃ τοὔνομα] (*De myst.* 7.5.1–3). Iamblichus grants that if names were set down according to convention [κατὰ συνθήκην], then it would not matter whether a person used one or another, "but if they are suspended from the nature of things, those names which are more adapted to it are also more dear to the gods" [εἰ δὲ τῇ φύσει συνήρτηται τῶν ὄντων, τὰ μᾶλλον αὐτῇ προσεοικότα καὶ τοῖς θεοῖς ἐστι δήπου προσφιλέστερα] (*De myst.* 7.5.8–10). Iamblichus tells us that the divine symbols are the things "most united" [τὰ μάλιστα συνηνωμένα] to the gods themselves, and that they "attach" [συνάπτοντα] us to them (*De myst.* 7.5.26–27). Given what we have uncovered about Iamblichus's views on symbols generally, his metaphysics, and his liturgical theories, we can conclude that Iamblichus sees the word as a final link in the chain of Neoplatonic emanation. He says that it rests below the "nature" of the thing it names—and so he makes it out to be a final link in a chain of being that has its source, ultimately, in the transcendent One.

To summarize, then, Iamblichus uses the same language (1) to mark the ontological connection between lower-order parts of the universe and the higher powers on which they depend; (2) to link the mysterious, material, divine symbols and the gods to which they are connected; and (3) to indicate the tie between a thing's physical nature and the word that hangs from it. This concatenation of the ontological, the ritual, and the linguistic will prove extremely productive in the work of the later Neoplatonists. Its most influential expositor will be Proclus, the fifth-century thinker to whom we will turn next.

Though Iamblichus seems to restrict his theory of language to divine names used in a ritual, he leaves the door of the symbolic open to other forms of speech and representation. Some of the "symbols" over which Iamblichus and Porphyry argue are not simple divine names but short narrative elements that are parts of traditional Egyptian myths, specifically those in which a god "unfolds into light from the mire" and "is seated above the lotus," or "sails a ship," or "changes his forms every hour, according to the signs of the Zodiac" (*De myst.* 7.3.23–24). That certain mythic scenes are classed as symbols clearly suggests that they might have powers similar to the soteriological elements of ritual. At this point, we are reapproaching the deep well of conceptual resources developed by the classical allegorists for reading "symbolic" myths. Whether Iamblichus himself tapped it we do not know, but his follower Proclus certainly did.

7

MOONSTONES AND MEN THAT GLOW: PROCLUS AND THE TALISMANIC SIGNIFIER

PROCLUS WAS born in Constantinople, where his family was located temporarily on business, on February 8, in 410 or 412 C.E., two years after Alaric sacked Rome.[1] We know the day and month of his birth with relative precision because of his interests in the astrological arts. He received a thorough classical training in Lycia, Alexandria, and Constantinople before assuming the mantle of "successor" to the Platonic Academy in Athens.[2] He took his place in a two-centuries-old tradition of Neoplatonic thinkers, including Plotinus, Porphyry, Iamblichus, Syrianus, and others, who styled themselves as Plato's true heirs.

In his copious writings on language and literature, Proclus marries the theurgical innovations of Iamblichus with traditional allegorism and brings the talismanic symbol into the mainstream of Western literary theory. "Mainstream" is not a term one hears often in conjunction with Proclus, but in the epilogue I hope to justify its use. Here let us begin with some general remarks on the unique problematics of representation in the work of Proclus. In the first pages of the *Life of Proclus*, written near the end of the fifth century C.E., Proclus's devoted student Marinus describes his master's physical appearance:

> The third bodily quality he possessed is comparable to temperance, which some see fit to consider as having to do with beauty of the bodily kind, and this is reasonable. For just as the former is observed in the harmony and agreement of the faculties of the soul, so also beauty of the body may be

[1] Perhaps the most accessible overview of Proclus and his work remains John M. Dillon, "General Introduction," *Proclus' Commentary on Plato's* Parmenides (Princeton: Princeton University Press, 1987), xi–xliv. Also helpful is E. R. Dodds, introduction to Proclus, *The Elements of Theology*, 2d ed. (Oxford: Clarendon Press, 1963), ix–xxxiii. A detailed and lucid overview in English can be found in Lucas Siorvanes, *Proclus: Neo-Platonic Philosophy and Science* (New Haven: Yale University Press, 1996).

[2] For a critical review of the status of the Athenian Academy in imperial Roman times, see John Glucker, *Antiochus and the Late Academy* (Göttingen: Vandenhoeck and Ruprecht, 1978).

discovered in a certain symmetry of its practical parts. He was very lovely to look on, for not only did he possess the beauty of just proportions, but from his soul a certain living light bloomed upon his body, and shone so wondrously, it is quite impossible to put into words. He was so lovely to look upon, that no painter caught his likeness, and all of his portraits that are in circulation, although they may be very lovely, they still fall far short of a representation of his true form.

τρίτη δὲ αὐτῷ ὑπῆρξεν ἀρετὴ σώματος, ἡ κατὰ τὴν σωφροσύνην τεταγμένη, ἣν δὴ περὶ τὸ κάλλος τὸ σωματικὸν θεωρεῖν ἀξιοῦσι, καὶ τοῦτο εὐλόγως. καθάπερ γὰρ ἐκείνη ἐν συμφωνίᾳ καὶ ὁμολογίᾳ θεωρεῖται τῶν τῆς ψυχῆς δυνάμεων, οὕτω καὶ τὸ ἐν σώματι κάλλος ἐν συμμετρίᾳ τινὶ ὁρᾶται τῶν ὀργανικῶν αὐτοῦ μορίων. ἰδεῖν δὲ ἦν σφόδρα ἐράσμιος· καὶ γὰρ οὐ μόνον αὐτῷ τὰ τῆς συμμετρίας εὖ εἶχεν, ἀλλὰ γὰρ καὶ τὸ ἀπὸ τῆς ψυχῆς ἐπανθοῦν τῷ σώματι οἱονεὶ φῶς ζωτικόν, θαυμάσιον ὅσον ἀπέστιλβε καὶ οὐ πάνυ φράσαι τῷ λόγῳ δυνατόν. Οὕτω δὲ ἦν καλὸς ἰδεῖν, ὥστε μηδένα τῶν γραφόντων ἐφικέσθαι αὐτοῦ τῆς ὁμοιότητος, πάσας δὲ τὰς φερομένας αὐτοῦ εἰκόνας, καίπερ καὶ αὐτὰς παγκάλους οὔσας, ὅμως ἔτι λείπεσθαι πολλῷ εἰς μίμησιν τῆς τοῦ εἴδους ἀληθείας. (*Vit. Procl.* 3)

The hagiographic biographers of late antiquity commonly claim that great philosophers and saints were impervious to being captured by simple representations. However, the biographers offer different reasons why. For example, two centuries before Marinus, Porphyry tells us that Plotinus told his would-be portraitist:

Why really, is it not enough to have to carry the phantom image [εἴδωλον] in which nature has encased us, without your requesting me to agree to leave behind me a longer-lasting phantom of the phantom [εἰδώλου εἴδωλον], as if it were something genuinely worth looking at? (*Vit. Plot.* 1)

To fend off the eager painter, Plotinus cites an argument that Plato had first forwarded in the *Republic* six centuries earlier, and one that nobody had since been able to lay to rest. As was well known to all the Neoplatonists, Plato considered the world as it appears to us to be already a copy of the higher, stable, and true realm of being, where the Forms dwell. And since the artist imitates the world as it appears to us, the artist makes copies of copies, and must therefore inevitably lead us farther away from, not nearer to, the real truth.[3]

[3] Plotinus's terminology is a direct echo of *Republic* 10.599a, 599d, 601b, 605c. Plotinus himself made the most far-reaching rethinking of the problem up to his time: When the artist wants to make a representation, he says, he is able to consult not just physical reality but the Forms themselves. Artistic *mimêmata*, then, are not imitations of imitations but have the epistemological status of manifested reality (not great, but more than they had in Plato's scheme). Further, Plotinus's restructuring puts the work of the artist on a par with the demiurge who constructed visible reality from the Forms. Plotinus

But Marinus gives a different explanation for Proclus's resistance to representation. Unlike Plotinus, who is said to have a low estimation of physical bodies, Proclus bubbles over with beauty. He radiates light—a property that no mere likeness could duplicate. The prohibition against representing him stems from a concern about not being able to do justice to the stunning qualities of the original. Proclus's wondrous glow illuminates more than just his small circle of initiates. It also highlights two features of his distinctive ontology. The later Neoplatonists developed theories for understanding the material world that come to full flower in Proclus's work and are of no small importance in the history of theories of representation. Marinus tells us that his master's glow is beyond our powers of speech [οὐ πάνυ φράσαι τῷ λόγῳ δυνατόν]—a property that Proclus applies with unique insistence to the transcendent One. The vocabulary of radiance and light also was common in Neoplatonism as a description of the One. The master's light "blooms" out from his soul upon his physical body. The term ἐπανθέω suggests that the light comes forth from the "flower" [ἄνθος] of the soul, or in Proclean psychology, the soul's highest tip, which partakes (somehow) of the transcendent One.[4] But this trace of transcendence which escapes simple imitation also points up a counterposition which is highly distinctive of Proclus's particular version of Neoplatonic ontology. Although the One is beyond us, it is, at the same time, somehow, present to us—or at least to those lucky enough to have basked in Proclus's glow. Using the language of the One in referring to Proclus's material self, Marinus suggests that certain pieces of matter—the body of an inspired philosopher, for example—might break through to the higher levels of reality and become themselves sources of radiance, nodes upon which the font of the universe manifests itself. This is something Plotinus, handsome though he may have been, could not do. To understand where this glow comes from, we need to look more closely at the particular theories of matter that enable it. We will then examine the profound implications of this ontology for issues of language and representation.

Proclus's Ontology

The great chain of emanationist being operated with increasing complexity as Neoplatonism developed from the fourth to the sixth centu-

---

also reformulates the standard criteria of beauty. Whereas earlier thinkers had emphasized notions of proportionality, he tells us that a single stone might be beautiful (see Plotinus 1.6 and 5.8). Proclus and his followers push all of these developments further than Plotinus chooses to.

[4] *Procli Commentarius in Platonis Parmenidem*, ed. Victor Cousin (Paris, 1864), 1071.

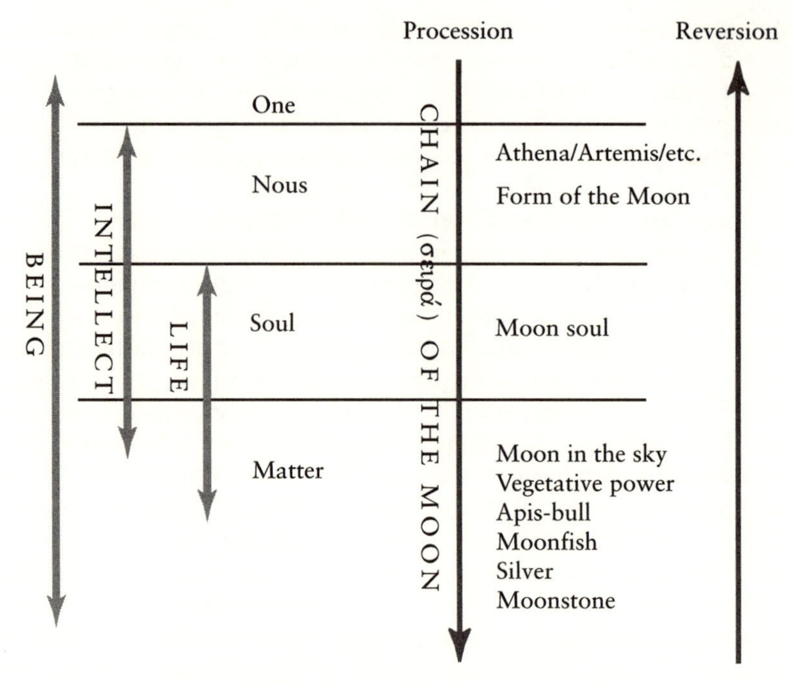

Figure 1. The Chain of the Moon in Proclus

ries.[5] As we mentioned in the previous chapter, however strongly they disagreed on the details, the Neoplatonists all agreed that the world emanates out from an infinite source, which unfolds into a hierarchy of several major strata of existence, usually expressed as layered on top of one another (see fig. 1) or sometimes as arranged in concentric circles. The material level sits at the bottom, the immaterial ones at the top. At the peak of the scheme rests the transcendent One, which radiates out from itself all the levels of the cosmos. The One is utterly beyond every conception of it we might have or every name we might give; it is be-

[5] Some of the more important works on Proclus's ontology and literary theory, which have influenced my readings, are: James A. Coulter, *The Literary Microcosm* (Leiden: E. J. Brill, 1976), 32–72; Anne D. R. Sheppard, *Studies on the 5th and 6th Essays of Proclus's Commentary on the Republic*, Hypomnemata, vol. 61 (Göttingen: Vandenhoeck and Ruprecht, 1980); Robert Lamberton, *Homer the Theologian: Neoplatonist Allegorical Reading and the Growth of the Epic Tradition* (Berkeley: University of California Press, 1986), 162–232; and Sara Rappe, *Reading Neoplatonism* (New York: Cambridge University Press, 2000), 167–96. E. R. Dodds's edition of Proclus's *Elements of Theology* remains indispensable to understanding his ontology. With regard to the notion of the symbol in particular, see Cardullo Loredana, *Il linguaggio del simbolo in Proclo. Analisi filosoficosemantica dei termini symbolon/eikôn/synthêma nel Commentario alla Reppublica* (Catania, Italy: University of Catania, 1985).

yond even being itself. Out of a spontaneous superabundance of goodness, it emanates out from itself all the levels of being that make up the hierarchical cosmos, including, in descending order, the Nous or Mind, which is pure intellectual reality; the Soul, which is the source of all life and self-motion; and Matter, which Plotinus considered so dull and lifeless that it did not even merit inclusion with the other layers of the world. The One's great outward flow, or procession, is matched by an automatic urge, within humans and everything else that exists, for return, or reversion, back to the perfect unity and simplicity of the One. This basic scheme gained many new sublevels from Iamblichus forward as successive thinkers discovered layer after layer of being, an ever-unfolding system of buffers between the world of base matter and the utterly transcendent One.

Proclus, among the last great figures in the Neoplatonic tradition, does more than his predecessors to earn the Neoplatonists' well-deserved reputation for ontological intricacy. But, as a consequence, he leaves behind a remarkably specific map of the way the world works. Most important for our purposes, he takes up the task, sensible enough in a mature theory of emanation, of trying to trace with precision the paths of the One's outstretching beams. Proclus believed that the One sent out individual rays (which he called "chains" [σειραί]) that manifested different immaterial and material beings, as they penetrated down through layer after layer of reality.[6] Proclus was confident that these beams could be tracked, and, with enough devotion and diligence, one presumably could arrive at a map of the ontological structure that lay behind (or above or within) all of sensible reality. An example or two might help. One ray, or chain, leaves the transcendent heights of the One and manifests itself, very near its source, as the traditional Greek god Apollo. When this same ray continues downward and enters the realm of Nous, it brings into being the Platonic Form of the sun. At the level of Soul, the beam manifests a sort of sun-soul that dwells immaterially beneath the sun's Form. Next, as it enters the outer limits of the material level, the beam brings into being the actual physical sun that we see in the sky. The beam does not stop there, however, but continues down to the lower substrata of material reality, into the plant level, where it manifests the heliotrope, and to the mineral level, where it appears as gold. Similarly a chain exists for the moon (fig. 1, right), beginning with the goddesses Athena, Artemis, Selene, or Hecate and proceeding downward through the Platonic Form of the moon, the moon soul, and the moon as a heavenly body, then further down to something called "vegetative power" (which is the general capacity of

[6] *Elements of Theology* props. 21, 97, 110–12; for further citations, see Dodds's index.

plants to grow), the Apis-bull, the moonfish, silver, and finally, at the lowest level, a humble rock called moonstone (which today is still known as selenite).[7] The property that runs through these chains, connecting the manifestations on the various levels, is "sympathy," a term of ontological linkage that we have seen in Stoic and divinatory contexts.[8]

A person strolling along through a Proclean world of moonstones and heliotropes sees a much different landscape than had existed in Plato's or even Plotinus's time. Stoic theorists of "sympathy," not to mention professional seers and traders in the magical arts, had long attuned a broad spectrum of the ancient population to hidden powers (divine or demonic) operating behind the visible scenes. But Proclus spelled out the breadth and depth of such powers with a heady precision that the Stoics lack; and unlike the magicians, he contextualized them rigorously within a sophisticated and broadly accepted philosophical language. Whether his peers would have agreed with Proclus on the details, many and perhaps even most of them accepted some version of the emanationist cosmos. His level of specificity, which his predecessors were either too critical to endorse or too circumspect to articulate, is the most distinctive and dynamic feature of his ontological speculations.

The Place of Matter in Proclus's Scheme

In perhaps any emanationist scheme, the world of appearances has a certain capacity to point us upward. Material beings carry some trace of the hidden immaterial powers that produced them. As we saw in the last chapter, we can see this tendency as early as the work of Plotinus. Though he often views brute, unformed matter [ἡ ὕλη] as an utter negativity and darkness, or even worse, he argues with equal vehemence in his treatise against the Gnostics that since the One is the source of *everything*, even unformed matter must carry some trace of transcendent goodness.[9] Proclus pursued this idea with more vigor and as a result, he slackened somewhat the tensions regarding matter that are apparent in Plotinus's work. Proclus came up with new defenses of matter. In his

[7] These sun and moon chains are reconstructed from the commentaries. See *In Parm.* 874 (selenite) and 903 (Apis-bull and moonfish); Proclus, *In Platonis Timaeum commentaria*, ed. E. Diehl, 3 vols. (Leipzig: Teubner, 1903–6), 1:43.6 (silver), 1:141.10 (Athena), 3:131.26 (Artemis and Hekate), 2:264.1 (Selene), 3:355.16 (vegetative power). For more on the chain of the sun, see Sheppard, 152–53.

[8] See *Elements* prop. 140. Further citations considered below. The notion of "sympathy" had a broad currency in the Late Republican and Early Imperial periods. As we have seen, the Stoics make use of the concept to justify divination, and the magicians claim to harness it for their own ends.

[9] Plotinus 2.9.3; cf. 1.8.7; 2.3.17; 3.4.1.

hands, the world that we see around us becomes less a misleading world of appearances and more an upward-leading, anagogic world of manifestations.

Proclus assigns a special status to the lowest extremities of his chains of being, paradoxically granting them a unique affiliation with the utterly transcendent One. As he makes clear in his *Elements of Theology*, Proclus thought that the One was especially responsible for imparting "being" to all parts of reality (that is, existence, considered in the abstract).[10] After the One, each level of the world added its own unique characteristics to the divine beam as it passed by. The level of mind or Nous imparts rationality to things, and the level of Soul imparts life. But Proclus observed that each of these latter characteristics traveled only a limited way down the chain. Rationality existed for many beings below the divine Mind, including gods, daemons, and humans, but it stopped there. It did not penetrate into the lower levels; hence, animals, plants, and stones are nonrational. The characteristic of life had a band of applicability that ran down a little farther into animal and plant life, but it too eventually stopped. Only that characteristic imparted by the One—which again is being, pure and simple—penetrates all the way down to even the lowest levels of inert reality (fig. 1, left).[11] Other entities higher up the chain of being are more complex, having souls and intellects, while the basest matter shares its utter simplicity with the even purer simplicity of the One. In this qualified sense, the humblest pieces of matter have a more direct, less mediated trace of the transcendent inside them. They glowed a little more clearly with the One. In addition, in Proclus's understanding, matter now plays a pivotal role in the larger structures of the cosmos.[12] It is literally the farthest turning point of the whole order of things. Just as all things flow from the One, so all things contain inside themselves a drive to get back to the One. Proclus's literary commentary, as we will see, assumes that this process, called reversion, is catalyzed at the farthest limits of the chains of being.

At this point we might step back to see what is brewing in Proclus's metaphysical stew. If matter has an especially direct connection to the One, what of something below matter? Many thinkers in the Platonic tradition had placed a level of quasi-reality below the material world; the world of artistic representations. We remember that Plotinus (echoing Plato himself) set those phantoms of the phantoms, the artisans' copies of the sensible world, at a further remove from the shadow world of appearances. According to Proclus's scheme, where the lowest end of

[10] *Elements* prop. 59.

[11] *Elements* prop. 56.

[12] *Elements* props. 58–59, and Dodd's commentary. Siorvanes discusses this aspect of Proclus's thought (183–89 and 206, n. 130). He disagrees with Dodds and Armstrong and denies this position would have been relevant to theurgy, but not persuasively.

the chain of being has an affinity with the highest One, a new window on the divine is held open to the practitioners of the representational arts. Proclus takes advantage of this opening and grants the poets and the artisans the capacity to produce representations that have unique ties to the transcendent divine.

Proclus and the Arts of Representation

Proclus pursues these new possibilities for theories of representation in two main areas, which he regularly discusses in tandem: depictions of the gods in theurgic cult statues and literary renderings of the gods through a mysterious language of symbols and divine names. On the ritual side, Proclus practiced theurgy, like all the Neoplatonists after Iamblichus. As we saw in the last chapter, the theurgic ritual was understood to transform certain objects (notably, material representations of the divine, in the form of votive statues) into points of transcendent presence [παρουσία].[13] The devotee invoked the divine presence by inserting into a cultic likeness of the god a material token—a bone, an herb, a gem, a stone, or a plant—with some kind of special affiliation with the deity, which was called a σύμβολον or a σύνθημα interchangeably.[14] These symbols and the metaphysics behind them are prominent in many features of Proclus's work. They have a soteriological function, and are invoked regularly as tiny shards of saving grace, transcendent traces sown by the higher orders into the mundane world. From our earlier survey of his metaphysics, we might speculate that gold was especially useful for the purpose of evoking Apollo, and that Selene was particularly fond of moonstones. Such theories, of course, borrow on the whole *pars pro toto* economy of representation by which the magical arts had long operated.

Proclus's theories of the special powers of matter and his theurgic practice dovetail nicely into what must have appeared to him to be a cohesive and satisfying whole. Through all this, he insists, as any good Neoplatonist would do, that the One is utterly transcendent and beyond all representations we might make of it. In fact his *Commentary on the Parmenides* is one of the earliest and most elegant statements of negative theology in the history of Western thought.[15] Nevertheless, the theurgic statue, turned on a lathe, polished, and smoothed by the care-

[13] See *In Tim.*, 1.273.13; cf. *In Parm.* 781.12.

[14] For references to the practice, see chap. 6. On the interchangeablity of the terms, see Sheppard, 146.

[15] On Proclus's ongoing importance in this tradition, see Thomas A. Carlson, *Indiscretion: Finitude and the Naming of God* (Chicago: University of Chicago Press, 1999).

ful hands of a craftsman,[16] becomes a receptacle for the mysterious transcendent presence. Note that this process is not exactly representation, where a likeness is produced; it is invocation, based on real presence.

Proclus on Language

Proclus does not limit his theory of imaging strictly to liturgical tokens. Explicitly and repeatedly, he extends this very line of thinking into the realm of language and poetry.[17] When the subject of language in general comes up in his voluminous commentaries, he regularly states his theory that certain constructions in language, from individual words to whole poetic scenes, operate *precisely* like the symbolic tokens in the theurgic ritual. In his commentary on the *Republic*, which will soon detain us at some length, his protracted defenses of Homer against Plato's attacks make full use of his theory of the invocation of the divine by symbolic material language. He focuses on those scenes that had particularly bothered Plato and other critics, where Homer appears to be blaspheming the gods by depicting them as having corporeal forms, as subject to passions and desires, or as involved in indecorous or even shameful acts. But Proclus tells us that Homer—being a keen observer of all the strata of reality—uses the built-in connections that link material things to higher-order significances. What may appear to us, mired as we are in the material world, to be quarrels or illicit love affairs among the gods or even the physical binding in chains of an immortal divinity are, in reality, material symbols with higher-order immaterial referents. Just as the theurgists use symbolic matter to represent that which by definition is beyond every representation, so too the most skilled among the poets and mythmakers use symbolic language to name that which cannot be named.

We begin with language. Language that qualifies as being symbolic, he says repeatedly, is especially that which assigns material, or even sometimes vulgar, attributes to those hyperessences that are beyond every material attribute. We can look at an example or two, among many, where Proclus spells out his theories of language within his grander ontological and liturgical visions. In chapter 51 of the commentary on the *Cratylus*, he considers the general question of what the art of names really is:

> Let us briefly discuss what the poetic art of names is. . . . It is clear that there is a certain representational power in the soul (indeed, painting and

[16] Proclus *In Parm.* 847.

[17] See Sheppard, 145–61; Lamberton, 190–91.

other such skills are suspended from it), and this power assimilates lower-order things to higher-order ones. . . . By the same power, in turn, the soul is able to assimilate itself back up to its superiors—gods, angels, and daemons. But further, by the same power it also likens the things that descend from itself to itself and, further still, to those things superior to itself. On account of this it fashions statues of both gods and daemons. But wishing to bring into being similitudes of the things that exist that were in a certain way immaterial and born from intellectual substance only, . . . it brought forth from itself the substance of names. And just as the ritual art in this way makes statues like the gods through certain symbols and unspeakable *synthêmata* and makes them suitable for the reception of divine illuminations, so too by the same power of assimilation the lawgiver's art brings into being names as statues of their objects, when it represents through echoes of one sort or another the nature of things that exist.

Τίς δὲ ἡ τῶν ὀνομάτων ποιητικὴ τέχνη, συντόμως εἴπωμεν . . . ὅτι μὲν οὖν ἐστί τις ἐν ψυχῇ εἰκαστικὴ δύναμις, δῆλον (καὶ γὰρ ἡ ζῳγραφία καὶ αἱ τοιαῦται ταύτης ἐξήρτηνται τῆς δυνάμεως), ἀφομοιωτικὴ οὖσα τῶν δευτέρων πρὸς τὰ κρείττονα . . . καὶ πάλιν κατὰ τὴν αὐτὴν δύναμιν ἡ ψυχὴ δύναται ἑαυτὴν ἐξομοιοῦν τοῖς κρείττοσιν ἑαυτῆς θεοῖς ἀγγέλοις δαίμοσιν· ἀλλὰ καὶ τὰ δεύτερα ἀφ' ἑαυτῆς ἐξομοιοῖ πρὸς ἑαυτὴν διὰ τῆς αὐτῆς δυνάμεως, καὶ ἔτι πρὸς τὰ κρείττω ἑαυτῆς, διὸ θεῶν τε ἀγάλματα καὶ δαιμόνων δημιουργεῖ· βουλομένη δ' ἀΰλους τρόπον τινὰ καὶ μόνης τῆς λογικῆς οὐσίας ἐγγόνους ὑποστῆσαι τῶν ὄντων ὁμοιότητας, ἀφ' ἑαυτῆς . . . τὴν τῶν ὀνομάτων παρήγαγεν οὐσίαν· καὶ ὥσπερ ἡ τελεστικὴ διὰ δή τινων συμβόλων καὶ ἀπορρήτων συνθημάτων τὰ τῇδε ἀγάλματα τοῖς θεοῖς ἀπεικάζει καὶ ἐπιτήδεια ποιεῖ πρὸς ὑποδοχὴν τῶν θείων ἐλλάμψεων, οὕτω δὲ καὶ ἡ νομοθετικὴ κατὰ τὴν αὐτὴν ἀφομοιωτικὴν δύναμιν ἀγάλματα τῶν πραγμάτων ὑφίστησι τὰ ὀνόματα διὰ τοίων καὶ τοίων ἤχων ἀπεικονιζομένη τὴν τῶν ὄντων φύσιν. (*In Crat.* 18.27–19.18)[18]

In this particular articulation, Proclus speaks of the language-making soul as a cog in the machinery of emanation. Like other midlevel beings, it receives higher-order effluxions, translates them, and passes them on down the chain of being, preserving the special characteristic of the chain. A person's power to do this with regard to names is precisely the same as the statue-making power. Both are artistic productions working with matter, whether in the form of letters and sounds or wood and gemstones.

Again, in the seventy-first chapter of the commentary on the *Cratylus*, in a discussion on the notion of divine names, Proclus or his unknown

[18] Text from Proclus, *In Platonis Cratylum commentaria*, ed. G. Pasquali (Leipzig: Teubner, 1908). Given the central importance of Proclus in this tradition, and the relatively small circle in which he is well-known, I have sometimes given extensive citations.

editor ponders the theory both of names and of theurgic statues from the viewpoint of Proclus's broader ontology of matter:

> Well, each existing thing has a *synthema* from the unspeakable cause itself [the One], which is beyond the intelligibles, all the way down to the furthest extremes, through which everything is attached to that cause—some more loosely, some more tightly, according to the clarity and the obscurity of the *synthema* in them. This is the thing moving everything toward the desire of the good and this wanting produced in things is unquenchable. It is not knowable (for it has come through even to things unable to know it), it is stronger than life (for it is present even to soulless things), and it does not involve intellectual power (for it lies in those things that have no share of thinking). . . . Such are the things called symbols of the gods. They are uniform in the higher orders and multiform in the inferior ones. By imitating these things, theurgy also displays symbols through uttered, or inarticulate, expressions. The third type of property which has also come down from the intellectual hypostases to all individual things and proceeds all the way to us is the divine names. Through these the gods are invoked and by them they are praised. They have been revealed from the gods themselves, return back to them and, to the extent that they are revealed, advance us in a human kind of knowledge.
>
> ἀλλὰ αὐτῆς τῆς ἀρρήτου καὶ ἐπέκεινα τῶν νοητῶν αἰτίας ἐστὶν ἑκάστῳ τῶν ὄντων σύνθημα καὶ μέχρι τῶν ἐσχάτων, δι' οὗ πάντα εἰς ἐκείνην ἀνήρτηνται τὰ μὲν πορρώτερον τὰ δ' ἐγγύτερον κατὰ τὴν τρανότητα καὶ τὴν ἀμυδρότητα τοῦ ἐν αὐτοῖς συνθήματος, καὶ τοῦτό ἐστιν τὸ πάντα κινοῦν εἰς τὸν τοῦ ἀγαθοῦ πόθον καὶ ἄσβεστον τὸν ἔρωτα τοῦτον παρεχόμενον τοῖς οὖσιν, ἄγνωστον μὲν ὑπάρχον (διήκει γὰρ καὶ μέχρι τῶν γινώσκειν μὴ δυναμένων), κρεῖττον δ' ὂν ζωῆς (πάρεστι γὰρ καὶ τοῖς ἀψύχοις), νοερὰν δὲ τὴν δύναμιν οὐκ ἔχον (ἔγκειται γὰρ τοῖς ἀμοίροις τοῦ νοεῖν). . . . τοιαῦτα δ' ἐστὶν τὰ καλούμενα σύμβολα τῶν θεῶν· μονοειδῆ μὲν ἐν τοῖς ὑψηλοτέροις ὄντα διακόσμοις, πολυειδῆ δ' ἐν τοῖς καταδεεστέροις· ἃ καὶ ἡ θεουργία μιμουμένη δι' ἐκφωνήσεων μέν, ἀδιαρθρώτων δέ, αὐτὰ προφέρεται. τὰ δὲ δὴ τρίτα καὶ ἀπὸ τῶν νοερῶν ὑποστάσεων ἐπὶ πάντα καθήκοντα ἰδιώματα καὶ μέχρις ἡμῶν προϊόντα τὰ ὀνόματά ἐστι τὰ θεῖα, δι' ὧν οἱ θεοὶ καλοῦνται καὶ οἷς ἀνυμνοῦνται, παρ' αὐτῶν τῶν θεῶν ἐκφανέντα καὶ εἰς αὐτοὺς ἐπιστρέφοντα, καὶ ὅσον ἐστὶν αὐτῶν φανόν, εἰς γνῶσιν ἀνθρωπίνην προάγοντα. (*In Crat.* 30.19–32.3)

Here the descending symbols of the One, which are beyond even intellect and life, descend all the way to the lowest orders. The representational arts of theurgy and the production of divine names are treated as arts that join in the processions of these mysterious, ineffable chains of being. The term ἀναρτάω is significant in this context. Like the term συναρτάω, which Iamblichus used similarly,[19] it is a term of ontological attachment used to express the connection between a manifested thing and the higher-order powers of which it is a manifestation.[20] Though Proclus here limits his remarks to language about the gods, one would expect them to apply to his general language theory as well, but the issue is not entirely clear. Since the essence of even the most mundane thing is its hidden σύμβολον, the trace of the divine, all names that capture essences of things will be names of something divine. Moreover, Proclus shifts easily from talking about the names we use to describe the divine world and names in general. However, he does not commit himself to the position that the words of our everyday language all have "symbolic" power. In the *Parmenides* commentary (848–53) he seems to suggest that our run-of-the-mill names operate by convention when they name sensible things but by direct ontological connection when they designate the higher-order beings of which physical beings are a mere reflection. Complicating this picture further, not all names are run-of-the-mill. Taking off from Homer's suggestions that there are some things that have "divine names,"[21] a position that Plato picks up in the *Cratylus*,[22] Proclus develops a theory that there are names that operate at all the different levels of the cosmos, from the material world to the highest intellectual realms. In the *Parmenides* commentary, the class of higher-order names seems to be limited to the names of the gods, but the *Timaeus* commentary expands the class to include secret designations of sensible things as well. The divine names "unfold the whole essence of the things named, but those of men only partially come into contact with them" (*In Tim.* I 274.6–9). In this same section of the *Timaeus* commentary, Proclus tells us that these divine names are "symbols" that are impressions left by the One on every existing thing. They are a trace of each thing's participation in the "being" that undergirds the whole world.

Proclus and the Invocation Theory of Literature

Proclus differs from Iamblichus, and from all the Neoplatonists except Porphyry, in his attentiveness to the strictly literary implications of Neoplatonic emanationist ontology. In his commentary on the *Republic*, Proclus produces the first surviving systematically formulated alterna-

[19] See above, chap. 6.

[20] See, e.g., *Elements* prop. 9 (Dodds, p. 10, n. 15). Further references can be found in Dodds's index.

[21] See, for example, *Il.* 20.74 and 14.291.

[22] *Crat.* 391e–392b.

tive to the notion that literature is an imitation of the world (a mainstream idea in the classical period as well as now). As we mentioned above, Proclus and his peers knew book 10 of the *Republic* very well. Plato had banished the poets from his ideal state on the same grounds that Plotinus refused to sit for his portrait. In this reckoning, the poets are twice removed from the truth, since they produce phantom images of the sensible world, which is itself already a copy of the realm of the Forms.[23] Plato concentrates his attack on poetry based on his view of it as a form of mimesis, but Proclus already has a theory to supplant the mimetic model, something no one before him had made a sustained effort to do, and to replace it with what he calls a "symbolic" one. Speaking of the portions of Homer's work that had most offended critics, that is, the various disharmonies and indiscretions among the gods, Proclus asks:

> How could one call the poetry that interprets divine matters by means of symbols "imitation"? For symbols are not imitations [μιμήματα] of those things of which they are symbolic. For things could never be imitations of their opposites, the shameful of the beautiful, the unnatural of the natural. But the symbolic mode indicates the nature of things even through what is most strongly antithetical to them. If, then, a poet is inspired and reveals by means of symbols the truth of existent things, or if someone uses sure knowledge and reveals the very order of things, such a poet is neither an imitator nor can he be disputed by the aforesaid arguments.
>
> καὶ πῶς γὰρ ἂν ἡ διὰ συμβόλων τὰ θεῖα ἀφερμηνεύουσα μιμητικὴ προσαγορεύοιτο; τὰ γὰρ σύμβολα τούτων, ὧν ἐστι σύμβολα, μιμήματα οὐκ ἔστιν· τὰ μὲν γὰρ ἐναντία τῶν ἐναντίων οὐκ ἄν ποτε μιμήματα γένοιτο, τοῦ καλοῦ τὸ αἰσχρόν, καὶ τοῦ κατὰ φύσιν τὸ παρὰ φύσιν· ἡ δὲ συμβολικὴ θεωρία καὶ διὰ τῶν ἐναντιωτάτων τὴν τῶν πραγμάτων ἐνδείκνυται φύσιν. εἴ τις ἄρα ποιητὴς ἔνθους ἐστὶν καὶ διὰ συνθημάτων δηλοῖ τὴν περὶ τῶν ὄντων ἀλήθειαν, ἢ εἴ τις ἐπιστήμῃ χρώμενος αὐτὴν ἡμῖν ἐκφαίνει τὴν τάξιν τῶν πραγμάτων, οὗτος οὔτε μιμητής ἐστιν οὔτε ἐλέγχεσθαι δύναται διὰ τῶν προκειμένων ἀποδείξεων. (*In remp.* 1.198.13–24)[24]

[23] The best current reevaluation of this topic is Elizabeth Asmis, "Plato on Poetic Creativity," in Richard Kraut, ed., *Cambridge Companion to Plato* (New York: Cambridge University Press, 1992), 338–64.

[24] Text from Proclus, *In Platonis rem publicam commentarii*, ed. G. Kroll, 2 vols. (Leipzig: Teubner, 1899). Translations based on the still extraordinarily helpful second volume of Robert Drummond Lamberton's "Homer the Theologian: The Iliad and the Odyssey as Read by the Neoplatonists of Late Antiquity" (diss., Yale University, 1979). (His translation there of Pseudo-Plutarch's *Life of Homer* is of course now superceded by the edition published by Scholars Press [1996].) The appendices to Lamberton's disserta-

This curious passage sums up the most important attempt to develop an alternative to the mimetic theory of literature in the extant writing of the ancient period.[25] It is also a decisive moment in the life of the literary "symbol." As a preliminary step to unraveling the manifold implications of Proclus's theory, we need to recognize the boldness of his claim.

Though post-Romantic literary critics are perhaps accustomed to literary theories that claim to be nonmimetic, such theories are exceedingly rare in the classical period. There are perhaps good reasons for this, given the lack of viable alternatives to imitation-based theories of literature. Modern alternatives are generally some variation on the claim that the poet has the power to create wholly new worlds, and not just to copy the one we see. This vision might be labeled an "invocation" theory of literature. Rather than imitating the world as we see it in day-to-day life, the poet calls a new world into existence, through a creative power uniquely reserved for imaginative literature.[26] Such a stance has an intuitive appeal but raises a number of tricky issues.[27] Just how new can a literary "creation" be?[28] No matter how creative they may be, poets still inhabit the same material landscape that the rest of us do. However fancifully they manipulate it, they must work within a world we all know and see. Even if such a thing as totally new creation were possible, an audience would not recognize it, since it is logically impossible to recognize something that is *wholly* unfamiliar. Difficulties such as these keep the imitation model at the center of literary studies in many periods. But such concerns do not apply to Proclus's exuberant literary visions. His key innovation is his elaborate ontology. The entities we see in the world are only the tips of so many ontological icebergs. They have concrete ties to a great chain of seemingly disconnected features of the universe. The poets' power to invoke new worlds rests in their ability to trace through to reality's hidden layers. They lay bare, and actually invoke, unseen worlds. The ontological visions that

---

tion can be recommended as an anthology (not elsewhere matched) of allegorical criticism in English translation.

[25] Lamberton calls this view "perhaps the most striking and original point in Proclus's poetics" (*Homer the Theologian*, 190).

[26] The new category for the Romantics, of course, is the notion of the "imagination." In classical literary criticism, the equivalent Greek term, *phantasia*, does not enjoy anything like the prominence of imagination, though one can find a positive evaluation of it in Philostratus *Life of Apollonius of Tyana* 6.19.

[27] For the most interesting contemporary treatment of imitation-based theories and their detractors, and extensive references to other figures in the discussion, see Paul Ricoeur, *Time and Narrative*, vol. 2 (Chicago: University of Chicago Press, 1992).

[28] A thorough reevaluation of this question in the postromantic literary world is presented in Françoise Meltzer's, *Hot Property: The Stakes and Claims of Literary Originality* (Chicago: University of Chicago Press, 1994).

Iamblichus developed to justify divine names (see chapter 6) suggest to Proclus similar arguments regarding the larger literary constructions of the poets.

Proclus is the first to articulate the paradigm of imitation versus invocation. The fulcrum of his literary thinking, in the passage above and elsewhere, is the category of the symbol. He marks the literary symbol with curious powers which it had not had before him and which it would retain for centuries to follow. Though Proclus's particular rendition of the category is new, it draws on a number of "symbolic" traditions in ancient thought. In the previous chapters, we have looked in some detail at the various services, literary and nonliterary, that ancient Greek symbols performed. They served as passwords, talismans with magical powers, philosophical aphorisms with odd potencies, and they were the oblique language that the gods used to communicate with mortals through oracles, omens, and dreams. Symbols were also, from the Hellenistic period forward, the language of a few inspired poets. With these various traditions as an inheritance, Proclus arrives at a new and powerful articulation of the nature of literary language, one that is as influential as it is strange.

Proclus proposes that the literary symbol does not resemble its referent, but rather carries a direct and ineffable ontological link to it. He claims that in shaping the raw material of language into "symbols," the inspired poet does not imitate his subject but invokes its real presence. The literary symbol, Proclus says, operates like a magic talisman. That is, like a voodoo doll or the consecrated Host in the Eucharist, the material token actually becomes that which it is supposed to represent; it invokes or summons the real presence of its referent. Literary symbols that depict the gods as having material attributes, for example, invoke the actual immaterial presence of divine beings. Symbolic literary images whose literal surfaces seem to suggest one thing actually carry an ontological link to a more profound and immaterial hidden meaning. This idea provides a philosophical heft to Proclus's allegorism that outweighs even the Stoics' complex theories.

Hierarchy of Poetry

Proclus is well known for his urge toward systematization.[29] In his poetics, the designation of "symbol" is generally reserved for the highest

[29] His *Elements of Theology*, for example, takes a Euclidean approach to ontology and lays out the entire structure of the cosmos in a series of 211 propositions and proofs that are supposed to build irrefutably from proposition to proposition.

of four main levels of poetry.[30] The lowest two categories in Proclus's scale of poetic modes are "mimetic." Mimetic poetry imitates the world of appearance that we see around us. If it does so inaccurately, it is designated "phantastic"; if accurately, "eikastic." Proclus draws this distinction from Plato's *Sophist* (246c). An example of the lowest "inaccurate" sort is where Homer says the sun rises from a lake.[31] For the next sort of mimetic poetry, the "eikastic" type, Proclus does not cite specific passages but speaks generally about those places where Homer "imitates the heroes fighting, or taking counsel, or speaking according to their various characters, some wisely, some bravely, some ambitiously."[32] He seems here to draw from Plato's *Republic* 2 (392d–394b), where Plato defines "mimetic" poetry as the production of direct quotations, in which the poet "imitates" the voice of his characters rather than telling a simple narrative in his own voice.[33] Proclus's third type of poetry is the didactic.[34] Didactic poetry teaches what we might call today facts, about the nature of the soul, or distinctions within natural or civic life, or the arrangement of the elements in the universe. It gives human souls, stuck in material bodies, the kinds of knowledge they need to negotiate their way through a life embedded in nature and society.

Proclus's highest category of poetry will get the bulk of our attention, as it got the bulk of his. The most characteristic feature of this poetry is its use of arcane, mystical "symbols." According to Proclus, the symbols are usually jarring, corporeal, sometimes even vulgar depictions of divine natures involved in the material world. The "symbolic" category of poetry seems clearly to have been developed in a defensive context. Those things that will count as symbols in Proclus's thinking are those that most offended the poets' traditional critics, including Plato: the castration of Ouranos, the binding of Zeus, Ares' tryst with Aphrodite, the expulsion of Hephaestus from Heaven. Proclus consistently invokes these infamous scenes as examples of the poets' greatest achievements. They are proofs of their inspired, hyperrational wisdom. Symbolic poetry arises from a divine madness that is higher than reason; it emanates from the Muses, possesses the poet, and then radiates out to the poet's readers. The parallels to the *Ion* are clear. When writing "symbolic"

[30] On these levels, see Sheppard, 162–202.

[31] Proclus *In remp.* 1:192.22–28.

[32] Proclus *In remp.* 1:192.28–193.4.

[33] This may appear to be an oddly narrow definition of a term that seems to have broad resonance in Plato's visions of poetry. Mimesis takes on a broader sense in *Republic* 10 (though perhaps not as broad as is generally thought), but in bk. 2, Plato defines it as specifically as Proclus does here. On this topic, see Asmis.

[34] Proclus *In remp.* 1:193.4–193.9.

poetry, the poet is no longer an imitator of mere appearances, rather he acts according to a higher principle. The poet produces base images, just as the demiurge of nature takes the unified world of the higher principles and stamps them into inert matter, and, precisely like the theurgist, fashions statues that carry a trace of divine presence.

The Poet as a Cog in the Machinery of Emanation

According to Proclus, the poet who writes the highest kind of poetry, the giver of names, and the theurgist all operate according to the very principle that governs and sustains the material world itself. All three figures are seen as working parts in the ontology of emanation. He compares their activities with the demiurgic forces that do the work of fabricating the cosmos. These figures, when inspired, observe the hidden ontological links that unite the immaterial and material orders, create mysterious material/verbal/literary "symbols," and render invisible entities into visible form. We have seen these views with reference to the theurgist and the namegiver, and they are set out even more clearly with reference to the inspired poet.

> The fathers of myth[35] observed that nature was creating images of nonmaterial and noetic Forms and embellishing this cosmos with these imitations, depicting the indivisible by means of fragmented things, the eternal by means of things that proceed through time, the noetic through that which the senses can grasp, and portraying the nonmaterial materially, the nonspatial spatially and depicting through things subject to change that which is eternally the same. When they saw this, in line with the nature and the procession of those things which have only apparent and imagelike existence, they themselves fabricated images of the divine in the medium of language, expressing the transcendent power of the models by those things most opposite to them and furthest removed from them: that which is beyond nature is represented by things contrary to nature; that which is more divine than all reason, by the irrational; that which transcends in simplicity all fragmented beauty, by things that are considered ugly and obscene.
>
> κατιδόντες γὰρ οἱ τῆς μυθοποιΐας πατέρες, ὅτι καὶ ἡ φύσις εἰκόνας δημιουργοῦσα τῶν ἀΰλων καὶ νοητῶν εἰδῶν καὶ τόνδε τὸν κόσμον ποικίλ-

[35] This category suggests a separate figure from the poet, who then appropriates and reconfigures the mythic material passed down by the mythmaker. We saw such a scheme in the work of Cornutus (see chap. 4). But in practice, Proclus does not put the distinction to use. Here, the phrase "fathers of myth" refers to Homer and Hesiod, whom he discusses in the previous paragraph. He tends to slip back and forth between poets and mythmakers, without being overly concerned about the differences between them.

λουσα τοῖς τούτων σισήσασιν τὰ μὲν ἀμέριστα μεριστῶς ἀπεικονίζεται, τὰ δὲ αἰώνια διὰ τῶν κατὰ χρόνον προϊόντων, τὰ δὲ νοητὰ διὰ τῶν αἰσθητῶν, ἐνύλως τε τὸ ἄϋλον ἀποτυποῦται καὶ διαστατῶς τὸ ἀδιάστατον καὶ διὰ μεταβολῆς τὸ μονίμως ἱδρυμένον, ἑπομένως τῇ τε φύσει καὶ τῇ προόδῳ τῶν φαινομένως ὄντων καὶ εἰδωλικῶς, εἰκόνας καὶ αὐτοὶ πλάττοντες ἐν λόγοις φερομένας τῶν θείων τοῖς ἐναντιωτάτοις καὶ πλεῖστον ἀφεστηκόσιν τὴν ὑπερέχουσαν τῶν παραδειγμάτων ἀπομιμοῦνται δύναμιν, καὶ τοῖς μὲν παρὰ φύσιν τὸ ὑπὲρ φύσιν αὐτῶν ἐνδείκνυνται, τοῖς δὲ παραλόγοις τὸ παντὸς λόγου θειότερον, τοῖς δὲ φανταζομένοις ὡς αἰσχροῖς τὸ παντὸς μεριστοῦ κάλλους ὑπερηπλωμένον· (*In remp.* 1.77.13–27)

A few points here will bear our close attention. The first is the general comparison of the fathers of myth with the demiurgic creation of the cosmos itself (see *In Tim.* 1.310.3ff). Proclus follows Syrianus in understanding that this figure sits at the highest point of the intellectual realm. The Demiurge takes the higher immaterial realities and makes material representations of them (*In Parm.* 844–45).

Second, Proclus's list of incompatible opposites—indivisible and fragmented, timeless and time-bound, material and immaterial—mark traditional problems in the general ontological scheme that Plato left to his heirs. The advocate of a theory like Plato's, which suggests that an immaterial, transcendent stratum of reality is the template for the material world, must eventually face interrogation over how, precisely, immaterials become material.[36] Proclus adds a new pair of incompatible opposites: images, in language, of the imageless divine. What is divine, by Proclus's own reckoning, transcends our categories of language and thought, but the poet, somehow, renders the extralinguistic into language. This aspect of Proclus's theory is critical to the notion of the symbol. The "symbol" is consistently Proclus's term for that language that defies the prohibition against speaking the unspeakable. In this way he contextualizes the problem of representing the divine through language into larger issues of cosmology and ontology. This is shrewd argumentation. While many of Proclus's peers would be quick to dismiss the poets' material fabrications as contrary to the divine nature, they could not easily do the same with the demiurgic creations given how seriously the *Timaeus* treats them. In the *Republic* commentary, Proclus tells us that to blame Homer for making corporeal representations of the incorporeal is as absurd as blaming the Demiurge for making material creation.[37]

[36] Even Plato himself recognized the problem. In the *Parmenides*, as the Neoplatonists knew well, the shrewd Eleatic philosopher attacks the theory of the Forms on just such grounds as these.

[37] Proclus *In remp.* 1:75.20–28; 205.4–21.

Third, we should highlight Proclus's claim that symbolic language expresses "the transcendent power of the models by those things most opposite to them and furthest removed from them." This rule, embedded in Proclus's views of the material world, dovetails nicely with his defensive strategy. We recall Proclus's distinctive view that lowliest matter has a special affiliation with the highest principle of the cosmos. Since only the simplest property of "being," which derives only from the One itself, penetrates all the way through to the lowest links in the chains of reality, these lowest links carry a less mediated trace of the divine in them than intermediary beings. This principle provides Proclus with an ontological basis for explaining why Homer sometimes uses the basest, most corporeal of images for the greatest gods. He makes the point finer in the section of text following the longer citation above:

> Moreover, when we consider each chain of the gods descending from above down to the lowest creatures and passing through all the ranks of beings encountered in reality, we can see that the ends of these chains manifest properties like those the myths assign to the gods themselves and that they produce and maintain aberrations comparable to those by which the myths have hidden the secret doctrine of first causes.
>
> πρὸς δὲ αὖ τούτοις καθ' ἑκάστην τάξιν θεῶν ἄνωθεν ἄχρι τῶν τελευταίων ὑφιζάνουσαν καὶ διὰ πάντων ἐπεξιοῦσαν τῶν ἐν τοῖς οὖσιν γενῶν ἔξεστιν θεᾶσθαι τῶν σειρῶν ἀποτελευτήσεις τοιαύτας ἰδιότητας προστησαμένας, ὁποίας οἱ μῦθοι τοῖς θεοῖς αὐτοῖς ἀπονέμουσιν, καὶ τοιούτων πραγμάτων ὑποστατικὰς καὶ συνεκτικάς, δι' οἵων ἐκεῖνοι τὴν περὶ τῶν πρωτίστων ἀπόρρητον θεωρίαν κατέκρυψαν. (*In remp.* 1.77.29–78.6)

Far from blaspheming the gods, according to Proclus's logic, these base corporeal images appropriately render the highest principles through material images that sit at the extremities of the ontological chains, which in their baseness possess a paradoxical affinity with transcendent.[38] Indeed, Proclus tells us, the gods actually like to be represented in base material images. Echoing Iamblichus's statement that the gods take joy in being represented "symbolically" by the theurgists, Proclus says: "Furthermore, the gods enjoy hearing these symbolic formulas and favor the invokers and reveal their specific properties through them on the grounds that they are appropriate to them and most in harmony with them." [καὶ γὰρ οἱ θεοὶ τῶν τοιῶνδε συμβόλων ἀκούοντες χαίρουσιν καὶ τοῖς καλοῦσιν ἑτοίμως πείθονται καὶ τὴν ἑαυτῶν ἰδιότητα προφαίνουσιν διὰ τούτων ὡς οἰκείων αὐτοῖς καὶ μάλιστα γνωρίμων συνθημάτων] (*In remp.* 1.83.18–22).

[38] For a similar logic, see Proclus *In remp.* 1:76.28–77.4.

The Nonmimetic Symbol, the Signifying Power of Sympathy, and the Poet as Theurgist

We have already seen Proclus explicitly contrast symbols with imitations [μιμήματα]. He uses the symbol to supplant what had, since Plato, been the dominant understanding of the way literature works. The traditional view relies on a rhetoric of resemblance and establishes a set of poetic values based on accuracy of rendering. A good poem will produce an "accurate likeness" of the way the world is. Proclus explicitly denies that the representational model applies to the highest type of inspired poetry, the "symbolic" type. He grants Socrates' point that Homer's myths do not accurately "imitate" the gods: "It is reasonable, then, to claim that the myths of Homer do not give a good imitation of the divine" and "clearly bear no resemblance to those things that truly exist" [εἰκότως ἄρα τοὺς Ὁμηρικοὺς μύθους οὐκ εὖ μεμιμῆσθαι λέγομεν τὸ θεῖον· . . . ἀλλὰ ταύτῃ μὲν οὐδὲν ἐοικότες φαίνονται τοῖς οὖσιν] (*In remp*. 1.80.4–8). And yet, the symbol still indicates its referent. Proclus finds a new basis for semantic connection, on analogy to theurgic rites, in the force of sympathy. The same mysterious power that connects Apollo to gold and Selene to moonstones is now claimed to link a transcendent truth to a material literary representation.

> Just as the hieratic art necessarily distributes cult practices among the gods and their attendants [demons], so that none of those in the eternal following of the gods may be deprived of an appropriate cult, attracting the goodwill of the gods by holy initiations and mystical symbols, and inviting the contribution of the demons by using the passions manifest in the ceremonies, which work by some ineffable sympathy—in the same way the fathers of these myths, taking into consideration the whole extent, so to speak, of the procession of divine beings and wanting to relate the myths to the entire chain issuing from each god, conceived the surface which the myths project, with its images, by analogy to the lowest classes that preside over the lowest level of experience, rooted in the material world, but the secret (hidden from the masses of men and beyond their comprehension) of the inaccessible transcendent essence of the gods, they translated into perceptible form for those who aspire to such visions.

> ὥσπερ οὖν ἡ τῶν ἱερῶν τέχνη κατανείμασα δεόντως τὴν σύμπασαν θρῃσκείαν τοῖς θεοῖς καὶ τοῖς τῶν θεῶν ὀπαδοῖς, ἵνα μηδὲν ἄμοιρον τῆς ἐπιβαλλούσης θεραπείας ἀπολείπηται τῶν ἀϊδίως ἑπομένων τοῖς θεοῖς, τοὺς μὲν ταῖς ἁγιωτάταις τελεταῖς καὶ τοῖς μυστικοῖς συμβόλοις προσάγεται, τῶν δὲ τοῖς φαινομένοις παθήμασιν προκαλεῖται τὰς δόσεις διὰ δή τινος ἀρρήτου συμπαθείας, οὕτως ἄρα καὶ οἱ τῶν τοιῶνδε μύθων πατέρες εἰς πᾶσαν ὡς

εἰπεῖν ἀποβλέψαντες τὴν τῶν θείων πρόοδον καὶ τοὺς μύθους εἰς ὅλην ἀνάγειν σπεύδοντες τὴν ἀφ' ἑκάστου προϊοῦσαν σειρὰν τὸ μὲν προβεβλημένον αὐτῶν καὶ εἰδωλικὸν ἀνάλογον ὑπεστήσαντο τοῖς ἐσχάτοις γένεσιν καὶ τῶν τελευταίων καὶ ἐνύλων προεστηκόσι παθῶν, τὸ δὲ ἀποκεκρυμμένον καὶ ἄγνωστον τοῖς πολλοῖς τῆς ἐν ἀβάτοις ἐξῃρημένης τῶν θεῶν οὐσίας ἐκφαντικὸν τοῖς φιλοθεάμοσιν τῶν ὄντων παρέδοσαν. (*In remp.* 1.78.18–79.2)

The inspired poet and the theurgist operate by the same nonmimetic mode: the symbol which does not resemble its hidden referent, but has a "sympathy" with it. In the last chapter, we mentioned very briefly that Iamblichus had a nuanced stance toward the notion of "sympathy." He wanted to claim a higher-order connection between his symbols and the divinities to which they were attached.[39] I suspect that the widespread use of the notion of sympathy among magicians made Iamblichus wary of the term and prompted him to try to generate a new one. Sympathy worked for him on the level of the physical cosmos, whereas higher, nonphysical beings were not subject to it. Proclus does not feel such compunctions: In his thinking, the term "sympathy," broadly speaking, marks the power or energy that suffuses the chains that emanate from the One. It is the energy that links the higher-order manifestations to the lower-order ones along the cosmos's ontological rays. All of this makes reading and interpretation look very much like a sacramental act. One need only note the fate of Hypatia to be reminded of the real risks of pagan religious affiliation in Proclus's day. It is therefore reasonable that he would shift modes of worship into the more private realm of reading the poets. Here we see an extension and modification of ideas that we have already located in both the Derveni Papyrus in the classical period, and in the Stoics, as attested by Cicero's *De natura deorum*. Both these texts contrasted true piety, based on a full understanding achieved through texts, to the simple ritualism of those who go through the motions.[40]

Another passage from the *Republic* commentary expands on the modes by which the often jarring symbolic scenes convey their meanings, and gives us a somewhat clearer picture of a literary "sympathy":

In fact, what has happened to these mythic fictions [τὰ μυθικὰ πλάσματα] is like what Plato says happened to the most divine and august doctrines. For they are a matter for laughter for the masses of men, but to the few who rise to the level of intellect they reveal the myths' sympathy with their refer-

[39] Iamblichus tends to limit the use of this term to the material world; in higher realms, he renames the power φιλία. See Peter Struck, "Pagan and Christian Theurgies," *Ancient World* 32.1 (2001): 28.

[40] See chaps. 1 and 5.

> ents [ἐκφαίνει τὴν ἑαυτῶν πρὸς τὰ πράγματα συμπάθειαν] and give proof, based on the very operations of the hieratic art, of their power derived from natural unity with the divine [τῆς πρὸς τὰ θεῖα συμφυοῦς δυνάμεως.] (*In remp.* 1.83.12–18)

As we have seen before, in discussions of language theory, τὰ πράγματα especially indicates the referents as opposed to the words that are supposed to point to them. This is clearly the context in which it is intended here. And again, the symbolic myths "emphasize the sympathy which, throughout the universe, binds the last effects to the causes that engendered them" [τῆς ἐν τῷ παντὶ συμπαθείας τῶν ἀποτελεσμάτων πρὸς τὰ γεννητικὰ αὐτῶν αἴτια] (*In remp.* 1.84.8–10). In a remarkable synthesis, Proclus elides any substantive difference between the liturgical activities of the theurgist and the inspired poet's production of verse. The force of sympathy permeates this new and powerful mode of symbolic discourse.

The Symbol as "Anagogic"

In Neoplatonic ontology, as we have seen, the downward reach of the One is consistently paired with an upward striving on the part of all its creations. All things, from the humblest stone to a human being to the highest divine being, have an automatic urge to reach back upward toward their source in the process of reversion. While reversion is the natural urge of all things, it is continually thwarted by the tendency of beings enmeshed in matter to stay where they are and wallow around in their material natures. Since Plotinus, the goal of philosophy had been to free the human soul from these retarding impulses and allow it to take wing to where it naturally wanted to go. Plotinus advocated a discipline of pure contemplation. Iamblichus supplemented contemplation with ritual, which he deemed a necessary part of the devotee's discipline. Proclus supplements the Plotinian scheme yet further with his view of the soteriological power of symbolic poetry. While his position is extreme, it is also relevant to many later mainstream visions of the transformative and salvific power of poetry. Aristotle's *katharsis* is often the basis for later critics who claim that poetry can transform the emotions of an audience. But the grander views that one sees articulated in Boccaccio, Dante, or in some of the Romantics, in which poetry is held out as a vehicle for transporting the soul to higher planes of knowledge and awareness—these visions owe some debt to Proclus.

Proclus uses Plato's *Ion* as a prooftext for his thoughts on inspired poetry and its effect on its audience. In this dialogue, Socrates makes his famous remarks regarding poetic inspiration. The poet is drawn toward the Muse just as a piece of metal is drawn toward a magnet. And just as the metal becomes an attracting agent as long as it is in contact with the magnet, so too the poet exerts a force of attraction on the rhapsodes who sing his poetry. And further, the audience who hears the rhapsode's performance shares in the energy of attraction and passes it on. Proclus interprets the magnetic chain as nothing other than one of the chains of emanation that radiate out from the transcendent One; and the force that courses through it, he understands as "sympathy":

> In all these passages [from the *Ion*], he [Plato] says that inspired poetry is seated right in the middle, between the divine cause, . . . the origin of inspired impulses, and the last echoes of inspiration seen operating by sympathy in the rhapsodes. Here in the middle Socrates has placed the madness of the poets. This madness receives its impulse from outside and imparts it to others, brought to fulfillment from above and transferring the illumination it receives from above to other beings, providing a single bond uniting the most remote participants with the unity in which they participate.
>
> ἐν δὴ τούτοις ἅπασιν τὴν ἔνθεον ποιητικὴν μέσην ἀτεχνῶς ἱδρῦσθαί φησιν τῆς τε θείας αἰτίας . . . τῆς ἀρχῆς τῶν ἐνθεαστικῶν κινήσεων καὶ τῶν τελευταίων ἀπηχημάτων τῆς ἐπιπνοίας τῶν ἐν τοῖς ῥαψῳδοῖς κατὰ συμπάθειαν δρωμένων ἐν μέσῳ τὴν τῶν ποιητῶν μανίαν ἔταξεν, κινουμένην τε καὶ κινοῦσαν καὶ πληρουμένην ἄνωθεν καὶ εἰς ἄλλα διαπορθμεύουσαν τὴν ἐκεῖθεν ἔλλαμψιν, ἕνα τε σύνδεσμον παρεχομένην τοῖς ἐσχάτως μετέχουσι πρὸς τὴν μετεχομένην μονάδα. (*In remp.* 1.184.25–185.7)

Again, this is the language of emanation used in the service of poetics. But the *Ion* example points out the potential for the forces of sympathy to connect not only signifying chains of signs and referents but also the divine Muses, poets, rhapsodes, and the audience:

> For just as [the Muses] fill all the other creations of the father, both visible and invisible, with harmony,[41] even so in the souls of which they take possession they illuminate the trace [ἴχνος] of divine symmetry and bring divine poetry to perfection. Since the entire action of the illuminator consists in divine presence [παρουσία], and the illuminated one gives itself over to the impulses that come from it and steps out of the divine and uniform, this, I believe, is why he called such illumination "possession" and "madness." It is "possession" because it takes power over all things that are moved by it and "madness" since it causes the illuminated ones to depart from their own usual actions and enter its identity.
>
> ὡς γὰρ τὰ ἄλλα πάντα τά τε ἀφανῆ καὶ τὰ ἐμφανῆ δημιουργήματα τοῦ πατρὸς τῆς ἁρμονίας πληροῦσιν καὶ τῆς ἐνρύθμου κινήσεως, οὕτως δὴ καὶ ταῖς

[41] Whereas Proclus tells us that Apollo had a special affiliation with the sun and sent a solar power through his chain, the Muses send a force of "harmony" through theirs.

κατόχοις <ἐξ> αὐτῶν ψυχαῖς τὸ τῆς θείας συμμετρίας ἴχνος ἐλλάμπουσαι τὴν ποιητικὴν ἀποτελοῦσιν τὴν ἔνθεον. ἐπεὶ δὲ ὅλη μὲν ἡ ἐνέργεια τοῦ ἐλλάμποντός ἐστιν ἐν ταῖς θείαις παρουσίαις, τὸ δ' ἐλλαμπόμενον ἑαυτὸ ταῖς ἐκεῖθεν κινήσεσιν ἐπιδίδωσιν καὶ τῶν σφετέρων ἠθῶν ἐξιστάμενον ὑπέστρωται ταῖς τοῦ θείου καὶ μονοειδοῦς ἐνεργείαις, διὰ ταῦτα οἶμαι κατοκωχήν τε καὶ μανίαν ὁμοῦ τὴν τοιαύτην προσείρηκεν ἔλλαμψιν· ὡς μὲν κρατοῦσαν τῶν ὑφ' ἑαυτῆς κινουμένων ὅλων κατοκωχὴν αὐτὴν ὀνομάσας, ὡς δὲ ἐξιστᾶσαν τῶν οἰκείων ἐνεργημάτων εἰς τὴν ἑαυτῆς ἰδιότητα τὰ ἐλλαμπόμενα μανίαν προσειπών. (*In remp.* 1.180.19–181.2)

The "trace" of the passage above sounds very much like other statements Proclus makes regarding the secret σύμβολον or σύνθημα that the One places, as a trace of itself, inside of all beings, including human souls. In the introduction to book 2 of his *Commentary on the Timaeus*, Proclus tells us that the One implants in each existing thing a σύνθημα of itself appropriate to that thing.[42] There is a clear parallel here to the *Chaldean Oracles*, where the father of the universe sowed symbols all through the cosmos (a passage for which Proclus is our source, and which he references here).[43] These shards of the divine nature are the cause of the "sympathy" that unites the various chains of being together. Those things in the chain of Apollo will have a sunlike symbol in their souls, those in that of Selene will have a moonlike symbol, and those who are especially attuned to the melodies of the Muses will carry a harmony symbol.[44] With this psychology in mind, Proclus seems to mean something quite specific when he suggests that the seemingly offensive "symbolic" stories of the poet "establish a secret sympathy in us, leading to participation with the gods" [συμπάθειαν ἡμῖν ἄρρητον προπαρασκευάζουσιν εἰς τὴν μετουσίαν τῶν θεῶν] (*In remp.* 1.84.1–2). The poet's mythic symbols here operate on that part of the soul that carries a trace of the divine and reawakens the symbol to the divinity with which it is linked. Once again, precisely like the symbol of the theurgic rites, the literary symbol is the mechanism that spurs the upward-stretching process of reversion. Like matter, which serves as the ontological turning point and catalyst for reversion; the poet's words are "uplifting" in a very concrete sense indeed. Through sympathetic connection they raise the souls of the poets, rhapsodes, and audience toward anagogic union with the One. Proclus claims this explicitly in a number of places: Though they bear no resemblance to the things that exist, the symbolic myths are "in harmony with the gods and raise up

[42] Proclus *In Tim.* 1:210.2–31.

[43] The oracle is quoted in Proclus *In Crat.* 52.11, it is referenced at *In Tim.* 1:211.1–2.

[44] See Lamberton, 218.

[ἀνάγουσιν] to contemplation of the gods those who are naturally suited" (*In remp.* 1.80.9–11). "Such myths [the symbolic myths] reveal a holy mystery and constitute an anagogic initiation [τελετὴν ἀναγωγόν] for the listener" (*In remp.* 1.80.21–23). And finally, in a comment on the *Phaedrus*, Proclus makes his most passionate statement of the soteriological power of poetry:

> This arousing and enrapturing [of the soul by poetry] is indeed the task of both [Muse and soul] and contributes to the fulfillment of a single entity—composed of the illuminated and the illuminating, I mean—for the one moves downward and the other is spread out below to receive its giving. The "awakening" is a straining by the soul and unswerving movement, a turning away from the fall into the created world back toward the divine; the rapture is inspired movement, and a tireless dance around the divine, bringing the possessed to perfection. (*In remp.* 1.181.19–27)

The Invocation Theory in Practice

In his commentary on the *Republic*, Proclus defends Homer at length against Plato's specific charges, making full use of his theory of the invocation of the divine by symbolic material language. His particular symbolic readings, which Lamberton has systematically investigated, focus on those indecorous scenes that had especially bothered Plato and other critics.[45] Yes, he will concede, if they are understood as mere imitations, they are blasphemous, for the gods would be represented as doing impious things. But these scenes are σύμβολα, which are only the lowest links in long ontological chains that lead, with an arcane directness, to the divinities themselves:

> The casting out of Hephaestus exhibits the procession of the divine from above down to the lowest creations in the realm of the senses, moved and achieved and guided by the creator and father of the universe, and the chains of Kronos show the union of the whole of creation with the noetic and paternal transcendence of Kronos, and the castration of Ouranos hints at the separation of the Titanic chain from the order that maintains the universe. . . . For all that which among us is associated with the worse and belongs to the inferior realm the myths take to refer to that nature which is precisely the superior and more effective, when reference is made to the gods. For example, "bondage" among us is a hindrance and checking of activity; there, it is a connection and ineffable union with the causes. "Cast-

[45] Lamberton, 197–232. Lamberton also shows that Proclus's practice does not always mirror his theory, so that properly "symbolic" poetry sometimes functions by εἰκόνες.

ing out" here is violent movement caused by someone else, but among the gods it indicates generative procession and a free-ranging, easy presence everywhere, not separated from its own source but proceeding from this in succession through all things. "Castration" in the context of fragmented and material things constitutes a diminution of power, but in the context of the first-working causes it hints at a procession of second-order entities from their own causes to a lower level of being, while the first-order beings remain undiminished in themselves and neither are displaced on account of their procession nor diminished by their departure nor divided on account of the differentiation into the lower levels.

ἡ μὲν Ἡφαίστου ῥῖψις τὴν ἄνωθεν ἄχρι τῶν τελευταίων ἐν τοῖς αἰσθητοῖς δημιουργημάτων τοῦ θείου πρόοδον ἐνδείκνυται, κινουμένην καὶ τελειουμένην καὶ ποδηγετουμένην ὑπὸ τοῦ πάντων δημιουργοῦ καὶ πατρός, οἱ δὲ Κρόνιοι δεσμοὶ τὴν ἕνωσιν τῆς ὅλης δημιουργίας πρὸς τὴν νοερὰν τοῦ Κρόνου καὶ πατρικὴν ὑπεροχὴν δηλοῦσιν, αἱ δὲ τοῦ Οὐρανοῦ τομαὶ τὴν διάκρισιν τῆς Τιτανικῆς σειρᾶς ἀπὸ τῆς συνεκτικῆς διακοσμήσεως αἰνίσσονται. . . . πάντα γὰρ τὰ παρ' ἡμῖν κατὰ τὸ χεῖρον ἐμφανταζόμενα καὶ τῆς καταδεεστέρας ὄντα συστοιχίας ἐπ' ἐκείνων οἱ μῦθοι κατ' αὐτὴν τὴν κρείττονα φύσιν καὶ δύναμιν παραλαμβάνουσιν. οἷον ὁ δεσμὸς παρ' ἡμῖν μὲν κώλυσίς ἐστι καὶ ἐπίσχεσις τῆς ἐνεργείας, ἐκεῖ δὲ συναφὴ πρὸς τὰ αἴτια καὶ ἕνωσις ἄρρητος. καὶ ἡ ῥῖψις ἐνταῦθα μὲν κίνησίς ἐστι βίαιος ὑπ' ἄλλου, παρὰ δὲ τοῖς θεοῖς τὴν γόνιμον ἐνδείκνυται πρόοδον καὶ τὴν ἄφετον ἐπὶ πάντα παρουσίαν καὶ εὔλυτον, οὐκ ἀφισταμένην τῆς οἰκείας ἀρχῆς, ἀλλ' ἀπ' ἐκείνης διὰ πάντων ἐν τάξει προϊοῦσαν. καὶ αἱ τομαὶ τοῖς μὲν μεριστοῖς πράγμασιν καὶ ἐνύλοις ἐλάττωσιν ἐμποιοῦσιν τῆς δυνάμεως, ἐν δὲ ταῖς πρωτουργοῖς αἰτίαις πρόοδον τῶν δευτέρων εἰς ὑφειμένην τάξιν ἀπὸ τῶν σφετέρων αἰτίων αἰνίσσονται, τῶν πρώτων ἀνελαττώτων ἐν ἑαυτοῖς ἱδρυμένων, καὶ μήτε κινουμένων ἀφ' ἑαυτῶν διὰ τὴν τούτων πρόοδον μήτε ἐλασσουμένων διὰ τὸν τούτων χωρισμὸν μήτε διαιρουμένων διὰ τὴν ἐν τοῖς καταδεεστέροις διάκρισιν. (1.82.10–1.83.7)

When Hephaestus falls from Olympus and lands on Lemnos, the scene is not indecorous but symbolic of the procession of the divine through all the hierarchically arranged levels of reality. And the binding of Kronos to a rock in Tartaros is actually a symbol of ineffable union between Kronos, who is traditionally associated with Nous by the Neoplatonists, and the material world. And though on a material level castration seems to constitute a diminution of power, on a higher level it indicates the aloofness of the upper orders from the process of generating the lower orders. Since it relies on ontological connection and not resemblance, the symbol can represent through unlikeness; it can serve, to use a notion put to work by an influential Christian follower of Proclus, to whom we will turn in a moment, as a dissimilar symbol.

Conclusion

While Proclus's theories of language and poetry are undeniably intricate and heavily dependent on an idiosyncratic metaphysics, we ought to grant that they make a certain amount of internal sense given the ontological positions that were sketched out above. They also give history's perhaps most rigorous philosophical explanation and justification for the theory that poetry is an inspired vehicle of divine truth. They have, I will suggest in the epilogue, shown a long endurance in the history of literary theory, though precisely how and under what guises is sometimes difficult to see. People seem to *want* to believe that the poets cross bridges that we all wish were crossable, and Proclus satisfies this desire with uncommon precision. Readers in various periods return to the poets to provide some insight, if only a glimpse, into a world that only the gods know. And theorists in various periods return to Proclus to explain precisely how the poet might do this. The durability of this wish and the consistent intuitive appeal of Plotinus's emanationist cosmology, which enables Proclus's theory, may go some way toward explaining the otherwise curiously long legacy that this rather grand theory has in the history of literary theory. Though Proclus's "symbol" makes little sense outside his ontology, its later proponents rarely subscribe to the full set of metaphysical propositions that justifies it. But the belief that a "symbol" is able to indicate things that are not at all like it, or that it has *some* kind of mysterious ontological link with its referent, or that it is a privileged vehicle for raising us up to the divine—all these Proclean habits of thought will ring true to many later thinkers. More often than we currently recognize, these later visions owe some debt to Proclus.

EPILOGUE

SYMBOL TRACES: POST-PROCLEAN THEORIES

IN RECENT TIMES Proclus has not generated the interest that he once did. Though, perhaps even more than the other Neoplatonists, he has consistently received lavish attention from enthusiasts of the occult sciences, his fortunes in the classicists' canon have waxed and waned. But his relative obscurity today should not lead us to gloss over the importance he has had for pivotal thinkers in a number of periods. Those who specialize in Proclus have long been familiar with the breadth of his influence on the cosmologies of premodern Europe, East and West, but his legacy can be tracked in literary studies as well. These observations are meant as a survey of a few discrete moments in post-Proclean "symbol" history, which, while not systematic or exhaustive, will indicate the fruits that are waiting to be plucked.

The main points, which will be discussed below, are as follows. First, through the writings of "Dionysius the Areopagite," an invented identity for a shadowy sixth-century Christian, Proclus's thought, cosmetically adapted to Christianity, was held in high esteem in Europe and Byzantium through the greater part of the Middle Ages.[1] Thomas Aquinas cites Dionysius more frequently than any authority except Augustine, invoking him some 1,700 times in the *Summa*.[2] Dionysius's general influence on medieval cosmology and theology has been covered in illuminating detail in recent years. Though he is no simple parrot of

[1] Close to a century of philological scrutiny has determined the extent of Pseudo-Dionysius's debt to Proclus, down to repetition of key segments of text, phrases, and individual technical terms. For a good summary of it, see E. R. Dodds's introduction to his translation of Proclus's *Elements of Theology*, 2d ed. (Oxford: Clarendon Press, 1963), xxvi–xxviii. On the great importance of Dionysius's concept of the symbol for literary theory in the Middle Ages, see A. J. Minnis, "The Dionysian Imagination," in *Medieval Literary Theory and Criticism c. 1100–c. 1375: The Commentary Tradition*, eds. A. J. Minnis and A. B. Scott (Oxford: Clarendon Press, 1988), 165–73, and Minnis, "General Introduction: The Significance of the Medieval Commentary-Tradition," in *Medieval Literary Theory and Criticism*, 1–11.

[2] On the connections, the bibliography is vast. See the recent contribution of Fran O'Rourke, *Pseudo-Dionysius and the Metaphysics of Aquinas* (Leiden: E. J. Brill, 1992).

Proclean ideas,[3] it has been well understood for the last hundred years that Dionysius appropriates nearly his entire ontological system of thought, and his literary theory as well, for a Christian purpose. We will find that the theory of the symbol is another trace of the Neoplatonic world that Dionysius passes on. In his treatise *On the Divine Names*, Dionysius finds Proclus's theory of the symbol useful in tackling the hermeneutic problems involved in reading the Christian Bible. Using Proclus's theory, Dionysius assures us that the places where God appears in corporeal form are not μιμήματα of events that actually occurred, but σύμβολα of higher immaterial referents, which they signify by a more arcane means than simple imitation. Dionysius also recapitulates the symbol's role in ritual. He uses the term to mark the Host's power of invocation in the Eucharist. With this symbol theory (which recapitulates Proclus's ontological, liturgical, and literary forms), Dionysius becomes one of the most important authorities in the medieval period on figurative language in the Bible.

Second, when Platonic thought was reintroduced to Europe, Proclus became a central figure for Ficino. As has happened at other points in the history of Plato's reception, Ficino understood Proclus's commentaries as the key to the varied and difficult Platonic corpus.[4] Ficino owned and translated Proclus's commentaries on Plato as well as his synthetic works of theology and philosophy. Among the rich collection of classical ideas Ficino bequeathed to the European Renaissance was the literary theory of the symbol, explicitly opposed to mimesis, and

[3] For the most efficient summary of the differences between Proclus and Pseudo-Dionysius, see "Pseudo-Dionysius," in *Oxford Dictionary of Byzantium* (New York: Oxford University Press, 1991).

[4] Michael Psellus, a Byzantine philosopher who revived the study of Plato in eleventh-century Constantinople and was a key figure in the transmission of classical Greek texts, read Plato's works through the Neoplatonic commentators, especially Proclus. He called Proclus a "great haven" in which he could find all knowledge (*Chronographia* 1.136, cited in Dominic J. O'Meara, *Pythagoras Revived: Mathematics and Philosophy in Late Antiquity* [New York: Oxford University Press, 1992], 54). Proclus's prominence for nineteenth-century English-speaking intellectuals was secured by Thomas Taylor. Taylor (1758–1835)—a student of Proclus so devoted to him that he named his son after him—produced the first complete English translation of Plato's dialogues, literally surrounding them with Proclus's commentaries, which he includes as sidebars, footnotes, and appendices. Emerson, for example, came across his Plato in these translations (see Albert J. von Frank, *An Emerson Chronology* [New York: Macmillan, 1994], 162). Also from Taylor's translations, Emerson developed a great admiration for the commentaries of Proclus. Perhaps Proclus's recurrent popularity as a guide to understanding Plato, more than any other factor, explains the neglect of his corpus in more recent periods. When nineteenth-century philologists took up the patently worthwhile project of separating the ideas of Plato himself from his later interpreters, those interpreters became understood primarily as obfuscators of Plato, not as thinkers in their own right.

recapitulating Proclus's symbol in its major and even minor details.[5] Third, Proclus's symbolic thinking played a role in the works of three Romantics: Schelling, Novalis, and Coleridge. The Neoplatonists' general influence on the Romantics has received a good bit of attention,[6] but the connection could be fleshed out in further detail by a specific focus on the category of the symbol.

Finally, though I will not investigate it in any more detail below, the German philosopher Hegel seems to owe some debt to Proclus.[7] Hegel notes his esteem for Proclus's *Commentary on the Parmenides* (the dialogue being of great importance to him) in the preface to the *Phenomenology of Spirit* (1807). Also, in 1821, Victor Cousin dedicated the editio princeps of Proclus's *Parmenides* commentary to none other than G.W.F. Hegel. No mere set of explanatory notes, Proclus's commentary extends to over six hundred pages and contains long excurses, in book 7, into the dialectics of negation. On the basis of these indications, further study on the Proclus-Hegel connection appears to be warranted. Another Proclus enthusiast, Ralph Waldo Emerson, was convinced. In his "Origin and Originality," he considers the question of whether there is anything new under the sun:

> The originals are not original. . . . The first book tyrannizes over the second. Read Tasso and you think of Vergil; read Vergil, and you think of Homer; and Milton forces you to reflect on how narrow are the limits of human invention. . . . Hegel pre-exists in Proclus, and, long before, in Her-

[5] For a helpful summary of Ficino's theory of the symbol, see Paul Oskar Kristeller, *The Philosophy of Marsilio Ficino*, trans. Virginia Conant (New York: Columbia University Press, 1943), 92–99. Though Kristeller does not mention Proclus here, Ficino's theory bears a resemblance in all its major features, and even in its minor ones, to Proclus's. See, for example, Ficino's view that the symbol indicates along the "sympathies" that exist between different orders of the universe (see chap. 7; cf. Proclus, *In Tim.*, 1:205–14, esp. 210.16–19); that the interval to be spanned in symbolic representations decreases as one moves down the chain of being (cf. Proclus *Elements of Theology* props. 130, 117); that the symbol has an ontological connection with the higher reality that it signifies (see chap. 7). And given Ficino's intimate familiarity with Proclus's work (he translated the commentary on the *Alcibiades*, *De sacrificio et magia*, the *Elementa physica*, *the Elementa theologica*, and possibly also the hymns; and owned the *Theologia Platonica*), we have little room to doubt that Proclus is Ficino's source.

[6] See, e.g., M. H. Abrams, *Natural Supernaturalism* (New York: Norton, 1971), 146–51.

[7] See A. H. Armstrong, "Platonism and Neoplatonism," *Encyclopedia Britannica* (1979), 15: 541: "The rediscovery of Proclus by the great German Idealist G.W.F. Hegel (1770–1831) had an important influence on his thought and so on the whole history of nineteenth-century Idealist philosophy . . . the direct influence of the Neoplatonists on Idealist thought is undisputable." On the Proclean legacies in Hegel, see Thomas A. Carlson, *Indiscretion: Finitude and the Naming of God* (Chicago: University of Chicago Press, 1999).

aclitus and Parmenides. Whoso knows Plutarch, Lucian, Rabelais, Montaigne and Bayle will have a key to many supposed originalities.[8]

That Emerson invokes not only Proclus but the Presocratics (Heraclitus and Parmenides), weakens the comparison somewhat. But Emerson's mention of Proclus was not casual, given his own familiarity with and esteem for the Neoplatonist.

Pseudo-Dionysius and Dissimilar Symbols

In probably the next generation after Proclus, a figure known to modern scholars as Pseudo-Dionysius marries Proclean metaphysics with Christian theology and achieves a synthesis with enduring and widespread influence. His pivotal importance for the history of Catholic and Orthodox theology (though with somewhat different results)[9] has been reckoned with increasing diligence in the last decade. Though Pseudo-Dionysius's identity remains shrouded in mystery, we know a few things about him with certainty: his thought follows closely along many of the arcane ways of Proclus; he is deeply interested in explaining how the Bible is able to depict the transcendent divine in mere linguistic representation; the notion of the symbol is central to his work and appears with ontological, liturgical, and literary dimensions that mirror Proclus's in decisive ways;[10] and he becomes a central authority for medieval biblical hermeneutics. Historians of theology, such as Jaroslav Pelikan, are apt to say that Dionysius appropriates Proclean concepts for Christian ends. At the other end of the spectrum lies E. R. Dodds's pungent position: Dionysius, he tells us, dresses Proclean metaphysics "in Christian draperies." However we decide to put it, the vast influence of Proclus on Dionysius is beyond doubt.[11]

Early in the sixth century, this writer took on the identity of Paul's

[8] Ralph Waldo Emerson, "Quotation and Originality," in *Works* (Cambridge, Mass.: Riverside Press, 1883), 8:172.

[9] In the medieval West, Dionysian hierarchies were adduced to justify the structure of ecclesiastical authority; by contrast the East saw in them the justification for a theology of the individual soul's ascent toward and communion with God. See John Meyendorff's review of Gheorghe I. Dragulin, "Eclesiologia tratatelor Areopagitice si importanta ei pentru ecumenismul contemporan" (Bucharest, 1979), a Romanian doctoral dissertation, in *St. Vladimir's Theological Quarterly* 24 (1980): 272.

[10] The term appears some ninety times in the few hundred pages of his corpus. He wrote a work, sadly lost, under the title *The Symbolic Theology*, though it is perhaps significant that the churchmen chose not to preserve it, especially since he himself chose to reference it nine times in the surviving corpus.

[11] The issue is still alive; see the ongoing debate in *St. Vladimir's Theological Quarterly* concerning the Orthodoxy of Dionysius.

Athenian convert, Dionysius the Areopagite, mentioned at Acts 17.34. Though the disguise was somewhat flimsy, due to careless references in his works to later thinkers, it remained intact, in no small part because of the exculpatory commentaries of John of Scythopolis (a likely collaborator in the ruse) as well as the more ingenuous backing of an unimpeachable defender of Orthodoxy, Maximus the Confessor. Dionysius did not choose his pseudonym at random. The Dionysius in the Book of Acts lived in Athens, the fabled well-spring of the philosophy that the later Dionysius found so compelling. But more pertinent to the topic at hand, Dionysius converts very shortly after Paul makes the following cautionary statements to the Greeks: "we ought not to think that the Deity is like gold, or silver, or stone, a representation by the art and imagination of humans." Pseudo-Dionysius shares with the one in Acts an acute concern for the problems involved in divine representations. He was familiar with the distinctive problematics of divine representation set out in the Hebrew Bible and the New Testament. If Proclus had his Plato, warning against the inevitable epistemological decay of image making, the later Dionysius surely had his Moses, warning him against the idolatry of graven images. However, Dionysius shows a marked preference for the Platonic means of casting the issue and the specifically Proclean defense. He shows no concern for the problem of idolatry. This is somewhat remarkable.

Unlike his Platonizing Christian predecessors (like Origen or the Cappadocian Fathers), Dionysius weds firm negative statements regarding representations with equally firm positive ones. Like Proclus, Dionysius tells us insistently that the traces of divine presence in the material world enable us to articulate the ineffable and to represent that which is emphatically beyond representation. This dialectic between representation and non-representation courses through the whole of the Dionysian corpus in its treatment of literary (biblical) depictions in the *Divine Names*, of ontology in the *Celestial Hierarchy*, and of liturgy in the *Ecclesiastical Hierarchy*. His statement at the beginning of the *Divine Names* is characteristic:

> And as many of the other theurgic[12] enlightenments, which accord with Scripture, as the hidden tradition of our inspired spiritual guides revealed to

[12] Paul Rorem and Colm Luibheid, who translated Pseudo-Dionysius for the Classics of Western Spirituality Series, do not render θεουργικός here as "theurgic," nor do they translate any cognate of the Greek term "θεουργία" with cognates of "theurgy," as classicists normally do. "Our author used the term 'theurgy' to mean 'work of God,'" Rorem and Luibheid argue, "not as an objective genitive meaning a work directed to God [i.e., ritual magic] (as in Iamblichus *De mysteriis* 1.2.7:2–6) but as a subjective genitive meaning God's own work" (52, 11.11). An argument for such a pronounced difference between Dionysius and his Neoplatonic predecessors faces a heavy burden, given the overwhelming weight of technical vocabulary from late Neoplatonism, including theurgy, and

> us, these also we have been initiated into, during this life, analogically through the sacred veils of the benevolent power of the sacred writings and of the traditional structure of the priesthood. And this benevolence clothes for our benefit intelligibles in sensible things and things beyond being in things that exist, and assigns shapes and contours to things without shape and contour and fills and divides the supernatural and formless simplicity with the manifold of individual symbols. . . . And in this life, as far as we are able, we use symbols that are fitting for the divine, and from these in turn we are analogically stretched up to the simple and unified truth of the intelligible visions, and when we put in check every intellectual thought of the divine forms, as far as we are able we cast our intellectual energies upon the transcendent ray, as much as divine law permits. (*Divine Names* 1.4; *CD* 1:113.12–115.10)[13]

The Proclean resonances here are clear. Here and elsewhere in his writings, Dionysius consistently marries the economy of representation that governs literary depictions to the ontology of the unfolding of the cosmos and to schemes of liturgical representation. With regard to ontology, Proclus's chain has become a ray, and Dionysius tells us that the transcendent divine leaves traces of itself in the form of σύμβολα or συνθήματα in the existing things that unfold from it.[14] With regard to ritual practice, he follows Iamblichus and Proclus in claiming that the One replicated its unfolding hierarchy in the liturgical practices of earthly celebrants.[15] The One passes down into Christian rituals secret and mysterious material symbols that become nodes upon which the divine presence manifests itself.[16] Dionysius's version of the Eucharist—one of Christianity's earliest full commentaries on the liturgical practice—comes off sounding provocatively theurgical, especially when one

---

from the school of Proclus in particular, that appears in Dionysius's work. The issue of precisely what Iamblichus and Dionysius mean by "theurgy" is a complex one. For specific consideration of it, see Peter Struck, "Christian and Pagan Theurgies," *Ancient World* 32 (2001): 25–38. Though the term θεουργία and its variants appear repeatedly in the corpus, and some thirty times in Dionysius's main treatise on liturgy alone, the English term "theurgy" appears nowhere in the Classics of Western Spirituality translation (*Pseudo-Dionysius*, trans. Colm Luibheid, forward, notes, and translation collaboration by Paul Rorem, Classics of Western Spirituality Series [New York: Paulist Press, 1987]).

[13] Translations my own. Citations are to Dionysius's work, by book and chapter, and then to the critical edition of the texts, *Corpus Dionysiacum*, ed. Beate Regina Suchla, Günter Heil, and Adolf Martin Ritter, 2 vols (Berlin: de Gruyter, 1990–91).

[14] *CH* 124a.

[15] *Ecclesiastical Hierarchy*, chap. 1.

[16] The "symbols" are mentioned dozens of times in the main liturgical treatise, the *Ecclesiastical Hierarchy*. They are ritual implements or scriptural images, which are regularly described as "gifts" from the divine (376d, 377b, 444c). As a concession to our nature, they give shape and form to that which is beyond shape and form.

compares it with Cyril of Jerusalem's (c. 315–86) close analysis of liturgical texts and Theodore of Mopsuestia's (c. 350–428) detailed typological reading onto the historical events of the crucifixion. Dionysius, by contrast, reads the Eucharist like Iamblichus and Proclus read the theurgical act, as the One's descent into plurality and then reversion back toward unity.[17] Given the superficial similarities between the theurgic rite and the Christian Eucharist, it is noteworthy that Dionysius calls the Eucharistic host a "symbol" that, through ritual, invokes the full presence of the divine.[18]

In his theory of literary representation, specifically treated in the *Divine Names*, Dionysius brings the better part of Proclus's new ontological world, and the symbolic habits of mind that it provides, to the text that emerged supreme from the Mediterranean culture wars of the first few centuries of the common era, the Christian Bible. Dionysius reads the Bible the way Proclus read Homer. As if he were answering Plato, Dionysius picks up Proclean theory, and even his precise language, to justify those passages where the holy text assigns various predicates, down to lowly material ones, to the utterly transcendent divinity. Dionysius explains, like Proclus, that the transcendent One cannot be represented through any kind of simple imitation. He shares this opinion not only with Proclus but with earlier Christian apophatic theologians, like the fourth-century Cappadocians, who tell of their preference for describing God with alpha-privative attributes: God is boundless, timeless, indivisible, immaterial, invisible, ungraspable, inscrutable, and so on.[19] But with a vigor unlike any Christian thinker before him, Dionysius believes that this utterly ineffable God can *also*, as it happens, be articulated and represented through a mysterious language of divine symbols that assigns, not negative characteristics, but seemingly inappropriate positive material attributes to the transcendent godhead. Why is this? As is the case with Proclus, the answer lies in the ontology:

> And so it is fitting for the cause of everything and the being beyond being to be both nameless and to have every name, of all things that exist. . . . For the unnamable goodness is not only the cause of cohesion or life or perfection, so that from this or that one of its designs it might be given a name. Rather the unnamable goodness enfolds in itself beforehand all things that exist, simply and without division. . . . and so it is fittingly praised and named by all things that exist. (*Divine Names* 1.7; *CD* 1:119.10–120.8)

[17] See Paul Rorem, *Pseudo-Dionysius: A Commentary on the Texts and an Introduction to Their Influence* (New York: Oxford University Press, 1993), 118–21.

[18] *EH* 444a–c.

[19] *DN* 865b–c.

Not only does the One transcend all, it suffuses all. Hence, it is fittingly named with the names of everything that is, including even base things. This Proclean territory provides Dionysius with a grounding for his examination of the places in Scripture where the transcendent God appears in all manner of material images, sometimes infelicitous ones: for example, when God is said to have eyes, ears, hair, a face, hands, a back, or wings; or when God is said to be fire, water, a cloud, or even a stone.[20]

Dionysius elaborates his theory of the symbolic through the concept of dissimilar symbols (*CH* 2.3–4), his most important and lasting literary legacy. Just as Proclus had claimed, Dionysius asserts that the most base and material things are sometimes the most fitting means of representing the divine. Such lowly images jar us away from attributing any material characteristics to the godhead, an error into which we might be tempted if we use only pleasing images like "light" or "love":

> I do not suppose that anyone of those who think straight would deny that dissimilar images anagogically raise our human mind better than similarities. For it is likely that an admirable representation of the sacred would lead people astray, into thinking that heavenly beings are some kind of golden and gleaming men and that they sparkle and are attractive. It was in order that those who have no thought beyond pretty appearances might not be affected that the imposing wisdom of the holy theologians sacredly descended even to dissimilar similarities, and made a concession to our inclination toward matter and to remain fixed on lowly images. But they were mindful of the upward-stretching part of the soul, and they goad us by the ugliness of the symbols [*synthemata*] in order that, when they seem neither permitted by divine law nor true, it does not seem right even to those very much inclined to material things, that supercelestial and divine sights, which approach to truth, resemble things so shameful. (*Celestial Hierarchy* 2.3; *CD* 2:13.7–21)

Dionysius continues, echoing Proclus's specific line of argument, and claims that certain qualities and characteristics that appear to be deficiencies when viewed on the material plane are actually indications of greater powers when they are assigned to the divine (we recall especially Proclus's reading of the castration of Ouranos):

> Even the quality of irrationality itself and insensibility when applied to animals or to inert matter we rightly call a lack of rationality and sense, but when it is applied to immaterial and purely intellectual beings, in a way that befits the divine, we acknowledge their transcendence, as being above the heavenly sphere, and beyond our discursive and embodied reason and

[20] *DN* 596c, 597a–b; *MT* 1033b.

our senses, which are material and estranged from their disembodied intellects. (*Celestial Hierarchy* 2.4; *CD* 2:14.19–24)

Further, Dionysius tells us that even brute matter bears divine traces and is able to raise us up to the divinity (we need to pay particular attention to the notion of beauty here):

> So then, it is possible to fashion forms that are not unfitting to the heavenly beings, even from the most shameful parts of the material world, because even matter, since it is disposed toward the substance of the truly beautiful throughout its every material order, contains certain traces of the intellectual majesty, and it is possible through them to be led up anagogically to the immaterial archetypes. (*Celestial Hierarchy* 2.4; *CD* 2:15.1–5)

Elsewhere Dionysius tells us that the Beautiful is precisely that aspect of the One that suffuses and holds together the cosmos. He equates it with Proclus's Good beyond being. Beauty, he says specifically, is the cause of the sympathy that binds the world (*Divine Names* 4.7—he uses Iamblichus's variant of the idea of sympathy, φιλία [*CD* 1.152.2]). For Dionysius, then, beauty serves as the basis and ground of semantic/sympathetic connection between what appear to be incongruous elements: base matter and the transcendent divine. The divine is not (cannot be) signified by imitation or resemblance, but only by pointing out the ontological trace of itself that it leaves in the very being of the elements that we use to invoke it. Representations are not phantoms but manifestations. They have the anagogic power to lift us up.

> As I have said, then, one ought not to speak about this transcendent and hidden divinity, nor indeed to apply any of our thoughts to it, beyond what has been divinely revealed to us out of the sacred writings [Scripture]. . . . However, the Good is not entirely incommunicable to everything that exists, but by itself it permanently sets up the transcendent beam and reveals by enlightenments proportionate to each of the things that exist and stretches divine minds upward toward the contemplation of itself that is appropriate to them and to participation and a state of becoming like itself. And the minds who devote themselves to the effort, as far as is holy and in accord with divine law . . . they are stretched upward steadfastly and unswervingly toward the ray that enlightens them, and they fly upward in accordance with the desire of holy enlightenment in proper proportion, with pious reverence, with temperance, and with holiness. (*Divine Names* 1.2; *CD* 1:110.2–2:111.2)

At another point Dionysius recapitulates Proclus even more specifically. As H. D. Saffrey has noted, at the beginning of book 9, Dionysius drops a notably Proclean turn of phrase.[21] In discussing the pairs of divine names—"great/small," "same/different," "similar/dissimilar," and "rest/motion"—Dionysius tells us, "Well, we must examine also all that is manifested to us from these statues that are the divine names" [φέρε καὶ τούτων τῶν θεωνυμικῶν αγαλμάτων, ὅσα ἡμῖν ἐμφανῆ, θεωρήσωμεν] (*Divine Names* 9.1, *CD*, 207.8–9). As we have seen, this comparison of names and statues is standard in Proclus, a distinctive mark of his blending of the representational schemes of ritual theurgy and literary language. Saffrey has argued convincingly that the equation of words and statues is sufficiently strange to mark it as an indisputable link between Proclus and Dionysius.

John of Scythopolis, Dionysius's exculpatory commentator, tries to Christianize this passage—an effort that can only be said to have backfired.[22] In explaining Dionysius he makes an even more provocative comparison with pagan practices:

> It is with perfect wisdom that he [Dionysius] speaks of the statues that are the divine names, for he extends this notion, which he borrows from the Greeks, by applying it to the truth. The Greeks, as a matter of fact, made up objects resembling statues without feet or hands which they called Hermes; they made them hollow with a door in the style of cupboards. Inside these statues they placed statues of the gods they adored. . . . It is in this way, then, that this passage too must be understood: those names from sacred Scripture, such as "small," "being seated," etcetera, which are used concerning the God who alone exists and who alone is real, are not worthy to be spoken of God; but if these names are explained and if they are interpreted in a manner worthy of God, then they contain, within, the statues and the divine imprints of the glory of God.[23] (Migne, *Patrilogiae Cursus, series Graeca* 4.368d–369a)

Saffrey thinks John's ethnographic data is drawn from Plato's *Symposium*; I read here also some variant of the theurgic rites, sufficiently fudged to fit Dionysius's adopted chronology.

The language of ineffable words, devotional statues that represent what is beyond all representation, and traces of the transcendent divine buried inside the mundane world—all three of these transactions com-

[21] Henri-Dominique Saffrey, "New Objective Links between the Pseudo-Dionysius and Proclus," in Dominic J. O'Meara, ed., *Neoplatonism and Christian Thought* (Albany: State University of New York Press, 1981), 64–74.

[22] On John's commentary, see Paul Rorem and John C. Lamoreaux's *John of Scythopolis and the Dionysian Corpus: Annotating the Areopagite* (Oxford: Clarendon Press, 1998).

[23] Translation based on Saffrey.

bine and recombine in the works of Proclus and Pseudo-Dionysius. The implication of equivalence between these three representational economies carries profound implications for later theories of representation. Theories of ontological connection between sign and referent, which had been suggested earlier by the Stoics, are here given a concreteness and detailed justification that they had not known before and in turn provide a uniquely powerful justification of what had been known traditionally as the mimetic arts. Whereas imitations had been vulnerable to the charge of lack, of not quite fitting the original, of epistemological decay, Proclus and Dionysius grant them the power to reveal, to be not just misleading appearance but revelatory manifestation. Through Dionysius this Proclean theory reverberates for many centuries to come in both East and West. We will now make brief forays into two authors for whom it becomes relevant: John of Damascus, in his defense of icons, and Dante, in his justification of representing the divine in secular poetry.

Symbolization in the Greek East: John of Damascus

Writing over two centuries after Dionysius, John of Damascus (700?–754) hands down one of the three major justifications of icon veneration that survive from the iconoclastic period.[24] In *On the Divine Images* he cites Dionysius to support his case for the spiritual benefits of religious art.[25] Each of the three discourses that make up John's work is followed by copious citations from a dozen or so authorities, leading off with several passages from Dionysius, including one from the *Divine Names*, one from the *Ecclesiastical Hierarchy*, and several from the letters. In language we have heard before, John cites Dionysius as saying that Scripture and liturgy "clothe with shapes and forms things which are shapeless and formless, and by a variety of symbols fashion mani-

[24] A selected bibliography: Paul J. Alexander, "Hypatius of Ephesus: A Note on Image Worship in the Sixth Century," *Harvard Theological Review* 45 (1952): 177–84; Ernst Kitzinger, "The Cult of Images in the Age before Iconoclasm," *Dumbarton Oaks Papers* 8 (1954): 85–150; Hans Von Campenhausen, "The Theological Problem of Images in the Early Church," in *Tradition and Life in the Church*, trans. Av. V. Littledale (London: Collins, 1968), 171–200; Peter Brown, "A Dark-Age Crisis: Aspects of the Iconoclast Controversy," *English Historical Review* 88 (January 1973): 1–34; Robert S. Nelson, "The Discourse of Icons, Then and Now," *Art History* 12 (June 1989): 144–57; David Olster, "Byzantine Hermeneutics after Iconoclasm: Word and Image in the Leo Bible," *Byzantion* 64 (1994): 419–58.

[25] St. John of Damascus, *On the Divine Images: Three Apologies against Those Who Attack the Divine Images*, trans. David Anderson (Crestwood, N.Y.: St. Vladimir's Seminary Press, 1980). For citations of Dionysius, see 1.10, 1.11, 3.21.

fold attributes of the immaterial and supernatural simplicity."[26] While Dionysius follows Proclus in justifying the actual practice of rendering the transcendent godhead by material representations, John uses Dionysius to support a more modest position. He comments that if Dionysius endorses the practice of making images of the imageless, it is certainly acceptable for the icon makers to fashion representations of Jesus, the incarnate God, and the living saints. Since God became flesh in Jesus of Nazareth, the argument goes, we can portray that flesh in our icons; we are not thereby assigning material characteristics to God but merely representing those characteristics that God himself took on.

And yet, it should be noted, John does not dissociate himself fully from the stronger Dionysian position. He closes his second oration by stating it without reservation, as his own interpretation of the construction and adornment of the tabernacle as described in the Book of Exodus: "You see that the law and everything it commanded and all our own practices are meant to sanctify the work of our hands, leading us through matter to the invisible God."[27] More important, John cites Dionysius as his authority for two of the six different kinds of icons he lays out in his famous typology.[28] The imaging of the imageless that takes place in Scripture and God's creation of the material world now stand alongside the devotional icons as members of the same extended family of representation.

John is no Dionysius. He does not exhibit the cohesive and highly theorized representational visions of the late Neoplatonists. Furthermore, he develops fully the opportunities that Christology offers for the justification of divine representations, something that Dionysius curiously (and perhaps tellingly) does not do. But John gives Dionysius a prominent place in the controversy over icons that engaged the attention of so many during the eighth and ninth centuries, for he puts Dionysius's strongest formulations on the power of representations on the iconodule agenda. As we have seen, these strong positions are enabled by an intermingling of ontological, liturgical, and literary processes, for which Proclus is the most important precursor.

If we compare John's more elaborated justification of icons with that of an earlier figure, the Dionysian dimension comes more clearly into view. Writing in the mid-sixth century, only a short time after the Dionysian corpus popped up in various Byzantine libraries, Hypatius of Ephesus was skeptical of its genuineness. Though much more work would be necessary to prove the point, his anti-Dionysianism is, I sug-

[26] *DN* 592b.

[27] John of Damascus *On the Divine Images* 2.23

[28] John of Damascus *On the Divine Images* 3.18–23.

gest, of a piece with what we know was his tentative position regarding the practice of icon veneration. We have a short but enlightening correspondence between Hypatius and one of the priests in his see. The local priest writes for advice on how to handle his parishioners' apparent tendency to venerate icons. Hypatius writes back with a message of cautious tolerance.[29] He allows that the practice may serve a pedagogical purpose for the illiterate. The definitive anagogic promises of Dionysius are absent, as are the heady comparisons, cited by John, between the images used in liturgical practice and the representational scheme by which the universe unfolds. The differences between Hypatius's moderate position and John of Damascus's more expansive one must be at least partially attributable to the influence of the Dionysian corpus. Earlier Orthodox authorities had simply been too wary of idolatry to embrace a comprehensive iconology of language, image, and material thing. Dionysius feels no such compunction. Soon after he receives the imprimatur of Maximus the Confessor (580–662), he offers his bountiful anagogic resources to a tradition in need of them (to justify icon worship) and open to them (as shaped by the upward-stretching vision of the Cappadocians).[30]

Symbolization in the Latin West: Dante

The writings of the Neoplatonists did not fare well in the West after the Christian emperor Justinian closed the Neoplatonic academy at Athens in 529. Moreover, and more importantly, fewer and fewer people in the Roman West could read Greek. Though not widely studied, several of Proclus's texts survived perfectly well in the Byzantine East, despite their obvious departures from Orthodoxy. But it was only after a hiatus of three centuries that Proclean ideas reentered the Latin West, in September of 827, when the Eastern emperor Michael the Stammerer presented to Louis the Debonair a gift of the Dionysian corpus at Compiègne.[31] The text was deposited at St.-Denis, where the abbot, Hilduin, made an abortive attempt at translation, but it was not until after 860 that it began to make an impact on Western thinking. In that year, Charles the Bald commissioned a new translation from John Scotus Eriugena, an Irishman who had fled to Paris to escape the Viking raids.

[29] The document is translated and commented on by Alexander (relevant citation at 179).

[30] On this whole topic, see Jaroslav Pelikan, *Christianity and Classical Culture* (New Haven: Yale University Press, 1993).

[31] On this history, see Jean Leclercq, "Influence and Noninfluence of Dionysius in the Western Middle Ages," in Luibheid and Rorem, 25–32.

John rendered the texts of Dionysius into a Latin that was comprehensible and compelling, made a number of commentaries, and wrote his own extensive works of theology and ontology along Dionysian lines.

Two hundred and fifty years later, the Dionysian corpus was given new stature by Abbé Suger (1081?–1151) of St.-Denis. Suger reinvigorated an old tradition that Dionysius the Areopagite, whom the French called Denis, made a trip to Gaul to evangelize and became the first bishop of Paris. (His relics were, and still are, thought to be buried in the cathedral.) Suger promoted Dionysius's theory, which, because it allowed for symbolization of God, gave the abbot a theoretical explanation for the rich decorations and massive architectural renovations with which he remade his cathedral—and enhanced his stature as a public figure and friend of kings. His cathedral is the first example of the combination of European architectural styles now called the Gothic, in which the metaphysics of light and other Neoplatonic principles played a formative part.[32] A new Dionysian translation and commentary were produced at St.-Denis, and interest was sparked at nearby St.-Victor and Chartres. Many commentaries and translations were made, and Dionysius's corpus took its place, alongside the distinctly Neoplatonic Plato of Calcidius's *Timaeus* and Bernard Silvestris's philosophical *Aeneid*, as a central text in the so-called twelfth-century Renaissance.

The newly prominent Dionysian writings percolated through the libraries around Paris and affected the churchmen's thinking in a number of important ways. Among Dionysius's more prominent legacies was his approach to reading the Bible. According to A. J. Minnis, Dionysius quickly took his place as "perhaps the single most important source of medieval notions of imagery and symbolism."[33] The theory of the "symbol" that Proclus had originally developed to defend Homer against Plato became a crucial resource for medieval Bible commentators. The specific notion of dissimilar symbols, for example, recurs, under Dionysius's authority, in the works of Hugh of St.-Victor and Thomas Aquinas.[34] We will look here more closely only at Thomas.

Albert the Great, Thomas's teacher and one of the elder statesmen among the Scholastics, devoted a significant portion of his career to studying Dionysius and extended his considerable prestige in defending

[32] See Erwin Panofsky, ed. and trans., *Abbot Suger on the Abbey Church of St.-Denis and Its Art Treasures* (Princeton: Princeton University Press, 1946).

[33] A. J. Minnis, "The Dionysian Imagination," in *Medieval Literary Theory and Criticism c. 1100–c. 1375: The Commentary Tradition*, ed. A. J. Minnis and A. B. Scott (Oxford: Clarendon Press, 1988), vii.

[34] For references to Hugh, Thomas, and others, see Minnis and Scott, 165–73, and Minnis's "General Introduction," in Minnis and Scott, 1–11.

Dionysius's corpus from accusations that it was "oriental."[35] He published influential commentaries and gave two years' worth of lectures on Dionysius, of which Thomas's minute transcriptions still survive.[36] Thomas himself published commentaries on Dionysius and cited him as an authority in the *Summa*, in his article "Should sacred writing use metaphorical or symbolic language?" (one of his 1,700 citations of the Christian Neoplatonist):

> As Dionysius says in the first part of his *Celestial Hierarchy*, "The divine ray cannot shine upon us in any other way except up in a large number of sacred veils." . . . It is therefore appropriate that spiritual things should be set before us under bodily likenesses. . . . It must be said that the ray of divine revelation is not destroyed by the sensible images with which, as Dionysius says, it is veiled. But it remains rooted in its own essential truth, so that the minds to which it is revealed are not permitted to remain in the realm of images, but it raises them up to a recognition of intellectual truths.[37]

In the twelfth and thirteenth centuries Dionysius became *the* authority on the use of figurative language in Scripture, particularly on those passages where the divine is anthropomorphized or put into some other physical form. Via Dionysius, Proclus's theory of the symbol began to enter the wider philosophical inquiry surrounding biblical interpretation that accompanies the recovery of classical texts.

In addition to the works of Dionysius, the Scholastics became interested in a work attributed to Aristotle, the *Liber de Causis*. As later generations discovered, this text is actually an epitome of Proclus's summa of Neoplatonic metaphysics, the *Elements of Theology*. It survived in Arabic, and in the twelfth century was translated into Latin by Gerard of Cremona (d. 1187). The *Liber* gives back what Justinian had taken away, a cohesive and undiluted statement of Neoplatonic emanationist ontology, which until then had existed in a Christianized form in Dionysius and in traces in a variety of other sources (like Boethius, Augustine, and Calcidius). The thirteenth-century reader of the *Liber* must have had an uncanny feeling, reading a codified statement of beliefs that were already at some level present in his or her understanding

[35] Simon Tugwell, *Albert and Thomas*, Classics of Western Spirituality Series (Paulist Press: New York, 1988), 55. The charges that the theory of the symbol, of nonmimetic representation, is "oriental" in origin recur with some regularity in its history. In the thirteenth century this notion probably means not much more than "Byzantine," but, curiously, it takes on a series of other inflections in later scholarship on Proclus. The idea that the Neoplatonists as a whole were marked by oriental influences (whether Syrian, Egyptian, or Persian) resurfaces in the nineteenth and early twentieth centuries.

[36] Ibid., 208–9.

[37] Minnis, 239–40.

of the universe. The text influenced Aquinas (though perhaps less so after he discovered its Aristotelian pretensions to be fraudulent). It had a tremendous impact on Dante as Charles Singleton's work makes clear, and through him the ideas it contains remained eminent for the rest of the Middle Ages.[38]

In the High Middle Ages the Proclean theory behind the symbol in Pseudo-Dionysius is reunited with a systematic statement of Proclean metaphysics in the *Liber de Causis*, and both are reappropriated from the scholastics for secular poetics by Dante, greatly broadening poetry's spiritual reach. The *Liber* is perhaps the single most important source of Dante's distinctly emanationist cosmology. He cites it several times in book 3 of the *Convivio*:

> Every substantial form proceeds from its first cause, which is God, as is stated in the book *On Causes*, and these forms receive their diversity not from it, which is most simple, but from the secondary causes and from the matter into which it descends. Thus in the same book, in treating the infusion of divine goodness, the following words appear: "And the goodnesses and the gifts are made diverse by the participation of the thing which receives them."[39]

Here we see the Neoplatonic scheme of emanation and note the distinguishing characteristic of diversity being generated at the lower levels through procession. In the following, the movement of recession back up the metaphysical levels comes into view as well:

> Since every cause, as is stated in the book *On Causes* already cited, infuses into its effect a part of the goodness which it receives from its own cause, the soul infuses into and gives to its body a part of the goodness of its own cause, which is God. Consequently, since wonderful things are perceived in her [his Lady], as regards her bodily part, to the point that they make all those who look on her desirous to see these things, it is evident that her form (that is, her soul), which directs the body as its proper cause, miraculously receives the goodness of God's grace.[40]

A Neoplatonic, particularly Proclean, emanationist metaphysics is rearticulated as Dante stands at the entrance to heaven, in cantos 1–4 of the *Paradiso*. He begins canto 1 with, "The glory of the All-Mover penetrates through the universe and reglows in one part more, another part

[38] See Singleton's notes to the *Commedia* (Dante, *The Divine Comedy*, trans. and ed. Charles S. Singleton (Princeton: Princeton University Press, 1970–75), where the *Liber* is cited throughout. Patrick Boyde, *Dante, Philomythes and Philosopher: Man in the Cosmos* (Cambridge University Press, 1981), details Dante's borrowings from the *Liber*.

[39] Dante *Convivio* 3.2. Translation from Richard H. Lansing, Dante's *Il Convivio* (New York: Garland, 1990).

[40] Dante *Convivio* 3.6.

less."[41] As Dante and Beatrice are about to enter, Beatrice gives him a famous theoretical explanation for why he will be able to understand the formless divinities he is about to see:

> These showed themselves here, not because this sphere is allotted to them, but to afford a sign [*segno*] of the celestial grade that is least exalted. It is needful to speak thus to your faculty, since only through sense perception does it apprehend that which it afterwards makes fit for the intellect. For this reason Scripture condescends to your capacity, and attributes hands and feet to God, having other meaning.[42]

Though the word symbol (*simbolo* in later Italian) is not used, the ideas are those of Dionysius's theory of dissimilar symbols.[43] The formless divine natures are given forms, which are somehow connected with them, in a way that makes discursive sense within a literary mode, nonmimetically. It is done as a concession to our nature. The importance of the emanationist ontology, which is dramatically restated in canto 4 of the *Paradiso*, should be understood here. The lower-order realities are manifestations, and not mere appearances, of the higher ones. They share in the goodness of the higher levels from which they came and back to which they recede. The translation of the higher worlds, and in this case the highest world, into the world of sense (Proclus's world of matter) proceeds along the illuminating rays of Dante's universe. Proclus's theory helps Dante open the gates to heaven.[44]

The author of the *Epistle to Can Grande* comments on the beginning of Dante's *Paradiso* in the following:[45]

> It is evident that every essence and every virtue proceeds from a primal one; and that the lower intelligences have their effect as it were from a radiating body, and, after the fashion of mirrors,[46] reflect the rays of the higher to the one below them. Which matter appears to be discussed clearly enough by Dionysius in his work *On the Celestial Hierarchy*. And therefore it is stated in the book *On Causes* that "every intelligence is full of forms." Reason,

[41] Dante *Paradiso* 1.1–4. All translations are from Singleton.

[42] Dante *Paradiso* 4.37–45.

[43] In his source notes for this passage, Singleton quotes the section of Thomas's *Summa* cited above (at n. 37), with its reference to Pseudo-Dionysius's *Celestial Hierarchy*.

[44] This is not to mention the influence that Proclus, through Pseudo-Dionysius's hierarchy had in shaping that heaven.

[45] Trans. from Minnis, 464–65. In his notes on lines 2–3 of canto 1, Singleton cites this passage also.

[46] It is interesting that a mirror, *the* mimetic device, reenters the cosmos. Possibly—though I cannot pursue the subject here—the theory of nonmimesis makes pretensions that it cannot live up to; for the nonrepresentational symbol, from Proclus to the Romantics, consistently reverts to mimetic points of reference.

then, as we have seen, demonstrates that the divine light, that is to say the divine goodness, wisdom, and virtue, shines in every part.

Whether Dante was the author of this part of the epistle is not crucial. What is important is that this Dante commentator brings together specifically these two texts to explicate the section of Dante's journey where he is about to enter the realm of heaven. The doctrine of Pseudo-Dionysius would naturally find corroboration in the *Liber*, since both descend from Proclus. And the author of the epistle understandably enough invokes them as justification. The theories they articulate had no small part in making possible the feat that they are invoked to justify: the representation of the divine.

The *Commedia* reaffirms the capacity of nonbiblical literature to transmit divine knowledge. It is often noted that Dante appropriates the tools of biblical interpretation for the study of secular poetry. What is not often noted is that certain of these tools were developed for the study of secular poetry in the first place, and that Dante is only reappropriating what Dionysius had earlier taken from Proclus. The divine is once again made available to nonscriptural poetic representation, and, once again, through what is understood to be a nonmimetic mode. In Dante's wake, Petrarch and, especially, Boccaccio reap the theoretical benefits of Dante's bold literary practice.[47] They codify literature's wider spiritual reach and formulate the argument for the general defense of poetry by drawing on its power to articulate the divine. Pseudo-Dionysius's theory of the symbol provides a critical resource to which they both turn. In a letter to his brother Gherardo, Petrarch tries to justify poetry by claiming that scripture uses poetic devices too and makes a Dionysian argument: "I would almost say that poetry is theology written about God. When Christ is called, now a lion, now a lamb, and again a worm, what is that if not poetic?"[48] In other words, If Scripture can be excused its apparent representational excesses, why can't we excuse secular poetry also? The Proclean legacies behind the *Divine Names* come to Petrarch's aid.

Boccaccio will ask the same question, more pointedly. The last two books of his *Genealogy* repeatedly plead that if representing god by poetic devices does not diminish the status of the Bible, then it should not diminish the status of secular poetry either. It seems clear to Boccaccio, moreover, that the poetic mode is especially suited to the greatest truths. Poetry becomes theology and theology poetry. He also cites Dionysian symbols of God with the same implication: in the Bible, God

[47] Petrarch downplays any debt to Dante. But whatever his familiarity with the *Divine Comedy*, Petrarch articulated his theory on a literary landscape reshaped by it.

[48] Minnis, 413.

can be a "sun, fire, lion, serpent, lamb, worm, or even a stone."[49] He then goes on to cite Dionysius himself, in John Scotus's translation:

> Again, let them examine the words of Dionysius the Areopagite, a disciple of Paul, and glorious martyr of Christ, in his book on the *Celestial Hierarchy*. He takes the matter up from the first premise, and gives complete proof that divine theology employs, with its other instruments, poetic inventions. He says: "For in truth Theology with much skill hath employed sacred poetic forms and figures to convey nonfigurative meaning, at the same time opening our minds, as I have already said, providing them with means of right conjectural interpretation, and presenting Holy Scriptures in anagogical form."[50]

> Insuper perscrutentur, quid scripserit Dyonisius Ariopagita Pauli discipulus et Christi martir egregius, in suo Ierarchi celestis libro. Ex intentione quippe dicit, prosequitur atque probat divinam theologiam poeticis fictionibus uti, inter alia ita dicens: "Et enim valde artificialiter theologia poeticis sacris formationibus in non figuratis intellectibus usa est, nostrum, ut dictum est, animum revelans, et ipsi propria et coniecturali reductione providens, et ad ipsum reformans anagogicas sanctas scripturas."[51]

Note that the major features of Proclus's theory are indicated here: poetic forms are sacred; figures are assigned to what is above all figuration; these figures open our minds and raise us up anagogically to the divine. This, in a nutshell, is the theory behind Boccaccio's claim that poetry is theology.[52] Here, the broad allegorical claims for the knowledge that poetry can convey are firmly ascendant.

The Symbol among the Romantics

I close with a few thoughts on the Romantics.[53] It is a truism that the Romantics displace "classical" poetics—but it holds true only if one understands classical poetics to be coextensive with Aristotelian poetics.

[49] Translation from Giovanni Boccaccio, *Boccaccio on Poetry*, trans. Charles Osgood (Indianapolis: Bobbs-Merrill, 1956) 71.

[50] Osgood, *Boccaccio*, 87.

[51] Text from Giovanni Boccaccio, *Genealogie deorum gentilium libri*, ed. Vincenzo Romano, Scrittori d'Italia, *Giovanni Boccaccio Opere XI* (Bari, 1951), 2: 737.17–25.

[52] See Minnis, 494, including references.

[53] The topic has been treated by Wesley Trimpi, *Muses of One Mind: The Literary Analysis of Experience and Its Continuity* (Princeton: Princeton University Press, 1983). See also a brief mention of it by Robert Lamberton, in *Homer the Theologian* (Berkeley: University of California Press, 1986), 195 and 301–2. On a related topic, see Jon Whitman, "From the Textual to the Temporal: Early Christian 'Allegory' and Early Romantic 'Symbol,'" *New Literary History* 22 (1991): 161–76.

If the study I have undertaken here proves compelling, it seems more accurate to say that the Romantics, rather than overturning classical notions of poetry, displace one classical model (the Aristotelian) for another (the symbolic/allegorical). The Romantics lever the "symbol" into prominence, specifically as opposed to what they know as "allegory." But "allegory" by their time was a (by their assessment) mechanistic genre of *writing*, worked over thoroughly in the medieval and Renaissance periods. This tradition bears only a little resemblance to the classical traditions of *reading* we have reassembled here. The Romantic "symbol" definitively shares a synecdochic logic, as well as a rather grand power of invocation, with the ancient "allegorical" one.[54]

The general indebtedness of the Romantics to the Neoplatonists has been established for decades.[55] Abundant parallels have been suggested between Romantic notions of a divine spirit that pervades the world and Neoplatonic emanation theories.[56] The Romantics also seem to have borrowed Proclus's theory of the symbol.[57] Though there are many internal debates and divisions among Romantic theorists of literature, in general their inflections of the category of "mimesis" bear important similarities to those of Proclus and the ancient Neoplatonists. For the Romantics, the "mirror" of the neoclassical poets produced only dry, mechanistic, lifeless reproductions of reality. This characterization of the earlier periods is part of a desire to circumvent the neoclassical

[54] On this whole aspect of the romantic "symbol," a pivotal study is Paul de Man's "Rhetoric of Temporality," in *Blindness and Insight: Essays in the Rhetoric of Contemporary Criticism*, 2d ed., Theory and History of Literature, vol. 7 (Minneapolis: University of Minnesota Press, 1983), 187–228.

[55] See M. H. Abrams's landmark study, *The Mirror and the Lamp* (New York: Oxford University Press, 1953), 169–95, where Abrams accepts but refines the opinion of Paul Reiff that Plotinus is the only figure who might be called the "key" to understanding Romanticism. Of course, several central Romantic concerns have no analogs among the ancient Neoplatonists, including a Fichtean emphasis on the notion of will, a centering of the dialectics between the "I" and the "not-I," between the subject and object, and a struggle with particularly Kantian inflections of the notion of transcendence.

[56] See Abrams, 146–95. See also Thomas McFarland, *Coleridge and the Pantheist Tradition* (New York: Oxford University Press, 1969), esp. 107–90.

[57] A fuller account of the Neoplatonic history behind Romantic notions of the symbol would certainly have to take account of the many (but not infinite) indirect sources for the wealth of ideas that the Neoplatonists bequeath to European thought. These mediating sources include the Christian mystical tradition, especially the German mysticisms growing from Meister Eckhart's work (which takes Pseudo-Dionysius as its starting point); Renaissance magic and occult traditions, from Ficino through Boehme and Paracelsus (for which the Neoplatonists Iamblichus and Proclus are the most prominent Greek authorities); and traditions of allegorical biblical commentary (which grew up in conversation with the Neoplatonic allegorists). Even without tracing these traditions in detail—a difficult but perhaps not impossible task—the Romantic notion of the symbol resonates at a few observable points with that first synthesized by Proclus.

mimetic model of literature, drawn along strongly Aristotelian lines, in order to reconceptualize literature as no mere or slavish copy of the existing world but rather as the creation of a new world by the imagination.[58] For this purpose, the category of the "symbolic" (construed equally as *Symbol* in German and "symbol" in English), as opposed to the mere mimesis of the neoclassical critics, was a potent tool. It may be the case that the Romantics inherit the whole conceptualization of the mimetic "problem," as well as its solution, from the Neoplatonists.

Around the turn of the eighteenth century the German Romantics reinvigorate the symbol. The category had been in obscurity for some time. The term *Symbol* has no entry in Adelung's *Wörterbuch der hochdeutschen* of 1780.[59] It experiences a rebirth concurrent with the most intense periods of Romantic theorizing and with the reemergence of interest in Neoplatonic texts in Germany. The repetition of the term "symbol" by this or that thinker means little in and of itself. For example, Kant uses the term in the third *Critique* in 1790 (par. 59) as clearly an "arbitrary" sign, like a mathematical one (a far cry from Proclus's symbol, and more in keeping with what Aristotle had in mind). But Novalis's unsystematic musings on magic in the ninth book of his *Encyclopedia* present a more pertinent case.[60] In this work, Novalis tells us, among other things, that the symbolic [*Symbolisch*] is representative, but also that it works not through mimesis but through magic (1670) and that magic and art are the same thing in the sense that both transform the sensual world by means of force exerted by the will (1667). The sign [*Zeichen*] has a sympathy [*Sympathie*] with the thing it represents, in a system of theurgy [*Theurgie*] in which the spirits infusing the universe are coerced into service through talismans [*Amulette*, *Talismane*] that tap into the higher powers (1697). A thing becomes clear only through symbolization, through nonmimesis (1670, 1694). One finds some inconsistency in the terminology here, which suggests that

[58] A number of modern studies of the Romantics make this point. It could be said to be the main thesis of Abrams's *The Mirror and the Lamp*. More recently, Ernst Behler concludes his *German Romantic Literary Theory* (New York: Cambridge University Press, 1993) with the following: "We could also characterize this basic shift [made by the Romantics] in the appreciation of art and literature as a move away from the model of representation to that of creation, from mimetic imitation to creative production" (301).

[59] On the emergence of the term in Germany in this period, see Gerhard Kurz, "Friedrich Schlegels Begriff der 'symbolischen Form' und seine literaturtheoretische Bedeutung," in *Aspekte der Romantik*, ed. Sven-Aage Jørgensen, Per Øhrgaard, and Friedrich Schmöe (Copenhagen: Wilhem Fink, 1983), 30.

[60] *Materialien zur Enzyclopädistik. IX*, in *Werke, Briefe, Dokumente [von] Novalis, Fragmente* 1, ed. Ewald Wasmuth (Heidelberg: Verlag Lambert Schneider, 1957), 435–67. An English translation is available: Novalis, *Encyclopedia IX*, trans. Karl Siegler (Coquitlam, B.C.: Archaí, 1973).

Novalis has derived these Neoplatonic ideas from mediating sources rather than directly from ancient authors but the main points of overlap could not be clearer.

But Schelling may have in fact revived the Neoplatonic symbol proper, drawing on the original sources. In his work the symbol [*Symbol*] is uniquely able to render the immaterial by means of the concrete, the bodiless by means of bodies, and it becomes through his influence the primary engine by which the Romantic poet is able to invoke a new world of the imagination.[61] It is not impossible that Schelling knew Proclus's thoughts on the subject of "symbols." Several of Proclus' works were available in manuscript form at Jena. In 1821, Victor Cousin edited the first modern edition of Proclus's *Commentary on the Parmenides*—a work in which the symbol figures prominently—and dedicated it to F.W.J. Schelling (along with Hegel).[62] Furthermore, in 1820, Creuzer also dedicates the editio princeps of Proclus's *Commentary on the First Alcibiades* to Schelling.[63] Granted, these editions appear some years after Schelling articulates his concept of the symbol and may only be a sign of respect. It is possible that Schelling came up with his theory and terminology on his own, and then confirmed them by reading Proclus, but this scenario is not entirely satisfying either.[64]

The theme of Coleridge's indebtedness to his German colleagues has been well covered in modern treatments of the period. Coleridge too asserts that the symbol is a powerful mode of literary production. In fact, it is uniquely able to render the transcendent in the material. It is "consubtantial," using Coleridge's term, with its referent.[65] The symbol is characterized by a "translucence of the Special in the Individual or of the General in the Especial or of the Universal in the General. Above all by the translucence of the Eternal through and in the Temporal. It always partakes of the Reality which it renders intelligible; and while it enunciates the whole, abides itself as a living part in that Unity, of

[61] See, e.g., Friedrich Wilhelm Joseph Schelling, *The Philosophy of Art*, trans. Douglas W. Stott, Theory and History of Literature, vol. 58 (Minneapolis: University of Minnesota Press, 1989), 46, 49.

[62] Vols. 4 and 5 of *Procli Philosophi Platonici Opera*, ed. Victor Cousin (Paris: J.-M. Eberhart, 1821).

[63] *Procli Successoris in Platonis Alcibiadem Priorem Commentarii*, ed. F. Creuzer (Frankfurt, 1820).

[64] There is some reason to think Schelling knew Proclus's *Commentary on the Republic*. His answer to Plato's charges against the poets bears a resemblance to that which Proclus articulates there. Schelling claims that Plato's objections had to do only with "realistic" genres of poetry, in other words, those that aimed at representations of nature. That poetry that "displays the character of the infinite," which Schelling will later define as the "symbolic," is free from Plato's sanctions (Schelling, 4–5).

[65] Samuel Taylor Coleridge, *The Statesman's Manual*, in *Works*, ed. Shedd, 1: 436–37.

which it is the representative."[66] Proclus could have described his devotional statues in just such terms, and we know with no doubt that Coleridge admired Proclus: "The most beautiful and orderly development of this philosophy, which endeavours to explain all things by an analysis of consciousness, and builds up a world in the mind out of materials furnished by the mind itself, is to found in the *Platonic Theology* of Proclus."[67] Coleridge did not rely on the Germans for his knowledge of the great master of Neoplatonic metaphysics. He had access to the works of Proclus, in manuscript as well as in the English translations of Thomas Taylor,[68] as early as the 1790s.[69] While other thinkers contributed in an important way to Coleridge's innovations in language theory, I would also suggest a precursor in Proclus.[70]

The Endurance of the Symbolic

Though the force of the Neoplatonists' symbol is felt in many subsequent literary developments, its history and the modes of thinking that made it possible have remained hidden. Due to its circuitous and difficult background the symbol has remained something of a foundling among the standard turns of literary thought. Though I have only been able to make a few suggestions, we have every reason to believe that those modern versions of the "symbol" that make claims of ontological connection to their referents owe some debt to the bold and sometimes curious developments of postclassical literary theory and to the traditions of allegorism, divination, Pythagoreanism, magic, and emanationism that enable them. The readers we have examined appropriate and reshape the notion of the symbol for their own idiosyncratic ends, to be

[66] Coleridge, *Statesman's Manual*, 30.

[67] Samuel Taylor Coleridge, *Memorials of Coleorton, Being Letters from Coleridge, Wordsworth and His Sister, Southey, and Sir Walter Scott to Sir George and Lady Beaumont of Coleorton, Leicestershire, 1803 to 1834*, ed. William Knight (Edinburgh: D. Douglas, 1887), 2: 107.

[68] The relationship of Thomas Taylor (the self-styled Platonist who named his son "Proclus") with William Blake has been a theme in Blake scholarship since Samuel Foster Damon's *William Blake, His Philosophy and Symbols* (Boston: Constable and Company, 1924). For a more recent critic who has taken up the question, see Kathleen Raine's work, including *Blake and Tradition* (Princeton: Princeton University Press, 1968), 1: 73–74, and passim. His relationship with Coleridge has not been as well documented.

[69] See Thomas McFarland, *Coleridge and the Pantheist Tradition* (Oxford: Clarendon Press, 1969), 356, n. 37.

[70] For example, Robert N. Essick has shown the great importance of the work of Jacob Boehme for Coleridge's language theory. See Robert N. Essick, "Coleridge and the Language of Adam," in Frederick Burwick, ed., *Coleridge's Biographia Literaria: Text and Meaning* (Columbus: Ohio State University Press, 1989).

sure. The concept has been constructed and reconstructed over centuries, across cultures, and always for particular purposes, but, as I have tried to suggest, never ex nihilo. For all the readers examined here, the "symbol" becomes the key to establishing a vocabulary of ontological immediacy, of indication that somehow transcends mere imitation. Since the time of Proclus, and his bold claims based on the power of the theurgic rites, symbolic language has been granted the power to invoke and create the world, right before our eyes. In this sense, the "symbol" as an invocation speaks with unique relevance to contemporary theories of language.[71] Contemporary thinkers in the traditions of Nietzsche and Heidegger have been uniquely attuned to the role of language not simply in reflecting the world that we see but in shaping it. Proclus may have lived with the comforting assurance that the world invoked and constituted by language is precisely the real one. We post-Romantic readers are perhaps not so sure.

[71] For further references to modern contestations surrounding the "symbol," see Jon Whitman, "Allegory," in T.V.F. Brugan, ed., *New Princeton Encyclopedia of Poetry and Poetics* (Princeton: Princeton University Press, 1994), 10, which includes references to Benjamin and De Man.

APPENDIX

CHRYSIPPUS'S READING AND AUTHORIAL INTENTION: THE CASE OF THE MURAL AT SAMOS

TO THOSE involved in current literary-theoretical debates, the issue of "authorial intention" may seem somewhat nostalgic. The question was a heated one a half-century ago, when M. C. Beardsly and W. K. Wimsatt, Jr., published "The Intentional Fallacy," *Sewanee Review* 54 (1946). The debate has since shifted in many different directions, but in general the question of intentionality is still relevant for the study of allegory, because it recurs in current valuations of this material,[1] and also (more importantly) because it was alive for ancient readers themselves. As was pointed out earlier, the charge that a critic reads into a text what belongs on the outside relies on some stable sense of where to draw the text's boundaries. Unfortunately, the allegorists' ancient detractors rarely address themselves to this issue, though often the default position is some notion of authorial intention. They generally pass off as a simple and obvious proposition that a text has natural boundaries that all will recognize, and that the allegorists are by definition outside of them.[2] The allegorists' own views on the issue of authorial intention help us situate more fruitfully their views on the boundaries of the text. As we saw in chapter 3, Balbus, in Cicero's *De natura deorum*, suggested that the Stoics were happy to distance themselves from poets who might have mishandled traditional myths. This implies a skepticism on their part toward the poets' ability properly to handle and control the meanings that naturally inhere in the stories with which they

[1] See A. A. Long, "Stoic Readings of Homer," in Robert Lamberton and John J. Keaney, eds., *Homer's Ancient Readers* (Princeton: Princeton University Press, 1992), 65. Cf. the slightly different view of George A. Kennedy, in his preface to *The Cambridge History of Literary Criticism, vol. 1, Classical Criticism*, ed. George A. Kennedy (New York: Cambridge University Press, 1989), xi.

[2] This was the position of Aristarchus and of Cicero in *De natura deorum* (see chapter 1). One occasionally finds a similar view among contemporary commentators. West's treatment of the Derveni commentator, for example, is rather pronounced in this regard (M. L. West, *The Orphic Poems* [New York: Oxford University Press, 1983], 78–79).

are working. We also saw that one later Stoic, Cornutus, is more explicit on this point (chap. 4). When the poet's relationship to his material is viewed in this way, authorial intention is of little help in arbitrating the boundaries of a text or determining what properly belongs "inside" it and what properly belongs "outside."

A famous example of Chrysippean reading will shed more light on this issue. Perhaps Chrysippus's most notorious allegorical reading is not of a text but of a mural painted on the walls of the temple of Hera on the island of Samos.[3] In this mural, Hera is depicted fellating Zeus,[4] and we are told by Origen and others that Chrysippus interpreted the painting allegorically:[5] it depicted matter receiving the *spermatikoi logoi* of the divine.[6] This interpretation, of course, seems forced at first blush. Later Christian writers clearly found the painting scandalous and assumed that Chrysippus did also, that he was embarrassed by it and was attempting somehow to explain it away. Diogenes Laertius, writing probably five hundred years after Chrysippus, also casts the reading in a negative light. But it is hard to claim in any secure way that at the time Chrysippus was writing, when sexual practices were still very much an element in the traditional repertoire of ritualizable actions, the mural would have been embarrassing to him or to his contemporaries.

We might try another question as a guage of interpretive fidelity: Is Chrysippus's reading faithful to the intention of the artist? One wonders what the intention of the artist would have been in such a case. We have no good evidence, so far as I am aware, so we are left to speculate. It is most doubtful that the artist was attempting to shock; this simply would not make sense at the largest and most important (and expensive) center of active worship of the Greeks' highest-ranking goddess. If the drawing were offensive, embarrassing, or sacrilegious in the eyes of the priests or worshipers, we can safely assume it would not have lasted more than a minute on the wall. What did the artist, the priests, and the worshipers see when they looked at this image? We can never know for

[3] According to Vergil, Samos was Juno's second favorite place (*Aeneid* 1.16). The sanctuary was located on a plane in the south of the island, about two hundred yards inland from Cape Colonna, which the Genovese named for the single column of the temple still standing. Strabo tells us that the temple and its chapels were an elaborate picture gallery (*Geography* 14.1.14). See *Smith's Dictionary of Greek and Roman Geography*, under "Samos."

[4] *SVF* 2: 1071–74 (see Origen *Contra Cels.* 4.48; Clement of Alexandria *Rom. Homil.* 5.18; and DL 7.187)

[5] There is no reason to think that Chrysippus was idiosyncratic in reading the votive representations of artists allegorically. See Plutarch *On the Oracles at Delphi* 400a–b.

[6] Long suggests that Chrysippus might not be serious, but Plutarch presents contrary evidence: "Chrysippus is quite often petty, although he does not indulge in jesting, but wrests the words ingeniously, but unconvincingly" (*On How to Study Poetry* 31E).

sure—but can we rule out the possibility that the painter himself had some sort of meaning as Chrysippus's in mind? The temple itself dates to the sixth century B.C.E.,[7] but the first evidence for the mural independent of Chrysippus's reading comes from Strabo. This leaves open the possibility that an artist from the period when Stoicism was on the rise (early third century B.C.E.) depicted the scene with Stoic principles in mind. The archaeological record suggests that while the fifth and fourth centuries brought few additions to the Heraion, in the third, second, and first centuries the temple saw a marked increase in artisanal embellishments.[8] A *terminus post quem* of around 300 B.C.E. is therefore not unreasonable, while the fact that Chrysippus saw the painting gives us a *terminus ante quem* of circa 210. During this period Stoicism was establishing itself in the Greek-speaking world, and the artist might very well have had Stoic principles in mind when painting the scene. Furthermore, whether or not the painter was consciously and specifically influenced by Stoic allegorism, allegorical reading was an established tradition by the time the temple was built, so whenever the mural was painted, the painter could have relied on this tradition to suggest more than a straightforward sexual act.

As for Chrysippus's interpretation, we know it to accord well with his broader positions. He has in mind here the pneumatic conception of the soul. As we recall, the Stoics consider that the commanding faculty extends its pneuma, its collective logoi, throughout the body, like the tentacles of an octopus (chap. 3). Five of these are the senses; another is our capacity to speak; still another is the male capacity to emit generative sperm. According to the Stoics, the emission of sperm (like sensory perception of the enunciation of words) is at root a transference of logoi. This sexual transference of logoi suggests to Chrysippus the ontological process by which logoi (pneuma) enter unqualified matter and bring things into existence. Furthermore, he is drawing on a tradition that figures Zeus's logoi as ordering agents that suffuse and structure unformed matter, figured as Hera.[9] If one can allow that the ancients saw logoi in sperm and sperm as logoi also, his interpretation is actually quite traditional.

This is all by way of saying that the question of whether Chrysippus's reading of the mural is an imposition on the "text" is highly complex

[7] The Polycratean Temple (c. 540–530). Graham Shipley, *A History of Samos, 800–188 B.C.* (New York: Oxford University Press, 1987), 78–79.

[8] Shipley, 203. There may have been pictures in the Heraion from early on. Herodotus tells us that a Samian engineer, who spanned the Danube for Darius, dedicated a painting of himself in the Heraion (Shipley, 107).

[9] Celsus (according to Origen *Contra Celsus* 6.42) allegorized Zeus and Hera in this manner, attributing the interpretation to Pherecydes (sixth century B.C.E.).

and depends on a whole range of normative judgments about the artist, the original audience, and the common sense of the one evaluating the interpretation. There is another question to ask, for which an answer is more forthcoming, and perhaps more fruitful. Do Chrysippus's readings make sense within the larger context of his thought, or is he, out of some assumed embarrassment, passing off a hermeneutical whopper? The former seems to me much more likely.

BIBLIOGRAPHY OF ANCIENT AUTHORS

Citations to classical texts are from the Oxford Classical Texts series, unless otherwise noted. Journals and standard reference works, when abbreviated, follow *l'Année philologique*.

Artemidorus. *Onirocriticon*. Ed. Roger Park. Leipzig: Teubner, 1963.

Boccaccio, Giovanni. *Boccaccio on Poetry*. Trans. Charles Osgood. Indianapolis: Bobbs-Merrill, 1956.

———. *Genealogie deorum gentilium libri*. Ed. Vincenzo Romano. Scrittori d'Italia, nos. 200–201, *Giovanni Boccaccio Opere* X–XI. Bari: G. Laterza, 1951.

Clement of Alexandria. *Stromata I–VI*. Ed. O. Stählin and L. Früchtel. Berlin: Akademie-Verlag, 1960.

Cornutus. *Theologiae Graecae compendium*. Ed. C. Lang. Leipzig: Teubner, 1881.

Dante. *The Divine Comedy*. Trans. Charles S. Singleton. Princeton: Princeton University Press, 1970–75.

Fragmente der Vorsokratiker. 6th ed. Ed. Diels, H. and W. Kranz. Berlin: Weidmann, 1951.

Galen, *On the Doctrines of Hippocrates and Plato*. Part 1, books 1–4. Ed., trans. and comm. Phillip DeLacy. *Corpus Medicorum Graecorum* 5.4.1.2. Berlin: Akademie-Verlag, 1978.

Hellenistic Philosophers. Ed. A. A. Long and D. N. Sedley. New York: Cambridge University Press, 1987.

Heraclitus [the Allegorist]. *Allégories d'Homère*. Ed. Félix Buffière. Paris: Belles Lettres, 1962.

———. *Quaestiones Homericae*. Ed. F. Oelmann. Leipzig: Teubner, 1910.

Hermetica. Ed. and trans. Walter Scott. 4 vols. Boston: Shambhala, 1985.

Iamblichus. *De vita Pythagorica*. Ed. L. Deubner. Leipzig: Teubner, 1937.

———. *In Platonis dialogos commentariorum fragmenta*. Ed. John M. Dillon. Leiden: E. J. Brill, 1973.

———. *Les mystères d'Égypte*. Ed. E. des Places. Paris: Belles Lettres, 1966.

———. *Protrepticus*. Ed. Ermenegildo Pistelli. Stuttgart: Teubner, 1967.

Macrobius. *Commentarii in Somnium Scipionis*. Ed. James Willis. Leipzig: Teubner, 1963.

Orphic Poems. Ed. M. L. West. New York: Oxford University Press, 1983.

[Plutarch]. *De Homero*. Ed. Jan Fredrik Kindstrand. Leipzig: Teubner, 1990.

———. *Essay on the Life and Poetry of Homer*. Ed. Robert Lamberton and J. J.

Keaney. American Philological Association American Classical Studies, no. 40. Atlanta: Scholars Press, 1996.
Porphyry. *Opuscula Selecta*. Ed. A. Nauck. Leipzig: Teubner, 1886.
———. *Philosophi Fragmenta*. Ed. Andrew Smith. Stuttgart: Teubner, 1993.
———. *Quaestionum Homericarum liber I*. Ed. A. R. Sodano. Napoli: Giannini, 1970.
———. *The Cave of the Nymphs in the Odyssey*. Ed. L. G. Westerink (Seminar Greek 609). Arethusa Monographs 1. Buffalo: SUNY, 1969.
Posidonius. Ed. L. Edelstein and I. G. Kidd. 2d ed. New York: Cambridge University Press, 1989.
Presocratic Philosophers: A Critical History with a Selection of Texts. Ed. G. S. Kirk, J. E. Raven, and M. Schofield. Cambridge: Cambridge University Press, 1983.
Proclus. *Commentarius in Platonis Parmenidem*. Ed. Victor Cousin. Paris, 1864.
———. *Elements of Theology*. Ed. E. R. Dodds, 2d ed. Oxford: Clarendon Press, 1963.
———. *In Platonis Cratylum commentaria*. Ed. Georg Pasquali. Leipzig: Teubner, 1908.
———. *In Platonis rem publicam commentarii*. Ed. G. Kroll. 2 vols. Leipzig: Teubner, 1899–1901.
———. *In Platonis Timaeum commentaria*. Ed. E. Diehl. Leipzig: Teubner, 1903–1906.
———. *Opera*. Ed. Victor Cousin. Paris: J.-M. Eberhart, 1820–1827.
Pseudo-Dionysius. Trans. Colm Luibheid. Classics of Western Spirituality. New York: Paulist Press, 1987.
Stoicorum veterum fragmenta. Ed. J. Von Arnim. 4 vols. Stuttgart: Teubner, 1964.

BIBLIOGRAPHY OF MODERN AUTHORS

Abrams, M. H. *The Mirror and the Lamp*. New York: Oxford University Press, 1953.

———. *Natural Supernaturalism*. New York: Norton, 1971.

Alexander, Paul J. "Hypatius of Ephesus: A Note on Image Worship in the Sixth Century." *Harvard Theological Review* 45 (1952): 177–84.

Armstrong, A. H., ed. *The Cambridge History of Later Greek and Early Medieval Philosophy*. Cambridge: Cambridge University Press, 1970.

Asmis, Elizabeth. "Plato on Poetic Creativity." In Richard Kraut, ed., *Cambridge Companion to Plato*, 338–64. New York: Cambridge University Press, 1992.

Atherton, Catherine. *The Stoics on Ambiguity*. New York: Cambridge University Press, 1993.

Atkins, J.W.H. *Literary Criticism in Antiquity: A Sketch of Its Development*. Cambridge: Cambridge University Press, 1934. Rprt. Gloucester, Mass.: Peter Smith, 1961.

Beard, Mary. "Cicero and Divination: The Formation of a Latin Discourse." *Journal of Roman Studies* 76 (1986): 33–46.

Beardsley, M. C., and W. K. Wimsatt, Jr. "The Intentional Fallacy." *Sewanee Review* 54 (1946): 468–88.

Becher, Ilse. "Tiberüberschwemmungen: Die Interpretation von Prodigien in Augusteischer Zeit." *Klio* 67 (1985): 471–79.

Behler, Ernst. *German Romantic Literary Theory*. New York: Cambridge University Press, 1993.

Bergren, A.L.T. "Helen's 'Good Drug' (*Odyssey* 4.305)." In S. Kresic, ed., *Contemporary Literary Hermeneutics and the Interpretation of Classical Texts*, 201–14. Ottawa: Ottawa University Press, 1981.

Bouché-Leclercq, Auguste. *Histoire de la divination dans l'antiquité*. 4 vols. Paris: E. Leroux, 1879–82.

Bowersock, G. W. *Roman Arabia*. Cambridge, Mass.: Harvard University Press, 1983.

Bowman, Alan K. *Egypt after the Pharaohs*. Berkeley: University of California Press, 1986.

Boyde, Patrick. *Dante, Philomythes and Philosopher: Man in the Cosmos*. New York: Cambridge University Press, 1981.

Bremond, A. "Notes et documents sur la religion neoplatonicienne." *Recherches de Science Religieuse* 23 (1933): 102–6.

Brown, Peter. "A Dark-Age Crisis: Aspects of the Iconoclast Controversy." *English Historical Review* 88 (January 1973): 1–34.

Bruns, Gerald L. "The Problem of Figuration in Antiquity." In Gary Shapiro and Alan Sica, eds., *Hermeneutics: Questions and Prospects*, 147–64. Amherst: University of Massachusetts Press, 1984.

———. "The Hermeneutics of Allegory and the History of Interpretation." *Comparative Literature* 40 (Fall 1988): 384–95.

———. *Hermeneutics Ancient and Modern*. New Haven: Yale University Press, 1992.

Buffière, Félix. *Les mythes d'Homère et la pensée grecque*. Paris: Belles Lettres, 1956.

Burkert, Walter. "La genèse des choses et des mots." *Études Philosophiques* 25 (Oct.–Dec. 1970): 443–55.

———. *Lore and Science in Ancient Pythagoreanism*. Cambridge, Mass.: Harvard University Press, 1972.

———. *Die orientalisierende Epoche in der griechischen Religion und Literatur*. Sitzungsberichte der Akad. der Wissenschaften in Heidelberg: no. 1. Heidelberg: Winter, 1984.

———. *Greek Religion*. Trans. John Raffan. Cambridge, Mass.: Harvard University Press, 1985.

———. "Der Autor von Derveni: Stesimbrotos Περὶ τελετῶν?" *Zeitschrift für Papyrologie und Epigraphik* 62 (1986): 1–5.

———. *Oedipus, Oracles, and Meaning: From Sophocles to Umberto Eco*. Samuel James Stubbs Lecture Series. Toronto: University of Toronto Press, 1991.

———. *Creation of the Sacred*. Cambridge, Mass.: Harvard University Press, 1996.

Calame, Claude. "Sexuality and Initiatory Transition." In André Laks and Glenn W. Most, eds., *Studies on the Derveni Papyrus*. New York: Oxford University Press, 1997.

Campenhausen, Hans Von. "The Theological Problem of Images in the Early Church." In *Tradition and Life in the Church*, trans. Av. V. Littledale, 171–200. London: Collins, 1968.

Cardullo, Loredana. *Il linguaggio del simbolo in Proclo: Analisi filosofico-semantica dei termini symbolon/eikôn/synthêma nel Commentario alla Repubblica*. Catania, Italy: University of Catania, 1985.

Carlson, Thomas A. *Indiscretion: Finitude and the Naming of God*. Chicago: University of Chicago Press, 1999.

Chrysostomou, Pavlos Ch. "*Ἡ Θεσσαλικὴ θεὰ Εη(ν)οδία ἢ φεραία θεά*." Dissertation, University of Thessalonica, 1992.

Clarke, Howard. *Homer's Readers: A Historical Introduction to the* Iliad *and the* Odyssey. Newark, Del.: University of Delaware Press, 1981.

Coleridge, Samuel Taylor. *Works*. Ed. Shedd. New York: Harper, 1863–64.

———. *Lectures 1795, On Politics and Religion*. Ed. Lewis Patton and Peter Mann. Princeton: Princeton University Press, 1971.

———. *Memorials of Coleorton, Being Letters from Coleridge, Wordsworth and His Sister, Southey, and Sir Walter Scott to Sir George and Lady Beaumont of Coleorton, Leicestershire, 1803 to 1834*. ed. William Knight. 2 vols. Edinburgh: D. Douglas, 1887.

Copenhaver, Brian P. *Hermetica*. New York: Cambridge University Press, 1992.

Coulter, James A. *The Literary Microcosm: Theories of Interpretation of the Later Neoplatonists*. Columbia Studies in the Classical Tradition, vol. 2. Leiden: E. J. Brill, 1976.

Cremer, Friedrich W. *Die Chaldäischen Orakel und Jamblich* De mysteriis. Meisenheim am Glan: Hain, 1969.

Cumont, Franz. *Oriental Religions in Roman Paganism*. London, 1911. Rprt. New York: Dover Publications, 1956.

Curtius, E. R. "The Poet's Divine Frenzy." In *European Literature and the Latin Middle Ages*, 474–75. Princeton: Princeton University Press, 1973.

Damon, Samuel Foster. *William Blake, His Philosophy and Symbols*. Boston: Houghton Mifflin 1924.

Dawson, David. *Allegorical Readers and Cultural Revision in Ancient Alexandria*. Berkeley: University of California Press, 1992.

De Jong, Irene J. F., and J. P. Sullivan, eds. *Modern Critical Theory and Classical Literature*. Leiden: E. J. Brill, 1994.

DeLacy, Phillip. "The Epicurean Analysis of Language." *American Journal of Philology* 60 (1939): 85–92.

———. "Stoic Views of Poetry." *American Journal of Philology* 69 (1948): 241–71.

De Man, Paul. *Allegories of Reading: Figural Language in Rousseau, Nietzsche, Rilke, and Proust*. New Haven: Yale University Press, 1979.

———. "Rhetoric of Temporality." In *Blindness and Insight: Essays in the Rhetoric of Contemporary Criticism*, 2d ed., Theory and History of Literature, vol. 7, 187–228. Minneapolis: University of Minnesota Press, 1983.

Denniston, J. D., ed. *Greek Literary Criticism*. New York: E. P. Dutton, 1924.

Derrida, Jacques. "White Mythology: Metaphor in the Text of Philosophy." In *Margins of Philosophy*, trans. Alan Bass, 207–71. Chicago: University of Chicago Press, 1982.

Detienne, Marcel. *Homère, Hésiode et Pythagore: Poésie et philosophie dans le pythagorisme ancien*. Bruxelles-Berchem: Latomus, 1962.

———. *Les maîtres de vérité dans la Grèce archaïque*. Paris: F. Maspero, 1967. Trans. Janet Lloyd as *The Masters of Truth in Archaic Greece*. New York: Zone Books, 1996.

Dillon, John. "Image, Symbol, and Analogy: Three Basic Concepts of Neoplatonic Allegorical Exegesis." In R. Baine Harris, ed. *The Significance of Neoplatonism*, 247–62. Norfolk, Va.: International Society for Neoplatonic Studies, 1976.

———. *The Middle Platonists: A Study of Platonism, 80 B.C. to A.D. 220*. London: Duckworth, 1977.

Dillon, John. "Iamblichus of Chalchis." *ANRW* 2.36.2 (1987): 826–909.

Dillon, John, and A. A. Long, eds. *The Question of "Eclecticism": Studies in Later Greek Philosophy*. Hellenistic Culture and Society, vol. 3. Berkeley: University of California Press, 1988.

Dodds, E. R. *The Greeks and the Irrational*. Berkeley: University of California Press, 1951.

Emerson, Ralph Waldo. "Quotation and Originality." In *Works*, vol. 8. Cambridge, Mass.: Riverside Press, 1883.

Essick, Robert N. "Coleridge and the Language of Adam." In Frederick Burwick, ed., *Coleridge's Biographia Literaria: Text and Meaning*. Columbus: Ohio State University Press, 1989.

Faraone, Christopher A. *Talismans and Trojan Horses: Guardian Statues in Ancient Greek Myth and Ritual*. New York: Oxford University Press, 1992.

Faraone, Christopher A., and Dirk Obbink, eds. *Magika Hiera: Ancient Greek Magic and Religion*. New York: Oxford University Press, 1991.

———. "Taking the Nestor's Cup Inscription Seriously: Conditional Curses and Erotic Magic in the Earliest Greek Hexameters." *Classical Antiquity* 15 (1996): 77–112.

Farrell, Joseph. *Vergil's Georgics and the Traditions of Ancient Epic*. New York: Oxford University Press, 1991.

Finan, Thomas, and Vincent Twomey, eds. *The Relationship between Neoplatonism and Christianity*. Dublin: Four Courts Press, 1992.

Fletcher, Angus. *Allegory: Theory of a Symbolic Mode*. Ithaca: Cornell University Press, 1964.

Fontenrose, Joseph. *The Delphic Oracle*. Berkeley: University of California Press, 1978.

Ford, Andrew. "Performing Interpretation: Early Allegorical Exegesis of Homer." In Margaret Beissinger et al., eds., *Epic Traditions in the Contemporary World*. Berkeley: University of California Press, 1999.

———. *Origins of Criticism: Literary Culture and Poetic Theory in Classical Greece*. Princeton: Princeton University Press, 2002.

Foucault, Michel. *The Care of the Self. Vol. 3 of the History of Sexuality*. Trans. R. Hurley. New York: Pantheon Books, 1986.

Fowden, Garth. *The Egyptian Hermes*. Princeton: Princeton University Press, 1986.

Funghi, Maria Serena. "The Derveni Papyrus." In André Laks and Glenn W. Most, eds., *Studies on the Derveni Papyrus*. New York: Oxford University Press, 1997.

García, J. F. "Ritual Speech in Early Greek Song." In Ian Worthington and John Miles Foley, eds., *Epea and Grammata: Oral and Written Communication in Ancient Greece*, 29–53. Leiden: E. J. Brill, 2002.

Gauthier, Philippe. *Symbola: Les étrangers et la justice dans les cités grecques*. Nancy, France: University of Nancy II, 1972.

Gersh, Stephen. *KINHSIS AKINHTOS: A Study of Spiritual Motion in the Philosophy of Proclus*. Leiden: E. J. Brill, 1973.

———. *From Iamblichus to Eriugena: An Investigation of the Prehistory and Evolution of the Pseudo-Dionysian Tradition*. Studien zur Problemgeschichte der antiken und mittelalterlichen Philosophie, vol. 8. Leiden: E. J. Brill, 1978

———. *Middle Platonism and Neoplatonism: the Latin Tradition*. Publications in Medieval Studies, vol. 23. Notre Dame, Ind.: University of Notre Dame Press, 1986.

Gersh, Stephen, and Charles Kannengiesser, eds. *Platonism in Late Antiquity*. Vol. 8 of *Christianity and Judaism in Antiquity*. Notre Dame, Ind.: University of Notre Dame Press, 1992.

Geudtner, Otto. *Die Seelenlehre der chaldäischen Orakel*. Meisenheim am Glan: Hain, 1971.

Glucker, John. *Antiochus and the Late Academy*. Göttingen: Vandenhoeck and Ruprecht, 1978.

Graeser, Andreas. "The Stoic Theory of Meaning." In John M. Rist, ed., *The Stoics*, 77–99. Berkeley: University of California Press, 1978.

Graf, Fritz. "Prayer in Magic and Religious Ritual." In Christopher Farone and Dirk Obbin K., eds., *Magika Hiera*, 188–213. New York: Oxford University Press, 1991.

———. "An Oracle against Pestilence from Western Anatolia." *Zeitschrift für Papyrologie und Epigraphik* 92 (1992): 267–79.

———. *Greek Mythology*. Baltimore, Md.: Johns Hopkins University Press, 1993.

———. "Excluding the Charming." In M. Meyer and P. Mirecki, eds., *Ancient Magic and Ritual Power*, 29–42. Leiden: E. J. Brill, 1995.

Greenblatt, Stephen J. *Allegory and Representation*. Baltimore: Johns Hopkins University Press, 1981.

Grube, G.M.A. *The Greek and Roman Critics*. London: Methuen, 1965.

Hadot, Pierre. "Fragments d'un commentaire de Porphyre sur le Parménide." *Revue des Études Grecques* 74.351–53 (1961): 410–38.

———. *Porphyre et Victorinus*. Paris: Études Augustiniennes, 1968.

Halliwell, Stephen. *Aristotle's Poetics*. Chapel Hill: University of North Carolina Press, 1986.

Hankey, W. J. *God in Himself*. New York: Oxford University Press, 1987.

Harris, Roy, and Talbot J. Taylor. *Landmarks in Linguistic Thought: The Western Tradition from Socrates to Saussure*. New York: Routledge, 1989.

Hays, Robert Stephen. "Lucius Annaeus Cornutus' "Epidrome" (Introduction to the Traditions of Greek Theology): Introduction, Translation, and Notes." Dissertation, University of Texas at Austin, 1983.

Henrichs, Albert. "Die Kritik der stoischen Theologie im PHerc. 1428." *Cronache Ercolanesi* 4 (1974): 5–32.

———. "Changing Dionysiac Identities." In Ben F. Meyer, E. Sanders, eds., *Jewish and Christian Self-Definition*, vol. 3. Philadelphia: Fortress Press, 1982.

Henry, M. "The Derveni Commentator as Literary Critic." *TAPA* 116 (1986): 149–64.

Hopkins, Vivian C. *Spires of Form: A Study of Emerson's Aesthetic Theory*. Cambridge, Mass.: Harvard University Press, 1951.

Irvine, Martin. *The Making of Textual Culture: "Grammatica" and Literary Theory, 350–1100*. Cambridge Studies in Medieval Literature, vol. 19. New York: Cambridge University Press, 1994.

Johnston, Sarah Iles. *Hekate Soteira: A Study of Hekate's Roles in the* Chaldean Oracles *and Related Literature*. Atlanta: Scholars Press, 1990.

———. "Riders in the Sky: Cavalier Gods and Theurgic Salvation in the Second Century A.D." *Classical Philology* 87 (October 1992): 303–21.

Kahn, Charles. "Was Euthyphro the Author of the Derveni Papyrus?" In André Laks and Glenn W. Most, eds., *Studies on the Derveni Papyrus*, 55–63. New York: Oxford University Press, 1997.

Kapsomenos, S. G. "The Orphic Papyrus Roll of Thessalonica." *Bulletin of the American Society of Papyrology* 2 (1964): 2–31.

Keaney, J. J., and Robert Lamberton. *[Plutarch], Life of Homer*. American Philological Association American Classical Studies, no. 40. Atlanta: Scholars Press, 1996.

Kennedy, George A. *Classical Criticism*. Vol. 1 of *The Cambridge History of Literary Criticism*. New York: Cambridge University Press, 1993.

Kern, O. "Brimo." *PRE* 3 (1887): 853–54.

Kett, P. "Prosopographie der historischen griechischen Manteis bis auf die Zeit Alexanders des Grossen." Dissertation, University of Nuremberg, 1966.

Kidd, I. G. "The Relation of Stoic Intermediates to the *Summum Bonum*, with Reference to Change in the Stoa." *Classical Quarterly*, n.s., 5 (1955): 181–94.

Kieckhefer, Richard. *Magic in the Middle Ages*. New York: Cambridge University Press, 1989.

Kirby, John T. "Aristotle's *Poetics*: The Rhetorical Principle." *Arethusa* 24 (1991): 197–217.

Kitzinger, Ernst. "The Cult of Images in the Age before Iconoclasm." *Dumbarton Oaks Papers* 8 (1954): 83–150.

Knox, Bernard. "Author, Author." *New York Review of Books* 42.18 (November 16, 1995).

Kotansky, Roy. "Incantations and Prayers for Salvation on Inscribed Greek Amulets." In Christopher Faraone and Dirk Obbink, eds., *Magika Hiera*, 107–37. New York: Oxford University Press, 1991.

Kretzmann, Norman. "Plato on the Correctness of Names." *American Philosophical Quarterly* 8 (April 1971): 126–38.

Kristeller, Paul Oskar. *The Philosophy of Marsilio Ficino*. Trans. Virginia Conant. New York: Columbia University Press, 1943.

———. "Neoplatonismo e Rinascimento." *Il Veltro* 35 (Jan.–Apr. 1991): 25–37.

Kroll, J. H., and F. W. Mitchel. "Clay Tokens Stamped with the Names of Athenian Military Commanders." *Hesperia* 49 (1980): 86–96.

Kurz, Gerhard. "Friedrich Schlegels Begriff der 'symbolischen Form' und seine literaturtheoretische Bedeutung." In *Aspekte der Romantik*, ed. Sven-Aage Jørgensen, Per Øhrgaard, and Friedrich Schmöe, 30–43. Copenhagen and Munich: Wilhem Fink Verlag, 1983.

Laks, André, and Glenn W. Most, eds. *Studies on the Derveni Papyrus*. New York: Oxford University Press, 1997.

Lamberton, Robert Drummond. "Homer the Theologian: The *Iliad* and the *Odyssey* as Read by the Neoplatonists of Late Antiquity." Dissertation, Yale University, 1979.

———. *Homer the Theologian: Neoplatonist Allegorical Reading and the Growth of the Epic Tradition*. Berkeley: University of California Press, 1986.

Lamberton, Robert Drummond, and John J. Keaney, eds. *Homer's Ancient Readers*. Princeton: Princeton University Press, 1992.

Lamedica, A. "La terminologia criticò-litteraria dal Papiro di Derveni ai Corpora scoliografici." *Lessici Tecnici Greci e Latini*, Atti del 1° Seminario di

Studi, "Accademia Peloritana dei Pericolanti." *Cl. Lett. Filos.* 66, suppl. 1 (1990): 83–91.

Lebedev, A. V. "Heraclitus in P. Derveni." *Zeitschrift für Papyrologie und Epigraphik* 79 (1989): 39–47.

Lee, Guy. "An Aristarchan Maxim?" *Proceedings of the Cambridge Philological Society* 201 (1975): 63–64.

Lévêque, Pierre. *Aurea catena Homeri*. Paris: Belles Lettres, 1959.

Lewy, Hans. *The Chaldean Oracles and Theurgy: Mysticism, Magic, and Platonism in the Later Roman Empire*, ed. Míchel Tardieu. Paris: Étude augustiniennes, 1978.

Linderski, J. "Cicero and Roman Divination." *Past and Present* 36 (1982): 12–38.

———. "Watching the Birds: Cicero the Augur and the Augural Templa." *Classical Philology* 81 (1986): 330–40.

Lloyd, A. C. *Anatomy of Neoplatonism*. Oxford: Clarendon Press, 1990.

Lloyd-Jones, Hugh. "The Delphic Oracle." *Greece and Rome* 23 (1976): 60–73.

Long, A. A. "Dialectic and the Stoic Sage." In John M. Rist, ed., *The Stoics*, 101–24. Berkeley: University of California Press, 1978.

———. "Stoic Readings of Homer." In Robert Lamberton and John J. Keaney, eds., *Homer's Ancient Readers*, 41–66. Princeton: Princeton University Press, 1992.

Mahé, Jean-Pierre. *Hermès en haute-Égypte*. Quebec: Presses de l'Université Laval, 1978–82.

Majercik, Ruth. *The Chaldean Oracles: Text, Translation, and Commentary*. New York: E. J. Brill, 1989.

Manetti, Giovanni. *Theories of the Sign in Classical Antiquity* Trans. Christine Richardson. Bloomington: University of Indiana Press, 1993.

Marrou, H. I. *A History of Education in Antiquity*. Trans. George Lamb. New York: Sheed and Ward, 1956.

Martin, F. X., and J. A. Richmond, eds. *From Augustine to Eriugena: Essays on Neoplatonism and Christianity in Honor of John O'Meara*. Washington, D.C.: Catholic University of America Press, 1991.

Massenzio, M. "La poesia come fine: La desacralizzazione della tragedia: Considerazioni sulla 'Poetica' di Aristotel." *Religione e Civiltà* 1 (1972): 285–318.

Maurizio, L. "Anthropology and Spirit Possession: A Reconsideration of the Pythia's Role at Delphi." *Journal of Hellenic Studies* (1995): 69–86.

McCown, Chester C. "The Ephesia Grammata in Popular Belief." *Transactions and Proceedings of the American Philological Association* 54 (1923): 129–40.

McFarland, Thomas. *Coleridge and the Pantheist Tradition*. Oxford: Clarendon Press, 1969.

McKeon, Richard. *Rhetoric: Essays in Invention and Discovery*. Woodbridge, Conn.: Ox Bow Press, 1987.

Meijering, Roos. *Literary and Rhetorical Theories in the Greek Scholia*. Groningen: E. Forsten, 1987.

Meltzer, Françoise. *Hot Property: The Stakes and Claims of Literary Originality*. Chicago: University of Chicago Press, 1994.

Menn, Stephen Philip. *Plato on God as Nous*. Journal of the History of Philosophy Monograph Series. Carbondale: Southern Illinois University Press, 1995.

Meredith, A. "Porphyry and Julian against the Christians." *ANRW* 2.23.2 (1980): 1119–49.

Merlan, Philip. *From Platonism to Neoplatonism*. 3d ed., rev. The Hague: Martinus Nijhoff, 1968.

Meyer, M., and P. Mirecki, eds. *Ancient Magic and Ritual Power*. Leiden: E. J. Brill, 1995.

Miller, Patricia Cox. *Dreams in Late Antiquity: Studies in the Imagination of a Culture*. Princeton: Princeton University Press, 1994.

Minnis, A. J., and A. B. Scott, eds. *Medieval Literary Theory and Criticism c. 1100–c. 1375: The Commentary Tradition*. Oxford: Clarendon Press, 1988.

Modrak, Deborah K. W. *Aristotle's Theory of Language and Meaning*. New York: Cambridge University Press, 2001.

Most, Glenn W. "Pindar, O. 2.83–90." *Classical Quarterly* 36.2 (1986): 304–16.

———. "Cornutus and Stoic Allegoresis." *ANRW* 2.36.3 (1989): 2014–65.

Mouraviev, S. N. "The Heraclitean Fragment of the Derveni Papyrus." *Zeitschrift für Papyrologie und Epigraphik* 61 (1985): 131–32.

Münzel, Robert. *De Apollodori περὶ θεῶν libris*. Bonn Typis Caroli Georgi Universitatis, 1883.

Müri, Walter. "Symbolon." In *Griechische Studien*. Schweizerische Beiträge zur Altertumswissenschaft, vol. 14. Basel: Friedrich Reinhardt, 1976.

Murrin, Michael. *The Veil of Allegory: Some Notes toward a Theory of Allegorical Rhetoric in the English Renaissance*. Chicago: University of Chicago Press, 1969.

———. *The Allegorical Epic: Essays in Its Rise and Decline*. Chicago: University of Chicago Press, 1980.

———. Review of *Allegory: The Dynamics of an Ancient and Medieval Technique*, by Jon Whitman. *Journal of Religion* 69 (April 1989): 295–97.

Nagy, Gregory. *Best of the Achaeans*. Baltimore: Johns Hopkins University Press, 1979.

———. "Early Greek Views of Poets and Poetry." In George A. Kennedy, ed., *Cambridge History of Literary Criticism,* vol. 1, *Classical Criticism*. Cambridge: Cambridge University Press, 1989.

Nelson, Robert S. "The Discourse of Icons Then and Now." *Art History* 12 (June 1989): 144–57.

Novalis. *Encyclopedia IX*. (= *Materialien zeur Enzyclopädistik. IX*). Trans. Karl Siegler. Coquitlam, B. C.: Archaí, 1973.

Obbink, Dirk. "Cosmology as Initiation vs. the Critique of the Orphic Mysteries." In André Laks and Glenn W. Most, eds., *Studies on the Derveni Papyrus*. New York: Oxford University Press, 1997.

Olster, David. "Byzantine Hermeneutics after Iconoclasm: Word and Image in the Leo Bible." *Byzantion* 64 (1994): 419–58.

O'Meara, Dominic J., ed. *Neoplatonism and Christian Thought*. Studies in Neoplatonism, vol. 3 Norfolk, Va.: International Society for Neoplatonic Studies; Albany: State University of New York Press, 1981.

———. *Pythagoras Revived: Mathematics and Philosophy in Late Antiquity*. New York: Oxford University Press, 1989.

O'Meara, John J. *Porphyry's Philosophy from Oracles in Augustine*. Paris: Études Augustiniennes, 1959.

O'Rourke, Fran. *Pseudo-Dionysius and the Metaphysics of Aquinas*. Leiden: E. J. Brill, 1992.

Panofsky, Erwin, ed. and trans. *Abbot Suger on the Abbey Church of St.-Denis and Its Art Treasures*. Princeton: Princeton University Press, 1946.

Parke, H. W., and D.E.W. Wormell. *The Delphic Oracle*. 2 vols. Oxford: Blackwell, 1956.

Pease, Arthur, ed. *M. Tulli Ciceronis De divinatione*. Darmstadt: Wissenschaftliche Buchgesellschaft, 1963.

Pelikan, Jaroslav. *Christianity and Classical Culture: The Metamorphosis of Natural Theology in the Christian Encounter with Hellenism*. Gifford Lectures at Aberdeen, 1992–93. New Haven: Yale University Press, 1993.

Pépin, Jean. *Mythe et allégorie: Les origines grecques et les contestations judéo-chrétiennes*. 2d ed. Paris: Études Augustiniennes, 1976.

———. *La tradition de l'allégorie de Philon d'Alexandrie à Dante*. Paris: Études Augustiniennes, 1987.

Pfefferkorn, Kristin. *Novalis: A Romantic's Theory of Language and Poetry*. New Haven: Yale University Press, 1988.

Pfeiffer, Rudolph. *History of Classical Scholarship*. Oxford: Clarendon Press, 1968–76.

Pharr, C. "The Interdiction of Magic in Roman Law." *TAPA* 63 (1932): 269–95.

Porter, James. I. "Philo's Confusion of Tongues." *Quaderni Urbinati di Cultura Classica* 24 (1986): 55–74.

———. "Hermeneutic Lines and Circles: Aristarchus and Crates on the Exegesis of Homer." In Robert Lamberton and John J. Keaney, eds., *Homer's Ancient Readers*. Princeton: Princeton University Press, 1992.

Pratt, Louise. "Odyssey 19.535–50: On the Interpretation of Dreams and Signs in Homer." *Classical Philology* 89 (1994): 147–52.

Pritchett, W. K. *The Greek State at War*. Vol. 3. Berkeley: University of California Press, 1979.

Rahner, Hugo. *Greek Myths and Christian Mystery*. Trans. Brian Battershaw. New York: Biblo and Tannen, 1971.

Raine, Kathleen. *Blake and Tradition*. Princeton: Princeton University Press, 1968.

Raine, Kathleen, and G. M. Harper, eds. *Thomas Taylor the Platonist: Selected Writings*. Princeton: Princeton University Press, 1969.

Rappe, Sara. *Reading Neoplatonism*. New York: Cambridge University Press, 2000.

Reynolds, L. D., and N. G. Wilson. *Scribes and Scholars: A Guide to the Transmission of Greek and Latin Literature*. 3d ed. New York: Oxford University Press, 1991.

Richardson, N. J. "Homeric Professors in the Age of the Sophists." *Proceedings of the Cambridge Philological Society* 201 (1975): 65–81.

———. "Literary Criticism in the Exegetical Scholia to the *Iliad*: A Sketch." *Classical Quarterly* 30 (1980): 265–87.

Ricoeur, Paul. *Time and Narrative*. Chicago: University of Chicago Press, 1992.

Riley, Mark. "Theoretical and Practical Astrology: Ptolemy and His Colleagues." *TAPA* 117 (1987): 235–56.

Roemer, Adolf. *Die Homerexegese Aristarchs in ihren Grundzügen dargestellt*. Paderborn: F. Schöningh, 1924.

Romilly, Jacqueline de. *Magic and Rhetoric in Ancient Greece*. Cambridge, Mass.: Harvard University Press, 1975.

Rorem, Paul. *Pseudo-Dionysius: A Commentary on the Texts and an Introduction to Their Influence*. New York: Oxford University Press, 1993.

Rosen, Ralph. "The Ionian at Aristophanes *Peace* 46." *Greek, Roman and Byzantine Studies* 25.4 (1984): 389–96.

Rosenmeyer, Th. G. "Gorgias, Aeschylus, and *Apate*." *American Journal of Philology* 76 (1955): 225–60.

Runia, David. "Naming and Knowing: Themes in Philonic Theology with Special Reference to the *De mutatione nominum*." In R. Van den Broek, T. Baarda, J. Mansfeld, eds., *Knowledge of God in the Graeco-Roman World*, 69–91. Leiden: E. J. Brill, 1988.

Russell, D. A., and M. Winterbottom, eds. *Ancient Literary Criticism: The Principal Texts in New Translations*. New York: Oxford University Press, 1972.

———. *Criticism in Antiquity*. Berkeley: University of California Press, 1981.

Rusten, Jeffrey S. "Interim Notes on the Papyrus from Derveni." In *Harvard Studies in Classical Philology*, vol. 89, 121–40. Cambridge, Mass.: Harvard University Press, 1985.

Saffrey, Henri-Dominique. "New Objective Links between the Pseudo-Dionysius and Proclus." In Dominic J. O'Meara, ed., *Neoplatonism and Christian Thought*, 64–74. Albany: State University of New York Press, 1981.

Schelling, Friedrich Wilhelm Joseph. *The Philosophy of Art*. Trans. Douglas W. Stott. Theory and History of Literature, vol. 58. Minneapolis: University of Minnesota Press, 1989.

Schibli, Hermann Sadun. *Pherekydes of Syros*. New York: Oxford University Press, 1990.

Schlunk, Robin R. *The Homeric Scholia and the Aeneid: A Study of the Influence of Ancient Homeric Literary Criticism on Vergil*. Ann Arbor: University of Michigan Press, 1974.

Schofield, Malcolm. "Cicero for and against Divination." *Journal of Roman Studies* 76 (1986): 47–65.

Scodel, Ruth. "Tantalus and Anaxagoras." *Harvard Studies in Classical Philology* 88 (1984): 13–24.

Scott, Walter. *Hermetica*. 4 vols. Boston: Shambhala, 1985.

Segal, Charles P. "Gorgias and the Psychology of the Logos." *Harvard Studies in Classical Philology* 66 (1962): 99–155.

Shaw, Gregory. *Theurgy and the Soul: The Neoplatonism of Iamblichus*. University Park: Pennsylvania State University Press, 1995.

Sheppard, A.D.R. *Studies on the 5th and 6th Essays of Proclus' Commentary on the Republic*. Hypomnemata, vol. 61. Göttingen: Vandenhoeck and Ruprecht, 1980.

———. "Proclus' Attitude to Theurgy." *Classical Quarterly* 32.1 (1982): 212–24.

Shipley, Graham. *A History of Samos, 800–188* B.C. New York: Oxford University Press, 1987.

Sider, David. "Heraclitus in the Derveni Papyrus." In André Laks and Glenn W. Most, eds., *Studies on the Derveni Papyrus*. New York: Oxford University Press, 1997.

Silverman, Alan. "Plato's Cratylus: The Nature of Naming and the Naming of Nature." Oxford Studies in Ancient Philosophy, vol. 10 (1992).

Simonsuuri, Kristi. *Homer's Original Genius: Eighteenth-Century Notions of the Early Greek Epic (1688–1798)*. New York: Cambridge University Press, 1979.

Siorvanes, Lucas. *Proclus: Neo-Platonic Philosophy and Science*. New Haven: Yale University Press, 1996.

Sluiter, Ineke. "The Greek Tradition." In *The Emergence of Semantics in Four Linguistic Traditions*. Amsterdam/Philadelphia: John Benjamins, 1997.

Smith, Andrew. *Porphyry's Place in the Neoplatonic Tradition: A Study of Post-Plotinian Neoplatonism*. The Hague: Martinus Nijhoff, 1974.

Smith, Nicholas D. "Diviners and Divination in Aristophanic Comedy." *Classical Antiquity* 8 (1989): 140–58.

Struck, Peter T. "Iamblichus, *De mysteriis*, book 1." In Richard Valantasis, ed., *Religions of Late Antiquity in Practice*, 489–505. Princeton: Princeton University Press, 2000.

———. "Pagan and Christian Theurgies." *Ancient World* 32.1 (2001): 25–38.

———. "Speech Acts and the Stakes of Hellenism in Iamblichus, *De mysteriis* 7." In Paul Mirecki and Marvin Meyer, eds., *Magic and Ritual in the Ancient World*, 289–303. Religions of the Graeco-Roman World. Leiden: E. J. Brill, 2002.

Tate, J. "On the Beginnings of Greek Allegory." *Classical Review* 41 (1927): 214–15.

———. "Cornutus and the Poets." *Classical Quarterly* 23 (1929): 41–45.

———. "Plato and Allegorical Interpretation." [1] *Classical Quarterly* 23 (1929): 142–54; [2], *Classical Quarterly* 24 (1930): 1–10.

———. "On the History of Allegorism." *Classical Quarterly* 28 (1934): 105–14.

Taylor, Thomas, trans. and comm. *The works of Plato, viz. his fifty-five dialogues, and twelve epistles, translated from the Greek; nine of the dialogues by the late Floyer Sydenham, and the remainder by Thomas Taylor: with occasional annotations on the nine dialogues translated by Sydenham, and copious notes by the latter translator; in which is given the substance of nearly all the existing Greek ms. commentaries on the philosophy of Plato, and a considerable portion of such as are already published*. 5 vols. London: T. Taylor, 1804.

Thom, Johan Carl. "The Golden Verses of Pythagoras: Its Literary Composition and Religio-Historical Significance." Dissertation, University of Chicago, 1990.

Thompson, C. L. "Stoic Allegory of Homer: A Critical Analysis of Heraclitus' Homeric Allegories." Dissertation, Yale University, 1973.

Thompson, David. *Dante's Epic Journeys*. Baltimore: Johns Hopkins University Press, 1974.

Thorndike, Lynn. *History of Magic and Experimental Science*. 8 vols. New York: Macmillan, 1923–58.

Trimpi, Wesley. *Muses of One Mind: The Literary Analysis of Experience and Its Continuity*. Princeton: Princeton University Press, 1983.

———. "Konrad Gesner and Neoplatonic Poetics." In Arthur Groos, ed., *Magister Regis: Studies in Honor of Kaske*, 260–72. New York: Fordham University Press, 1986.

Tugwell, Simon. *Albert and Thomas*. Classics of Western Spirituality Series. New York: Paulist Press: 1988.

Van der Valk, M. *Researches on the Text and Scholia of the Iliad*. 2 vols. Leiden: E. J. Brill, 1963–64.

Von Frank, Albert J. *An Emerson Chronology*. New York: Macmillan, 1994.

Watson, Gerard. *The Stoic Theory of Knowledge*. Belfast: Queen's University, 1966.

West, M. L. *The Orphic Poems*. New York: Oxford University Press, 1983.

———. "Hocus-Pocus in East and West." In André Laks and Glenn W. Most, eds., *Studies on the Derveni Papyrus*. New York: Oxford University Press, 1997.

Whitaker, C.W.A. *Aristotle's De interpretatione*. New York: Oxford University Press, 1996.

Whitman, Jon. *Allegory: The Dynamics of an Ancient and Medieval Technique*. Cambridge, Mass.: Harvard University Press, 1987.

———. "From the Textual to the Temporal: Early Christian 'Allegory' and Early Romantic 'Symbol.'" *New Literary History* 22 (1991): 161–76.

———, ed. *Interpretation and Allegory: Antiquity to the Modern Period*. Leiden: E. J. Brill, 2000.

Wilkinson, L. P. "Cicero and the Relationship of Oratory to Literature." In *Latin Literature*, ed. W. V. Clausen and E. J. Kenney, vol. 2 of *The Cambridge History of Classical Literature*, New York: Cambridge University Press, 1982.

Winkler, John J. *The Constraints of Desire*. New York: Routledge, 1990.

INDEX LOCORUM

GENERAL INDEX